Italy's Economic Revolution

Italy's Economic Revolution

Integration and Economy in Republican Italy

SASKIA T. ROSELAAR

OXFORD
UNIVERSITY PRESS

OXFORD
UNIVERSITY PRESS

Great Clarendon Street, Oxford, OX2 6DP,
United Kingdom

Oxford University Press is a department of the University of Oxford.
It furthers the University's objective of excellence in research, scholarship,
and education by publishing worldwide. Oxford is a registered trade mark of
Oxford University Press in the UK and in certain other countries

First Edition published in 2019

Published in the United States of America by Oxford University Press
198 Madison Avenue, New York, NY 10016, United States of America

British Library Cataloguing in Publication Data
Data available

Library of Congress Control Number: 2019933998

ISBN 978–0–19–882944–7

DOI: 10.1093/oso/9780198829447.001.0001

Acknowledgements

This project has been a long time in the making and has benefited from the advice of many people along the way. Here I would like to thank them all for showing an interest in my work and taking the effort of helping me improve it.

I first started to research integration processes in the Roman Republican period during a two-year Newton International Fellowship at the University of Manchester in 2009–10, funded by the British Academy and Royal Society. I am honoured that these two august bodies found my research worthy of funding, which allowed me to come to the UK. I was able to develop my career in a way that would not otherwise have been possible. My host at Manchester was Tim Cornell, whom I cannot thank too much for all his help and support during the first stages of this research project, and for his discussions and comments on various drafts.

The project was then continued during a Teaching Fellowship at the University Reading in 2011 and a Nottingham Advanced Research Fellowship at the University of Nottingham in 2011–13. I would like to thank all my colleagues at Manchester, Reading, and Nottingham for their help and support, especially Peter Kruschwitz, Helen Lovatt, Judith Mossman, Tim Parkin, and Alison Sharrock. My time at Nottingham also gave me the opportunity to teach on subjects related to this work, and I thank my students for their interest in the subject and for asking questions that pointed out the difficulties of my argument.

For their comments on various drafts and for valuable discussions, I am indebted to Wim Broekaert, Michael Crawford, Massimiliano Di Fazio, Paul Du Plessis, Paul Erdkamp, Marian Helm, Daniel Hoyer, Paul Kloeg, Egbert Koops, Myles Lavan, Luuk de Ligt, Kathryn Lomas, Jean-Paul Morel, John Rich, Nathan Rosenstein, Roman Roth, Rafael Scopacasa, Marleen Termeer, and Koen Verboven. I am especially grateful to Michael Crawford for allowing me to study his personal archive relating to coin hoards from Italy and to Jean-Paul Morel for his detailed comments on the archaeological section of this book. John Rich deserves thanks for buying me lunch and tea, and of course for reading the whole manuscript in just one week. For introducing me to the practical difficulties of archaeological fieldwork and its interpretation, I thank Tesse Stek and Marleen Termeer and all the participants of the Colonial Landscape Project campaign in San Giovanni in Galdo, September 2011.

A big thank you goes to all those attending the conferences 'Integration and identity in the Roman Republic' in Manchester, 2010, and 'Processes of integration in the Roman world' in Nottingham, 2013. My work has greatly benefited from the discussions there. Various parts of this book were first presented at research seminars and conferences; I would like to thank audiences in Amsterdam, Bochum, Brussels, Cambridge, Cardiff, Clermont-Ferrand, Cologne, Edinburgh, Glasgow, Groningen, Manchester, Nottingham, Oxford, Paris, Rome, Seville, and St Andrews, where many helpful comments were made.

This book comes with an interactive map displaying the distribution of Italians and Romans in the Mediterranean, intended to present large amounts of data in a new way. Olivier Hokke and Bas Dado of OrbitGames programmed the map exactly according to what I had in mind, and were always ready to answer questions and run updates; they made the map much clearer than I could have done on my own.

For assistance with obtaining permissions for the illustrations in this book, I would like to thank Lindsay Holman at the Ancient World Mapping Center, Davide Monaco at sanniti.info, Steve Lansdale at Heritage Auctions, Liz Taylor at the Institute of Classical Studies, Egidio Incelli at the Soprintendenza Archeologia, belle arti e paesaggio del Molise, and the Museo Archeologico Nazionale di Aquileia.

This book has benefited from the assistance of many helpful and efficient people at Oxford University Press; I would like to thank the three anonymous reviewers for their helpful comments, which led to a significant overhaul in the manuscript. For finally seeing it through to press, I would like to thank Charlotte Loveridge, Georgina Leighton, Céline Louasli, Keerthana Sundaramoorthy, and Juliet Gardner.

Last but not least, I would like to thank my family. My mother stimulated my interest in history from an early age, even if I did not always want to listen, and my father's academic career has always been an inspiration to me. My brother Jan was always ready to find historical references in obscure science fiction movies. My husband Mark created the maps for this volume, and was always there for me to talk about my work. Finally, our daughter Eleonora constantly reminds me of the most important question in the study of history: 'But why, Mommy?'

Contents

List of Figures

Whilst every effort has been made to secure permission to reproduce the illustrations, we may have failed in a few cases to trace the copyright holders. If contacted, the publisher will be pleased to rectify any omissions at the earliest opportunity.

List of Maps

Maps

Map 1: Northern Italy.

Map 2: Southern Italy and Sicily.

Ancient World Mapping Center © 2018 (awmc.unc.edu). Used by permi

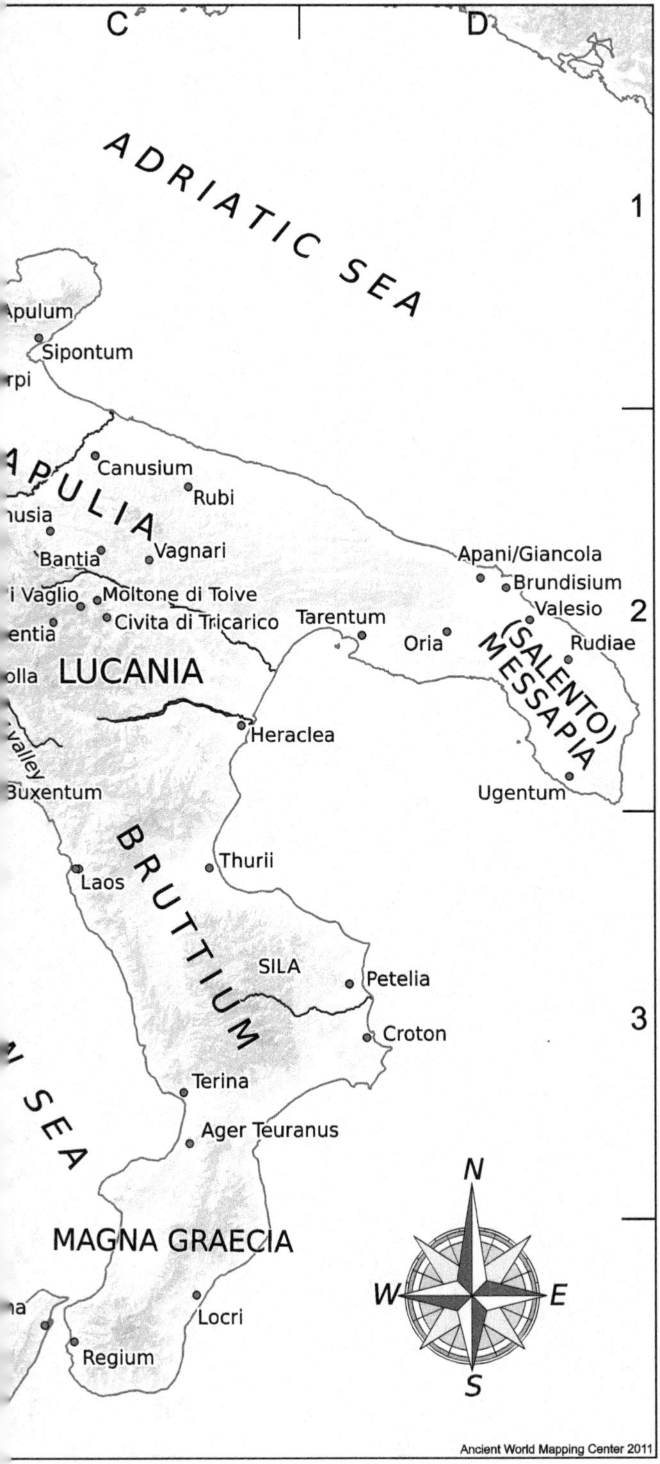

C
D
1
2
3
ADRIATIC SEA
Sipontum
Canusium
Rubi
APULIA
Bantia
Vagnari
Apani/Giancola
Brundisium
Valesio
Moltone di Tolve
Civita di Tricarico
Tarentum
Oria
Rudiae
LUCANIA
MESSAPIA
(SALENTO)
Heraclea
Ugentum
BRUTTIUM
Thurii
Laos
SILA
Petelia
Croton
Terina
SEA
Ager Teuranus
MAGNA GRAECIA
Locri
Regium
N
W
E
S
Ancient World Mapping Center 2011

1
Introduction
Economy and Integration in the Roman Republic

1.1 Introduction

During the last four centuries BC,[1] the peoples of Italy came to be united under Rome's dominion. The political unification of first Italy and then large parts of Europe, Africa, and Asia under Roman political dominance had far-reaching consequences for the conquered peoples: together with political unification came social, economic, religious, linguistic, and cultural change. Some elements of culture became universal, especially in the Imperial period: 'Roman'-style theatres appeared in Brittannia and Syria, 'Roman' baths in Germania and Africa. In the Republican period, on the other hand, uniformity was scarce, at least until the first century. Not just cultural uniformity, but also legal, institutional, and linguistic uniformity did not exist in Italy for most of the Republican period. This book will investigate these processes of integration of Italy during the period of the Roman Republic, between roughly 400 and the mid-first century.

Often 'integration' is seen as a cultural process, by which two or more different peoples come to share the same culture and identity: 'the action or process of successfully joining or mixing with a different group of people'.[2] When this definition of integration is applied to the Roman world, 'integration' can be seen as a synonym for cultural change, often called 'Romanization': the process by which the different peoples in Italy 'joined' or 'mixed with' the Romans. However, it is important to emphasize that many different types of integration can occur—for example, political, linguistic, economic, social, cultural, and religious. All these types of integration are interrelated, but not all necessarily occur at the same time and at the same pace.

This book will focus on the economic integration of Italy in the Republican period. In particular, it will explore the connection between economic activity and integration—how did economic activities contribute to the unification of Italy in the civic, legal, social, and cultural sense? On the one hand, this book will investigate whether Italy became more integrated in an economic sense during the gradual expansion of Roman hegemony. Economic integration is defined here

[1] All dates are BC unless stated otherwise.

[2] Cambridge Dictionary 2018.

Italy's Economic Revolution. Saskia T. Roselaar, Oxford University Press (2019). © Saskia T. Roselaar.
DOI: 10.1093/oso/9780198829447.001.0001

as an increase of economic contacts between the different regions of Italy: did more long-distance economic relations emerge between the various regions of Italy? On the other hand, this book will investigate whether and how economic relations between Romans and Italians contributed to the integration of the Italic peoples in the Roman framework. Together with political dominance and economic interaction came cultural change among the Italic peoples: eventually they abandoned their own languages in favour of Latin, and a more uniform material culture emerged. How, if at all, were economic interaction and cultural change related? Did Italians build social relations with the Romans they traded with, leading to the social integration of Italy? And did the economic integration of Italy contribute in any way to the political integration of Italy, defined here as the grant of Roman citizenship to all Italians after the Social War of 91–88 BC?

1.2 The Structure of this Book

A brief overview of the structure of this book will shed light on the argument and rationale proposed. In the current introductory chapter, a number of preliminary discussions point out the main avenues of investigation of the volume. Firstly, section 1.3 gives a brief overview of the theories regarding economic developments and economic integration that underpin the volume. An important place is assigned to New Institutional Economics (NIE), which emphasizes the importance of institutions for economic developments. These institutions can be either formal—laws, government systems, property rights systems—or informal, such as social customs. As we will see throughout the book, economic developments were accompanied and often stimulated by changes in institutions, such as laws, currency, and language, as well as the creation of social relationships within and outside the Italian peninsula. The next section, 1.4, focuses on the concepts of 'integration' and 'identity'. As will become clear, what it meant to be Roman changed considerably in the last centuries BC, as did the identities of the various Italic peoples. Related to this, section 1.5 examines the concept of 'Romanization'—a term often used to describe the developments in Italy in the later Republic, but now increasingly questioned in scholarly debates. In section 1.6, the administration of Republican Italy will be discussed; a complicated patchwork of administrative statuses existed in Italy, and this may have affected the economic, social, and cultural developments that occurred in these respective areas. Finally, section 1.7 gives an overview of the methodology of this volume; a large variety of information, of many different types—literary, archaeological, epigraphic, and numismatic—has been used, so that a brief explanation of the methodology behind the argument is necessary.

Chapter 2 focuses on the interactions that took place between Romans and the peoples of Italy. A lacuna in current research is that most studies on Republican

Italy focus on cultural change. They describe the consequences of increased contact between the Italic peoples and Rome, namely the appearance of a more uniform culture and the spread of the Latin language—in other words, integration in a cultural and linguistic sense. Such studies often attribute these changes simply to the Roman conquest. Many assume that when an area had been 'Romanized' politically, i.e. was conquered by Rome and/or had received Roman citizenship, its 'Romanization' was complete.[3] However, it is not clear how exactly the conquest led to cultural change. There is therefore a significant gap in our knowledge of the integration processes in the Republic: we know that the peoples of Italy were united under Roman dominion and that the Italian cultures eventually became more similar, but we do not know how such changes resulted from day-to-day contacts between Romans and Italians and between Italians from different regions. We will investigate first, therefore, which interactions exactly took place between Romans and Italians and between various Italic peoples. Only if we know where and how different peoples interacted with each other can we understand how such contacts led to cultural and linguistic change.

The growing number of contacts between Romans and Italians, as described in chapter 2, led to economic change in Italy, which will be the subject of chapter 3. We will first look at economic activities carried out by Italians, independent from Roman interference. Still, these activities changed as Rome's power grew. Many Italians were quick to take advantage of the possibilities offered by their association with Rome, such as the opening up of new markets for Italian products and safer sailing because of Roman control of the Mediterranean. These economic activities had important consequences for economic developments in Italy itself: many far-reaching changes took place in the third to first centuries—for example, in settlement patterns and the scale of agricultural production. These developments varied widely from region to region, but at the same time, some developments occurred all over Italy. To test the connections between contacts with Rome and economic developments of Italy, four areas will be taken as case studies; the economic developments in each of these areas will be traced. This chapter will highlight the importance of non-Roman citizens in the economy of Republican Italy. There is still a tendency in Republican historiography to focus on Rome and the impact of the conquest on Italy. For example, Kay's 2014 book is called *Rome's Economic Revolution*. His work focuses almost completely on the activities of Roman elites; Italians receive only ten pages.[4] Of course, Roman senators, *equites*,

[3] Some recent examples include Celuzza 2002, who describes cultural changes in various towns after the Roman conquest under the heading 'La romanizzazione', and Cambi 2004, entitled 'Le campagne di Falerii e di Capena dopo la romanizzazione', as if the Roman conquest equalled cultural 'romanization'.

[4] Kay 2014, 206–12 on trade, 221–4 on public building, 231–2 on manufacture. His focus is consistently Roman: when discussing Hellenistic farms, Kay states (p. 151) that these were introduced into the 'Roman world' in the third century, while in fact many of them were located in allied Italy (see chapter 3.2.3).

and other elites accumulated great amounts of wealth and invested this in economic activities, but so did the Italians. In this book, we will therefore give more attention to the agency of the Italians and the economic developments they experienced during the Roman Republican period.

Chapter 4 investigates the long-term consequences of the association between Rome and Italy. This chapter will look, first, at changes in institutions and laws that occurred in the Republican period. Roman law gradually developed ways to enable trade between peoples with different legal systems. It also became necessary to deal efficiently with local systems of weights, measures, and coinage, which varied widely throughout Italy. Secondly, this chapter will discuss how wealth was invested in Italy. As discussed in chapter 3, the Italians were commercially active in a variety of ways. The investment of their income in public and private building gradually changed the landscape of Italy. Chapter 4 will also look in more detail at cultural change in Italy in the Republican period. Many new building types appeared in Italy, often inspired by Hellenistic models. Trendsetters may have been Italian *negotiatores* (merchants), who traded in many areas of the Mediterranean. However, this change in cultural expression did not necessarily indicate changes in the identity experienced by the Italians, as will be explored in this chapter. Therefore, chapter 4 also examines the concept of *Italia* and of an Italian identity, which emerged in the third and second centuries. Finally, this chapter discusses the attempts of the Romans to protect the economic well-being of the Italians. To maintain the Italians' loyalty, the benefits of association with Rome must outweigh the disadvantages. This section will discuss how the Romans managed—or failed—to achieve this aim.

For a long time the Italians were satisfied with their position in the Roman framework. They had to serve in the Roman army, but this duty was offset by the material benefits accruing from their association with Rome. However, as the Republican period progressed, Italian dissatisfaction with this state of affairs grew. Chapter 5 looks into the reasons for the growing discontent in the second century; it traces the development from the first signs of discontent to the eventual grant of citizenship in the first century. Firstly, this chapter examines the disadvantages that the Italians experienced because they did not have Roman citizenship, with regard to both prejudice from Romans and negative effects on their economic position. Italian frustration in the late second and early first centuries led to a demand for Roman citizenship. Rome's reluctance to share the Roman citizenship and its material benefits with Italians eventually culminated in the Social War of 91–88.[5] The Italians were granted Roman citizenship after the Social War, thus completing their civic integration, but this was not the final culmination of the process of cultural change. In fact, the largest changes in the culture of Italy

[5] The most important works on the Social War are Gabba 1954; Salmon 1958; 1962; Brunt 1965; Nagle 1973; Mouritsen 1998; Kendall 2013; Dart 2014.

occurred only after the political unification of the peninsula.[6] It seems that the Italians voluntarily adopted elements of Roman culture to create a 'Roman' identity for themselves, but having a 'Roman' identity did not exclude maintaining an 'Italian' identity as well (see section 1.4).

1.3 Economic Activities and Institutions

The focus of this work is the economic integration of Italy in the Republican period and the connection between economic activity and other types of integration. This means that the nature of the economy of Republican Italy should be discussed, as well the economic developments that occurred in this period.

The nature of the Roman (and implicitly, the Italian) economy has been much debated. Traditional studies of the Roman economy attempted to characterize the Roman economy as either 'primitive' or 'modern'. Primitivists, most prominently Finley[7] and Hopkins,[8] argued that the ancient economy was fundamentally different from, and much less developed than, the modern capitalist market economy. It was assumed that the market was dominated not by rational laws, but by social and political conventions, such as gifts and redistribution. On the contrary, modernists argued that the ancient economy and economic thought were similar to modern capitalist societies, in that they were ruled by economic laws such as supply and demand and dominated by the desire to make a profit. Implicitly, the economy of the Italian peninsula as a whole was classified either as equal in potential and achievement to the Roman economy (in modernist works), or as fundamentally poorer than the economy of Rome (in primitivist discourse).[9] In my view, this dichotomy is unhelpful. It is hardly possible to judge the ancient economy using modern standards, as the technological limitations severely limited its possibilities for profitable gain.[10] Instead, we should look at all available evidence in order to reconstruct, as far as possible, the performance of the Italian economy and the living standards of people in ancient Italy. As shown by the example of Pompeii, it was indeed possible for ancient towns to reach a fairly high living standard.[11]

Furthermore, the degree of integration in the Roman (and by implication Italian) economy has been the subject of intense discussion. Finley argued that the ancient economy was 'cellular': most regions lived off their own produce and imported little from elsewhere, so that the economy consisted of a large number of self-sufficient cells. Finley argues therefore that longer-distance trade was intermittent and periodic, and involved only those items which could not be produced

[6] Wallace-Hadrill 2008. [7] Finley 1999. [8] Hopkins 1978.
[9] Tol & De Haas 2017, 3. [10] Bang 1997.
[11] Flohr & Wilson 2017, 13–15; Jongman 2017, 18–24.

in the area itself, such as non-essential foodstuffs and luxury items.[12] It will be shown, however, that many parts of Italy saw fairly large amounts of import (see chapter 3) and were served by a dense network of periodic markets (chapter 2). This network allowed people, from simple peasants and small-scale manufacturers to professional traders and large landowners, to do business with each other and to distribute agricultural surpluses and manufactured goods throughout Italy.[13] This most likely was sufficient to create an average economic growth of about 0.1 per cent per year from 200 BC to AD 100, raising the living standards of most Romans and Italians.[14]

Although the ancient economy cannot simply be classed as 'modern', modern economic theory can assist ancient historians in the interpretation of the available data. Particularly important for the study of economic developments in Italy is an investigation into the institutions that underpinned economic activities in Republican Italy. Institutions can be formal—laws, government systems, property rights systems—as well as informal, such as social customs. Together, these institutions to a great degree determine the economic relations that take place. Economists have given much attention to the importance of institutions, as is shown by the perspective of New Institutional Economics (NIE).[15]

A central concept within NIE are transaction costs, which are directly affected by a society's institutions. Transaction costs can be defined as all costs incurred in making an economic exchange, and can be divided into three types:

- Information costs, i.e. costs in money and time that are necessary to find out where a required good is available on the market, where demand is highest, which supplier offers the lowest price, etc.
- Bargaining costs, i.e. costs required to reach an agreement with the other party. Reaching an agreement can take up valuable time, as well as requiring the services of specialized middlemen.
- Policing and enforcement costs, i.e. the costs of making sure the other party adheres to the contract, and taking appropriate action in case of a conflict.

This means that the free market is never completely free; neither individuals, businesses, nor governments can make a free and completely rational economic choice, since they are constrained by the rules of the economy and its institutions. Moreover, they do not have full, complete, and reliable information available on

[12] Finley 1999, 158–62. [13] De Ligt 1993, 109, 114.

[14] Morris, Saller, & Scheidel 2007, 5–6.

[15] For modern theories of NIE, see North 1990; Harriss, Hunter, & Lewis 1995. For the ancient world, see Lo Cascio 2006; Bang 2009. Criticism can be found in Steiger 2006; he argues that NIE is unable to deal with non-individual rights, e.g. rights to common land, which were very important in the ancient world (see Roselaar 2010, 209–13). Despite these objections, NIE is important in emphasizing the importance of transaction costs and the effects of lowering them, which was certainly relevant for the Roman Republic.

which to base their choice. Furthermore, no system of redistribution is totally efficient, since most parties aim to maximize their own profits, rather than cooperating to ensure an efficient redistribution of goods. This means that despite the presence of efficient institutions, transaction costs never sink to the lowest possible level, since there is always a degree of inefficiency present in the available institutions.

On the one hand, the presence of institutions raises transaction costs slightly, since legal requirements, such as making a written contract or going to court to solve a dispute, are not free. If an individual could gain complete and perfect information and carry out transactions in the most efficient way, without needing institutions, his transaction costs would be lower. On the other hand, as long as institutions function efficiently, their presence will lower transaction costs for most individuals, since institutions simplify transactions and create access to information that would otherwise be unavailable. Thus, the creation of institutions is the best solution to lower transaction costs to the lowest possible level for most individuals.

Thus, according to NIE, formal institutions are created partially to simplify the acquisition of information and to reduce transaction costs. However, informal institutions also play an important role, since they can reduce the cost of finding reliable information. For example, businessmen received information from their business contacts about trade opportunities, such as food shortages in specific areas, and gained information about the reliability of potential business partners. On the other hand, maintaining a good name in such a network involves higher transaction costs: for example, informal customs demand gifts to prospective business partners.[16]

Some of the tenets of NIE are clearly applicable to the Republican period. In the early Republic, barriers for trade existed, which raised transaction costs. For example, the absence of a shared coinage raised transaction costs. Firstly, money-changers were needed to deal with different types of coin, and expected a fee for their services. Secondly, if people accepted foreign coins as the equivalent of their own, or valued them by weight, there was always the risk of being underpaid. To cover this risk, all prices might be set at a higher level. Similarly, because not all states used the same laws, it took a great amount of time and money to take disputes to the courts. This might be mitigated by raising the prices for all exchanges. Thus, inefficient institutions may have led to higher transaction costs and therefore to higher prices overall. Whether all these mechanisms were at work in the Roman Republic cannot be determined; for example, there is no evidence that prices were raised in order to mitigate high transaction costs. However, we can be sure that the variety of institutions existing throughout

[16] See Broekaert 2013 for the importance of trust in the networks of the Caecilii from Pompeii and the Sulpicii from Puteoli.

Italy meant that it cost time and effort to conclude contracts with people from other states.

The expansion of the Roman state lowered transaction costs throughout Italy, since it reduced the risk of armed conflict, created access to the Roman legal system, and eventually provided a shared currency and metrological systems. On the other hand, the Roman state was pursuing its own interests and those of its leading oligarchy, namely to increase its own power and the glory of its leaders—including the Italian elites, who had to be convinced to remain loyal to Rome. Therefore, being conquered by the Romans on the one hand brought advantages to the Italians, e.g. being able to use Roman institutions and to trade in new areas, but it was not a universal blessing. Not everyone was able to profit from inclusion in the Roman state; if local elites wanted to profit, they had to adapt to Roman institutions and culture. Thus, on average the Italians experienced greater economic well-being. However, we will see that eventually the Italians felt they were unable to profit fully from their association with Rome. In other words, the unequal relationship with Rome had become too costly for them to sustain in economic terms—and perhaps also in other terms, as we will see.

1.4 Integration and Identity

As stated above, one focus of this work is the connection between economic activity and other types of integration. In fact, integration is closely connected to the concept of identity. The processes of integration in the Republic are often assumed to have led to a change in identity among the Italians: it is thought that they came to feel more 'Roman' and eventually identified themselves as such. These are important issues for this book, so it is necessary to explore them in more detail. First, we must clarify what exactly will be meant by the terms 'identity', 'culture', etc, and how these can be transformed in a situation of political and economic change. We will, furthermore, analyse how processes of integration occur and how they are experienced by individuals living in a situation where multiple ethnic, cultural, or linguistic groups interact.

Identity has been described as 'a social category, a set of persons marked by a label and distinguished by rules deciding membership and (alleged) characteristics features or attributes'.[17] Several forms of identity exist at the same time: a sense of personal identity gives meaning to 'I', while social identity creates a sense of belonging to a group, a 'we'. The most important features that determine identity are race, ethnicity, religion, language, and culture, although none of these is essential; they are just outside markers that may indicate the identity of the person

[17] Fearon 1999, 2.

displaying them.[18] It is not even necessary that people share the same language or material culture in order to share an identity.[19] Language can, however, become an important part of identity, especially when this is threatened. During the Social War, for example, the Italians opposing Rome used the Oscan language to set them apart from the Romans, even if not all Italians who opposed Rome actually spoke Oscan (see chapter 5).

The terms identity and ethnicity are often used as synonyms, although ethnicity is better defined as one specific part of identity relating to a self-conscious identification with a particular sociocultural group.[20] Six elements of shared ethnicity have been identified: a common name for the group, common myths of descent, a shared history, shared cultural elements (often including language), a sense of coming from a specific territorial homeland, and the sense of belonging to the same group.[21] The latter may be the most important: ethnicity revolves around 'beliefs about one's obligations to the group, the acceptance of behavioural prescriptions arising from membership in the group, feelings about belonging to the group and about participating in the formal and informal institutions and activities'.[22]

Expressions of culture are important to display one's identity. Culture may be defined as the tangible aspect of identity: the objects and values that are used to display one's identity to others. Often, one ethnic group shares one culture; for example, all Etruscans share what can be described as Etruscan culture. However, within one ethnic group there can be several subcultures, so that one ethnic group does not necessarily share all elements of a specific culture. Culture must be expressed or performed through objects and activities. The most important function of such performances is the enactment of community: they strengthen the perception of commonality that is created and maintained through social practice, and distinguish members from non-members.[23]

In older scholarly literature, Roman culture and identity were assumed to have been fixed: a set package of values, beliefs, and material expressions, which was transferred wholesale to people in Italy and the provinces. People were believed to have accepted this package and thus to have been turned into 'Romans', giving up their old values and cultures. A Roman identity was seen as incompatible with a 'native' one.[24] However, it is now recognized that identities and the accompanying cultural and material expressions are not fixed, but change over time. Objects and behaviour that identify a specific culture need to have a function in order to be

[18] Hall 2002, 9–12.

[19] Dench 1995, 213; Wallace-Hadrill 2008, 64. Which elements of identity are most important for a people or individual depends on the situation; for example, the Greek language was an important part of what it meant to be Greek, while one did not necessarily have to speak Latin in order to be a Roman citizen. See Woolf 1995, 14–16.

[20] Hodos 2010, 4.

[21] Smith 1986. For ethnicity in the Greek world, see Hall 2002.

[22] Smolicz 1981, 85.

[23] Mac Sweeney 2011, 35–41.

[24] E.g. Haverfield 1908.

performed. There has to be a social rationale that explains why they are important for the community that performs them, otherwise they will cease to be relevant and disappear.[25]

This means that the identity of a group or person can change according to circumstances. A person may feel himself to belong to more than one (sub) culture, and therefore have more than one identity. Thus, the identity that someone chooses to adopt can vary according to circumstance: someone can be at the same time a son, a father, a husband, a wealthy farmer, a Lucanian-born Roman citizen, a local town councillor, and the guest friend of a Roman, and consider himself 'all, some, or none of these at any given moment'.[26] This man presents himself differently to his own family than to a Roman magistrate; sometimes he prefers to call himself a Roman—for example, when dealing with Roman courts of law or pursuing a career in Rome—while at other times he expresses pride in his Italian heritage—for example when celebrating a local town festival.[27] People often adjust their identity if it brings them profit, either materially or socially.[28] In ancient Italy, for example, an Italian engaging in Roman politics would be more successful if he presented himself as a Roman to other Romans. Still, in private circumstances his local identity could be the most important to him. Thus, Rome imposed a supplementary identity, but it was quite possible to have more than one identity.[29] The willingness of Italians to present themselves as 'Roman' varied according to time and circumstance. Language use is a good example of such behaviour: the shift from Italian languages to Latin did not progress in a uniform fashion. An Italian could choose to employ different languages in different situations, according to the identity he wanted to present (see chapter 3).[30]

The identity of a group or individual is often perceived differently by outsiders than by insiders. A person may claim one identity, but another may be imposed by others.[31] This is especially important with regard to prejudice: if immigrants are perceived by the receiving society as lazy and unreliable, they will have a hard time participating in the economic life of their new country. For the ancient world, prejudice was especially important when participating in Roman politics.[32] Nevertheless, when it suited their purpose, the Romans were quick to assert a shared identity with Italians. Cato's *Origines* is a good example: the author acknowledges the importance of Italians in the expansion of Rome's power.[33] In the Augustan

[25] Hodos 2010, 15; Wallace-Hadrill 2008, 29. [26] Huskinson 2000, 10.

[27] Huskinson 2000, 15; Hodos 2010, 26–7. As Wallace-Hadrill 2008, 5 suggests, cultural expression took the form of 'triangulation' between Greek, Roman, and local, so that a different end result could be displayed in each situation.

[28] Sweetman 2011, 4–5. [29] Witcher 2000; Harris 2007, 319. [30] Langslow 2012.

[31] Huskinson 2000, 10; Wallace-Hadrill 2008, 3–6. [32] Dench 1995.

[33] Jefferson 2012.

period, the contribution of Italy to the power of the Roman state was acknowledged even more explicitly (see chapter 5).

We will see throughout this book that the Romans made very little effort to alter the existing language, religion, or other cultural aspects of the Italians. The political integration of Italians into the Roman state did not mean that they had to adopt all elements of Roman culture. If they wished to participate in the economic networks that spanned the peninsula, and in politics in Rome, Italians benefited from learning Latin and adhering to the main elements of the cultural *koine* that was shared by Romans and Italians, but they did not have to give up their cultural identity completely (see chapters 4 and 5). Furthermore, cultural integration between Romans and Italians was not actively encouraged by the Roman state.

Material culture is the most visible aspect of ancient identity, since different kinds of material culture are well preserved in the archaeological record. Scholars are often quick to associate any and all material remains with a certain historically attested people. However, it has long been recognized that 'pots are not people': the use of a certain type of pottery or other object does not mean that the user identified with the people who produced these objects, nor does it mean that people using the same items shared the same identity.[34] The adoption of supposedly 'Roman' cultural elements has often been seen as 'self-Romanization': people adopted products associated with Rome, because they thought of themselves as Roman.[35] However, this cannot be maintained. For example, pottery imported from Greece appears at Italian sites from the eighth century onwards, but its presence does not mean that the people using these pots were Greeks, or thought of themselves as 'Greek'. They merely used these newly available objects for their own purposes, e.g. to display their social status to their local peers by using expensive and fashionable new items. Thus, the meaning associated with an object was not the same everywhere.[36]

In fact, people could use 'Roman' culture to express a local identity: the arrival of Rome widened the range of cultural choices of expression for the conquered, and thus provided more options to express regional identities.[37] Very importantly, cultural choices were not always a conscious response to Rome. Usually such choices were made in response to local circumstances and motivated by the desire to maintain or enhance one's local social position, without a direct reference to Rome.[38] People using such items were not trying to become Roman, but were 'retaining the core of their cultural identity, with the addition of certain powerful innovations that assisted them to perform their lives in new ways under the

[34] Witcher 2006. For the concept of 'style', see Versluys 2013, 432–4: styles were flexible, depending on the message displayed, and could be combined with other styles.

[35] See discussion in Cavalieri 2012, 171.

[36] Witcher 2000, 219; see Woolf 1998, 176–80.

[37] Roth 2012.

[38] Hingley 2005, 111.

changing political conditions'.[39] Furthermore, we must be aware that not all objects used in daily life were significant in expressing an identity. Factors such as the availability of objects, determined by the market, may have played an equally important role. Therefore, not every choice for a specific item should be seen as a conscious statement, either for or against Roman culture, or as an expression of identity.

Not all groups within the Italian communities engaged equally with the new opportunities that emerged after the conquest of Italy by Rome. Italian elites were more aware of Rome's presence and its impact than the average Italian; local elites engaged first-hand with Romans, both during the conquest and later, in connection with the Roman administration. They were also aware of the benefits that could accrue from association with Roman rule, such as new economic opportunities that resulted from the growing Roman dominion in the Mediterranean. Local elites often had to walk a fine line between protecting their own interests and those of their people. They had to obey Roman demands for soldiers, food supplies, etc, because a refusal could bring Roman retribution, but they also had to protect the local population from Roman exploitation.[40] Elites could, furthermore, reinforce their local status by spending money—some of which they had earned in the new, Roman-created Mediterranean markets—on public buildings and other gifts.[41] Close association with Rome and its representatives was not attractive for the elites because of the 'Roman' culture on offer, but especially because of the political and military—and, I argue, economic—opportunities. Integration into the Roman state offered opportunities to make money, e.g. by using Roman communication routes, through the development of a town into an economic centre. Thus, association with the Roman state offered opportunities to maximize one's economic potential.[42]

However, this did not mean that elites who associated with Rome were trying to represent themselves as Romans, rather than as members of their respective Italian groups. For most local elites, their position in their hometown was paramount, since this was the main political arena for most Italians. Italians holding Roman citizenship and aspiring to acceptance in Roman society had to walk a fine line between displaying cultural behaviour acceptable in Rome, and adhering to their identity as Italians from local communities. They could not completely give up their local identity, since this would mean that they would lose their local powerbase. Even when all Italians had received Roman citizenship, politicians from an Italian background often maintained strong bonds with their hometowns,

[39] Hingley 2005, 99. See Woolf 1998, 11; Wallace-Hadrill 2008, 10; Versluys 2013, 429.
[40] Huskinson 2000, 19; Hingley 2005, 79.
[41] Huskinson 2000, 97; see Woolf 1998, 156–7; Perkins & Nevett 2000, 217; Hingley 2005, 50; Meijer 2011, 25.
[42] Sweetman 2011, 4–5.

acting as patrons and benefactors, in exchange for their townsmen's support in elections at Rome (see chapter 5).

There are few sources written from an Italian point of view, but it is clear that the conquest of Italy by Rome led to changes in identities across Italy, and in the material artefacts and the language in which the Italians expressed this (see chapter 4). In this study, I frequently use the term 'Italians', and it is therefore important to explain what this term means. In most studies, the Italic peoples are defined in ethnic terms, e.g. Lucanians or Samnites. It is debated at what time the Italic peoples came to be grouped into these clearly defined units. Some argue that these cultural boundaries had already been defined in the fifth century or earlier.[43] Other scholars have argued that the Roman conquest in the fourth and third centuries was instrumental in creating ethnic boundaries between the Italic peoples. As individual Italian towns cooperated in the fight against Rome, they started to identify along ethnic lines, rather than by town.[44] It is important to remember that ethnic identities did not necessarily match political or cultural boundaries:[45] not all Samnites belonged to the same state, although they shared largely the same culture, with some local differences. It must be remembered that for most of the Republic, there was no common 'Italian' identity. There were tensions within and between communities, based on local rivalries, status differences, and the varying impacts of Roman authority. Therefore, the Italians were not able, before the Social War, to formulate an overall policy that could have formed an alternative to Roman rule (see chapter 5).[46]

Therefore, in this book I use 'Italians' as a general term for all people in Italy who did not possess Roman citizenship, including *cives sine suffragio* (see below), those with Latin rights and settlers in Latin colonies, and those who were nominally independent, i.e. Italian allies. Thus, 'Italian' is used exclusively to indicate a specific legal status, which is characterized by the absence of Roman citizen status, rather than by shared (legal or other) characteristics of Italians. The use of a single term for these various people, therefore, by no means implies that they shared the same culture and language. On the contrary, there were many different Italic peoples with different languages and cultures. A Hellenistic cultural *koine* was slowly spreading through Italy and many elements of this culture were shared throughout Italy from the fourth century onwards (see chapter 4.4), but there was no civic or ethnic unity among the Italic peoples until very late in the Republican period. Furthermore, even if some Italic peoples shared an ethnic identity, e.g. 'Samnite' or 'Etruscan', Italians in many cases identified more strongly with their individual towns than with their ethnic group. This meant that not all towns within an ethnic group shared the same political outlook. This is

[43] Bourdin 2012, 550–1.
[44] Cornell 2004 for the Samnites; see Dench 1995, 202–12; Isayev 2017, 89–92.
[45] Stek 2013a, 348–50. [46] Fronda 2010, 25–8.

shown by the conflicts within and between towns during the Second Punic War, when some chose Hannibal's side, while others preferred Rome.[47]

Despite the opportunities and possibilities offered to the Italians after the Roman conquest, it is very important to emphasize that the conquest was not a universally positive experience. In some recent books written for the general public, the Roman attitude towards integration has been presented as an ideal, an example for current multicultural societies struggling with the integration of immigrants.[48] Most of these representations focus on the Imperial period, when the Romans formulated a clearer mission of 'civilization'.[49] Often, scholars paint a picture of people happy to join the Roman state, leading to a general growth in well-being during the Roman period. Although it cannot be denied that living standards on average grew and that many people profited from their incorporation into the Roman state,[50] the conquest must not be forgotten. The Roman conquest of Italy was extremely violent, with as many as 70,000 people enslaved during the Samnite Wars (even if Livy's figures are exaggerated),[51] many towns destroyed, and great amounts of lands taken as *ager publicus*. After the conquest, rather than striving for 'integration and assimilation, connectedness and growth',[52] the main aim of Rome was to maintain its hegemony and collect material wealth from the conquered territories.[53] Those who did not cooperate with Rome were mercilessly punished, as the example of Fregellae shows: this town, a Latin colony with a blameless record of loyalty to Rome, revolted in 125 and was razed to the ground as punishment.[54]

Thus, any active discontent was punished, and the Romans did not share the privileges associated with Roman citizenship with their Italian allies. The integration of Italy and especially the provinces has been presented as the result of elite negotiation and native agency.[55] This is true in a sense, but it only applied to those elites who had survived the conquest and remained loyal to Rome.[56] Furthermore, if Italian elites who had received citizenship wanted to be accepted fully by the Roman elite, they had to conform to a certain behaviour ideal, without much leeway for deviant ideas; they 'negotiated' their identities, but within the context of 'rules that were not entirely of their own making'.[57] Moreover, the economic benefits of the conquest were not equally accessible to all; it may be that the Italian

[47] Fronda 2010.

[48] E.g. Meijer 2011, 12.

[49] Verg. *Aen.* 6.851–3: 'Remember, Roman, it is for you to rule the nations with your power, / (that will be your skill) to crown peace with law, / to spare the conquered, and subdue the proud' (*tu regere imperio populos, Romane, memento/(hae tibi erunt artes), pacique imponere morem,/parcere subiectis et debellare superbos*). See Plin. *NH* 3.39: Italy was 'chosen by the power of the gods...to gather the scattered realms and to soften their customs..., and to give civilization to mankind'. See Woolf 1998, 54–60.

[50] Jongman 2017.

[51] Liv. 10.29-17-18 for the battle of Sentinum. See Cornell 1995, 361.

[52] Meijer 2011, 13.

[53] Mattingly 2011, 164, 212. See Millett 1990, 6; Hingley 2005, 120.

[54] Liv. *Per.* 60; Vell. 2.6.4.

[55] E.g. Millett 1990; Woolf 1997.

[56] Mattingly 2011, 38.

[57] Hingley 2005, 48, 60; see Mattingly 1997, 19.

regions saw more economic inequality between rich and poor in the Republican period (see chapter 3.3.5).

It is clear that the formation of identities and processes of integration is complex, and involves negotiation from all parties. This book will investigate how economic relations between Romans and Italians and between different Italian groups affected the identity of the Italians and their integration into the Roman framework. Throughout this book, we will see that the incorporation of the allies into the Roman framework opened up new opportunities for those who managed to work together with the Romans. However, full integration into the Roman state, including social relations and participation in politics, required a certain degree of adaptation to Roman identity and culture. Therefore, while the Italians were certainly powerful agents in shaping their own culture and economic prosperity, they were still dependent on Rome's goodwill in allowing them to pursue these opportunities. Furthermore, certain options, such as gaining a share in ruling Rome's growing empire, remained closed to the Italians until the first century.

1.5 Integration and Romanization

In this book, I cannot avoid saying just a few words on the heated issue of 'Romanization'. This term has been used so often, with so many different meanings, that scholars have despaired of its usefulness and have proposed to abandon the term altogether.[58] However, I will argue that the term may be usefully applied to some of the developments we can discern in Republican Italy.

Early studies of the integration of Italy considered Roman culture and Latin language to be more 'civilized' than the various Italic languages and cultures, and Romanization was therefore seen as the inevitable consequence of military conquest.[59] Of course, this stance has long been abandoned, although the superiority of Roman culture is still often latently—or even overtly—present in scholarly literature. Even in recent works, any cultural change, such as a change in the type of material culture or the appearance of a more urbanized settlement pattern, is explained as a result of Romanization. A 2001 study of the sanctuary at Rossano di Vaglio in Lucania states: 'Sono presenti a Rossano dediche più impegnative, come statue in bronzo... e sculture a tutto tondo in marmo,... prodotti in botteghe di tradizione insulare microasiatica tra III e II sec. a. C., che testimoniano... l'avanzata fase di romanizzazione della Lucania che si esprime attraverso l'adozione di forme concettuali e modelli figurativi ellenistici.'[60] However, the authors

[58] E.g. Mattingly 2002; Sweetman 2011, 1. [59] E.g. Haverfield 1908.

[60] Masseria & D'Anisi 2001, 130. Another example is Greco 2004, 625–7, who explains that statues of women found at the Hera temple at Paestum were similar to other temples in Campania and Rome,

do not explain why the presence of art based on models from Asia Minor should be a sign of 'advanced' Romanization; it is simply assumed that this type of art arrived first in Rome and from there spread through Italy. The incorporation of an area by Rome is then considered sufficient explanation for all economic, social, and cultural changes taking place after the conquest, as we have seen above. Nevertheless, we must avoid such 'post hoc ergo propter hoc' explanations: political and cultural integration do not occur at the same pace, not can political incorporation explain wide-ranging economic and cultural changes.

Although some scholars still adhere to the idea that Rome had a great impact on every aspect of life in Italy, this has been severely criticized in the last decades. The most important result of recent studies, many based on essential archaeological research, is an awareness of the enormous variety of responses to Roman conquest. This variation existed not only on the provincial or regional level, but even from location to location. It is now clear that contacts between Romans and Italians were much more complex than previously thought, and that Italians, and later provincials, were active agents who created their own cultural identity, rather than passive recipients of 'Roman' culture[61]—although, as we have just seen, there were limits to this negotiation. Furthermore, it is impossible to identify 'Roman' culture spreading through the Mediterranean, at least in the Republican period: despite some shared characteristics, local responses were widely divergent. Most scholars therefore agree that processes of cultural change were complex and that different people of different social classes and in different locations actively engaged with Roman culture for their own reasons and purposes.[62]

Moreover, the Romans were in many cases not the instigators of cultural change: many areas of Italy already enjoyed elements of Hellenic culture, such as temples and theatres, while Rome as yet did not enjoy these amenities. Rome was not the driving force in the spread of these cultural elements, which instead appeared first in the towns of Campania, but also in rural sanctuaries such as Pietrabbondante in Samnium (see chapters 3 and 4).[63] In addition, since many items, such as pottery, arrived in Italy directly from Greece, rather than through Roman mediation, the presence of such items tells us nothing about 'Romanization' in Republican Italy.[64]

One of the main objections against the term 'Romanization' is that it is Rome-centred and does not take into account the various local and regional experiences throughout the peninsula. Mattingly, for example, argues that 'Romanization' does not take account of the variety of multidirectional cultural experiences, and

and concludes that this was the result of 'quell'imponente fenomeno di unificazione culturale promosso da Roma'. See also Salmon 1982, 100; Torelli 1983, 243.

[61] Millett 1990; Woolf 1998; Keay & Terrenato (eds.) 2001; Le Roux 2004.
[62] Stek 2014, 37–9. [63] See Zanker (ed.) 1976. [64] Dench 1997, 46–7.

that its use leads to the generalization of locally specific developments.[65] As just noted, in each location the response to contact with Rome was different: most people retained their own laws and institutions, culture, and language. The processes of cultural integration that occurred throughout the Italian peninsula were the result of complex interactions between the Roman state and its representatives (many of whom were not from Rome at all) and the indigenous populations, who of course were not homogeneous either. Geographical mobility on a large scale ensured that the populations of many regions, not only in the cities but also in the countryside, consisted of people from different cultural backgrounds.[66]

Some have therefore looked for alternative models to explain cultural change, such as 'creolization' or 'cultural bricolage',[67] which supposedly give a louder voice to the conquered peoples, and especially to the non-elite population. The term creolization is derived from linguistic studies and refers to a 'mastery of two cultural traditions, which can be drawn on in different degrees according to context'.[68] This would fit the idea that each individual possesses several separate identities, which can be used according to the needs of the situation. The problem with this theory is that creole languages are usually part of a sub-elite culture, while in Italy the 'mastery of two cultural traditions' was also displayed by the elites.[69] 'Cultural bricolage' sees cultural identity as built of many different building blocks, 'some old, some new, some local, some coming from outside'.[70] Thus, identity and its expression were made up of several building blocks, with each block receiving more or less attention, dependent on the situation. Despite the introduction of these new models, the fact remains that most of the primary sources are written from the perspective of the Roman elite. This problem is not easily solved by abandoning 'Romanization' for a different term.[71]

Recently, the concept of globalization has been applied to the processes of cultural change that took place in the Roman world.[72] During most of the twentieth century, cultural change was seen as a unification process, by which the territories under Roman rule became more uniform in culture. In the last quarter of the twentieth century, this approach was replaced by a focus on local studies, emphasizing the extreme variation of local responses to Roman conquest.

[65] Mattingly 1997, 9. [66] Isayev 2017, 108–38.

[67] Le Roux 2004, following the sociological concept of 'hybridity', proposes 'métissage', in which two cultures were 'blended'; however, this suggests that the end product was one uniform culture rather than a variety of cultural elements that were more or less important, according to the context.

[68] Webster 2001, quote at 218.

[69] Osborne & Vout 2010, 235–6. Furthermore, creolization did not apply to all aspects of life in the same way: administrative systems changed earlier and in a more direct way than culture.

[70] Terrenato 1998, quote on p. 24.

[71] Wallace-Hadrill 2008, 11–13. His work should be read with the insightful review by Osborne & Vout 2010.

[72] E.g. Pitts & Versluys (eds.) 2014; Witcher 2017. However, Stek 2014, 31 explains that globalization is not a completely new concept, and has been influenced by earlier models.

However, this created the danger of losing track of the common factors within Roman Italy. Globalization has been considered a new way to approach the cultural changes caused by the Roman state, without imposing old-fashioned imperialistic ideas. As we have seen, local society remained the focus of life for most people. Even though globalization leads to more connections with the outside world, this is often accompanied by a contrary trend of more emphasis on local identity.[73] Changes occurred on a 'global' level, some under the influence of Rome, others as a result of independent developments. These changes were processed differently in each locality, leading to a unique configuration of global and local elements.[74] Recent studies have acknowledged this combination of global and local in the neologism 'glocalization'.[75]

In discussing 'Roman' culture, it is important to remember that 'there is no such thing as a 'pure' Roman culture, because Rome and Italy were themselves trapped in a network of cultural references to the Hellenistic, Italic, and Mediterranean worlds'.[76] Thus, it is virtually impossible to trace the directions of cultural influence to a single source, since cultural elements of several origins affected Italy at the same time. Even before the Roman conquest, cultural aspects derived from the Greek world, with which the Italians had long maintained economic and social contacts, affected Italian cultures.[77] For example, the appearance of coined money in Samnium in the third century is sometimes ascribed to the influence of Latin colonies settled in the area.[78] However, already in the fourth century, money from Magna Graecia and Campania circulated in Samnium. The first Samnite coins were influenced not by Rome, but by Campanian and southern Italian coinage.[79] It is therefore difficult to draw a strict line between 'Roman' and 'Italian' culture; both were strongly influenced by Greek elements. This means that changes in cultural manifestations in Italy in the period of Roman dominance may not always be due to Roman influence, but should be ascribed to contacts with Greeks in southern Italy or with mainland Greece (see chapter 4).

Furthermore, many cultural developments in Italy that were once seen as the result of Roman influence have turned out to be not very Roman after all. Thus, the appearance of hill forts in mountainous areas of Italy in the fourth century, which has been ascribed to the Roman threat against Italic peoples, had little to do with Rome.[80] Buildings that are often considered typically 'Roman', such as baths and aqueducts, appeared in some Italian towns much earlier than in Rome itself. Stone theatres were built in various towns in Italy in the second century, but in Rome itself not until the year 55 (see chapter 4). Atrium houses appeared in Etruria and southern Italy long before they became part of the standard house

[73] Witcher 2000, 217. See Hodos 2010, 24.
[74] Naerebout 2014, 268–9.
[75] Pitts & Versluys (eds.) 2014, 13.
[76] Jiménez 2010, 57; see Woolf 1997; Hingley 2005, 55; Wallace-Hadrill 2008, 19–28, 73–143.
[77] Purcell 1994.
[78] Renda 2004, 404.
[79] Crawford 1985, 26–8.
[80] Oakley 1995, 135–8.

design in Rome. 'Hellenistic farms', i.e. relatively small commercial farm units, appeared in many parts of the Mediterranean, not just in Italy, in roughly the same period (see chapter 3).[81]

The nature and speed of these changes differed according to region and location, so that a uniform 'Italic' culture did not exist, despite the existence of a *koine* of shared cultural elements among the Italic peoples.[82] It cannot be denied that as Rome united the Italian peninsula under its rule, the cultures of the Italic peoples gradually became more uniform, but this process was not complete until the Augustan period. It is only in this period, which falls outside the scope of this book, that a true 'cultural revolution'[83] can be said to have occurred (see chapter 5). Since Rome's political dominance apparently had so little influence on the cultures of the Italic peoples for most of the Republican period, it is certainly incorrect to speak of 'Romanization' in a cultural sense. The inspiration for many cultural changes in Italy came not from Rome, but from Hellenistic Greece, so that we may speak of a 'Hellenization' of culture rather than a 'Romanization'.[84]

Still, it cannot be denied that many cultural developments in Italy would have been impossible without the presence of the Roman state. Although these objects were not necessarily an indication of cultural 'Romanization', they would not have arrived in Italy without the institutions and economic networks created by the Roman state. For example, the Italians used many Roman institutions, such as laws and coinage; although they did not use these to display a Roman identity, the fact that they used Roman institutions in itself created a closer connection between them and the Romans. Furthermore, much of the money used by Italians to pay for Hellenistic buildings was gained in overseas trade or in agricultural production, which enjoyed a great increase after Rome's conquest of the Mediterranean.

I therefore agree with Hingley's statement that 'despite such attempts to decentre the idea of Roman identity, the use of the term "Roman" for the constellation that formed the empire is justified by the fact that these highly variable individual cultures were incorporated into an entity that called itself by this term'.[85] The external politics and military policy of the Italian states were bound by Rome's demands. The institutions of the Italian states, such as administration and coinage, quickly adapted to Roman standards (see chapter 4). Rome therefore had a great impact on some parts of Italian life, so that we might speak of Romanization in the administrative, political, and legal sense.

By no means, however, did Romanization lead to a loss of local identity; on the contrary, Italians exploited the possibilities to express their identities for their own

[81] Terrenato 2001a, 18–20. [82] See Johannowsky 1976; Wiseman 1983.
[83] Wallace-Hadrill 2008. [84] Wallace-Hadrill 2008, 27.
[85] Hingley 2005, 56. See Wallace-Hadrill 2008.

purposes, as we have seen. Even though new buildings and other objects followed Greek cultural models and were financially dependent on Roman imperialism, they were still expressions of local identity. As Wallace-Hadrill states, they were 'investment[s] in local religiosity and local pride which [were] in no way diminished by the existence of stylistic evocations of the east, or dependence on participation in Roman imperialism and constructional technique'.[86] Thus, the interaction between Roman conquest, Hellenistic culture, and local Italic identity is much more complex than is often acknowledged by the adherents and opponents of 'Romanization'.

In my view, really to understand the processes of integration and identity transformation in Republican Italy, as well as cultural and linguistic change, it is more fruitful to study actual interactions between Romans and Italians, rather than continue the debate on the usefulness of the term 'Romanization'. Much of the aporia surrounding the 'Romanization' debate stems from the misapprehension that developments should be studied in a single holistic model or framework. It is more useful to look at the diverse research questions on their own merit, and approach the source material with these questions in mind, rather than try to make all sources fit into a preconceived model.[87] Therefore, this book will look at the economic, administrative, and legal changes in Republican Italy, and the effects of this 'Romanization' on Italian culture and identity.

1.6 The Administration of Conquered Areas

Before we can move on to study the integration of Italy, it is necessary to survey briefly the way the Roman state administered the areas it conquered. As the Romans conquered Italy, they devised various ways to deal with the defeated populations. A number of different civic statuses could be granted to the Italian people that were conquered by the Roman state.[88]

- A grant of full citizenship (*civitas optimo iure*) to the defeated people. These communities retained their own local magistrates, but their system of local government was adapted to the Roman system. Roman citizens had a number of privileges not shared by others. The most important of these were the rights to vote and to be elected as magistrates. Furthermore, Roman citizens had access to the *ius civile*, the system of Roman law, which was not available to non-citizens (*peregrini*, see chapter 4). Finally, as a result of their protection by the *ius civile*, Roman citizens enjoyed a variety of economic

[86] Wallace-Hadrill 2008, 106–43, quote p. 115. [87] Stek 2014, 32.

[88] Göhler 1939; Sherwin-White 1973; Galsterer 1976; Hantos 1983; Bispham 2007, 74–112. For the Latins, see Coşkun 2009a.

advantages (see chapter 5). Finally, Roman citizenship served as a marker of status, which was unattainable for *peregrini*.

- A grant of *civitas sine suffragio* (citizenship without the vote). The particulars of this status are still debated. As the term *cives sine suffragio* implies, these people were citizens of the Roman state without the right to vote, but with regard to legal matters, they could most likely avail themselves of the Roman *ius civile*.[89] Areas with this status were governed as *praefecturae*: a *praefectus* was sent at regular intervals from Rome to settle lawsuits. It might be assumed that for internal, day-to-day business, *cives sine suffragio* had their own magistrates, since it would be impractical if no business could be conducted without a *praefectus*.[90] It is often assumed that the *civitas sine suffragio* was a transitional phase; a community would receive full citizenship when it was sufficiently 'Romanized'.[91] However, according to some sources, this status was given to Italians as a punishment,[92] and it is therefore unlikely that all *cives sine suffragio* were expected to become citizens eventually.
- Recent debate has called into question the existence of the *civitas sine suffragio* as a well-defined legal status. Mouritsen points out that the term *civitas sine suffragio* is never explained in the ancient sources. He assumes it is more likely that the concept was only developed when political integration into the Roman state was a real possibility and came to be desired by allied communities, possibly in the second century.[93] On the other hand, and more likely, Tan argues that the *civitas sine suffragio* was consciously created by the Roman state as a separate category of allies after the Latin War of 341–338. It allowed the Romans to collect taxes from wealthy allies, without admitting them to full citizenship.[94] In any case, by the late second century

[89] Cornell 1995, 351; Fronda 2010, 22.

[90] Bispham 2007, 95–7. *Praefecturae* were not settlement categories, but areas of jurisdiction. Thus, some towns could be colonies, but also the seat of a *praefectus* to govern *cives sine suffragio* or viritane settlers living nearby. In the Imperial period, there were two types of *praefecturae* (Festus 262L), but it is unclear how these imperial *praefecturae* were related to the *praefecturae* of the Republican period. At the centre of a *praefectura* was often a *forum* or *conciliabulum*, a small town for local gatherings and markets. *Fora* and *conciliabula* were seen as a basic type of administrative unit for Roman citizens living in areas without their own magistrates, normally governed by prefects. Livy often refers to Roman decisions announced in *fora* and *conciliabula*, e.g. 25.5.5–9, 25.22.4, 29.37.3–4, 34.1.4–7, 39.14.6–8, 39.41.5, 40.19.1–4. See the *lex repetundarum*, l. 31. See Sherwin-White 1973, 51–3; De Ligt 1993, 113; Laurence 1999, 27–35.

[91] E.g. Toynbee 1965:1, 403–4; Humbert 1978, 38, 348; Brunt 1987, 20; 1988, 139. Sherwin-White 1973, 213–14 is undecided.

[92] Gell. *NA* 16.13.6–7 states that at first, the *civitas sine suffragio* was given as a reward, e.g. to Caere in 350, while other communities were given it as a punishment, e.g. Anagnia in 306 (Liv. 9.43.24; Hor. *Ep.* 1.6.62). It is more likely that the relationship between Caere and Rome was one of *hospitium publicum*, as Livy 5.50.3 states, while the status of *civitas sine suffragio* was only clearly defined later. See Sherwin-White 1973, 48–58; Galsterer 1976, 83; Cornell 1995, 316, 321.

[93] Mouritsen 2006; Coşkun 2009b, 20 n. 20.

[94] Tan forthcoming.

there were no more communities with this status; it is not mentioned in the *lex agraria* of 111, which lists all other existing statuses.

- Confiscation of part of the conquered territory as *ager publicus.* This land could be distributed to Roman citizens either in colonies with Roman or Latin rights or in viritane distributions, in which individual settlers were granted a piece of land. These colonies were fully independent with regard to their internal affairs, but had to obey Rome's demands for the recruitment of soldiers and other supra-local events. *Ager publicus* could also remain in the hands of its former Italian owners, until the Roman state decided to use it.[95]
- Grant of a *foedus* (treaty) to the defeated people. This meant that the local inhabitants remained *socii*, independent allies with their own governments. Their only duty to the Roman state was to supply soldiers for the Roman army. They did not have to pay direct taxes to Rome, but their citizens paid local taxes and paid for the outfitting of the soldiers they sent to Rome's wars. In return, they profited from spoils taken in these wars.[96] Unfortunately, we do not know whether all allied towns had treaties,[97] and whether the contents of these treaties differed from town to town.

Many areas therefore remained allied, with their own independent administrative systems. It is difficult to determine exactly what this administration looked like, especially in the less urbanized areas of Italy. It is often assumed, for example, that the Samnites and Lucanians were organized in a league at the time of the Roman conquest,[98] but the evidence for this is meagre. For some towns and territories, we have second-century inscriptions recording local institutions. At the sanctuaries at Rossano and Atina Lucana, for example, inscriptions record *senateis tanginud* ('decisions of the Senate').[99] Interestingly, some magistrates in allied areas adopted Latin titles, even if their government structures remained different from those of Rome (see chapter 4.2.2).

Even though many Italian communities were fully autonomous in the running of their internal affairs, this did not mean that Roman rule left them completely unaffected. The allies' duties, especially to supply soldiers, influenced how their towns were governed. Most important was the census, which had to be performed at certain intervals. The most important reason for the census was to enable the Roman state to determine how many soldiers could be demanded from each ally.[100] Although some Italian towns may have held censuses before the conquest

[95] Roselaar 2010. [96] Cornell 1995, 366–7.

[97] This is usually assumed, but Rich 2008, 69–70 points out that only fourteen states in Italy are reported as having a treaty with Rome.

[98] E.g. Cornell 1995, 345–6.

[99] *Imagines* Potentia 9–10=Rix Lu 6–7; *Imagines* Atina Lucana 1=Rix Lu 2. See Senatore 2004, 309.

[100] See e.g. Liv. 34.56.6. See Tan forthcoming.

by Rome, they were now obliged to do so.[101] Italian states were usually allowed to perform the census in any way they wanted; the Roman state only interfered in local procedure if it felt a need to assert its authority. This is visible for example in the treatment of twelve Latin colonies, which in 209 refused to furnish soldiers to the army, saying that they were exhausted from the war effort. It took Rome five years to get around to dealing with them, but then it acted harshly: the colonies were ordered to supply twice as many soldiers as they had done before, plus 120 cavalry each, selected from the wealthiest citizens. The magistrates and representatives of the colony were to be detained until they had done what the Senate required. They also had to pay a 0.1 per cent property tax annually, for which 'the assessment shall be made similarly to the one in force in Rome'.[102]

It was important for Rome's control over Italy that local elites remained in place and fulfilled their local magisterial duties; Rome did not have the manpower to govern Italy directly, nor to ensure that her commands were carried out by the local communities. Even in cases where a general directive was sent out from Rome, as in the Bacchanalian affair of 186 (see chapter 4), Rome had to rely on the local magistrates to carry out its orders. Thus, the Romans had to strike a careful balance between destroying any opposition against them, and maintaining local administrative structures. As we will see, they were eventually unsuccessful, leading to the Italian revolt during the Social War.

1.7 Sources and Methodology

It is clear that a work of this kind requires many different source materials. This section will give a brief overview of the various types of sources and a justification of the way in which they have been used. Firstly, there are literary sources; although no ancient works directly discuss the issues under debate in this book, individual passages from many works provide information about economic relations between Romans and Italians and about cultural integration. Of course, the usefulness of literary sources is limited in some ways. The main problem is that most sources were written long after the events they describe. Of the most important sources, only Polybius and Cicero describe contemporary events, although they are not always impartial. Polybius' theme, Rome's rise to world power, means that he is often too positive about the greatness of Rome's institutions and the personal qualities of the city's great men.[103]

Other historical writers, such as Livy, Appian, Plutarch, and Velleius Paterculus, wrote after the Republican period; moreover, each had their own focus. Livy, our most important source, wrote from a patriotic perspective, focusing on the

[101] Cic. *Clu.* 41–5; *Arch.* 8, 10. See Northwood 2008.

[102] Liv. 29.15.5–9.

[103] Walbank 1957, 6–34.

growth of Roman power—although few of Rome's politicians could live up to his ideals.[104] Appian's reliability has been much debated; although he probably used an eye-witness source, he had his own aims in writing his work, which as a result is full of inconsistencies. This is caused, most likely, by the focus of work: to describe the gods-ordained expansion of the Roman Empire and the creation of the monarchy.[105] Plutarch similarly aimed to show that Rome's dominance was preordained by the gods.[106] Velleius Paterculus is not always reliable regarding historical events, but his work is interesting for the information he provides about his own family's history, dating back to the time of the Social War.[107]

Other types of texts also provide useful information. The comedies of Terentius and Plautus referred to actual situations in Roman society, even if they were based on Greek examples. They were written in the late third and second centuries, a period for which we have few contemporary sources.[108] Cicero, as an Italian new man rising to the heights of Roman government, has much to say on the position of Italians in the Roman state. He was keenly aware of the differences between Romans and Italians, and how an Italic background influenced one's political career in Rome.[109] Other literary sources that provide information about the Italians in the Republican period have only survived in a fragmentary state, such as Cato the Elder's *Origines*, Lucilius' satires, and Ennius' *Annales*. The surviving fragments give us an insight into the views of these second-century eye-witnesses regarding the integration of the Italians.[110]

Information on legal instruments for trade can be found in preserved laws and treaties. Unfortunately, laws that were no longer relevant were usually not preserved, and therefore very few Republican laws have been transmitted, either in literary works or as (fragmentary) inscriptions. Fortunately, some laws have survived on inscriptions that are directly related to economic activities, e.g. the *lex agraria* of 111 on the use of *ager publicus* in Italy. Other inscriptions refer to relations between Rome and Italy or between Italian communities, such as the Cippus Abellanus, a treaty between the towns of Nola and Abella in Campania.[111]

Coinage produced by Italian towns in the fourth and third centuries can indicate trade relationships. For example, coins from one town found elsewhere can indicate economic contacts between the two locations.[112] Of course, the exact nature of such contacts is difficult to discern: coins travelled for many reasons—for example, as payment for military service—not just as a result of trade. Coin hoards are particularly difficult to use as evidence for economic contacts, since the coins were taken out of circulation not for 'natural' reasons, but in extraordinary circumstances. Still, they give some indication as to the distances travelled by

[104] Pausch 2011. [105] Gabba 1956; Bucher 2000, 442–54. [106] Swain 1989.
[107] Rich 2011. [108] Leigh 2004. [109] See Roselaar 2017.
[110] All existing fragments by Roman historians are published in Cornell (ed.) 2013.
[111] See Crawford (ed.) 1996 for the most recent edition of Roman laws.
[112] For colonial coinage, see Termeer 2015, 399–407.

coinage: some Italian currencies were used in many areas, while others were used only in the immediate surroundings of the minting town. Coin evidence also shows the gradual expansion of Roman coinage into Italy and the disappearance of local Italian currencies. Numismatic evidence suffers from the same problems as other types of evidence: coins that were no longer valid were melted down and reused, and therefore relatively few coins have survived. Furthermore, numismatic material has been published very haphazardly; many coin finds have not been published at all, or in niche journals, so that it is difficult to gain a clear overview of all finds.[113]

Epigraphic materials are also useful for this study. Inscriptions can, for example, help us trace the disappearance of the Italic languages and the rise of Latin, one of the most important cultural changes taking place in the late Republican period. Inscriptions are especially important because of the onomastic information they provide. Names recorded on inscriptions can, for example, indicate migration patterns, when the same person appears in different locations. Names recorded on amphorae, tiles, bricks, etc give an indication of who was involved in the production of these items. Inscriptions on buildings indicate who were the donors of such buildings. If these were Italians, this may indicate that Italian elites flourished economically after the Roman conquest. Inscriptions found abroad can help us trace Italian involvement in overseas trade: if typically Italian names are attested abroad, this shows that Italians could profit from the expansion of economic opportunities in the Mediterranean.

Despite these possibilities in using onomastic evidence, we must be very careful in drawing conclusions. Apart from the usual problems with inscriptions, such as their fragmentary nature and the problems of dating,[114] onomastic studies are complicated by further issues. Firstly, it would be unwise to assume that people with the same *gentilicium* were in fact related. Some names are so common that no connection should be assumed between two individuals with the same name. Furthermore, it is often difficult to establish the exact origins of many names. Some are directly attested in inscriptions in non-Latin languages, such as Oscan, Etruscan, or Messapian.[115] Others were only used in a small area of Italy. Many names, on the other hand, occur in a much larger region, and cannot be assigned to a specific area of origin. Even if we can determine the origin of a name, we must be aware that this does not mean that someone using this name identified himself as belonging to the ethnic group where the name originated. In the Faliscan area, for example, many people had Oscan names, but that does not mean that these people were immigrants, or even that they were aware that these names were not

[113] See Rutter 2001. [114] See Adams 2007, 39–113.

[115] The most recent collections of inscriptions in Oscan and related languages are Rix 2002 and Crawford (ed.) 2011. For Messapian inscriptions, see De Simone & Marchesini 2002; for Etruscan texts, see Rix 1991.

local. Even if they were immigrants, using a foreign name does not mean that they had maintained any other elements of Oscan identity.[116] Nevertheless, with careful analysis it will be possible to gain useful information from epigraphic materials. To this end I have put together an Appendix, which collects information about all individual Italians from the Republic whose names have been attested: a total of almost 10,000 individuals.[117] This makes it possible to trace the economic activities of the Italians abroad.

Archaeological sources are useful both for the study of economic developments and for tracing cultural change. First, survey archaeology continues to provide new information about economic developments in Italy. Archaeological surveys are of course usually very difficult to interpret—more so than some publications suggest. For example, if the number of sites in an area declines in a certain period, this is often ascribed to population decline, but this was not necessarily the case. Changes in building materials or in settlements habits can offer alternative explanations. Many sites are not detected by survey at all; recovery rates vary enormously according to the method that is used, making it difficult to compare surveys carried out with different methods.[118] This also makes it very difficult to compare economic developments in different regions, studied by different teams using different methods. Moreover, it is possible that settlement patterns were different in each region or even in each community: in colonies settled by Rome, for example, settlers may have lived in villages rather than in isolated farms in the countryside. This would explain why the landscapes of some colonies, such as Cosa, seem so empty.[119]

Material artefacts are equally difficult to interpret, as we saw above. It cannot be assumed that a change in the use of material objects, e.g. pottery, should always be ascribed to a change in culture of the existing inhabitants or the appearance of a new group in the area. Nevertheless, when handled carefully, changes in material culture can give some indication of changed identities. Burial assemblages can be especially useful in this respect, since rituals concerning death and burial were usually much slower to change than other elements of culture. A change in grave gifts may therefore indicate significant changes in the identity of the people who deposited them.[120] Furthermore, material artefacts can help us trace trade routes, since a change in the use of material artefacts is often caused by changes in supply and demand, rather than by cultural change. Thus pottery and other material artefacts can trace economic relations that existed between different parts of Italy.

[116] See Lejeune 1976 for Oscan onomastics; see also Brunt 1982, 2–4; Farney 2007, 37.

[117] When reference is made in this book to specific names, the reader is encouraged to check the sources in the Appendix. This Appendix can be found at [www.oup.co.uk/companion/Roselaa].

[118] For Cosa, a recovery rate of 20–33% is suggested (Cambi 2002, 140), but the third-century colony is almost invisible. For the *suburbium* of Rome, see Witcher 2006. Especially small farms are likely to be underrepresented; see Rathbone 2008. See Launaro 2011 for an overview of archaeological surveys in Italy and the methodological differences between them.

[119] Pelgrom 2008, 336–57.

[120] Riggs 2005.

Furthermore, they can help us identify the role of Italians in international trade: some items were produced in specific areas of Italy and traded throughout Italy and abroad. Some items can help to establish trade routes in the Mediterranean; amphorae, for example, were often marked with the name of the producers of the wine, so that it is sometimes possible to identify the origins and destinations of these products (see chapter 3).

All in all, there is a large amount of evidence of different types and qualities. In general, all materials are defective in one way or another; we should therefore approach the subject through as many different types of evidence as possible. Overall, as we will see, the evidence is sufficiently strong to create a new interpretation of the processes of integration and identity formation occurring in Republican Italy.

It is clear that a subject such as this must be clearly delineated in time; it covers a vast array of topics and geographical areas, and might easily get out of hand. At the same time, it is necessary to cover a sufficiently long period of time in order to make clear the significant developments that occurred during the Republican period. I have chosen to focus on the period after the Roman conquest of Italy, which was completed around 268. The most important opportunities for interaction between Italians and Romans presented themselves after the conquest. The Romans had to find ways to control an area that was larger than ever before, while the Italians found themselves faced with a foreign hegemon, even though many were nominally independent. Both realized that they had to adapt themselves to this situation in such a way as to secure the well-being of both parties. This led to the creation of social and economic relationships between Romans and Italians.

This mostly peaceful coexistence continued—briefly interrupted by the Second Punic War—until the late second century, when increasing resistance against Roman rule emerged among the Italians. This led to the Social War of 91–88, after which the Italians were given Roman citizenship. In a way, this completed the integration process, since all Italians were now Romans in the civic sense. The main argument of this book will therefore end shortly after the Social War, when the Italians had become Roman citizens and were able to participate fully in the duties and privileges connected to this status. However, political integration was not the end of the integration process in Italy, since other types of integration, such as social and cultural, were still ongoing. I will therefore end with a short outlook on the changes that occurred in the first century; it was only at the end of the century that the integration of Italy was completed.

2
Points of Contact
Interaction between Roman and Italian

2.1. Introduction

This chapter will explore the possibilities for interaction between Romans and the peoples of Italy, especially for the purpose of economic activity. If we know in which locations and under which circumstances Italians and Romans interacted, this will allow us to determine how these interactions may have affected the economic, political, and cultural integration of Italy. It is important to emphasize the role of economic activities in integration processes. Trade is often the first kind of interaction between different groups. It can occur even if the people involved do not share a common language, laws, coinage, or system of weights and measures.[1] Over a longer period, trade can lead to the creation of social ties and to cultural integration between different groups. However, this is not inevitable: the cultural identity of trading partners does not necessarily converge. Therefore, even if economic interaction between Romans and Italians occurred, this does not mean that any further integration resulted from this. The same goes for other kinds of interaction, such as Romans and Italians serving together in the army. We should therefore analyse carefully what kinds of economic interaction occurred and what the results of these encounters were.

This chapter will therefore discuss a number of 'points of contact' where interaction between Romans and Italians occurred, with a focus on economic contacts. Firstly, we will look at colonies founded by the Romans, generally seen as important locations of interaction. Secondly, we will investigate mobility within Italy, which existed for a variety of reasons, such as seasonal work, transhumant pasturing, etc. Other important meeting points were religious locales, such as sanctuaries. Local and regional fairs and markets also played an important role. Finally, we will discuss interaction between Romans and Italians that occurred for non-economic reasons, such as marriage and patronage relations. Throughout this chapter, it will become clear that there were many opportunities for interaction between Romans and Italians—but at the same time, individuals could avoid engaging with these opportunities. Therefore, despite growing interaction

[1] Hdt. 4.196.

Italy's Economic Revolution. Saskia T. Roselaar, Oxford University Press (2019).
DOI: 10.1093/oso/9780198829447.001.0001

between the peoples of Italy, cultural or political integration was not inevitable, as we will see in chapter 4.

2.2. Roman Colonization and Spatial Integration between Romans and Italians

After the Latin War (341–338) the Romans embarked on the settlement of colonies throughout Italy.[2] The presence of a large group of settlers representing 'Roman culture' is often assumed to have had profound influences on the area surrounding their settlement. Colonies were seen as small copies of Roman towns, as Aulus Gellius states: 'This condition [of a colony] . . . is thought preferable and more prestigious because of the greatness and majesty of the Roman people, of whom colonies seem to be little images, as it were, and a kind of representations.'[3] Gellius' statement has become enormously influential; it used to be assumed that the colonies showed the surrounding local inhabitants a more 'civilized' way of life, and that this caused the locals to 'self-Romanize'.[4] Torelli, for example, states that 'Latin colonies very soon became a vehicle of strong Romanization, establishing in these zones . . . a socio-economic model. . . . The superiority of the model . . . rendered easy and consequential the exportation of cultural forms.'[5] Thus, colonies would have functioned as 'outpost[s] of Romanization'.[6] Colonies are thought to have introduced the concept of urbanization itself to many non-urbanized areas of Italy, and provided an example of what a town should look like in terms of the layout of the town and territory, public buildings, and administrative structures of urban government. Colonies supposedly emulated the example of Rome itself, since they were supplied with several standard buildings, such as a *curia* (council building), *comitia* (assembly building) and a Capitolium temple, dedicated to the triad Jupiter, Juno, and Minerva.[7] Many aspects of material culture, such as polygonal masonry walls, votive terracottas in the so-called 'Etrusco-Latial-Campanian' style, and black gloss pottery (see chapter 4) are assumed to have spread throughout Italy from the colonies.[8]

[2] The argument in this section has been more fully discussed in Roselaar 2011. See Termeer 2015 for a detailed study of the impact of colonies on their surroundings. For regulations regarding Latin colonies, see Roselaar 2013a; 2013b. For regulations regarding colonies with Roman citizenship status, see Roselaar 2009.

[3] Gell. *NA* 16.13.9: *propter amplitudinem maiestatemque populi Romani, cuius istae coloniae quasi effigies parvae simulacraque esse quaedam videntur.*

[4] E.g. Salmon 1969, 54; 1982, 66; Torelli 1995, 9–12; 1999, 127, 173–5, 186–7.

[5] Torelli 1999, 122.

[6] Sherwin-White 1973, 99; Galsterer 1976, 60–2; Morel 1988, 53.

[7] Salmon 1969, 14; Galsterer 1976, 61–2; Brown 1980, 15–16; Patterson 2006b, 608.

[8] Torelli 2006, 86–7; Sisani 2007, 87–9.

However, many ideas about the role of colonies in cultural change in Italy have recently been questioned. The idea that colonies served as models for urban life and stimulated cultural change in Italy can no longer be maintained.[9] As for the urban layout of towns, this was not always the same; in pre-existing towns, the colony's layout was adapted to what was already there. Colonies built *ex novo*, such as Cosa, had more opportunity to shape the town layout as they saw fit, but this was a long-term process. Cosa, often assumed to have been an 'archetypical' colony, was in fact not so typical.[10] Here, as in many other cases, no standard set of public buildings was erected when the colony was founded. Most colonies indeed have a *curia* and *comitia*, but these were not usually built immediately after the foundation, and their architecture varies from town to town.[11] The Capitolium temple in most cases was not built until the second century, and even then not in all colonies.[12] In short, close resemblance between Rome and its colonies cannot be established in many cases; some colonies resembled Rome, but others did not.[13]

At the same time, impressive buildings were erected far away from colonies, such as the sanctuary at Pietrabbondante (see chapter 4). Such sanctuaries served as centres in non-urban areas, as discussed in section 2.4. Thus, even if the urban model was, at this time, not adopted in all areas of Italy, investment in public building occurred also in areas far removed from colonies established by Rome. Furthermore, there does not seem to have been much difference between cultural developments in areas located near colonies and those further away. Overall, the role of colonies seems to have been of marginal importance in cultural changes in Italy.[14]

A further important new insight concerns the fate of the local Italian population, which had inhabited the territory until the colonial foundation. It used to be assumed that the colonists lived in isolated farms throughout the colonial territory, each tending his own plot of land, in land distribution grids called centuriations. The local people are assumed to have been expelled from the centuriated land, to the marginal areas of the territory (see Fig. 2.1).[15]

However, in many colonies no regular centuriation pattern is visible. In fact, centuriation grids dating to the foundation of the colony have been found in only seven colonies. The oldest grids may of course have disappeared over time, but we should not assume that centuriation took place in every colony at the time of the foundation. Furthermore, in four out of these seven cases, the grids were measured not in the Roman *actus*, but the Greek *plethron* or the Oscan *vorsus*.[16] This makes

[9] Important revisionist works are Bispham 2006; Crawford 2006; Sewell 2014; Termeer 2015. The most recent scholarly views are summarized in Stek & Pelgrom (eds.) 2014.

[10] Fentress 2000, 12–14.

[11] Sewell 2014, 126–8.

[12] Greco 2004; Bispham 2006, 93–112; Crawford 2006, 65–7.

[13] Morel 1988; 1991b, 135–6.

[14] Bispham 2006.

[15] Salmon 1969, 25–6; Brown 1980; Grelle 2008, 369.

[16] The Roman *actus* measured 35.5 metres and the Greek *plethron* 30.8 metres. The Oscan *vorsus* was a surface measurement, amounting to 8,640 Roman square feet or about 756 square metres.

Fig. 2.1. Traditional reconstruction of a colonial landscape, with the local inhabitants expelled to the 'terre lasciate agli indigeni' at the top.
Drawing by G. Moscara, in Settis 1984, p. 150, fig. 129.

it difficult to see these interventions as typically Roman; they may not even have been related to colonial settlement at all. Indeed, in many cases centuriation systems seem to have been used for drainage or irrigation.[17] In some colonies, such as Cosa, there indeed seems to have been some spatial separation between colonists and local inhabitants, since evidence of the presence of indigenous inhabitants is very rare inside the centuriation grid. But this was not the case in all colonies, as we will see on page 33–36.[18]

In short, it seems unwise to adhere to the 'model-replica' idea, according to which colonies imitated Rome. It seems more useful, as recent studies have pointed out, to see them as communities with their own role in local and regional economic and cultural networks. Each followed its own historical trajectory after the foundation by Rome.[19]

Despite their limited importance for cultural change, I argue that colonies served as important 'points of contact' between Romans and the surrounding

[17] Pelgrom 2008, 362–3. [18] Roselaar 2010, 142–4; Pelgrom 2014, 79–81.
[19] Torelli 1999 (despite his insistence on Rome as a model); Bispham 2006; Sewell 2014.

Italian population. As we have seen, there is no evidence for the assumption that the local population was expelled from the town and the surrounding area. In fact, for many colonies there is evidence that Italians were living in the colonial city and the surrounding territory. If non-Romans were in regular contact with Roman settlers in colonies, this meant that they interacted on a regular basis.

This debate is related to the civic status of the Italians living in colonies settled by the Romans. I have argued elsewhere that Latins were regularly admitted as official settlers in colonies with the Latin status, but not in colonies with Roman status. Italians did not usually become settlers in either Latin or Roman colonies. However, it was quite possible for Italians to live in colonies, even if they were not admitted as official settlers.[20] These people could be either the original inhabitants, who remained in the area, or immigrants from elsewhere. I will discuss a few examples briefly, in order to show how common it was for Italians to live in colonies and what may have been the reasons behind this.

Fregellae, a Latin colony founded in 328, attracted many Italians with an Oscan background. As Livy states,[21] many of these had migrated into the colony after its foundation, probably in the early second century. At this time, Fregellae became a central location for the processing of wool and leather, attested by the many workshops built in the town. The town grew considerably in size; it measured 100 hectares by the early second century.[22]

For Alba Fucens, founded as a Latin colony in 303, the temple of Hercules is thought to have fulfilled a role in the integration between colonists and the surrounding population. Alba was an important centre for transhumant sheep breeding, with a migration route between summer and winter pastures (*tratturo*) passing through the town and a cattle market in the town centre. Hercules was a patron of pastoralism,[23] but, as Bispham has suggested, may also have been considered a deity of colonization.[24] Thus his temple in Alba may have been popular with Italians, who had already venerated Hercules before the conquest, as well as with the Latin colonists.[25] At the same time, Alba was an important market town and attracted many people for economic reasons, which contributed to interaction between various peoples.[26]

The Latin colony Brundisium in Messapia was founded around 245. Interesting in this case is that the local elite continued to play an important role in the town. For example, in the Second Punic War a Roman garrison was commanded by a man named Dasius, a typical Messapian name, who came from Brundisium.[27] In the second and first century, many direct Latinizations of Messapian names

[20] Roselaar 2011. [21] Liv. 41.8.8.

[22] Coarelli 1998, 53, 60–5; Broadhead 2002, 72–80. Interestingly, Carthaginian hostages in 199 requested to be moved to Fregellae, perhaps because it offered more amenities (Nepos, *Hann.* 7).

[23] Van Wonterghem 1992. [24] Bispham 2006, 113–17.

[25] Torelli 1999, 38–9; Bispham 2006, 106–8. See also Stek 2009, 55–8.

[26] Stek 2009, 165–70. [27] Liv. 21.48.8–9; see also Plb. 3.69.1.

appear in Brundisium, such as Statorius, Tutorius, and Visellius.[28] These people may therefore not have lived in the town originally, but migrated to Brundisium at a later date. Considering Brundisium's role as a major trade port, especially for the provisioning of Roman armies fighting in Greece, economic immigration must have been considerable.[29]

Another example of the importance of commerce is Aquileia, a flourishing trade community with a mixed population of Gauls, Veneti, and Etruscans, even before it was settled as a Latin colony in 181. Epigraphic evidence suggests that many non-Romans remained in the town, which developed into the major trading port for the Po valley. The Roman state was willing to let the new settlers profit from trade networks already established by the locals.[30] The town itself quickly grew beyond the walls established at the foundation.[31]

Similar developments are visible in colonies with the Roman citizen status. Minturnae was one of the first Roman colonies, founded in 296. The most important evidence for the presence of non-Romans consists of names of Oscan origin, of which a surprisingly large number is attested.[32] Most of these date from the second and first centuries. In this period, the town developed into one of the most important harbours of Latium, which led to a great increase in its size (see chapter 3).[33] It is likely that many people had moved to Minturnae because of its prosperous economy.

Puteoli, founded in 194, also shows much evidence for non-Roman names.[34] The continued importance of some locals, who even reached the highest local office of *duumvir*, suggests that they were included in the colony as official settlers, which was quite common in the period after the Second Punic War. Many others may have been attracted by the prosperity of the town, which had been the most important harbour in Campania from the late third century onwards.[35]

There does not seem to be much difference between Latin and Roman colonies with respect to the presence of Italians. In both Roman and Latin colonies, the evidence for the presence of Italians is strongest in the colonies that developed into important trade centres. Colonies that did not become flourishing commercial centres did not attract as many people, and therefore did not develop into the multi-ethnic communities that some colonies became. Famously, Sipontum and

[28] Silvestrini 1990, 257; Lamboley 1996, 388.
[29] Plb. 10.1.9. See Aprosio 2008, 89–90.
[30] Strazzulla Rusconi 1982; Bandelli 1983.
[31] Broadhead 2002, 113.
[32] CIL 1² 2678–706=ILLRP 728–42. See Guidobaldi & Pesando 1989, 68–73.
[33] Guidobaldi & Pesando 1989, 38.
[34] Liv. 34.42.5–6. A regulation regarding the building of a wall, the so-called *Lex de pariete faciundo* of 105, gives one Numerius Fufidius as one of the *duumviri*, the leading magistrates of the town. Both his *praenomen* and *gentilicium* are of Oscan origin. The guarantors for the work are Blossius, Granius, and Tetteius, all Oscan names (CIL 1² 698=10.1781=ILS 5317=ILLRP 518).
[35] See Soricelli 2007 on Eastern peoples at Puteoli—in 105 there was a temple of Serapis (CIL 10.1781=ILLRP 518=ILS 5317), and in the mid-first century there was a Nabataean community (CIS 2.158).

Buxentum were abandoned soon after their foundation in 194.[36] Considering their marginal location within Italy's economic networks, compared to towns like Brundisium or Puteoli, this is not surprising. This suggests that many Italians attested in economically important colonies, whether Latin or Roman, had only moved in after the colonies had developed into prosperous centres, because the Italians were attracted by the commercial opportunities that these towns offered. Some towns, such as Aquileia and Puteoli, had already been important centres before the colonial foundation, so the local population may simply have remained when the colony was created. Other colonies, such as Minturnae, only developed into prospering centres later on, especially in the second century, and did therefore not attract immigrants from the moment of their foundation.

Thus, in colonies Italians lived in close proximity to Roman settlers. This situation of copresence offered opportunities for interaction between different groups.[37] A first obvious point of contact between Romans and non-Romans in colonies was trade. It was quite common for people to move to locations in which trade was profitable. An interesting example is Agrigentum in Sicily, where 'great numbers of Roman citizens... live and trade... among the Agrigentes in the greatest harmony'.[38] Similar events most likely also occurred in colonies in Italy. Another type of interaction between Romans and Italians in colonies was social relations, including marriage.[39] For example, the sister of Ennius from the allied town of Rudiae married a Pacuvius from Brundisium.[40] The grandfather of L. Calpurnius Piso (*cos.* 58) was a Gaul, who had moved to the Latin colony Placentia in the mid-second century. Relations of patronage are likely as well: various Roman magistrates favoured the colonies with their attention. For example, the censors of 174, Q. Fulvius Flaccus and A. Postumius Albinus, organized public building at Potentia, Pisaurum, and Sinuessa.[41] Religious contacts may also have been common: local temples often remained in use after a colony had been founded, and would have attracted both locals and immigrants. An example is the temple at Telamon near Cosa, which remained Etruscan in style, even when it was redecorated after 273, suggesting that locals still attended it.[42] Sometimes the arrival of colonists led to changes in the items that were given as votives, e.g. at Luceria, where terracotta votives became common after the colonial foundation. However, older types of votives also remained in use.[43] In some ways, colonies resembled non-colonial towns, in that they were active in the

[36] Liv. 39.23.3–4.

[37] For the concept of copresence, see Isayev 2017, 108. It should be noted, however, that the presence of multiple social groups in the same location does not necessarily lead to cultural integration; in the modern world, there is often very little interaction between people of different groups, even when they live in the same town.

[38] Cic. *Verr.* 2.4.93. [39] Patterson 2006a. [40] Plin. *NH* 35.19.

[41] Liv. 41.27.11–12. A relative of Flaccus had been involved in the foundation of Potentia and Pisaurum, Liv. 39.44.10.

[42] Torelli 1999, 145. [43] D'Ercole 1990.

same regional economic and cultural networks. This led to changes in cultural expressions that originated in Rome. For example, *arulae* (small terracotta altars decorated with mythological scenes) in Brundisium were quite close to Roman examples, while in Hadria many of them have unique imagery, partially influenced by nearby Aquileia. Thus, the colonies did not simply copy Roman examples.[44]

We may conclude that there were many opportunities for contact between Romans and Italians in colonies. Thus, colonies played a very important role in the integration of Italy under the Republic, but their role was not that of 'outposts of Romanization'. Some colonies indeed played a role in expanding 'Roman' culture (see chapter 4), but others had very little effect on the surrounding area in the cultural sense. Their most important role was in providing opportunities for economic, social, and religious interaction between Romans and Italians. Thus the colonies contributed to greater knowledge about Rome and greater familiarity with its customs, language, and culture among the neighbouring Italians. Therefore, the foundation of colonies contributed to a certain degree to the cultural and linguistic changes in Italy between the fourth and first centuries, as we will see in chapter 4.

2.3. Migration and Mobility

Apart from colonization, there were many other opportunities for mobility and migration in the Republican period. Some of these were organized by the Roman state. The state settled its citizens not only in colonies, but also in individual settlements, without the creation of a central town as a colony. These 'viritane' settlers were governed by *praefecti* (see chapter 1). Sometimes *fora* were set up in such districts, villages that could serve as marketplaces and administrative centres. In most cases, however, the settlers had to rely on existing towns, many of which were inhabited by locals, which functioned as central places in the settlement.[45] The potential for integration between Romans and Italians was therefore even larger in viritane settlements than in colonies, since in viritane distributions, colonists had to interact with locals from the start.

A very different type of state-organized settlement of individuals occurred as well: the Roman state in some cases deported defeated peoples to a different region. Some migrations involved large numbers of people moving over long distances: in 180 and 173, the state moved 47,000 Ligures Apuani from northern Italy to the Fortore Valley in Samnium.[46] This did not mean that the previous

[44] Termeer 2015, 330–2. [45] Humbert 1978, 340–6.

[46] Liv. 40.38.3–8, 40.41.3–4. See Toynbee 1965:2, 279; Salmon 1967, 310; Pina Polo 2006, 185–8; Isayev 2017, 181.

inhabitants of this area were expelled; an Oscan inscription dating from the second century records their presence.[47] In 211, the population of Capua was resettled in various locations:

> Those who had not been in Capua during the war, nor in any rebellious Campanian city, were to be settled to the north of the Liris in the direction of Rome; those who had gone over to the side of Rome before Hannibal came to Capua were to be removed to this side of the Volturnus, and no one was to possess any land or building within fifteen miles of the sea. Those who had been deported beyond the Tiber were forbidden to acquire or to hold either for themselves or their posterity landed property anywhere except in the territories of Veii, Sutrium and Nepet, and in no case was such holding to exceed fifty *iugera*.[48]

This settlement was not organized by the state, in the sense that the Roman state assigned specific plots of land to each person, but it did cause large-scale migration within Italy. Thus, people from different areas of Italy were brought together by the actions of the Roman state.

Italians also migrated independently, without interference of the Roman state. It is likely that the level of mobility was very large,[49] but it is unfortunately very difficult to trace these patterns of migration, since there are few records in the sources. Epigraphic evidence provides some interesting glimpses into such movements. Some funerary inscriptions record explicitly that the deceased had not been born in the town in which he died. A text from Cumae, for example, records Dekis Hereiis Dekkieis Saipinaz ('Decius Herius, son of Decius, from Saepinum').[50] In such cases, migration is clearly attested: someone moved from one place to another, but still identified himself by his place of birth. In other cases, we can only surmise that migration may have taken place. For example, around 300 a pot was marked in Teanum Sidicinum in Campania by a man called Plator, a name that originated in Messapia.[51]

When such independent migration is mentioned, it is often in relation to economic opportunities. For example, Polybius describes how a newly discovered gold mine in the Alps attracted many Italians—unfortunately we do not know the civic status of these people—who worked the mine together with the locals, probably at some point in the early second century.[52] Another example is the arrival of the Roman army near Aquileia in 178, which immediately caused traders to flock to the camp.[53] Thus, the movements of the Roman armies offered

[47] *Imagines* Fagifulae 3=Rix Sa 30.
[48] Liv. 26.34.8–10. Uncertainty about the status of the Capuans remained; see Liv. 38.28.4, 38.36.5–6.
[49] Isayev 2017, 5.
[50] *Imagines* Cumae 8=Rix Cm 14.
[51] *Imagines* Teanum Sidicinum 25; see Crawford 2011, 2, 4.
[52] Plb. 34.10.10 (Strabo 4.6.12).
[53] Liv. 41.1–2.

economic opportunities for Italians, which far exceeded their normal trade income, and therefore led to increased mobility.[54]

For some towns we have evidence for the presence of *incolae*, a term used for people who did not hold civic rights in the town. They may have migrated to these towns from elsewhere, or have been local inhabitants who did not hold civic rights. In Aesernia, a Latin colony, an inscription dating to the second century records *Samnites inquolae.*[55] At Sena Gallica, a colony with Roman status, an inscription mentions *incolae,*[56] while in Sarsina—an allied town—someone made a donation *municipibus [su]eis incoleisque* ('to his fellow citizens and the *incolae*').[57]

Rome itself naturally attracted many immigrants, who contributed to its enormous growth in the last two centuries BC. Based on figures for mortality and fertility in the city, it has long been argued that a great influx of people from Italy and elsewhere would have been needed to sustain the growth of the city of Rome. Morley estimates that over 10 per cent of people from Italy must at some point have lived in Rome, even if they did not stay there permanently.[58] Often this migration is presented in a negative way: the people of Italy are supposed to have been deprived of their economic resources by the Roman conquest. Unable to feed themselves, they drifted to the city and formed an urban proletariat, fed by food distributions.[59] However, in many periods the city's growth was caused by pull factors, such as job opportunities in public building and shipping.[60] As we have seen, many other Italian cities also experienced population growth, especially those that were important economic centres.

Other types of voluntary migration also occurred in Republican Italy. For seasonal migration we have very little evidence, although it must have been very common. Many economic activities were seasonal, such as pasturing and the harvest. For example, Cato gives a great deal of advice on how to recruit temporary workers for the harvest, and emphasizes that a farm should be located in areas with plenty of wage labourers available.[61] He also gives arrangements for contracting out building work and for letting out land to tenants.[62] Temporary work was arranged by middlemen, according to Cato, who recruited labourers and sent them to the farms. A famous story about Vespasian's great-grandfather, who must have lived in the early first century BC, says that he 'came from the region beyond the Po and was a contractor for the day-labourers who come regularly every year

[54] Isayev 2017, 236–40. [55] CIL 1^2 3201; see Humbert 1978, 346.
[56] ILLRP 776=CIL 1^2 779=12.5388.
[57] ILLRP 662=CIL 1^2 2123=11.6528=ILS 7846. For the legal status of *incolae*, see Gagliardi 2006.
[58] Morley 1996, 53; Erdkamp 2008, 438–41.
[59] Toynbee 1965:2, 9–14; Gabba 1977, 275–9; 1989; Hopkins 1978, 11–13. [60] Coarelli 1977.
[61] Cato *Agr.* 1.1.3, 136, 144–5. See Garnsey 1980; Erdkamp 2008, 425–30.
[62] Cato *Agr.* 14, 136.

from Umbria to the Sabine district, to till the fields'.[63] The fact that middlemen specialized in providing labourers suggests that such arrangements were common.

Temporary work was also available in cities—for example, in public building. As we will see in chapter 4, public works took place in many locations in the second and first centuries. Such work needed labourers for a few months or years, depending on the type of building, and thus was ideal for wage labourers looking for temporary jobs. Harbour towns offered seasonal work, e.g. as porters or rowers, since the sailing season lasted from about March until October.[64] The temporary nature of the wool industry also attracted labourers who travelled around looking for work, including women: an early first century inscription from Aquileia commemorates a female travelling woolworker.[65]

Transhumant pasturing was another important type of migration that created ties between different areas of Italy.[66] In the second century, an increase in large-scale animal husbandry occurred, through both short-distance (vertical) and long-distance (horizontal) transhumance. In the Biferno valley in Samnium, for example, sheep farming became an important part of the local economy in the later second century, bringing considerable wealth to the local elites.[67] These activities could connect regions over considerable distances: Varro relates how 'Publius Aufidius Pontianus, of Amiternum, had bought some herds of sheep in furthest Umbria, . . . providing that the shepherds should take them to the pastures of Metapontum and to market at Heraclea'.[68]

We may conclude that a wide variety of possibilities existed for economic migration throughout Italy in the Republican period. The Roman state did not attempt to limit this mobility, except in the case of the inhabitants of Latin and Roman colonies (see chapter 4.2.1).[69] Although we cannot quantify these movements, the fact that people like Varro, Cato, and Suetonius find nothing odd in referring to wage labour or transhumant migration suggests that these activities were common. This must have had an enormous impact on the integration of Italy. If people were free to move wherever they wanted, there would be an increased need for a common language, which Latin could provide, as well as for a common coinage system, which gradually appeared (see chapter 4). The question remained whether this high level of mobility affected the development of identities within the towns that experienced high levels of immigration. In theory, towns were composed of the citizens, who held full citizen rights (*municipes*), as well as *incolae*, who did not. Even among the full citizens, people may have had different ethnic backgrounds; the composition of the *incolae* would have been even more varied. For most people, the town in which they lived was

[63] Suet. *Vesp.* 1.4. [64] Erdkamp 2008, 428–9. [65] *Inscr. Aq.* 1.69: *lanifica circlatrix.*
[66] Erdkamp 2008, 423–4; Roselaar 2010, 173–9. [67] Barker, Lloyd, & Webley 1978, 48–9.
[68] Var. *R.* 2.9.6. See also Var. *R.* 2.1.16 (Apulia-Samnium), 2.1.17, 2.2.9; Hor. *Epod.* 2.27–8 (Lucania-Apulia); Pall. 4.11–13.
[69] Isayev 2017, 38.

the most important focus of their daily lives. Local communities strengthened their communal identity through the celebration of local festivals, which included citizens as well as *incolae*.[70] At the same time, we have seen that some migrants emphasized their town of origin, such as Dekis from Saepinum. Others retained names from their area of origin, such as Plator from Messapia. On the other hand, locals may have emphasized their identity when large numbers of migrants moved in. For example, in the Faliscan area, which experienced a large influx of viritane settlers,[71] a few typically Faliscan *praenomina* occur. The use of these names may indicate a specific adherence to Faliscan identity as separate from Etruscan or Roman. On the other hand, this does not mean that these families also used other specifically Faliscan cultural markers.[72] This shows that identities could be remembered and recorded in a variety of ways, and that some people placed importance on their origins even in migration situations. It is to be noted that people in most cases referred to their home towns, or expressed their identity through the use of specific languages or names. As we will see in chapter 3.2.1, Italians abroad also referred to their home towns, not their ethnic groups. They did not usually identify themselves by referring to a people as a whole; there are no references to individuals calling themselves, for example, 'Samnite' or 'Lucanian', nor are there any references to an overarching Italian identity (see chapter 4.6).

Migration did not affect all towns and regions in Italy equally: towns that became important (economic) centres attracted immigrants, while those that were not well connected to the newly emerging economic networks experienced a decline in population. In areas that flourished economically, locals were more inclined to stay and contribute further to local economic prosperity.[73] All these developments, as we will see in chapter 4, were part of a general reorganization of the Italian economy in the second century: because Italy as whole was united into a more coherent economic network, the role of each town and region in this network changed. The role of Rome in the creation of these opportunities for migration was complex; on the one hand, mobility for seasonal work or transhumance, for example, had already occurred before the Roman conquest. At the same time, the expansion of Roman hegemony created more opportunities for interaction, on a larger scale than ever before.

2.4. Sanctuaries and Temples as Meeting Places

Sanctuaries were an essential part of the Italian countryside, both before and after the Roman conquest of Italy. Apart from their obvious religious functions, it is

[70] E.g. Brundisium's foundation day, as noted by Cic. *Att.* 4.1.4.
[71] Roselaar 2010, 320.
[72] Bakkum 2009, 254–5, 284–90.
[73] Cébeillac-Gervasoni 1978, 241–2; 1998, 249–50.

often asserted that sanctuaries fulfilled other roles as well. Since urbanization was low in many areas of Italy, it is thought that sanctuaries fulfilled some of the functions and services that are normally provided by cities, such as political gatherings and the facilitation of trade. Small sanctuaries are often described as commercial centres for people living in the surrounding countryside,[74] while large ones are envisaged as centres for trade at a regional and even an international level. Sanctuaries were especially suitable for such functions, because the gods oversaw the transactions, providing a deterrent against fraud. At the same time, sanctuaries provided a neutral and safe place in which elements from 'outside', including foreign merchants, could be received.[75] However, while many scholars make a connection between sanctuaries and trade,[76] the exact role of sanctuaries is not yet clear. In many cases, the actual occurrence of trade at sanctuaries cannot be attested. This section will explore to what degree sanctuaries played an important role in the integration between different peoples, through either trade or other interactions.

Already in pre-Roman Italy, sanctuaries served as important meeting points for members of different ethnic groups. In Graviscae, the material record reveals contacts with Egypt, various Greek cities, and southern Italy, while Pyrgi shows a Carthaginian presence.[77] Temples in Latium also served as meeting places, according to the literary sources. For example, Dionysius of Halicarnassus describes a temple of Jupiter which was used by Romans, Latins and other peoples:

> And as a means of providing that the treaties made with those cities might endure forever, Tarquinius resolved to designate a temple for the joint use of the Romans, the Latins, the Hernicans and such of the Volscians as had entered into the alliance, in order that, coming together each year at the appointed place, they might celebrate a general festival, feast together and share in common sacrifices.[78]

Archaeological evidence shows multicultural contacts: the temples of Satricum have yielded great amounts of imported pottery from the seventh century onwards, attesting to wide-ranging contacts.[79]

It might be assumed that sanctuaries continued to perform similar functions after the Roman conquest of Italy. Many areas were not urbanized, so that sanctuaries played a role as civic, social, and economic meeting places.[80] Indeed, for some temples we have explicit evidence that they were used as such. For

[74] Bradley 1997, 120; 2005, 1027; Andreau 2002, 122.

[75] Morel 1983b, 569; Edlund 1987, 85; Glinister 1997, 78–9; Malrieu 2005, 95. Thus sanctuaries constituted a 'middle ground' for contacts between different ethnic groups; see Malkin 2002.

[76] Glinister 1997, 79.

[77] Lesk 1999; Mazzei 2002; Bradley 2005, 130. For Pyrgi, see Edlund 1987, 73–4; for Graviscae, see Edlund 1987, 74.

[78] DH 4.49.1.

[79] Bouma et al. 1995; see Glinister 2003, 142.

[80] Bradley 2000, 62–7, 133 for Umbria.

example, the fair at Lucus Feroniae was connected to a religious festival and was expressly stated by Dionysius to bring together people from everywhere:

> There is a sanctuary, honoured in common by the Sabines and the Latins, that is held in the greatest reverence and is dedicated to a goddess named Feronia.... To this sanctuary people used to resort from the neighbouring cities on the appointed days of festival, many of them performing vows and offering sacrifice to the goddess and many with the purpose of trading during the festive gathering as merchants, artisans, and farmers.[81]

This sanctuary clearly was an important meeting place for various peoples. Its importance is illustrated by the fact that it was reconstructed in the second half of the second century in a monumental Hellenistic style.[82] A fair also took place at the temple of Voltumna near Volsinii in 389: 'Traders were bringing in reports of an assembly at the shrine of Voltumna, where the leading men from all the Etruscan cantons were forming a hostile league.'[83]

This shows that sanctuaries fulfilled important roles as meeting places between various peoples. Thus, they contributed to the integration of different peoples in Italy. However, for actual economic functions taking place within sanctuaries, the evidence is rather limited. In the temple of Juno at Gabii, *tabernae* have been found, indicating a permanent commercial function for the sanctuary.[84] For many sanctuaries, a commercial function is only assumed on the basis of their location near crossroads or rivers, without any real evidence.[85] Nevertheless, many show evidence for networks of exchange that created relationships over long distances. Material artefacts from a large variety of places, from Italy and abroad, have been found in Italian sanctuaries. Several finds show wide-ranging Mediterranean connections; the sanctuary at Pyrgi, for example, has yielded a Punic-type vase, produced in the third century in western Sicily, as well as a glass pendant and a ram's head from Carthage.[86] Statues from Asia Minor and Rhodes were found in the temple at Rossano di Vaglio in Lucania, dating to the third and second centuries.[87] The presence of coins may provide further clues. Many Italian sanctuaries have yielded coins from distant areas; for example, at Campochiaro and San Giovanni in Galdo in Samnium, the most common coins came from Neapolis,

[81] DH 3.32.1. See Liv. 1.30.5, 6.2.2, 26.12, 27.4; Strab. 5.2.9. DH 4.49.1–2 and Plin. *NH* 3.69 mention a festival at Mons Albanus, shared by Romans, Latins, Hernicans, and Volscians. Liv. 32.1.9 shows that the festival still took place in 199. See Bodei Giglioni 1977, 49; Edlund 1987, 87.

[82] Cambi 2004, 79.

[83] Liv. 6.2.2. See for its earlier importance Liv. 4.23.5, 5.17.6. Plin. *NH* 34.34 mentions that in 264 the Romans took 2,000 bronze statues from the sanctuary. See Edlund 1984, 279.

[84] Coarelli 1987, 15.

[85] Some examples are Croton (Edlund 1987, 108), Colfiorito (Bradley 1997, 111), Montegiordano (Guzzo 1984, 206), Armento (Russo Tagliente 1995), and Rossano di Vaglio (Masseria & D'Anisi 2001, 131–3).

[86] Michetti 2007, 331.

[87] Torelli 1977, 58. See Battiloro 2010, 224–7.

followed by coins from other Campanian and Apulian towns.[88] This kind of evidence is not direct proof of trade occurring at these sanctuaries: these finds could have been sacrifices left by local people, who had acquired these items through trade or as spoils of war.[89] A good example of the latter is a fourth-century Greek bronze corselet, inscribed with the Italian name Novios Bannios, dedicated to the gods in an unidentified Italian location.[90]

An important way in which sanctuaries fulfilled a function in the redistribution of goods was through the economic activities that they undertook themselves. The temple of Hera Lacinia at Croton owned 'a herd of every kind of cattle, sacred to the goddess... The profit from the stock was great, and from it was made and dedicated a column of solid gold, and the temple was gloried for its riches as well as for its sanctity.'[91] The so-called 'tablet of Heraclea' from the late fourth or early third century records regulations for the local temples of Athena and Dionysus. Athena's lands were leased for short periods and planted with vines; Dionysus' temple leased out land in long-term contracts, so that young vines and olive trees could be planted.[92]

Land ownership by temples is not often attested; secure evidence exists only for the temple of the Vestals in Rome, Diana Tifatina in Capua, Hercules Victor at Tibur, Angitia near Alba, and the temple shared between Nola and Abella.[93] Other temples were also rich, such as the temple of Fortuna at Praeneste, but it is not always clear what their sources of wealth were.[94] It is likely that much of the wealth of temples came from worshippers' donations. Varro explains how 'people give money to the gods, placing it in *thesauri*, [and] call it *stips*'.[95] In many cases, there is evidence for the existence of a treasury; one is mentioned on the *Cippus Abellanus*, for example.[96] Some votive deposits contain great numbers of coins.[97] Furthermore, many sanctuaries have yielded large numbers of small bronze statuettes, which

[88] Terzani 1991, 111. Rossano di Vaglio in Lucania has yielded coins from various Campanian and Apulian towns, as well as Rome; see Crawford 1985, 37–8.

[89] Battiloro 2010, 227, 258.

[90] SEG 29.1026. See Colonna 1984; Purcell 1994, 398. Dedications of helmets from the fifth century were found at many sanctuaries in Samnium; see Tagliamonte 1989–90, 528.

[91] Liv. 24.2–3; Cic. *Div.* 1.48. See Bodei Giglioni 1977, 41–2; Franchi de Bellis 1990, 111–12; Malrieu 2005, 103.

[92] Uguzzini & Ghinatti 1968; Brun 2000, 284.

[93] For Diana Tifatina, see Vell. Vell. 2.2.4, 2.25.4; CIL 1^2 635=ILS 22=ILLRP 332; AE 1894, 146=ILS 3240; AE 1971, 80=ILS 251; CIL 10.3826=ILS 79; CIL 10.4564=ILS 6306. For its *aerarium*, see CIL 1^2 1463. For the treasures of Diana's temple, see Athen. 11.466e, 489b; Paus. 5.12.3; CIL 10.3828. For Hercules at Tibur, see CIL 1^2 1486=14.3574=ILLRP 510. For Nola and Abella, see *Cippus Abellanus* l. 15–24. In Alba, a boundary stone (AE 1996, 632) marked the *fines populi Albensis, Marsorum*, and *Angitia*, showing that Angitia's temple owned land. See Bodei Giglioni 1977, 37–8, 49–51, 68–9; Carlsen 1994, 9–15; Granino Cerere 2009, 51–62.

[94] Liv. 24.3.3. Cic. *Div.* 2.87 calls it 'the most fortunate Fortuna ever seen'.

[95] Var. *L.* 5.182.

[96] *Cippus Abellanus* lines 10–12, 22–8. See Franchi De Bellis 1990, 112; La Regina 2000, 219–21.

[97] *Imagines* Interpromium 4. *Thesauri* have been attested in many locations; see Estienne & De Cazanove 2009, 22–7; Granino Cerere 2009, 44–7; Battiloro 2010, 227–8. Some coins were even made especially for donation: a coin found at Collepietro, in the Marsi area, has the legend *Diouis/stipe* ('for the treasury of Jupiter'), while another reads *Fortunai/stipe* (ILLRP 114).

represent considerable value.[98] Traders considered their activities to be under the protection of the gods and therefore rewarded gods, and thus temples, for successful business ventures. One tenth of the profit was often dedicated to the gods, as shown by a donation from the Vertulei brothers at Sora in the mid-second century.[99]

Other sources of income for temples were fees to priests for performing sacrifices.[100] Some temples provided a comprehensive package of services: the temple of Hercules Victor at Tibur not only sold votive gifts, but also dispensed justice, spoke oracles, and served as a base for tourism to the springs of the Anio river.[101] The fact that temples were important owners of wealth became clear in times of war. Hannibal, for example, plundered the temple at Lucus Feroniae.[102] In the civil wars of the first century, temple treasuries were an important source of cash for competing generals, indicating that the treasuries' wealth was considerable.[103]

Temple possessions were assigned to the upkeep of the temple and could not be used for other purposes. For example, the *lex Furfensis* of 58 laid down that 'if something is given to the temple as a dedication, let it be permitted to use it and to sell it... With the money which is raised, let it be permitted to buy, to take, and to give, as a fair gift, for the improvement and promotion of the temple.'[104] This kind of work created job opportunities for many people, both skilled and unskilled; thus temple building played an important role in economic networks in the second century.

A final important aspect of the economy of temples was 'religious industry'. The most important industry at sanctuaries was the production of votive gifts, which were sold to worshippers. These votives were produced in great numbers, often using clay moulds. It is difficult to establish exactly who controlled the production of such items: the temple itself, or craftsmen—whether itinerant or permanent residents—who worked near the temple, but were not employed by it.[105] This aspect of temple economy may have been very important for the local economy:

[98] See e.g. CIL 6.820. See Malrieu 2005, 99–103; Estienne & De Cazanove 2009, 9.

[99] CIL 1^2 1531=ILS 3411=ILLRP 136. CIL 1^2 632; 833=ILS 3410 records L. Munius from Reate, who donated money to Hercules. Other monetary donations are mentioned in CIL 14.3541=ILLRP 134; CIL 9.6153=ILLRP 142; CIL 1^2 2645=ILLRP 155; Liv. 5.21.2; CIL 6.29; CIL 1^2 37=6.29=ILS 3216=ILLRP 51. See Bodei Giglioni 1977, 52–3.

[100] Granino Cerere 2009, 39–44.

[101] Bodei Giglioni 1977, 64–5, 75.

[102] Liv. 26.11.8–9. See Malrieu 2005, 106–7, 114.

[103] Oros. 5.18.27, 6.15.5; App. *BC* 2.41, 5.97; VM 7.6.4; Plin. *NH* 33.16, 55–6; Diod. 38/9 fr. 14; Caes. *BC* 1.33.3; Plu. *Caes.* 35.6–11, *Ant.* 21.3; Dio 43.47.4, 48.12.4; Strab. 13.1.30, 14.1.14. See Bodei Giglioni 1977, 35–6; Malrieu 2005, 96–8; Estienne & De Cazanove 2009, 7.

[104] CIL 9.3515=1^2 603=ILLRP 508. See Malrieu 111–12; Granino Cerere 2009, 43–4. In the temple of Apollo in Pompeii, around 140, a pavement was laid out *Apelluneis eituvi[ad]* ('from the money of Apollo' (*Imagines* Pompei 23=Rix Po 14). In Lucus Angitiae, a wall was built *ex p(ecunia) p(ublica) Angitiae* (CIL 9.3885=ILS 4024). See Dench 1995, 165. In Capua in 108, a new temple was built, paid for *de stipe Dianai* ('by the treasury of Diana'; ILLRP 721; see Pobjoy 1997).

[105] Bromberg 1940, 131; Bodei Giglioni 1977, 46; Edlund 1984, 284; Lesk 1999, 129. Isayev 2010, 219 assumes that the craftsmen who produced these items were itinerant, but permanent production sites near temples are certainly attested; see Di Giuseppe 2012, 95–9 (although she also assumes that many of the producers were itinerant artisans, without any real evidence).

many temples show some evidence for the production of *ex votos*. At Lavinium, for example, a kiln was found near the Thirteen Altars, suggesting the local production of votives for the sanctuary.[106] Sometimes the same matrices were used at several temples, for example, at both Orvieto and Vignale in Umbria. This indicates that these temples participated in a supra-local economic and sacred network. Similarly, a loom weight from the Coppa Mengoni sanctuary in Teanum Apulum carries the same initials as terracottas from the Belvedere temple at Luceria and pottery matrices from Tarentum. This suggests a trade network with potters producing various products for a specific market.[107] Not only votives were produced at sanctuaries, but also building materials such as roof and floor tiles and bricks.[108] Temples not only produced items related to the cult: in the fourth and third centuries, a stunning 69 per cent of production sites of black gloss pottery were located near a cult site.[109] Clearly, these kilns produced not just votives, but also pottery for general use. Thus, many temples generated an income, which could be used to maintain the functioning of the sanctuary.

There was, finally, a lively business for travelling salesmen of semi-religious items such as amulets and potions. Cicero mentions 'a man of Ancona, Lucius Clodius, a travelling quack (*pharmacopolam circumforaneum*), who . . . had many more market towns (*fora*) to visit'.[110] This remark only gives us a small glimpse into what must have been a complex 'religious economy'; such informal contacts between various towns must have been quite common.

From all this, it is clear that sanctuaries played an important role in the distribution of goods and services both before and during the Roman Republican period. We may conclude, furthermore, that sanctuaries, and the economic functions they fulfilled, played an important role in bringing people together; thus temples and sanctuaries were important 'meeting points' between Romans and Italians. With sanctuaries playing such an essential role in economy and society, it makes sense that they remained the focus point of interaction after the Roman conquest of Italy. Many pre-existing sanctuaries were monumentalized in the second and first centuries. There was thus a great degree of continuity in the function of sanctuaries before and after the Roman conquest. Local elites functioned as priests in local sanctuaries, so that such temples were a logical choice for the investment of wealth gathered by local elites. Local elites paid for the maintenance and embellishment of local temples, in order to reinforce their social status in their communities. This indicates the importance of the continuity of

[106] Lesk 1999, 87. Many other sanctuaries show evidence of votive production; see Edlund 1984, 284–5; Battiloro 2010, 276.

[107] Antonacci Sanpaolo 2001, 31–3.

[108] CIL 10.8059; see Bodei Giglioni 1977; Morel 1983a, 29.

[109] Di Giuseppe 2012, 95–9. Many sanctuaries have yielded finds of loom weights; see Gleba 2009.

[110] Cic. *Clu.* 14.40.

local social and economic structures after the Roman conquest. These developments will be discussed in more detail in chapter 4.3.

2.5. Fairs and Markets

An important part of the economic networks that tied together Republican Italy was markets and fairs. These were usually held in towns that functioned as centres for their immediate surroundings, although trade could also take place in non-urban locations, such as rural sanctuaries. For urban markets, we need to distinguish several types of market. One type was local towns or other meeting places that provided markets for the people of the immediate hinterland. These were probably small-scale and served mainly the local economy. Then there were larger towns, which brought together people from a larger area. These regional centres not only served their immediate hinterland, but also provided services to people from adjacent regions. Finally, a few large towns played a role in the economy of Italy as a whole, such as Puteoli, Brundisium, and Aquileia. They served as import and export harbours for goods from the whole Mediterranean, and at the same time developed into consumer centres serving a large part of the surrounding territory. As we have seen in section 2.2, these towns attracted many people, who moved there in the hope of profiting from their economic prosperity. Of course, a strict distinction between local, regional, and supra-regional markets is artificial, since the exact function of each market differed; even large fairs attracted small farmers from the neighbourhood.

In an influential study of markets in the Roman world, De Ligt defines three types of markets: local, regional, and interregional. Local markets are defined as markets taking place regularly in a set location. They were characterized by the fact that the catchment area was no more than 50 kilometres; they lasted one day or a few days; a low volume of goods, of a relatively low value, was exchanged; and there was often direct trade between producers and final consumers. These markets attracted both small farmers, who sold their surplus and bought items they could not produce themselves, and local elites, who exchanged goods of higher value. Such markets, known as *nundinae*, were held in many locations. The *nundinum* was a period of eight days, which played an important role in law and government: new laws had to be announced during three consecutive *nundinae*, for example. Several *nundinae* calendars have survived from the early to mid-first century AD. Each contains a list of eight towns, 15 to 25 kilometres distant from each other, which were connected in a commercial network. This confirms De Ligt's catchment area of 50 kilometres.[111] Rome and Capua appear most often,

[111] CIL 6.8863; CIL 6.4.2, 32505.

suggesting that commercial networks were focused on these towns. Rome itself was obviously the most important market; Capua played an important role as a distribution centre for surrounding towns. Such fixed networks of markets are not attested for the Republican period, but the towns mentioned on the calendars—including major centres such as Capua and Minturnae, as well as smaller local centres such as Interamna Lirenas, Aquinum, and Casinum—certainly played an important economic role already in the second and first centuries BC.

At these small markets, peasants could sell their surplus to other locals,[112] or to *circumforanei*, travelling merchants who bought goods from small producers and sold them at larger weekly or seasonal markets.[113] Especially during harvest time, wealthy traders visited local markets in order to buy surplus crops for further distribution, e.g. at Rome.[114] Such markets tied together town and country, and served not only for commercial transactions, but also to distribute information, e.g. regarding legislation. In addition, they offered a platform for Roman politicians canvassing for votes.[115] In particular markets taking place in colonies, whether Latin or Roman, were important: they fulfilled the role of a central place for surrounding inhabitants, thus bringing both colonists and locals to the market to trade with each other. The foundation of colonies was therefore an injection of new producers and consumers into an area, creating new business opportunities for local producers and traders.

De Ligt's second category are regional markets, which had a much larger catchment area, bringing people together from distances of up to 300 kilometres; they lasted one or two weeks; they had a larger volume of trade, of a higher monetary value; and they involved specialized producers and large-scale merchants. Such fairs allowed for the sale of goods produced in the area to specialized merchants and goods from elsewhere to local consumers. These markets were especially important for the distribution of specialities from specific areas that were sold throughout Italy and the Mediterranean by specialized merchants.[116] A late-Republican example is the fair at Campi Macri near Mutina, which attracted customers looking to buy new animals for their flocks.[117] Thus such markets stimulated the distribution of agricultural products from the hinterland to the coastal areas and Rome, and also of products that had arrived by sea into the hinterland of Italy.[118] De Ligt emphasizes the distribution of luxury goods, such as

[112] *Moretum* 78–80; Col. *R.* 10.313–19; Verg. *Georg.* 1.273–5; Plaut. *Rud.* 296–300, 979–80, *Epid.* 198–9; *Aul.* 370–2; Var. *R.* 3.2.11, 3.3.4; Col. *R.* 7.3.13. On peasants and their engagement with the market, see Morley 1996, 75–7, 166–74; Holleran 2012, 181–3, 208–15.

[113] Cic. *Q.* 3.1.3. See Andreau 2002, 117 for large-scale trade at *nundinae.*

[114] Apul. *Met.* 1.5: a merchant in cheese and honey travelling around markets in Greece; *Vita Aesopi* 12: a trader travelling through the country buying pack animals. See De Ligt 1993, 107, 131; Holleran 2012, 188.

[115] Macr. *Sat.* 1.16.33–4; Liv. 7.15.13. See De Ligt 1993, 110–11.

[116] De Ligt 1993, 83, 86–7.

[117] Var. *R.* 2.pr.6; Strab. 5.1.11; CIL 10.1401. See De Ligt 1993, 83–4, 99.

[118] Andreau 1985, 188–9.

jewellery, and the importance of such markets for the elites, who came to sell specialized products and buy luxury items and expensive agricultural resources. However, as we saw above, there was no strict separation between small and medium-sized markets; regional fairs also played a role in the distribution of goods among the lower classes. Peasants could certainly attend regionals markets to buy non-food items. They may have been especially important in areas that were less urbanized and where no regular weekly markets were held.[119]

A third type of market identified by De Ligt is interregional fairs, which brought together people from even larger catchment areas (1,000–1,500 kilometres) and focus mostly on entrepôt commerce, i.e. the sale and purchase of goods that were neither produced nor consumed nearby.[120] The evidence for the existence of this type of fair dates mostly from the Eastern Empire, and is not attested for Republican Italy. However, it is difficult to make a strict distinction between regional fairs, De Ligt's second category, and yearly fairs. They shared many characteristics and differed only in scale.

Markets did not only take place on a weekly basis; in many towns permanent market facilities existed in the form of shops (*tabernae*) or market halls (*macella*). These locations served to bring together traders from many areas and to redistribute their goods to merchants, who would distribute them further.[121] Puteoli was an important market centre in the Republic. Long-distance trade from across the Mediterranean put in here, as well as ships from the nearby Bay of Naples.[122] Minturnae was also an important centre, serving as the export harbour for the products of Fregellae. The forum, built in the early second century, had *tabernae* where permanent trade could take place.[123] Capua, a central market town for Campania, had not only permanent markets for daily goods, but also the Seplasia, a specialized market for perfumes and medicine.[124] In many towns, markets were housed in *macella*, which are attested in the Republic in many places, e.g. Fidenae, Gabii, and Pompeii.[125] It is likely that the sellers at such markets were not local farmers, but professional traders who bought their goods from farmers.[126] *Fora pecuaria* ('cattle markets') were used especially for trade in animals; they are attested in several Italian towns.[127]

We may conclude that weekly markets and seasonal fairs played an important role in the economic distribution networks of Italy. At the same time, many towns—as well as sanctuaries, as we have seen—housed *tabernae* and *macella*,

[119] Frayn 1993, 49. [120] De Ligt 1993, 88–9. [121] De Ligt 1993, 100–1.

[122] Cic. *Att.* 5.2.2; see Strab. 5.4.6. See Frayn 1993, 90–1. [123] Frayn 1993, 47.

[124] Cic. *Pis.* 24–5, *Agr.* 2.76, 93–4; Plin. *NH* 16.40–1, 33.164, 34.100–8; Festus 458L; VM 9.1.ext.1. Plaut. *Rud.* 629–32 notes that some items sold here came from Cyrene, attesting to contacts with a wide variety of Mediterranean regions. See Frayn 1993, 81.

[125] Fidenae: Cato *Agr.* 135.2; Hor. *Epist.* 1.11.7; Strab. 5.3.2; Gabii: Hor. *Epist.* 1.11.7.

[126] De Ligt 1993, 93, 112.

[127] Frayn 1993, 151. Larinum was an important livestock market (Cic. *Clu.* 198), while Reate was the centre of the mule-breeding business in Sabinum (Var. *R.* 2.14).

in which exchange could take place at any time. Many of these buildings were erected in the last two centuries BC, showing the increase in economic transactions in this period.[128]

2.6. Other Interactions between Romans and Italians

2.6.1. Military service

Military service has often been considered one of the most important mechanisms for integration between Rome and its Italian allies. Here I will briefly review the arguments in order to determine how important military service may have been for the integration of Italian soldiers.

How the Italians were recruited into the Roman army is not entirely clear. From the mid- to late third century, it is likely that a fixed number of soldiers was requested every year from specific communities, according to a list called the *formula togatorum*.[129] For the earlier period, there is no evidence that the obligations of the allies were strictly delineated, apart from the general obligation to support Rome in war.[130] Recruitment of specific groups could be organized by personal relationships between Roman and Italian commanders. For example, L. Papirius Cursor in 293 had 'a remarkable power of command . . . that was equally effective with citizens and allies'.[131] Thus, relations between Rome and Italic peoples, as well as between different Italic peoples, were often mediated by personal relationships between the elites.

Italians usually served in their own cohorts with their own local commanders (*praefecti cohortis*), so that during battle they did not have much contact with Romans. On the other hand, not all allies fought separately from the Roman legions. There were also mixed units like the *extraordinarii*, who were composed of the best soldiers from all Italian allies, although Latin colonists were possibly the most numerous in this group. Latin was certainly the *lingua franca* in this group, so that soldiers who did not already speak it learned it here.[132] Italians from different peoples could also be assigned tasks together; in 208, for example, allied Etruscans served together with people from the Latin colony Fregellae,[133] bringing together people from different parts of Italy and different civic statuses.

As for army life, it has been argued that by serving with Romans and people from other parts of Italy, Italians learned Latin and gained familiarity with Roman culture.[134] On the other hand, the importance of the army as a location for

[128] See the ongoing project *Building tabernae* by Flohr at Leiden University: https://www.universiteitleiden.nl/en/research/research-projects/humanities/building-tabernae.

[129] Baronowski 1984; Erdkamp 2011, 120–3. [130] Hantos 1983, 165. [131] Liv. 9.16.6.

[132] Plb. 6.26.6–9. See Pfeilschifter 2007, 34–5.

[133] Plb. 10.31.1–6; Liv. 27.26–7; Plu. *Marc.* 29.

[134] Toynbee 1965:2, 110; Keaveney 1987, 11–14; Gabba 1976, 28; Dyson 1992, 53–4; Jehne 2006.

interaction between Romans and allies has recently been questioned, since the allies served not in the legions, but in their own contingents led by their own officers, and they did not live in the same barracks as Roman soldiers.[135] Nevertheless, although Romans and allies fought in their own units and had their own spaces in camp, they still lived in close proximity for extended periods of time. Italians could easily have socialized with Romans when off duty, and would have gained a basic idea of who the Romans were and what their culture and language looked like.[136]

The most important material benefit that Italians received from their service for Rome was a share in the spoils. It seems to have been normal that allies received the same amounts as Romans, although this is only stated explicitly for three occasions: in 180, 178, and 167.[137] When, in 177, 'the allies got only half as much as those with Roman citizenship,... they followed Claudius' chariot in such silence that you could feel their resentment'.[138] The sharing of spoils with allies may already be attested by a late-fourth century bronze breastplate from Lucus Angitiae, which was dedicated to the gods with the inscription 'on behalf of the Marsic legions' (*pro le[cio]nibus martses*). It is possible that these Marsi had served in the Roman army and had received a share of the spoils.[139] An inscription from Marruvium, in the Marsi area, records a temple being built by Scipio *Carthagine capta* ('after the capture of Carthage'). Apparently, Scipio set up buildings in various parts of Italy, to recognize the contribution made by the allies to his campaign.[140] Similarly, Lucius Mummius in 146 set up statues in various parts of Italy, indicating that the Italians shared in the spoils of his war in Greece. Some even carried inscriptions in Oscan, indicating Mummius' intention to communicate his message to the Italians: if they remained loyal, they could expect to be well rewarded, not just materially, but also in prestige.[141] Not so long ago it had been the Italians who were despoiled, with the spoils taken to Rome to be displayed—for example, statues taken from Volsinii in 264, which were displayed in the temples of Fortuna and Mater Matuta[142]—but now Italy did the same to the defeated peoples in the provinces.

The material benefits of service were the most important advantage that the Italians reaped from their association with Rome; many wars were extremely successful, so that the Italians could count on a steady inflow of wealth into their communities.[143] They would not have had access to this if they had not

[135] Mouritsen 1998, 67–8; Pfeilschifter 2007. [136] Rosenstein 2012, 93–103.
[137] Liv. 40.43, 41.7, 45.43.4–8 (Latins only).
[138] Liv. 41.14.2. [139] *CIL* 1² 5=ILLRP 7. See Dench 1995, 159. [140] ILLRP 326.
[141] Zevi 1996, 128. [142] Var. *L.* 5.46; Prop. 4.2. See Patterson 2006b, 610–11.
[143] Military service may have been one of the most important job opportunities; see Rosenstein 2004, 79–81. However, donatives varied from 7 to 200 *denarii*, so that allies would not always receive a large amount of spoils; see Gauthier forthcoming. Harris 1984, 91 argues that the Italians preferred not to fight at all. However, before the Roman conquest, martial prowess was certainly an important part of many Italian cultures.

been associated with Rome, so there were tangible benefits to maintaining loyalty to the Roman state. Distribution of spoils in the form of coins contributed to the monetization of Italy, and especially the spread of Roman coinage, as discussed in chapter 4: soldiers with Roman coins spent them at home, leading to a larger acceptance of Roman currency in the allied regions.

For Italian elites, the army offered more possibilities for integration than for the average soldier, since they had to communicate with Roman commanders regularly, especially with the *praefecti socium*: six elected Roman officers charged with coordinating the allied troops.[144] This enabled them to build ties of friendship and patronage with Roman leaders. The loyalty of the Samnite leader Herius Potilius is illustrated by the fact that when his unit of Samnites plotted a revolt in 259, he immediately reported this to the Roman command—his loyalty to Rome was more important than the respect of his countrymen.[145]

Another important aspect of military service was the opportunity for Italians to show off their martial prowess by their actions in battle, which was important in militaristic societies such as ancient Italy. The Marsi prided themselves on the fact that the Romans could achieve 'no triumph without or over the Marsi'[146]—clearly they were proud of their achievements in service of the Romans. Often Italians took the heaviest part of the fight, leading to higher casualty figures, but also to a martial reputation. At the battle of Pydna in 168, for example, the Paeligni and Marrucini were the first to engage the Macedonian phalanx.[147] During the Second Punic War, a Paelignian cohort refused to retreat; its commander hurled the cohort's standard into the enemy camp and challenged his men to follow him. Then 'the commander of the third legion berated the Romans for their cowardice in letting the allies have the glory of capturing the camp' and exhorted his men to follow the allies' example.[148] The valiant acts of allies were clearly acknowledged, but there was also a strong sense that the Romans should not be outmatched by their allies. In this case, this competition led to an unexpected victory, but disagreement between Roman and Italian commanders could also lead to disaster. In the First Punic War:

> Hamilcar... heard that in the Roman camp the allies and the Romans were at variance as to which had most distinguished themselves in the battles, and that the allies were encamped by themselves... Suddenly falling on them with his whole force as they were breaking up their camp, he killed about 4,000 men.[149]

[144] Suolahti 1956, 200 thinks that three of the *praefecti socium* were Romans and three were allies, while Galsterer 1976, 149 thinks all were allies. To judge from their names, it seems more likely that the *praefecti socium* were Roman citizens. Most of their names are common Roman names; only a few men had a non-Roman background, judging from their names: N. Decimius (Liv. 22.24.11), Vibius Accaus (Liv. 25.14.4, 13; VM 3.2.20), C. and L. Arrenius (Liv. 27.6.1–11, 27.8), and C. Ampius (Liv. 31.2.59). In any case, they had already been granted citizenship, or they could not have been elected *praefecti socium*.

[145] Zon. 8.11. [146] App. *BC* 1.46; Strab. 5.4.2. [147] Plu. *Aem.* 20.1–3.

[148] Liv. 25.14.4–6. [149] Plb. 1.24.3–4.

Thus, through service in the Roman army, the Italians could achieve glory. However, they often used this to reinforce the status of their own people, in competition with Rome, rather than to create a stronger association with the Romans.

On the other hand, it must be remembered that military service not only was an instrument of integration, but also sometimes formed an important source of discontent for Italian allies (see chapter 5). It could be argued that Italians had reason to resent the obligation to serve in the Roman army, which had so recently defeated them. The loyalty of the allies could therefore never be taken for granted: for example, in around 280, Decius Vibellius, a Samnite who commanded a garrison of Campanians at Regium under Roman orders, killed the inhabitants and seized control of the town.[150] During the Second Punic War, Dasius, commander of a garrison at Clastidium in Apulia, handed the town over to Hannibal.[151]

Furthermore, Italians usually furnished more soldiers than the Romans. Indeed, according to Livy's figures, allies furnished about one third more soldiers than the Romans on average, although the numbers varied from year to year.[152] Livy in one place refers to the 'regular number of allies and members of the Latin League, that is 15,000 infantry and 800 cavalry' per year,[153] but this number could be raised or lowered as necessary. His figures include both Latins and Italian allies, so it is difficult to determine how important this aspect of service was as a source for discontent among the allies. The Latins were mostly loyal to Rome during the Second Punic War and Social War, so they clearly had different feelings than the allies. It may be that Latins usually formed the largest part of the allied contingents: their loyalty was more secure than that of other allies, they knew the language and the fighting style of the Romans, and they lived closest to Rome, making recruitment easier.[154] Of the allied Italians, some seem to have served more often than others—for example, the Paeligni and Marsi, who are frequently mentioned in the sources.[155] In any case, only a small number of allies was needed each year, so that many Italians did not serve with Rome regularly, if ever.[156]

Sometimes allied contingents were kept under arms longer than Roman soldiers; this could have been another cause for resentment. In 200, for example, the governor of Gaul 'demobilized his entire army with the exception of 5000 allies

[150] App. *Samn.* 9; Liv. *Per.* 12.7; Plb. 1.7.7; Diod. 22.2.3. [151] Liv. 21.48.8–9; Plb. 3.69.1–4.

[152] Ilari 1974, 174 thinks that Latins made up more than 25 per cent of the whole army, but it is difficult to see how many of the allied soldiers were Latins and how many were Italians. Pfeilschifter 2007, 33 estimates two thirds allies; see Rosenstein 2012, 85–91.

[153] Liv. 40.36.7. [154] Tan forthcoming.

[155] The only groups actually mentioned by name are the Fregellans (Latin colonists) and the Italian allies the Marsi, Paeligni, Marrucini, and Etruscans. See Liv. 26.26–7, 44.40.5; Plu. *Aem.* 20.1–3; Front. *Str.* 2.8.5; see Erdkamp 2007.

[156] Rosenstein 2012, 85–93.

and members of the Latin League'.[157] Furthermore, casualty figures seem to have been slightly higher for allies than for Romans. In 181, for example, 'from the two legions slightly more than 200 Roman soldiers lost their lives, along with 830 allies and members of the Latin League, and some 2400 foreign auxiliaries'.[158] There also is some suggestion that allied casualties were considered less serious than Roman ones: 'There were fewer than a hundred casualties among the victors, and by far the majority of them were Paeligni.'[159] This loss of allied life was an important cause for discontent in the late second century. Between 133 and 91, the Romans suffered seven serious defeats, most importantly the battle of Arausio in 105, in which 80,000 soldiers were killed, the majority of them allies (although Valerias Antias, the source of this figure, usually exaggerates such numbers).[160] The Italians did not approve of this squandering of Italian manpower. On the other hand, Italian allies were valued more highly than foreign auxiliaries: after a defeat in 170, 'the casualties were mostly emergency conscripts from [Macedonia] and not of Italian stock, [which] minimized the disgrace caused by Claudius' rashness'.[161] Furthermore, as we will see (chapter 4), when allies were taken prisoner, the Romans petitioned for their release, just as they did for Roman citizens.

The Italians not only furnished soldiers, but also were responsible for outfitting, supplying, and paying the soldiers they sent, if they were paid at all. In the case of the Roman citizen army, pay was funded from the *tributum*, a tax which Roman citizens paid every year. The allies had, until the second century, a considerable amount of latitude in deciding how they elected the men to serve in the army, and could grant exemptions of these duties of their own accord.[162] The Roman state only intervened in order to emphasize its hegemony. For example, in 204, twelve Latin colonies were punished for not supplying enough soldiers to the Roman army. They had previously complained that 'there was not a man left for conscription nor any money for his pay',[163] but this had not excused them in the eyes of the Roman state. They were punished by the introduction of 'a property tax (*stipendium*) of one tenth per cent... to be paid annually'.[164] This suggests that the allies and Latin colonies normally only paid tax in years in which they actually furnished soldiers. Since they outfitted and paid their own soldiers, they did not pay any monetary contribution when no soldiers were demanded of them. This was an advantage over Roman citizens, who paid *tributum* every year. However, this balance changed in 167. After this year, *tributum* was no longer demanded of Roman citizens, while the allies continued to pay for the gear and the salaries of their soldiers. Whether the soldiers paid for these themselves or their states did so,

157 Liv. 31.10.5. See 32.1.5. 158 Liv. 40.32.7; see 40.40.13. 159 Liv. 44.42.8.

160 Liv. *Per.* 67.2. See Brunt 1965; 1988. 161 Liv. 43.11.11.

162 Plb. 6.21.4–5. An inscription from Aletrium in honour of L. Betilienus Varus frees him from these duties (CIL 12.1529=ILLRP 528).

163 Liv. 27.9.13. 164 Liv. 29.15.9–10.

they paid more than the Roman citizens, most of whom were supplied by the state in this period.[165] The *lex Acilia repetundarum* of Gaius Gracchus exempted some allies from *munera publica* ('public services'),[166] which could very well refer to the obligation to pay taxes in their home towns. Thus, the allies in the second century probably contributed more to the Roman war effort than Roman citizens, in terms of both the number of soldiers as well as the cost of outfitting them. This may have been an additional reason for resentment against their obligations to serve.

We may conclude that military service offered ample opportunities for social contacts between Romans and Italians, and between Italians of different ethnic groups. Furthermore, it offered the Italians access to an important source of wealth in the form of spoils, as well as prestige by showing off their martial prowess to their fellows and to the Romans. For elite Italians, who interacted with Roman command, military service offered opportunities to create social ties with the Roman elites. Although the allies were at a disadvantage in some respects, such as a higher mobilization rate and higher loss of life, service in the Roman army was unavoidable. Thus, it brought them into contact with the Romans, whether they wished it or not. Most, in fact, seem to have been willing to engage in army life and to exploit the opportunities for glory and wealth that it offered. On the other hand, not all allies fought in the Roman army for the same amount of time. This meant that the impact of military service for Rome was not the same for all allies; this in turn might have had consequences for their further integration.

2.6.2. Social relations: intermarriage, friendships, elite networks

A dense network of social relations existed throughout Italy, connecting Roman citizens with Italians and Italians with each other. These relations offered a variety of benefits for both the Roman and the Italian parties. Often a relationship was officially laid down in an agreement of *hospitium* (guest-friendship), between two individuals and handed on to their descendants, and formalized by a *tessera hospitalis*, a token that documented the existence of friendship. It is sometimes difficult to distinguish between friendship between equal partners and patronage between unequal partners, but in either case, the parties had to offer each other assistance in various matters. Of course, not all friendships were formalized by a *tessera hospitalis* and transferable to the heirs of those who initiated the relationship. For example, Ti. Gracchus' friendship with Blossius, a philosopher from Cumae of Oscan descent, was most likely only personal.[167]

Hospitium could also be concluded between communities and individuals, usually between a member of the Roman elite and an Italian community.

[165] See Rathbone 1993; Roselaar 2010, 255–6 for the census qualifications of Roman citizens.
[166] Line 77–8. [167] Plu. *TG* 8.5.

A bronze *tessera hospitalis* in the shape of a fish head, dating to the late third or early second century, records an agreement of *hospitium* between a *praefectura*, perhaps Fundi, and a Roman official, T. C[—, *[i]n eius fidem om[nes nos tradimus et] convenimus*, 'in whose faith we have all placed and entrusted ourselves'.[168] In these cases, we may speak of patronage rather than friendship, since the power relations between those involved were not quite equal. Such relations and alliances had already existed from an early period. Caere in Etruria had been an ally of Rome for a long time; when Rome was threatened by the Gauls in 396, it sent the Vestals to Caere for safekeeping.[169] Social relations between Romans and Caeritans remained strong; in 310, the brother of consul Q. Fabius Maximus Rullianus went on a reconnaissance mission in Etruria, because he had been educated in Caere *apud hospites* ('among guest-friends'), and therefore knew the Etruscan language. According to Livy, this was normal for aristocratic boys at the time.[170]

Relations of patronage could start for various reasons. Often the commander who first conquered a territory in the name of Rome maintained links of patronage with the area; he could use his influence to promote the interests of local people who had supported him during the conquest. For example, the Coruncanii, who negotiated in the late third century with the queen of Illyria in order to prevent war, had played a role in the conquest of Apulia. It may be that the Senate sent them to Illyria because they had clients in Apulia, who had been suffering from Illyrian pirate raids (see chapter 4.7).[171] The brothers Minucius, who mediated in a land dispute in northern Italy in 117, were descended from the conqueror of the area, the consul of 197.[172]

The conquering commander could also exercise influence to gain Roman citizenship for Italian clients. For example, the Atilii Glabriones of Perusia were probably connected to Acilius Glabrio, who defeated a rebellion of slaves in Etruria in 196. He may have rewarded loyal Etruscans with citizenship, who then took his name.[173] Roman nobles often supported their Italian protégés when they set their first steps on the Roman *cursus honorum*. Marius was introduced into Roman society by the Caecilii Metelli, with whom the Marii maintained hereditary patronage relationships.[174] Smaller favours were common: when Archias in the early first century wanted to become a citizen of Heraclea, he received a recommendation from Lucullus. Archias was a client not just of Lucullus, but of many other leading Romans too, including the Metelli, the

[168] CIL 1² 611=10.6231=ILS 6093=ILLRP 1068; see Di Fazio 2006; Bispham 2007, 97–8. See on *hospitium* Patterson 2006a, 140–1; Fronda 2011; Bourdin 2012, 569–74; Lomas 2012, 202–9.

[169] Plu. *Cam.* 22.3.

[170] Liv. 9.36.1–8. See Cic. *Div.* 1.92; VM 1.1.1. See Cornell 1995, 355; Adams 2003, 166–8.

[171] App. *Samn.* 10. See Marasco 1986, 72.

[172] ILLRP 517=CIL 1² 584; Liv. 32.29–31. Harris 1984, 94 thinks that every Italian town and people had an official Roman patron, but this is not attested.

[173] Liv. 33.36.1–3; CIL 11.1934=ILS 2685=ILLRP 638. See Dondin 1979, 668–9.

[174] Plu. *Mar.* 4.1.

Aemilii, and the Octavii.[175] The number of Roman nobles that one could call patrons was an important source of status for an Italian, since it indicated that his character was noble enough for these people to associate themselves with him.

Ties of patronage could also begin through economic relationships. It has been argued, for example, that Appius Claudius Caecus gained many clients in Latium and Campania when he built the Via Appia in 312. Not only would this have created jobs for many people, but it also opened up a major trade route between Rome and Campania. The same was true of the Via Flaminia in 220, which created new ties between Flaminius and the people of Picenum.[176] The founder of a colony or viritane distribution or colony could count the settlers as his clients, so that Flamininus, who had been head of the commission that reinforced the colonies of Narnia and Cosa in 199, became a candidate for the consulship, and 'with the eager support of his colonists' managed to get elected.[177] As censor of 174, Q. Fulvius Flaccus commissioned building projects in many towns in Italy (see chapter 2.2), suggesting that he had long-standing ties with these towns.[178] If a Roman noble possessed a land in an Italian town, he would often be its patron and created social bonds with the local elite. An example is Gnaeus Fulvius Flaccus, who was exiled in the Second Punic War and fled to Tarquinii, suggesting that he had landholdings there.[179]

If a local noble had secured a position in Rome, he could use this to bring further benefits to his home town. Cicero mentions the assistance that Plancius from Atina has given to his people:

> Plancius was a popular man in his tribe, because he has been kind to many of them, because he has been security for many of them, because he has procured employment for many of them by means of the authority and interest of his father, and because he has bound the whole prefecture of Atina to himself by all the kindness displayed by himself, by his father, and by his ancestors.[180]

Thus, people who had made progress in Rome could use their influence to assist others further down the scale of patronage.

Patronage could become an embarrassment, however: Marius had been a client of the Herennii, but preferred his association with the more prestigious Metelli, who could bring him more social advancement than the Herennii could. He therefore declared that 'as soon as he had been elected (plebeian aedile) he had

[175] Cic. *Arch.* 5–6. The same applied to Roscius of Ameria; see Cic. *Rosc. Am.* 15. The poet Ennius was a client of several elite Romans (Cic. *Arch.* 27, *Acad. Pr.* 2.51; Liv. 38.56.4). See Gruen 1990, 79–123.

[176] Cic. *Att.* 1.1 states that the curator of the Via Flaminia has a good chance in the consular elections because he knows many people all over Italy. See Plu. *Caes.* 5. See Dench 1995, 144; Laurence 1999, 41. See for economic assistance between patrons and clients, Rauh 1986a; Verboven 2002.

[177] Plu. *Flam.* 2.1.

[178] Rauh 1986b, 146–57.

[179] Liv. 25.20–1, 26.2.7–3.12, 27.1.9; VM 8.4.3; Plu. *Marc.* 24. Gaius Matienus went into exile in Tibur in 171 (Liv. 40.18.7–8, 43.2.8–11; Lucil. 219M).

[180] Cic. *Planc.* 47.

ceased to be a client; which was not altogether true. For it is not every magistracy that frees its occupants—as well as their posterity—from their relations to a patron, but only that to which the law assigns the curule chair.'[181] This shows that patronage relations were hereditary and subject to strict regulations, which could become an embarrassment if one wanted to escape from them. Still, Marius managed to disassociate himself from the Herennii and climb the Roman *cursus honorum* with the assistance of the Metelli.

Many relationships of *hospitium* between individual Romans and Italians are attested in quite unexpected places, with no indication of when and how the relationship had started. In the second half of the third century, T. Staiodius from the Marsi was a *hospes* of the Roman noble T. Manlius Torquatus, as a *tessera hospitalis* indicates.[182] During the Second Punic War, Ti. Sempronius Gracchus had a guest-friend from Heraclea, Flavus, while T. Quinctius Crispinus was the *hospes* of a Campanian called Badius. Unfortunately, in these cases, the war sundered their relations, when the Italians chose to defend their own interests against those of Rome.[183] On the eve of the Social War, Q. Poppaedius Silo, the leader of the Marsi, had many friends in Rome, including Livius Drusus; again, this was not sufficient to stop the war.[184] In a final effort to prevent the war, the Senate sent out men to inquire about what was going on, 'choosing those who were best acquainted with each [town]', suggesting that many Roman officials had personal relations in Italian towns.[185]

An interesting person is L. Rammius from second-century Brundisium, who 'used to entertain the Roman generals and distinguished ambassadors from foreign nations', including King Perseus of Macedon.[186] It is very interesting that Rammius seems to have been part of the indigenous elite of Messapia—his name should probably be read as Rennius, a name exclusively attested in the area. He had managed to hold on to his elite position after the conquest of the territory and the foundation of Brundisium, possibly because he had chosen the Roman side during the conquest and was rewarded by the Romans.[187]

Marriage between Roman and Italian elites was common. Pacuvius Calavius, *meddix* (leading magistrate) of Capua—a *civitas sine suffragio*—was married to the daughter of P. Claudius Pulcher (*cos.* 249) and Calavius' daughter was married to M. Livius Salinator (*cos.* 219, 207).[188] The Claudii tried to protect their family when Capua's elite was deported and its land confiscated after the town's defection in the Second Punic War, but to no avail; only 'those daughters [of the Capuans] who had married into other communities' were not punished.[189]

[181] Plu. *Mar.* 5.5. See Verboven 2002, 54. [182] CIL 1^2 1764=ILLRP 1066.
[183] Liv. 25.18.4; App. *Hann.* 35; VM 1.6.8. See Cébeillac-Gervasoni 1978, 231; Patterson 2006a, 149–50.
[184] Plu. *Cat. Min.* 1–2; Diod. 37.2.9, 37.13, 37.15.3; VM 3.1.2; *Vir. Ill.* 80.11. [185] App. *BC* 1.38.
[186] Liv. 42.17.2; App. *Rom.* 9.7. See Fronda 2011, 250. [187] Yntema 2006, 104.
[188] Liv. 22.35.3, 23.2.6, 27.34–5, 29.37.
[189] Liv. 26.15–16, 26.27.9, 26.34.3; VM 3.2.ext.1, 3.8.1, 5.2.1; Zon. 9.6.

These relations not only benefited the Italian clients of Roman elites; Italians themselves also had much to offer. We have already seen that many Italians were very wealthy, so that a marriage with a rich woman from an Italian town could improve the finances of a young Roman nobleman. For example, the marriage of the daughter of C. Iulius Caesar to Marius around 111 gave the Iulii access to substantial wealth. Another Iulia married Pedius, from a wealthy Campanian merchant family.[190] This renewed access to money quickly enabled the Caesares to reach higher offices, which they had not held for many years. Caesar himself was betrothed to a Cossutia, of an equestrian family from Capua often attested in the East.[191] Clearly, Italian families had much to offer in terms of wealth to impoverished Roman aristocrats.

There was a dense network of relationships not only between Romans and Italians, but also between Italians of different towns. Marriage relations existed between the Eumachii of Pompeii and the Numistrii of Lucania, who were both active in wool production and lived at opposite ends of important transhumance routes.[192] The sister of Ennius from the allied town Rudiae was married to the poet Pacuvius, from the Latin colony Brundisium.[193] Oppianicus the Younger from Larinum was married to Papia from Teanum, about 30 kilometres away; he also was good friends with the brothers Fabricius from Aletrium, about 190 kilometres from Larinum.[194]

Wiseman concludes that there was 'an "international aristocracy" in Italy composed of the ruling families of Latin, Etruscan, Oscan, and central-Apennine towns, who intermarried freely among themselves and among their social equals, the Roman nobility'.[195] There were indeed very strong ties between the Roman and Italian elites already in the third century, as attested by the marriages of the Capuan leaders. Some areas had closer connections to Rome than others, such as areas with *civitas sine suffragio* and Latin colonies, for whom marriages to Romans were easier than for allies. However, there are examples of friendship even between people from Lucania and Apulia and Romans, so that indeed all areas of Italy were involved in these social networks. On the other hand, these relationships often broke down in war, showing that social relations could not prevent warfare.[196]

[190] Plu. *Mar.* 6.2; Suet. *Iul.* 83. 2; App. *BC* 3.22. See Farney 2007, 189.

[191] Suet. *Iul.* 1. See Cébeillac-Gervasoni 1978, 236–7. Scipio Asicaticus (*cos.* 83) married his daughter to P. Sestius (Cic. *Sest.* 6–7, *Fam.* 5.6.1). If she was related to the amphora-producing Sestii, she was certainly an attractive marriage partner. Catilina married Gratidia, from a merchant family from Arpinum, possibly in an effort to improve his financial situation (*Schol. Bern. ad Luc.* 2.173; Sall. *Hist.* 1 45M).

[192] Morel 1991a, 201.

[193] Grelle 2008, 386 sees this marriage as evidence of a grant of *conubium* by Rome (see chapter 4.2.1), but there is no reason why this should be the case. Italians were not subject to Roman law and were therefore free to marry whomever they wished. Fronda 2010, 320 n. 119 states that it is 'not clear' whether this was possible, but there is no reason why not.

[194] Cic. *Clu.* 27, 46. See Fronda 2011, 252.

[195] Wiseman 1971, 63.

[196] Mouritsen 1998, 72–3 rightly points out that the allies did not always follow the demands of Rome, even when patronage links existed with Romans.

It might be debated whether the Italians were really the 'social equals' of the Romans, as Wiseman asserts; there were ties not only of marriage, but also of patronage between them, in which Romans were the dominant partners. Certainly, in terms of political advantages, Roman elites had more to offer than Italian elites, creating an unbalanced relationship between the two groups.[197] Nevertheless, it cannot be denied that these social ties pervaded Republican Italy and stimulated integration between Romans and Italians, at least on the level of the elites. Again, it must be remembered that this did not mean that the Italians felt that they were 'Roman' in any sense, but they certainly felt that they were the social equals of the Roman elites.

2.7. Conclusion

This survey of the various locations of interaction in the Roman Republic suggests that social and economic contacts between Romans and Italians, and between Italians of different ethnic groups, were ubiquitous. Colonies created enduring links between colonists and surrounding inhabitants. Especially in areas that were not densely urbanized, colonies provided new opportunities for interaction. Many colonies developed into prosperous communities and attracted further immigrants. Viritane land distributions, as well as seasonal and permanent migration, created further links between the various peoples of Italy.

In the pre-Roman period, sanctuaries and temples had been important locations for trade; this continued in many cases after the Roman conquest of Italy. Furthermore, religious industry and the accumulation of wealth by temples meant that they played a significant role in redistribution networks. The same applied to local and regional markets and annual fairs, which took place in many locations in Republican Italy.

Finally, we have seen that military service offered ample opportunities for social contacts between Romans and Italians. Furthermore, it offered the Italians access to spoils, as well as prestige. On the other hand, we have seen that the impact of military service for Rome was different for different groups of allies; this in turn might have had consequences for their further integration. We have also seen that social ties pervaded Republican Italy and stimulated integration between Romans and Italians, at least on the level of the elites. Again, it must be remembered that this did not mean that the Italians felt that they were 'Roman' in any sense, but this may have made them feel that they were equals of the Roman elites in social status.

All these interactions brought together people from different ethnic groups. Thus, they contributed to the economic, social, military, and political integration

[197] Fronda 2011, 255.

of Italy in the Republican period, in the sense that the peoples of Italy came into contact with each other on a more regular basis. Eventually this would lead to civic and social integration of Italy, but this did not happen until relatively late (see chapters 4 and 5). The next chapter will consider the economic changes that occurred in Italy as a result of the increased opportunities for contact between Romans and Italians, and discuss to what extent these contacts led to economic integration in Republican Italy.

3

The Economic Integration of Italy

3.1. Introduction

In the previous chapter, we have seen that Romans and the Italic peoples interacted in a variety of ways during the Republican period. This led to changes in all spheres of life: in culture, language, and currency, as well as in politics, administration, and social relations. In this chapter, we will focus on the economic sphere. In the third and second centuries, trade, and especially export from the Italian peninsula, grew to unprecedented levels, as both Romans and Italians pursued profits in new markets and in new goods, as a result of new opportunities created by the expansion of Roman hegemony in the Mediterranean. Commercial relations between Romans and Italians also occurred more often and on a larger scale than ever before, offering opportunities for integration in the social sphere.

The title of this book, *Italy's Economic Revolution*, emphasizes the importance of the Italians in the economy of the peninsula. Older scholarship discusses economic developments in Italy mostly in a negative way: it was argued that much of the land held by Italians was taken by the Romans after the conquest of Italy as *ager publicus*, land owned by the Roman state. It is assumed that this deprived most Italians of their economic assets and marginalized the Italians in the economy of the peninsula.[1] However, archaeological surveys in recent decades have shown that there is no evidence for economic decline in most parts of Italy in the middle and late Republic. Furthermore, many Italian areas boasted unprecedented economic prosperity, as shown by the great number of monumental buildings erected in this period (see chapter 4.3). Nevertheless, the role of Italians in economic activities is still often neglected; for example, Kay's 2014 book, *Rome's Economic Revolution*, has a mostly Roman focus (see note 4 of chapter 1). However, as we will see, the evidence regarding Italy in this period indicates that members of the various Italian peoples were active in profitable economic activities and that many areas of Italy experienced great economic prosperity. This chapter will therefore trace in more detail the involvement of Italians in the economic developments of the peninsula in the middle to late Republican period. We will look first at the economic activities undertaken by Italians, in order to see where, when, and why Italians engaged in trade in Italy and overseas.

[1] Toynbee 1965:2, 9–14, 177–9; Hopkins 1978, 11–13; Gabba 1989.

Italy's Economic Revolution. Saskia T. Roselaar, Oxford University Press (2019). © Saskia T. Roselaar.
DOI: 10.1093/oso/9780198829447.001.0001

Next, we will investigate how the changes in the economic network of the Mediterranean affected economic developments in Italy itself. Some parts of Italy flourished, since they were able to profit from new economic opportunities. Others, however, were less successful. It is likely that, as the economy of Italy and parts of the Mediterranean became more integrated, each region and town developed more specific functions within the larger economic network, and this meant that some regions saw large changes, whether positive or negative, in their economies. Of course, the extent of such changes should not be overestimated, since in all regions of Italy subsistence agriculture remained the norm, but it cannot be denied that the emergence of new economic networks had a great impact on local and regional economies.

We will also investigate whether the economic developments in Italy were in any way related to the legal status of the land and its people. It has been suggested that regions with more administrative contact with Rome, such as areas that received full Roman citizenship, experienced different economic developments than allied regions, which had less contact with Romans.[2] In order to study the economic developments in Italy, this chapter will investigate a sample of areas with various legal statuses, in order to see if legal status was in any way connected to economic development. This will also show how and why some areas profited from new economic opportunities, while others were less successful. Thus, we will be able to identify possible connections between the conquest of Italy by Rome, and the economic integration of Italy through the creation of new economic networks within and beyond the peninsula. Finally, we will investigate how the economic activities undertaken by the Italians contributed to the economic integration of Italy: did the regions of Italy and the Mediterranean experience closer economic interaction? Did this lead to a decrease in transaction costs and an increase in economic integration, because it became easier and cheaper to trade with other regions?

3.2. Italian Commercial Activities in the Mediterranean

It has often been assumed that the economy of Italy experienced severe decline after the Roman conquest: land owned by Italians was taken as *ager publicus*, depriving them of a valuable economic asset and marginalizing their role in the economy. The description by Appian is often taken as a starting point for the situation of Italian agriculture in the middle and late Republic. He describes how the Romans confiscated land as *ager publicus*, which was then monopolized by

[2] Morel 1991b, 130; Torelli 1999, 122.

rich Roman citizens. They drove out small farmers by force and created large estates, which were worked by slaves. Therefore, Appian says,

> the powerful were becoming extremely rich, and the number of slaves in the country was reaching large proportions, while the Italian people were suffering from depopulation and a shortage of men, worn down as they were by poverty and taxes and military service. And if they had any respite from these tribulations, they had no employment, because the land was owned by the rich who used slave workers instead of free men.[3]

This reconstruction was, until recently, believed by many scholars; the most forceful description of the 'decline of Italian agriculture' was given in Toynbee's monumental work of 1965. Since even today, some scholars still assume that Italy suffered economic decline in the middle and late Republic,[4] it is worth discussing this theory. In this chapter, it will become clear which elements of the traditional reconstruction are still valid, and which should be discarded.

It is now recognized that the traditional reconstruction is in some parts exaggerated and in others simply wrong. Archaeological surveys have shown that small farmers did not disappear, even in the most commercially orientated regions of Italy. Furthermore, recent estimates for the number of slaves in Italy are much lower than Toynbee and Brunt suggested.[5] Moreover, in most areas of Italy there is little trace of depopulation, although settlement patterns changed in many regions (see section 3.3).[6] Finally, the role of *ager publicus* was in many respects different from what Appian describes: most commercial farms were located on privately owned land, while Roman state-owned land often remained in the hands of its former Italian owners.[7]

This brings us to the main issue of this section: the role of the Italians in these economic developments. The older reconstruction of economic developments in Italy places great emphasis on the role of the Roman elite. However, it has long been recognized that Italians were not passive recipients of Roman rule; as discussed in chapter 1, they actively adopted elements of foreign cultures that were useful in local contexts. It is to be expected, therefore, that they were not passive in economic affairs either. It has long been recognized that many Italians were active in business throughout the Mediterranean, a fact duly noted whenever the role of Italians in the economy of the Republic is considered.[8] However, in my view most scholars do not appreciate the extent and variety of the activities

[3] App. *BC* 1.7–8. See also Plu. *TG* 8.

[4] Toynbee 1965:2, 9–14, 177–9; Johannowsky 1976, 267; Hopkins 1978, 11–13; Grelle 1981, 193–8. Some recent studies still adhere to this view, e.g. Gabba 1989; Levi 1997, 467; Pareti 1997, 439–41.

[5] De Ligt 2004; Scheidel 2005.

[6] Hin 2013. However, see De Ligt 2012, 266: some areas of Italy, e.g. Lucania and parts of Etruria, seem to have experienced population decline, as indicated by the decreasing number of settlement sites (see also section 3.3.4).

[7] See Roselaar 2010, 146–220.

[8] E.g. Gabba 1954.

undertaken by the Italians in all economic spheres: agriculture, pastoralism, manufacture, trade, and banking were all carried out on a large scale by Italians. I wish to show that the Italians were fully engaged in the economic opportunities that emerged after the Roman conquest of Italy and part of the Mediterranean—so much so that we might speak of an 'Italian economic revolution' occurring in the third to first centuries. In order to evaluate the importance of the economic activities of Italians for integration between Romans and Italians, we must first investigate which economic activities Italians undertook. As we will see, some Italian regions were more involved in such activities than others, leading to different economic developments in the various regions of Italy.

3.2.1. Italians in the Mediterranean

General references in the literary sources to Italians active in the Mediterranean are numerous, attesting to the wide distribution of Italians all over the Mediterranean. Not all Italians travelling in the Mediterranean were merchants (*negotiatores*), as is sometimes assumed.[9] For example, mercenary service was an important reason for Italians to move abroad.[10] Especially for the fourth and third centuries, there are many literary references to Italic peoples fighting for foreign powers, e.g. Syracuse, Carthage, and Pyrrhus of Epirus.[11]

Nevertheless, in most references to Italians overseas, they seem to be traders. Italian merchants often appear in the context of wars. For example, in 182, Illyrian pirates abused Romans and allies: 'injuries had been inflicted on many Roman citizens and Latins and allies.'[12] It is indeed very likely that Italian merchants fell victim to Illyrian aggression in 182. They were active in trade across the Adriatic, as we will see; the allied town Tarentum was one of the towns that asked for assistance from Rome. To indicate these victims of piracy, Livy uses the phrase are called *civibus Romanis et sociis Latini nominis* ('Roman citizens and allies of the Latin name'). It is necessary to examine briefly here who were meant by the phrase *socii nominis Latini*. It may be translated as 'allies of the Latin name', suggesting that Latins only were involved.[13] However, some texts use the phrase

[9] E.g. Rauh 1986b.

[10] Tagliamonte 1994, but see Bourdin 2012, 560.

[11] E.g. Thuc. 7.33, 7.57.11; DH 20.1, 21.3; Diod. Sic. 13.43.4, 13.55.7, 13.80.4, 13.87.1–88.2, 20.11.1, 20.61.7, 20.64.2, 21.3; Liv. 4.53.1, 6.13.7, 7.11, 30.33.5; Plb. 15.11.1; Plu. *Fab. Max.* 21.4. Many inscriptions attest to the presence of mercenaries outside Italy, even in Carthage; see Tagliamonte 1994.

[12] Liv. 40.42.4–5. See Wilson 1966, 91–2; Gruen 1984, 310 n. 11; Derow 2003, 53.

[13] Livy uses the same phrase in 9.19.2, 31.8.10, 33.43.3, 39.38.10, 40.18.6, 40.42.4, 43.12.6, 44.21.6, 45.43.7, 45.12.11. Briscoe 1973, 77–8 (Liv. 41.8.9) assumes the phrase only refers to Latins. Coşkun 2009b, 172–4 states that the form with *ac* appears only in 41.8–9, due to an early modern emendation. However, the phrase with *ac* or *et* appears in many more passages.

socii ac Latini nominis ('allies and those of the Latin name').[14] This has led many scholars to suggest that the phrase *sociis Latini nominis* always includes both Latin and Italian allies.[15] I agree with this view, since in the oldest attestations of the term, the term *socius* is clearly distinguished from the term *nomen Latinus*. The epigraphic *Senatus Consultum de Bacchanalibus* of 186 reads *ceivis Romanus neve nominus Latini neve socium quisquam* ('neither a Roman citizen nor a Latin nor any ally'); the *lex Acilia* of 122 says—*ceivis] Romanus sociumve nominisve Latini* ('a Roman citizen or an ally or someone of the Latin name').[16] Therefore, I assume that the phrase as used in Livy refers to both Latins and Italian allies.

Not only Illyria, but many other regions attracted Italian merchants. Literary and epigraphic sources regarding their activities start in the late fourth century. Sicily was one of the first regions where a significant presence of Italians has been attested. The Entella tablets, dated to the late fourth or early third century, attest the presence of Campanian mercenaries, who had settled in Entella in 404. Many have typically Oscan names, such as Leukios Pakkios.[17] Similarly, the Oscan Mamertini settled in Messina in the late fourth century.[18] These groups settled on Sicily permanently, while other Italians came to Sicily temporarily for commercial reasons. The island was close to Italy and gradually became the grain basket for the city of Rome. It also had good pasture lands. Moreover, from the second half of the third century it was securely in Roman hands and thus offered a safe location for investment. Rome seems to have left the exploitation of Sicily free to everyone, including Italians. It was also quick to create mechanisms to regulate trade: already in the First Punic War, a harbour tax (*portorium*) was raised on goods transported to and from the island. There were also state-owned agricultural and pasture lands, which the Roman state rented out to anyone willing to pay the lease.[19] In 227, a special praetor was created for Sicily; this may have been necessary because of the high number of conflicts occurring on the island, often related to trade.[20] The interest of Italians in landownership in Sicily is shown by the fact that in 205, L. Scipio intervened for the inhabitants of Syracuse, because 'certain men of

[14] This occurs in Liv. 2.41.6, 28.32.6, 31.5.4, 32.8.7, 34.56.5–6, 37.2.6, 37.50.2–3, 39.3.4–6, 39.20.1–3, 40.36.6, 41.8.9, 41.9.9. See Wegner 1969, 102.

[15] E.g. Wegner 1969, 95–104; Galsterer 1976, 101.

[16] The *lex de provinciis praetoriis* (dated 100) contains the phrase *cives Romani, socii nominis Latini, exterarumque nationum quae in amicitia populi Romani sunt* ('Roman citizens, allies, and those of the Latin name, as well as those external nations who are in the friendship of the Roman people') (Knidos copy, col. III, l. 29–35=SEG 3.378). This law was intended to protect all allies, and since the Italian allies cannot be considered *exterae nationes* (Richardson 2008, 86–9), the Italian allies were probably included in the phrase *socii nominis Latini*.

[17] Diod. 14.9.8–9. See Loomis 1994, 138 n. 19.

[18] Tagliamonte 1994, 191; Hoyos 1998, ch. 3.

[19] App. *Sic.* 2.6. See for Italians in Sicily Basile 1979; Pinzone 1999, esp. 386–97.

[20] Pinzone 1999, 392. An honorary inscription from Halaesa by the *Italicei* to Scipio Asiaticus may have been erected in gratitude for a judgement by Scipio on a trade dispute (CIL 1^2 612=10.7459=ILS 864=ILLRP 320). See Càssola 1962, 388.

Italian nationality (*Italici generis*) had seized the property of some Syracusans, and, although the senate had ordered its restitution, they still retained it'.[21]

This Italian interest in Sicily continued throughout the second and first centuries; for example, many Italian amphora stamps are attested in Sicily.[22] An interesting piece of evidence is the *Elogium Pollae*, an honorary inscription found in Polla in Lucania, dating to the late second century. The text praised an individual whose name is lost, and states that he, as praetor in Sicily, 'restored 917 fugitive slaves belonging to Italians to their masters'. It is possible that these Italians owned land or had other commercial interests in Sicily, not in Polla. It would make sense if the praetor of Sicily sorted out affairs in his own province, rather than in Lucania.[23] Cicero's *Verrines* show that many people active in the exploitation of Sicily came from the south of Italy, especially from Puteoli and further down the Tyrrhenian coast.[24] Of course, by Cicero's time all Italians held Roman citizenship, but they may have been continuing business that their ancestors had set up in Sicily.

Sardinia also attracted Italians from an early stage; it was included in the *provincia* of the praetor of Sicily, created in 227. The island was an important intersection in Mediterranean trade routes, for example for the export of olive oil, wine, and grain from Italy to Gaul.[25] In the second century, many Italians and Romans invested in agriculture on Sardinia, leading to the appearance of large farms and more viticulture on the island.[26] An inscription of the second century attests to the presence of *Falesce quei in Sardinia sunt* ('people from Falerii [in Etruria] who are in Sardinia'), although it does not state why they were present on the island.[27] The level of Italian interest in Sardinia was much smaller than in Sicily; Sardinia was not as fertile as Sicily and therefore attracted fewer people interested in owning land here.

Africa attracted Italians from the second century onwards. The first references appear in connection with the Roman siege of Carthage in 146. The inhabitants of Carthage had given up their weapons and provided hostages, but despite this, the Romans announced they would raze the city to the ground. The Carthaginians blamed not just Romans, but also Italians for the Roman betrayal: '[Some Carthaginians], meeting certain Italians, who were caught among them in this sudden and unexpected mischance, maltreated them in various ways, saying that they would make them suffer for the fraud practiced upon them in the matter of the hostages and the arms.'[28] It appears that these Italians were living in Carthage, for reasons not specified, and were caught up in the warfare. The Carthaginians saw

[21] Liv. 29.1.16. [22] Empereur & Hesnard 1987, 29.

[23] Fraschetti 1981, 206–7; Pinzone 1999, 390; but see Verbrugghe 1973, 30.

[24] Cic. *Verr.* 2.5.32, 145, 194. Nicolet 1966, 293 thinks they were mostly Roman citizens, but Cicero's evidence does not support this.

[25] Var. *R.* 2.6.5. See Colavitti 1999. [26] Pietra 2010, 55–6. [27] CIL 1^2 364=ILLRP 192.

[28] App. *Pun.* 92; see Plb. 36.7.5.

the Italians as responsible for the Roman deceit; either the Italians were viewed as accomplices of Rome, or the Africans failed to see the difference between Italians and Romans. Both explanations are interesting: in the first case, people in the Mediterranean saw the advantages that Italians gained from associating themselves with Rome. That the Italians themselves had been the victims of Roman conquest was not relevant for their later choice to remain loyal to Rome. Alternatively, if the Carthaginians failed to see the difference between Romans and Italians, this is a telling example of a common phenomenon, namely a lack of distinction between Romans and Italians on the part of outsiders. This had important consequences for Italian feelings of identity (see chapter 4.6).

In 122, Gaius Gracchus founded a colony at Carthage, for which colonists were recruited from 'all over Italy', according to Appian. It is not clear how many were actually settled, since the project seems to have been abandoned before completion.[29] Further settlers were established in Africa in 103 and 100 by Marius.[30] Italian merchants are also mentioned during the Jugurthine war. Again, they became the victim of their association with Rome:

> The Italians on whose valour the defence of the town (Cirta) depended, were confident that in the event of surrender they would escape injury because of the prestige of Rome. They therefore advised Adherbal to deliver himself and the town to Jugurtha... Thereupon Jugurtha first tortured Adherbal to death and then made an indiscriminate massacre of all the adult Numidians and traders whom he found with arms in their hands.[31]

The Italian traders seem to have been well organized: they managed to influence Adherbal, who commanded the defence of the town. However, their association with Rome, which they chose to advertise, could not save them: they were slaughtered together with the Numidians.

Iberia also attracted traders from Italy. Already in the third century some trade between Italy and the Iberian peninsula occurred. This is attested by finds of Greco-Italic amphorae and Italian Black Gloss pottery in many locations in Iberia (see section 3.2.2).[32] After the Second Punic War, many Roman soldiers had apparently remained in southern Iberia, since in 171,

> there came also from Iberia another embassy, from a new race of men. They, stating that they were the offspring of Roman soldiers and Iberian women, to

[29] App. *BC* 1.24; Solinus 27.11; Plu. *CG* 10.2–11.2; Vell. 2.7.7–8. The colony is described as a failure in the sources, but some land seems to have been distributed here; see App. *Pun.* 136; Obs. 33; Fronto *Ad Marc.* 2.1. A possible Gracchan boundary stone was found here (CIL 1^2 696=ILS 28=ILLRP 475).

[30] *BAfr.* 56.3; *Vir. Ill.* 73.1. Other Italians settled here after the Marian-Sullan war, when many of Marius' supporters fled to Africa. Three boundary stones in Etruscan, found near Carthage, may have been set up by them: Heurgon 1969.

[31] Sall. *Iug.* 26.1. See also 64.5: 'the traders, of whom there were a great number in Utica...' and a (presumably Etruscan) *haruspex* in 63.1.

[32] Principal 1998.

> whom the Romans had not been united in wedlock, and that their number amounted to more than four thousand, petitioned for a grant of some town to be given them in which they might reside.[33]

These soldiers, although Livy calls them Romans, may have included Italians as well. It was decided that a colony with Latin status should be established; the men did not receive Roman citizenship. The reason for this may have been that these men were descended from Iberian women, or that their fathers had not been Roman citizens. From the late second century onwards, Romans and Italians became interested in the Iberian gold, silver, and lead mines. Diodorus states that 'a multitude of Italians have swarmed to the mines and taken great wealth away with them'.[34] However, the greatest Italian interest in Iberia dates to the first century and the Imperial period.

Italians also traded with Cisalpine Gaul. Already in the fifth century, many Etruscan names are attested in Gaul, e.g. on a lead plaque from the commercial entrepôt Pech Maho, recording a payment to be made in Massilia. Great amounts of Etruscan pottery have been found in southern Gaul and the Rhône valley from the late seventh century onwards, and in various shipwrecks that carried amphorae from Vulci and Caere.[35] After 170, many Apulian oil amphorae and Dressel 1 amphorae appeared,[36] but most Italian amphorae found in Gaul can be dated to the first century.[37] Diodorus, in the late first century, says that the Gauls were so addicted to wine that 'many Italian traders, induced by the love of money which characterizes them, believe that the Gauls' love of wine is a godsend'.[38] Thus, it is clear that Italian activity in the western Mediterranean was impressive, especially from the late second century onwards.

Despite the attraction of the western Mediterranean for Italians, Italian commercial interest mostly focused on the Greek East. Italians are attested in many towns in the East from the third century onwards. At Rhodes, for example, people describing themselves with the ethnics 'Bruttians' and 'Lucanians' appear in the third century.[39] Late-third-century inscriptions in the theatre at Buthrotum in Epirus, the main harbour for Italians arriving from Brundisium, show

[33] Liv. 43.3.1. See Isayev 2017, 325.

[34] Diod. 5.36.3; see also Plb. 34.9.8; Str. 3.147–8. See Gabba 1954, 56–7; Richardson 1976, 142. Also interesting is the large amount of coins from Ebusus (Ibiza) found in Pompeii and nearby towns. In previous scholarship, this was used to argue that traffic between Iberia and central Italy was common in the late second and first centuries (Stazio 1955). However, it is now clear that many of these coins were local imitations, and that actual Ebusan coins arrived in a one-off influx around 140–30; see Stannard 2013.

[35] Bourdin 2012, 554–7; Isayev 2017, 76–8.

[36] Will 1987.

[37] Tchernia 1983, 92; 1986, 86.

[38] Diod. 5.26.3. See Cic. *Font.* 11.

[39] Hatzfeld 1912, 155–6; Marasco 1986, 41; Bourdin 2012, 559. Commercial relations are also attested by finds of amphorae from Rhodes, Knidos, and Kos on many Italian sites, dating from the second century. See Càssola 1970–1, 308–9; Scopacasa 2015. Marengo & Paci 2008, 314–15 conclude that these amphorae show the rapid 'Romanization' of these Italian communities, but this is not necessary.

Italians as slave owners.[40] However, the largest influx of Italians into the East took place after 167, when the Romans declared the island of Delos a free port.[41] This meant that no taxes had to be paid on goods imported to or exported from the island. This soon attracted many Roman and Italian merchants, who traded especially in slaves. According to Strabo, the island could handle 10,000 slaves a day.[42] It was also a transit harbour for luxury items from Egypt and further East, such as perfumes, precious stones, and spices.[43] This trade attracted not only Italians, but also people from further East. Thus, the creation of Delos as an entrepôt harbour also led to a certain degree of economic integration within the Mediterranean as a whole. Long-term relationships were built between these people and Italians: the banker Philostratos from Ascalon in Palestine became a citizen of Neapolis.[44] Italians also moved further abroad: they have been attested in Alexandria and elsewhere in Egypt, for example, from amphora stamps (see section 3.2.2).[45] An Antonius was active as a banker in third-century Syene (modern Aswan in Egypt). Around 250, we find a reference to an Italian ship bound for Syria, presumably for trade.[46]

As mentioned above, it should not be assumed that all Italians in the East were traders. For example, the Cossutii from Capua worked as architects on the Olympieion in Athens.[47] The Stallii from Lucania built the Odeion.[48] Other Italians lived abroad as exiles: in 197, the Romans were assisted in capturing Leucas, an island in the Ionian Sea, by 'some exiles of Italian stock, living in Leucas'.[49] However, in most cases trade is especially attested, for example, by inscriptions recording *Rhomaioi hoi pragmateuomenoi en...* ('Romans trading in...'). These occur in many Greek and Asian cities, not just Delos, already from the third century onwards.[50] However, when Asia was made a province in 129, the number of inscriptions recording Romans and Italians grew quickly. The creation of provincial structures created more legal security, which reduced transaction costs and thus stimulated trade. Around 120, the *lex portorii Asiae* ('law on harbour taxes in Asia') was passed, which regulated tax collection by Romans in Asian communities.[51] This attracted many Romans eager to exploit the

40 Marasco 1986, 39.

41 Delos was already an important emporium before 167, otherwise this choice would have made little sense. The Staii, for example, are reported on Delos already in the last quarter of the third century (Hatzfeld 1912, 80). See Baslez 1996.

42 Strab. 14.5.2. See Kay 2014, 202–4.

43 Plin. *NH* 13.4. See Brun 2000, 286; Kay 2014, 204–6.

44 Gabba 1994, 108; Hasenohr 2007. ID 2245 and 2272 record a marriage between a man named Seius, of Oscan descent, and Kleopatra from Arados in Phoenicia; see also ID 1724 (dated 106–93).

45 ILLRP 343=ID 1699; CIL 10.1797=ILS 7273. Decius Magius from Capua fled to Alexandria in 216; possibly he had connections there (Liv. 23.5–7, 23.10.3; Vell. 2.16.1–2). See Lampela 1998, 50.

46 Plu. *Arat.* 12.4.

47 See the Appendix at [www.oup.co.uk/companion/Roselaar] for the names mentioned in this section.

48 Vitr. *Arch.* 7.pr.17; IG 2.2 3427. See Rawson 1975.

49 Liv. 33.17.11.

50 IG 7.1862, from Thespiae; IG 12.7, 515, l. 55, from Amorgos.

51 Rauh 1993, 23; Kay 2014, 200.

wealth of Asia, especially the *publicani*, who were contracted by the state to collect tribute from the province. Of course, *publicani* were Roman citizens, but they may have worked with Italian employees and investors (see chapter 5).[52]

Many Italians settled permanently in the East; some created estates for wine and olive oil production already in the second century.[53] In 88, when Mithridates attempted to kill all Romans and Italians in Asia and Greece, murders were carried out in many towns, including Ephesus, Pergamon, Adramyttium, Kaunos, Tralleis, Chios, Lydia, and Kos, showing the wide distribution of Italians in the East.[54] However, his actions did nothing to stop Italian interest in the East: the largest increase in trade and landholding by Romans and Italians occurred after the Mithridatic wars.

Considerable debate has focused on the origins of the Italians attested on Delos and elsewhere in the East. Hatzfeld argued that most Italians on Delos were from southern Italy and therefore not Roman citizens,[55] but Wilson and Càssola countered that most of them were from central Italy, especially Rome and Latium, and therefore mostly Roman citizens.[56] This question is important for our current argument: if Italians without Roman citizenship were active in the East, this means that they were engaging in economic activities abroad, which had partially been stimulated by the expansion of Rome's hegemony. Thus, Italian economic activities were dependent on Roman military and political expansion and facilitated by Roman military and legal protection. If, on the other hand, Roman citizens were the most active traders on Delos, Italians would have been excluded from this profitable trading emporium, possibly leading to resentment against Rome.

Unfortunately, the evidence does not allow us to determine the background of all Italians in the East. In some cases, people recorded their home towns on inscriptions, especially those from Magna Graecia and Apulia: examples are Bouzos

[52] Cottier et al. 2008.

[53] Chios: App. *Mith.* 46–7. See Càssola 1970–1, 310–11. Eleia and Olympia: IvO 333, 335; Messene: IG 5.1.1433–4, SEG 30.415; Kos: IGR 4.1087; Aktion: IG 9.1^2 208; Arkadia: IG 5.2.268, 307, 515. For Italians in Thessaly, see Helly 1983; for Boeotia, see Müller 2002; in general, see Eberle & Le Quéré 2017.

[54] App. *Mith.* 23, 47. See Hatzfeld 1919; Kirbihler 2007, 23–4; Terpstra 2013, 194–207; Isayev 2017, 49–56.

[55] Hatzfeld 1912; see Salmon 1962, 117; Nicolet 1966, 369. Hatzfeld argues (p. 131) that many were from Puteoli, but the names he mentions as evidence—Novius, Pacius, Pettius, Staius, and Tutorius—are not specifically Puteolan. Tutorius was Messapian, while the other names are Oscan and are not attested in Puteoli in the Republican period.

[56] Wilson 1966, 87–91, 108–10 correctly argues that people from Magna Graecia already traded in the East in the fourth century, and that from the second century more Oscan-speaking Italians appeared, but that Romans, Latins, and Campanians were dominant. Càssola 1970–1, 317 concludes that out of 155 names, eighty were Roman and more than twenty were certainly Italian. Cébeillac-Gervasoni 1998, 177–8, 189–90 agrees that the majority came from Latium and Campania. Müller & Hasenohr 2002, 14 suggest that many were from Capua, since they assume close parallels between the names of the members of religious *collegia* attested there and on Delos, but the similarities are not very close. Adams 2003, 677–9 concludes that the language of the inscriptions on Delos was standard Latin, and does not show any local Italian influences.

Orteiras and Blattos Matouroi from Canusium, Salsios Tagyllios from Arpi, and Gaius Statorius and Gaius Polfennios from Brundisium. Amphora stamps record trade carried out by Dazos from Azetium in Apulia.[57] Many of these names, such as Dazos, indicate a Messapian origin. It is striking that people from the Latin colony Brundisium also mentioned their home towns, since identification by home town was probably a Greek tradition. The names of the Brundisians were clearly not Latin: some were Oscan, such as Polfennios, while Statorius was derived from the Messapian Thaotoridas. It may be that these people were local leaders who had been accepted into the elite of the Latin colony. Other Italian places of origin mentioned in the East include Neapolis, Cumae, Velia, Petelia, Heraclea, Locri, Tarentum, and Ancona—that is, towns from Magna Graecia.

Unfortunately, the tradition of mentioning one's home town was not common in the rest of Italy. This means that in most cases, there is no definite evidence for the origins of the Italians attested in the East and we must rely on onomastic evidence. The main problem with this is that we cannot always determine the origin of a name, nor ascertain whether someone held Roman citizenship. We must resort to looking for places in Italy where a particular *gentilicium* is most often recorded, which may point to the possible background of the attested person, and look at the citizenship status of this area. In order to determine whether or not a person possessed Roman citizenship, we can look at the language used by people with the same name in inscriptions elsewhere: if this was in Oscan, Etruscan, Messapian, or another Italian language, it is possible that the person did not have Roman citizenship, or at least identified as a non-Latin speaker. If, furthermore, we want to be sure that this person was active in business, which was not the case for all Italians in the East, we might look for evidence of commercial activity, such as amphora stamps. Alternatively, investments in public buildings in Italy may suggest that the person in question had earned significant wealth overseas, especially if people with the same name are also attested in the East.

Unfortunately, there are not many *gentilicia* that can be convincingly tied to economic activities abroad. If we want to be sure that an Italian attested overseas was engaged in business and was not a Roman citizen, we need a relatively limited area of Italy, without Roman citizenship, where the name is attested, preferably in connection with public building or agriculture, in another language than Latin. These criteria are fulfilled for a relatively small number of cases. For example, the Annii are attested on Delos, in Oscan inscriptions in allied Capua, and in several other Italian towns as dedicators of public buildings. This makes it relatively certain that some of the Annii were of non-Roman descent, earned their money in overseas trade, and invested this in Italy. Of course, there are still some problems: for example, some Annii already functioned as magistrates in Rome

[57] Hatzfeld 1912, 102, 144; Silvestrini 1990, 257–9.

at the same time that other Annii dedicated buildings with Oscan inscriptions, so clearly some Annii already possessed Roman citizenship. There were of course different families with the same *gentilicium*, so we need not assume that an Oscan-speaking family was related to a Roman family of the same name. Alternatively, as pointed out in chapter 1, a Roman magistrate from an Oscan background may have used different identities in different situations, and therefore put up inscriptions in Oscan. Nevertheless, most of the *gentes* mentioned in the East and in non-Latin inscriptions were not active in Roman politics until much later (see chapter 5), so we may conclude they indeed engaged in trade and were most likely not yet Roman citizens. Thus, for some *gentilicia* attested abroad, we can determine that they were attested in Italy exclusively in non-Latin inscriptions from areas without citizenship, such as the Audii, Granii, Oppii, and Steii, and furthermore sponsored public buildings in Italy, suggesting that they had made their fortunes in trade.

When we are able to identify the background of the people attested in the East, the towns of Magna Graecia and Campania played a large role; especially harbour towns, such as Brundisium and Tarentum, were important.[58] Others came from the city of Rome, major Latin or allied towns, such as Brundisium and Praeneste, as well as Campania, Samnium, Apulia, and Etruria.[59] Clearly many people from Italy, with a variation of civic statuses, engaged in activities overseas. The large number of Apulians in the East is interesting; geographically, Apulia was closer to Greece than to most parts of Italy, so its association with the East is not surprising.[60]

The number of Italians and Romans abroad is brought out starkly by the fact that Mithridates reportedly killed 80,000 people from Italy in 88, even if the number is exaggerated.[61] It is not clear whether these were all Italians or only Roman citizens: Livy's epitomizer states that 'everyone in Asia with Roman citizenship was butchered in a single day',[62] while Cicero also states that the victims were Roman citizens.[63] However, Appian says that Mithridates ordered his officials to 'set upon all Romans and Italians in their towns, and upon their wives and children and their servants of Italian birth'.[64] Of course, Mithridates' henchmen had no way to find out who was a Roman citizen, so it is likely that both citizens and Italians were among the victims. We may conclude that Italians without Roman citizenship were present in many areas of the Mediterranean from the third century onwards. Some were extremely active, such as the Aufidii

[58] Solin 1982, 111–12.

[59] Keaveney 1987, 4–5; Rauh 1993, 28, 32. Traders in Macedonia were mostly from Latin and Campanian cities, but also from eastern and southern Italy, e.g. Lucania; see Wilson 1966, 152–3.

[60] Yntema 1995, 388. Curti, Dench, & Patterson 1996, 187 doubt whether *foedera* with Rome allowed Italians to continue contacts with their existing trading partners, but there is no reason why this should have been forbidden.

[61] App. *Mith.* 23, 47; Cic. *Flacc.* 60; Plu. *Sull.* 24. See Kirbihler 2007, 22; Isayev 2017, 49–56.

[62] Liv. *Per.* 78. [63] Cic. *Cn. Pomp.* 7. [64] App. *Mith.* 22.

and Saufeii, while other Italians appear only once or not at all, at least in the existing evidence.

These Italian traders profited from the favourable economic and political circumstances created by the Roman state, e.g. the conquest of Sicily, Sardinia, and Asia Minor, and the creation of a provincial structure for these areas. This brought the conquered areas under secure Roman control and established a legal system to solve conflicts; or at least established Rome as a mediator in disputes. The support of the Roman state opened up new markets for Italian products, both in Italy—since Roman dominance ended military conflicts between the different peoples and towns of Italy—and abroad, especially through the supply of Roman armies fighting abroad. There was also less competition for Italian merchants, since the defeat of Carthage meant that fewer Carthaginian merchants were present in Sicily, Sardinia, and Iberia. Rome also held out the promise of protection against piracy and other threats (see chapter 4.7). All these benefits meant that Italians had more trading opportunities than ever before.

However, once these military and legal frameworks were in place, Italians were not regularly in contact with Rome or its representatives. The Roman state did not often get involved in the economic activities of traders abroad, whether Roman citizens or Italians. Therefore, we cannot assume that the economic activities of the Italians created a bond between Romans and Italians. There was no need for the Italians to feel that they now belonged to the Roman state or to identify themselves with it—as we have seen, Italians often referred to their home towns, rather than a connection with Rome. Their local origin was clearly more important to them than a 'Roman' or 'Italian' identity. We may conclude that Roman expansion stimulated economic activities for Romans and Italians, but there is no reason to assume that this also led to integration in the social or cultural sense.

3.2.2. Commercial export

In the previous section, we have seen how Italians were active in trade throughout the Mediterranean. They not only imported goods to Italy, such as slaves and spices, but also produced a variety of crops and manufactured goods that were exported throughout the Mediterranean. These activities took place under the same circumstances described in the previous section: a favourable economic and military situation created by the Romans, but exploited by the Italians on their own initiative. By investigating these activities in more detail, we may be able to determine how important they were for the economic integration of Italy and the Mediterranean.

It is difficult to trace these movements exactly, since there is little information about individual Italian producers. If Italians from areas without citizenship produced items for export, and marked them in languages other than Latin, we could make reasonable assumptions about the level of involvement of non-Roman citizens in commercial export activities. However, such evidence is usually absent. The most popular items for export were wine and olive oil, which were transported in amphorae. In some cases, these were stamped with the name of the producer and/or merchant,[65] but in most cases such stamps are absent, so that we do not know who produced them. Also widely traded were various types of pottery, sometimes stamped with the name of the producer. In the absence of onomastic evidence, our only option is to look at the region of origin of these products. We can often determine where they were made, and if we can also identify the civic status of the area—Roman citizenship, Latin, or allied—we can estimate the level of involvement of Italians in overseas export of Italian agricultural and manufactured products. This will allow us to evaluate the commercial activities of Italians in the last three centuries BC.

3.2.2.1. Wine and olive oil

A very important export product of Italy was wine. The production of wine is fairly easy to detect archaeologically, through the remains of wine presses and the presence of amphorae. Unfortunately, in many cases the Republican phase of production sites was obliterated by later phases. Even so, an increase in such installations is visible from the third century onwards in many parts of Italy.[66] Fortunately, we have an enormous amount of information from amphorae used to transport wine, which form important markers for trade patterns in the Mediterranean.

The two most important types of vessel in the Republican period were Greco-Italic and Dressel 1 amphorae.[67] Greco-Italic amphorae originated in Sicily and Magna Graecia in the late fourth and early third centuries. The shape of this amphora was influenced by amphorae from Rhodes and Knidos, indicating a close trade relationship between these islands and Italy. Many Italian sites have yielded finds of actual Rhodian and Knidian amphorae—especially sites without Roman or Latin status, for example, in Samnium.[68] They were roughly five main different types of Greco-Italic amphora, named A-E.[69] Form A was produced in Sicily and

[65] There is some debate about the meaning of amphora stamps: some, e.g. Manacorda & Panella 1993, 63, assume that the stamps show the name of the owner of the production site, not of the actual maker of the amphora, who was often a slave. However, not all producers were slaves, as we will see.

[66] Rossiter 1981, 358–61.

[67] It should be noted that amphorae themselves were not trade items; they were only transported because of their contents. Moreover, they could be reused several times, so that, for example, an amphora from Campania found in Iberia does not necessarily indicate a direct trade route between the two areas. See Morel 1998, 498 n. 24.

[68] Scopacasa 2015. See a full list of Rhodian amphora find spots in Dell'Aglio & Lippolis 1989, 547.

[69] The traditional typology of Greco-Italic amphora was introduced by Will 1982, although this categorization has been criticized by others. Many scholars have created their own classification systems, so that the study of amphora types is rather complicated. Since the exact classification of amphora types is not essential to my argument, I will only briefly describe Will's conclusions. See Tchernia 1986; Empereur & Hesnard 1987; Olcese 2005/6, 68–71.

around the Gulf of Tarentum from the mid-fourth century to the early third century. Forms B and D developed around *c.*260/240 and remained in use until *c.*220/210. Form C emerged shortly afterwards, around 225, and was produced until *c.*175. Form E was produced in Iberia between 175 and 100. Greco-Italic amphorae were used for export mostly to the western Mediterranean, particularly southern France, Iberia, and northern Africa. Italian amphorae already arrived at many important *oppida* in Gaul and Iberia in the third century, for example, Pech Maho in Gaul and Emporiae in Iberia, although only a few pieces were found at each site in the third century.[70]

The number of Greco-Italic amphorae in Iberia grew in the second century. It is possible that the consumers of this wine were especially Italian soldiers who were stationed in Iberia from the Second Punic War onwards, although many amphorae also reached indigenous sites. Great volumes of wine also reached southern Gaul, as shown by the contents of shipwrecks in the waters off the Italian and French coast.[71] The Grand Congloué 1 wreck, found near Marseilles, provides the most impressive evidence of the volume of trade destined for the Gallic market. It dates to about 200 and carried over 400 Greco-Italic amphorae and 6,000–7,000 items of Black Gloss pottery.[72] Thus, from the third century, the wine trade regularly covered long distances, mostly to the north-western Mediterranean, but also to the East.[73]

Recent finds have shown that Greco-Italic amphorae were produced in a great number of locations in Italy, both on the western and eastern coasts, e.g. in Magna Graecia, southern Latium, Campania, southern Etruria, Lucania, Bruttium, Tarentum, the Salento, the Po Valley, and Sicily.[74] The civic status of the area seems to have been irrelevant: important production sites were Sinuessa and perhaps Minturnae (Roman colonies), Cosa and Suessa (Latin colonies), Pompeii (an allied town), and Fundi (first *civitas sine suffragio*, from 188 full Roman citizenship).[75] The variety in statuses of these towns is very interesting: it shows that not having Roman citizenship was no barrier for exploiting economic opportunities. The names on Greco-Italic amphorae are equally interesting. The earliest, type A, were often marked in Greek.[76] Later types, especially B/D, were often stamped with Oscan names, although the script was often Greek. Some have a mix of Greek and Oscan names, such as XEN TREBIOS. One of the earliest stamps in Latin script is TR(EBIOS) LOISIO(S).[77] This man, or his son, is also mentioned on

[70] Will 1982, 338–53; Peacock & Williams 1986, 84–5; Tchernia 1986, 94–8; Empereur & Hesnard 1987, 25–9; Loughton 2000, 18–23.

[71] Parker 1992; Loughton 2000, 51–66.

[72] Morel 1998, 505.

[73] Olcese 2004, 180: Greco-Italic amphorae were found in Greece, Syria, the Black Sea area, and at Berenice.

[74] Vandermersch 1994, 85–7.

[75] Morel 1988, 54; Olcese 2004, 175.

[76] Will 1982; Vandermersch 1994, 79. For Ischia, see Olcese 2005/6, 68–71.

[77] Olcese 2004, 177–80; 2005/6, 68–71.

an inscription from 162/1 on Delos.[78] The stamp M LURI, found at the important trading post of Pech Maho in Gaul, dates to 250–210; chemical analysis shows it to be from Campania, where the name is attested at Pompeii and Herculaneum.[79]

Thus, it seems that the civic status of a person or an area made no difference to whether they produced these amphorae and sold them abroad. Areas with Roman citizenship, Latin, and allied status engaged in this kind of production. The geographical location in relation to trade routes was more important than civic status within the Roman state. Production was mostly located in coastal areas, from where markets throughout the Mediterranean could be easily reached. It has been suggested that the first emergence of Greco-Italic amphorae was due to production increase after the Roman conquest of Italy, and that production was controlled by elite Romans,[80] but there is no evidence for this. The locations of their production certainly do not point to great involvement by Roman citizens.

This tendency becomes even stronger in Dressel 1 amphorae. Traditionally, Dressel amphorae of the Republican period have been divided into three types: Dressel 1A, 1B, and 1C, although this classification has been criticized.[81] Traditionally it was assumed that 1A was produced from around 150–140 and continued to be produced until the 80s. Dressel 1B appeared in the last quarter of the second century and remained in use until the late first century. Dressel 1C was in use from the late second century until the second quarter of the first century.[82] It seems that the change from Greco-Italic to Dressel 1 amphorae was caused by an increase in production and standardization of production. This change indicates a rational organization of workshops for large-scale production; certainly, at this time, the amount of wine exported increased enormously.[83]

It was traditionally assumed that Dressel 1 amphorae were produced in southern Etruria, Latium, and Campania. Indeed, the main focus of production was in central Italy: production occurred in great numbers along the coast south of Sinuessa, around Vesuvius and near Pompeii. In Latium, these amphorae were made on the coast at Astura, Fundi, and Minturnae. Some sites near Cosa, Volaterrae, and Pisae also produced them. However, Dressel 1 amphora were in fact produced as far away as Bruttium. In total, about 100 production sites have

[78] CIL 1^2 425=10.8051.21=ILLRP 1177; CIL 8.22637.32; ID 1408A. See Zoumbaki 1998, 1; Olcese 2004, 179.

[79] Heurgon 1952. M. and C. Lassius from Pompeii marked their amphorae in Oscan letters.

[80] Olcese 2005/6, 63–4.

[81] Empereur & Hesnard 1987, 29; Tchernia 1986, 44; Guerrini & Mancini 2007, 217. It must be noted that it is often very difficult to distinguish between Greco-Italic and Dressel amphorae and between the several types of Dressel amphora. Furthermore, the dating of find spots is problematic: often amphorae are the only way to date a site, but many amphorae are not dated securely in the first place. See Loughton 2000, 18–31.

[82] Tchernia 1983; Peacock & Williams 1986, 86–90; Cipriano & Carre 1989, 71.

[83] Manacorda 1981, 23; Curti, Dench, & Patterson 1996, 176.

been identified in Italy.[84] Again, areas producing Dressel 1 amphorae could be Roman colonies (Minturnae, Sinuessa, Terracina, Circeii), areas settled by Roman citizens (Ager Falernus), Latin colonies (Cosa), and allied territory (northern Etruria, the area around Vesuvius, Bruttium). Again, it did not make a difference whether an area had Roman citizenship status or not; areas that were suitable for wine production profited from new opportunities to produce and export wine commercially.

The fact that production of Dressel 1 amphorae took place in Italian regions without Roman citizenship indicates that many Italians were involved in such commercial activities. Onomastic evidence offers limited support for this. Some amphora stamps, found in the western Mediterranean, indicate the involvement of people with Italian names, such as Caedicius, Clovatius, Ennius, Maecius, Satrius, and Statius. Some amphorae carry one-letter stamps in the Oscan alphabet, indicating the involvement of non-Latin speakers in their production.[85] Stamps on *dolia*, vessels used for the storage of wine, are also revealing: a stamp from Orvieto in Etruria records that the vessel was made by a slave of Tossius in the *figlina* (kiln) of Tettius. Both these names are non-Roman in origin.[86]

Dressel 1 amphorae were especially common on the coast of southern Gaul and Iberia, and are also commonly attested in Morocco, Sardinia, Sicily, Britain, and Germany. This type is also present at some eastern sites, e.g. at Delos.[87] The establishment of the *provincia* of Gaul in the 120s seems to have been an important stimulus for trade to Gaul, since the number of amphorae in Gaul strongly increased after this time. The growth of the wine export from Italy in the late second century is attested by an increase in the size of Italian ships. Until the late second century, ships usually measured about 75 tons and were able to carry about 1,500 amphorae. Greater vessels then began to appear: the Albenga wreck, dated 100–90, carried some 10,000 amphorae.[88]

Other types of amphora were produced in many regions of Italy. So-called Lamboglia 2 amphorae appeared on the eastern coast of the peninsula around the same time as Dressel 1 in western Italy, i.e. the mid-second century. They were used for the transport of wine and olive oil until the late first century. These amphorae were produced all along the Adriatic coast, from Venetia to Apulia.[89] They are widely distributed in the western Mediterranean, especially Gaul and

[84] Manacorda 1981, 13–16; Empereur & Hesnard 1987, 31; Tchernia 1986; Peacock & Williams 1986; Hesnard et al. 1989, 21–30. Dressel 1 amphorae were also produced at several sites in Sicily, Gaul, and Iberia; see Loughton 2000, 36–40.

[85] Gianfrotta 1981, 229–30.

[86] CIL 1^2 2351=11.6691.23=ILLRP 1241.

[87] Empereur & Hesnard 1987, 32; Tchernia 1986, 74–5. For Iberia, see Nolla & Nieto 1989.

[88] Kay 2014, 143.

[89] Tchernia 1986, 54; Cipriano 1994, 207; Carre & Pesavento Mattioli 2003, 269; Guerrini & Mancini 2007, 217.

Iberia, and in the eastern Adriatic, the Balkan area, Delos, Greece, and Asia Minor.[90] It has been argued that the production of these amphorae started when the Adriatic coast of Italy was consolidated by the Romans, in the third century.[91] However, the Roman conquest of this area occurred more than a century before the increase in amphora production, so a direct connection between conquest and commercial production seems far-fetched. The growth in production should rather be ascribed to new economic opportunities emerging in the second century. Again, the production of these amphora, and by implication the wine and olive oil transported in them, was not mainly in Roman hands. Production took place in Latin colonies, such as Aquileia and Firmum Picenum, but also on various sites in allied territory. Name stamps on these amphorae are mostly Greek, although some Latin and Illyrian names are also attested.[92] The typically Messapian names Das(i) mi(us) and Dasius also appear on Lamboglia 2 amphorae, as do several Oscan names.

Around Brundisium and in southern Apulia, a specific type of amphora for olive oil and wine was produced from the mid-second to the late first century. This was produced at a number of sites, the largest at Giancola and Apani, but also further south.[93] They were distributed especially in the eastern Mediterranean, but also in the west.[94] These amphora production sites appeared at the same time that larger farmsteads emerged, around 170–150; this suggests that these farms produced the wine and olive oil transported in the amphorae.[95] There has been some debate about the civic status of the amphora producers. Among the earliest producers, attested in the late second century, were Vehilius and Visellius, Latinized Messapian names. The strong connection of Visellius to Messapia is attested by a third- or second-century grave inscription from Lecce, which records a Viselius. The grave may be connected to an amphora production site at nearby Masseria Ramanno, where Visellius employed labourers with both Greek and Messapian names.[96]

Thus, local elites were closely involved in the production of these amphorae from the start. Only in the later first century, when the production of these amphorae reached its largest extent, do many clearly Roman names appear.[97] More outside involvement in amphora production occurred at this time, although those attracted by the economic opportunities in Apulia were not only from

[90] Manacorda 1981, 11–13; Empereur & Hesnard 1987, 33; Cipriano & Carre 1989, 97–9; Loughton 2000, 47–8.

[91] Cipriano 1994, 213.

[92] Paci 2008, 317, 320.

[93] Empereur & Hesnard 1984, 34–5; Lamboley 1996, 490; Compatangelo-Soussignan 1999, 99–100, 105.

[94] Cipriano & Carre 1989, 72–7.

[95] Yntema 2006, 106.

[96] Peacock & Williams 1986, 69, 82–3; Manacorda 1988, 99–100; Palazzo 1994, 55–7. Manacorda 2003, 298 thinks that Visellius was an investor from elsewhere, or that an ancestor was a settler from Rome in Brundisium; but it is more likely that he was native to the area.

[97] Palazzo 1994, 56; *contra* Manacorda 1988, 100.

central Italy, but also people from previously allied areas. The well-attested Betilienus, for example, came from Aletrium, a town that had held *civitas sine suffragio* before the Social War.[98] Thus, many Italians quickly profited from new economic opportunities that opened up after they were granted citizenship (see chapter 5.7).

We may conclude that the production of wine and olive oil on a commercial scale was not monopolized by the Roman elite, nor were these products made only at large, slave-staffed estates in central Italy. Instead, amphora stamps indicate the importance of people of Italian descent in these activities, already from the first appearance of commercial Greco-Italic amphorae in the fourth century. The Italians continued to engage in these activities when opportunities for trade expanded in the second century, as a result of the Roman conquest of the Mediterranean.

3.2.2.2. Pottery

Another export product of the Italian peninsula was pottery. Because of its high visibility in archaeological research, pottery has often been used to draw conclusions about economic developments in Italy. It is therefore necessary to discuss, first, the way in which pottery can be used to reconstruct economic developments—many of the developments described in section 3.3, for example, are based on pottery evidence. Secondly, we will look at the role of pottery as an export product in its own right.

Developments in the spread of pottery are often used as an indication of population developments, and by extension economic developments—a decline in pottery finds is often taken as a sign of declining (free, rather than slave) population, caused by an economic downturn. However, there are many problems with using pottery in this way, as the following discussion will show.[99] Firstly, the most important type of pottery used in the Republican period is Black Gloss pottery. This was used for almost 300 years, which makes it difficult to distinguish the impact of specific political or military events on its distribution.[100] Furthermore, it is difficult to measure population developments using only pottery as a tool; a decline in its use may also be caused by other developments, whether positive (greater connectivity between areas or new techniques, leading to greater availability of alternative types of pottery) or negative (impoverishment of the population or population decline). Finally, the survival of sites, if attested by the pottery record, cannot be directly related to population figures, since the ownership of these farms is unclear. Small farms may have been owned by large

[98] Càssola 1970–1, 324; Palazzo 1994, 59–60; Cébeillac-Gervasoni 1998, 152.

[99] Of course, this short space is not sufficient to discuss population developments in the Republican period in full. See De Ligt 2012; Hin 2013. See Di Giuseppe 2012, 142–55 for the connection between pottery and population developments.

[100] Bellini, Launaro, & Millett 2014, 259–60.

landholders and worked by slaves, so that the survival of small farms does not mean that they were still worked by small independent farmers.

The use of Black Gloss pottery shows similar developments across Italy. In most areas from 325 to 275, a rapid rise occurred in the use of Black Gloss pottery, followed by a sharp decline from 275 to 150, a smaller rise from 150 to 125, and a slow decline from 125 onwards. There seem to be roughly two variations on this trend: in some areas, mainly in Latium, Apulia, and Lucania, the first decline was very sharp, with a slight rise around 150. In others, mainly in northern Etruria and Campania, the first decline was not very sharp and there was a greater increase in the use of Black Gloss in the mid-second century. Sites that retained much Black Gloss were not necessarily Roman, for example, the allied towns Civita di Tricarico, Pompeii, and Volaterrae, and the Latin colony Venusia.[101] These locations were not necessarily very prosperous economic centres, but neither were the ones where Black Gloss declined sharply, such as the allied Lucanian sites Torre di Satriano, Roccagloriosa, and Gravina, the former Greek colony Locri, as well as Rome itself.

Whether the decrease after 275 indicates a decrease in population remains debatable. The number of settlement sites does decline in some areas, such as southern Etruria, but this seems to have happened slightly later, in the late third century. Furthermore, since the peak in the use of Black Gloss pottery occurred around 300, with a sharp decrease around 275–250, it is unlikely that this decline should be connected to the assumed population decline in the second century. Unfortunately, it is not possible to date Black Gloss pottery to more specific periods, and therefore we cannot determine developments that took place within a few decades. To explain the decline in Black Gloss use in the third century, we might look at economic developments in this period, in which Rome's military and economic influence over Italy increased. This could have led to changes in supply and demand for items such as Black Gloss pottery, influenced by the wider availability of imported pottery. As for the changes in the second century, I have argued elsewhere that general population decline in the second century is unlikely.[102] Obviously, the Second Punic War had caused population decline, which meant that the demand for Black Gloss pottery remained low for some decades; as the population started to increase again, this could have caused the slight rise in the mid-second century, as imported pottery could no longer meet demand in Italy. The final disappearance of Black Gloss might then be explained by a further increase in imports of pottery from other areas of the Mediterranean and the production of other types of pottery in Italy. Thus, pottery can be related to population developments in some regards, but not all population developments can be traced through the pottery record.

[101] Di Giuseppe 2012, 142. [102] Roselaar 2010, 146–220.

If we return to economic activities, it is clear that pottery was an important export product; many different types have been found throughout the Mediterranean. Many types of pottery were produced in many areas of Italy in the fourth and third centuries, in a great variety of shapes, fabrics, and designs. Most of these had only a local or at best regional distribution, such as many local types of Black Gloss pottery.[103] Only a few types were exported overseas. For example, the Messapian 'Gnathia' ware was produced from *c.*360 until the early second century at many allied sites in southern Italy.[104] In the third century, it was exported to various parts of the Mediterranean, such as Latium, the Adriatic coast, Corsica, Iberia, Greece, and Africa, but always in small quantities.[105] The impact of this trade on the economy of the exporting locations would therefore have been small, but its distribution still indicates wide-ranging contacts between Italy and the Mediterranean world.

An early type of Black Gloss pottery was Calene ware, produced in the Latin colony of Cales roughly between 250 and 180. This was found especially in Etruria, as well as Latium, Sabinum, Umbria, and the northern Adriatic coast. This pottery was also exported in small numbers to Gaul and Iberia.[106] Calene pottery was often stamped by its producers. Some recorded explicitly that they were slaves, while others were free. Some names suggest that they were not of Roman descent; for example, the names Paconius and Gabinius are mostly attested in Campania, not in Rome itself. On the other hand, many names on Calene ware are also attested in Rome, which makes sense if the settlers in this colony had moved here from Rome.[107]

Some 20 kilometres from Cales, the allied town Teanum Sidicinum also produced pottery in the late fourth and early third centuries. This is widely distributed in northern Campania and a few sites in Latium, including Rome. It was exported in small quantities overseas, as far as Iberia.[108] Some of this pottery was inscribed in Oscan with the names of the producers, most importantly the Berius family. Another interesting producer here was Plator, whose typically Apulian name suggests that he was an immigrant at Teanum.[109] This pottery was similar in some ways to the products of nearby Cales, but in other ways very different, indicating the different traditions that could be at work in neighbouring towns. The fact that both towns produced pottery on a commercial scale shows

[103] Morel 1980, 96–9, 103–6 lists several types of local Black Gloss pottery.

[104] Green 1976; De Cazanove 2004, 767; Guerrini & Mancini 2007, 200.

[105] Morel 1980, 89; Yntema 1995, 388; Guerrini & Mancini 2007, 200.

[106] Morel 1980, 94–5; 1988, 55–7; 1998, 500.

[107] Pedroni 2001, 65–81; Di Giuseppe 2012, 88.

[108] Morel 1980, 94–5; 1988, 56–7; 1991b, 137; Gatti & Onorati 1992, 194; Guerrini & Mancini 2007, 201.

[109] *Imagines* Teanum Sidicinum 25. See Morel 1980, 90–1; Guerrini & Mancini 2007, 200; Crawford 2011, 2, 4.

that the legal status of a community did not play a large role in determining its economic activities.[110]

Rome itself also produced pottery in the fourth and third centuries, which was exported to other parts of Italy. This was the case, for example, with the Heraklesschalen, produced in the second half of the third century, which have been found in Latium, Etruria, Picenum, and Sardinia.[111] The distribution of pottery produced in Rome has often been described as a sign of 'Romanization'.[112] It has been argued that the importance of Rome as a producer, and the popularity of its products, is shown by the fact that they were imitated in other locations. For example, a type of Heraklesschalen was produced at Aesis on the Adriatic.[113] However, the spread of such pottery should not automatically be seen as a sign of 'Romanization'; it is equally possible that the popularity of these products caused a rising demand, encouraging local producers to profit from this growing market. Since locally made products were probably cheaper than imported wares, the local population may have welcomed a local workshop that produced these items. Importantly, the popularity of these products was not necessarily due to the fact that they were from Rome; as we have seen in chapter 1, items could be interpreted in different ways in different locations, with or without any association with Rome.

The *pocola deorum* were a type of Black Gloss pottery intended for dedication to deities, as indicated by inscriptions mentioning the name of specific deities. They were produced in Rome in the early third century and found in Etruria, Latium, and Campania. They occur in towns of various status; some were found in colonies, but other colonies, such as Cales, have yielded no finds of them. The fact that colonies had a closer relationship with Rome than other towns does therefore not mean that they followed Rome's cultural choices.[114] Thus, the distribution of pottery produced in Rome cannot be seen as a sign of 'Romanization'. It is likely that supply and demand played a more important role than the cultural connotations of such products. People bought and used such items for their own purposes, such as status display. That the items happened to be made in Rome does not mean that the users desired to be specifically associated with Rome.

The types of pottery discussed up to this point were produced and exported in small numbers. They were not produced with the express aim of large-scale export. This changed with the emergence of the various types of so-called Campana Black Gloss ware. Its introduction is often seen as one of the most important indications of radical economic transformation in the second century, and it is

[110] Morel 1988, 56–7; 1991a, 136–8; Gatti & Onorati 1992, 194.

[111] The Heraklesschalen, a type of pottery marked with an H, intended for dedication to Hercules, are found especially in colonies, but also at many allied sites in Latium and Etruria. See Morel 1980, 95; 1988, 56–9; Guerrini & Mancini 2007, 200–1; Nonnis & Sisani 2012, 49–50.

[112] Morel 1988, 57–8.

[113] Breccarioli Taborelli 2000, 18.

[114] Morel 1969, 89–99; 2007, 502.

therefore worthwhile to discuss this in some detail. This new type of Black Gloss pottery was originally divided into three main groups: Campana A, B, and C, although local variations were produced virtually everywhere, collectively termed 'Campana D'.[115] However, the idea that Campana A, B, and C formed homogeneous groups is now more and more frequently abandoned. Especially for the B-group, it has been recognized that there were many locations of production, with a great variety in products. Thus, all Campana B pottery shared some characteristics, but there was also a very large and heterogeneous group of Black Gloss pottery resembling Campana B, but different in some respects. These products are now collectively called Campana B-oid.[116] Because of the problems connected with it, the term 'Campana pottery' has fallen into disuse among archaeologists, who now prefer to use the general appellation 'Black Gloss'.

An important characteristic of the 'Campana' Black Gloss was that its shapes and decoration were more uniform than in earlier Black Gloss pottery, while the artistic quality of the decorations declined. Morel used these facts to argue that this Black Gloss was a mass-produced item intended for export.[117] Some scholars see the appearance and spread of this type of pottery as emblematic of the 'slave mode of production' and 'Roman socio-economic imperialism'. Large workshops are assumed to have been established in the cities, in which slaves produced Black Gloss pottery for export.[118] Another important characteristic of this new economic approach is assumed to have been large, slave-staffed estates for wine and olive oil in the countryside; however, as we will see, these were much less common than is often believed.

In fact, there is very little archaeological evidence for the existence of large workshops for Black Gloss pottery. As Di Giuseppe shows, Black Gloss pottery was mostly produced at cult sites, as well as many other sites, such as farms and urban workshops.[119] Therefore, it is difficult to see the emergence of Black Gloss pottery as a symbol of 'Roman socio-economic imperialism'. Furthermore, as the name 'Campana' indicates, Campania used to be seen as the main region for the production of pottery on a commercial scale. However, Campania was not the only region where this type of pottery was produced: in virtually all areas of Italy, evidence has been discovered for the local production of Black Gloss. It was

[115] Lamboglia 1952. [116] Morel 1998.

[117] See Morel 1980, 101–2; 1988, 53; Guerrini & Mancini 2007, 201–2.

[118] E.g. most contributions to Giardina & Schiavone 1981. Morel is often cited as the most important scholar representing these views, e.g. in Roth 2007a, 40–94; Di Giuseppe 2012, 56. Nevertheless, Roth 2007a, 49 points out that Morel himself was very careful not to adopt a blanket approach, as indeed appears from Morel 1980, 105–6; 1983a, 25–7; 2009, 482. Rather, other historians made use of Morel's work by drawing far-reaching conclusions about large-scale economic transformation. Carandini 1988, 294–300, for example, postulates that pottery production was removed from the countryside to the cities and simply assumes that the producers were slaves. He also assumes that this model was valid throughout Italy.

[119] Di Giuseppe 2012, 95–7. For example, the farm at Moltone di Tolve (Lucania) produced its own Black Gloss pottery (Isayev 2007, 75).

produced not just in a few workshops, but in many locations; each was most likely small, with only a local or regional distribution.[120] Despite the fragmentation of production, the vases produced by these workshops were remarkably similar. Local producers mixed local features with widely distributed characteristics of Black Gloss pottery, leading to a standardization in pottery shapes and decorations. The standardization that Morel identified can thus be discerned to a certain degree.[121] The standardization of Black Gloss pottery attests to a growing cultural *koine* in Italy: many local types of pottery were either replaced or supplemented by imported wares produced according to a standard design, which then were copied locally. Still, this does not mean that all local pottery types were now based on a few standard shapes produced by large workshops.[122] It is often suggested that this *koine* was caused by the spread of Latin traditions through Italy, as colonists from Rome and Latium settled in other parts of Italy.[123] Nevertheless, as we will see in chapter 4.4, not all colonies played an important role in the distribution of elements of Roman culture to the surrounding areas.

As for the identity of the producers of this pottery, stamps can provide very little evidence. Stamps from Praeneste, an allied town, show many of the names common in the town, such as Anicius, Orcevius, Samiarius, and Trebonius.[124] On the other hand, names such as Atilius, Marcius, and Minucius, widely attested in Rome itself, are also attested as pottery stamps. Unfortunately, most pottery was not stamped at all, in contrast to the earlier types of pottery discussed above.[125] This is one of the reasons why it was assumed that pottery production had been consolidated under the control of the Roman elite and that the producers were slaves; the anonymity of producers was seen as part of the 'slave mode of production'.[126] Roth rightly points out, however, that it is unclear whether the producers of Black Gloss pottery were slaves or free men. Given that some free men were named on pottery stamps, it is unsafe to conclude that most pottery was produced by slaves. Furthermore, it is quite possible that the process of production, from extraction of the clay to firing of the vases, was not controlled by one workshop. Perhaps small producers rented space in kilns owned by a workshop, as is attested in the Imperial period at La Graufesenque.[127] Thus, producers could engage in pottery production part-time, in combination with other activities such as agriculture or manufacturing.[128]

[120] Morel 1981, 96.

[121] Morel 1980; 1983a, 23–7; 2007, 507–8; Guerrini & Mancini 2007, 201; Roth 2007a, 40–94.

[122] Roth 2007a, 56, says that Morel stated this, but Morel 2009, 481 denies this.

[123] Van Kerckhove 2004, 62.

[124] Di Giuseppe 2012, 89–91.

[125] Morel 1983a, 23; Pedroni 2001, 64–81; Di Giuseppe 2012, 87.

[126] Roth 2007a, 45–60 vehemently argues against the suggestion that all producers were slaves, which he ascribes to Morel; however, Morel 2009, 483 emphasizes the distinction between central Italy and the rest of the peninsula. See Di Giuseppe 2012, 6–7.

[127] Marichal 1988.

[128] Roth 2007a, 77–84, although he does assume (77 n. 67) that Roman elites controlled production.

3.2.2.3 Conclusion: commercial export in the Mediterranean

This section has clearly shown the importance of export from Italy to the Mediterranean. Many of the exported products came from Italian regions that did not possess Roman citizenship, such as Etruria, Campania, and the Adriatic coast. Others were produced in areas with Roman citizen rights, such as Latium, or from Latin colonies such as Cosa and Brundisium. Thus, the legal status of an area seems to have had very little effect on the economic activities of the people living here. They made full use of the economic opportunities offered to them, and neither they nor their overseas trading partners cared about their civic status. More important was the location of the production area; for wine, good agricultural land was needed, near clay beds that could be used to produce transport amphorae. Furthermore, a good connection to transport routes, especially overseas, was necessary.[129] Thus, most coastal areas of Italy engaged in commercial production and export overseas. This kind of activity was stimulated by the growing Roman dominance of the Mediterranean, which ensured peaceful travelling and trading conditions and possibilities for settling trade disputes. This in time caused the Mediterranean, or at least the areas suitable for production and/or as markets, to become integrated in a more unified economic system.

3.2.3. Developments in agriculture and manufacturing

During the fourth to first centuries, significant developments were visible in the organization and scale of agricultural production: the number of larger farms producing for the market increased, as did the size of individual farms. Many became larger than necessary for subsistence, suggesting at least partial involvement in commercial production. We will now look in more detail at the people behind these activities, in order to see what role Italians played in them. The location of agricultural and manufacturing activity suggests that Italians were important producers. Many commercial sites were located in Latium, where many people possessed Roman citizenship, but also in Campania and Etruria and along the Adriatic coast, where citizenship was much less widespread.

Before we look into Italian activities in agriculture, we should determine what is meant by the term *villa*, which is often used to indicate a large commercial farm. However, this term is problematic: it is not always clear what different scholars mean by a *villa*, or by terms such as 'large farm'. The problem is made more complicated by the work of Cato the Elder, written around the mid-second century, which appears to be a manual for agriculture. It contains detailed descriptions of several types of *villa*. These were, apparently, quite large operations: Cato prescribes

[129] Morley 1996, 63–5.

that an estate producing olive oil should have five olive presses. Cato's detailed description of the ideal *villa* has led many scholars to look for such establishments in the archaeological remains; many second-century farms identified in the archaeological remains are therefore called 'Catonian villa'. Many scholars also assume that this was the typical *villa* at which most commercial production in the second century took place.[130] These assumptions are part of the same traditional reconstruction of economic development in the second century, described above: small farmers lost their land to wealthy members of the Roman elite, who then established 'Catonian villas', worked by slaves; at the same time, they established slave-staffed pottery production sites in the towns. Other elements of this reconstruction have turned out to be incorrect, and indeed the growth of commercial farms in the second century is more complicated than older scholarship suggests.

It is very difficult to match the archaeological remains to the description by Cato. Archaeological sites dating from the second century cannot be equated with the 'Catonian *villa*'. Cato's *villa* is much larger than most farms that have actually been found. *Villae* with five olive presses, for example, do not appear before the first century in most parts of Italy. This suggests that Cato's work is not a realistic description of agriculture as it occurred in the second century, but rather a moral and ideological treatise.[131] On the other hand, Cato emphasizes the simple nature of the farm, with simple whitewashed walls and no decoration—again a moral point, arguing against the opulence in many Roman elite houses in this period. However, many Italian farms were in fact more luxurious than the *villa* Cato describes: the farm at Moltone di Tolve in Lucania, for example, was decorated with mosaics and wall paintings.[132]

We should therefore not look towards 'Catonian *villae*' to understand developments in commercial agriculture in the third and second centuries.[133] Instead, from the third century, and in some areas even earlier, there appear what Terrenato calls 'Hellenistic farmsteads'. These farms were much smaller than the *villae* described by Cato, but show evidence of commercial production.[134] Several sites that match Terrenato's description of 'Hellenistic farmsteads' have been excavated, the best-researched being Giardino Vecchio and Villa Sambuco in Etruria, Via Gabina in Latium, Moltone di Tolve in Lucania (see Fig 3.1), and San Vito in Salapia (Apulia). The size of these buildings is limited: Villa Sambuco measured 530 m^2, Giardino Vecchio 400–500 m^2.[135]

Some scholars dismiss these farms as unlikely places for export production.[136] However, since no larger *villae* have been identified for the second century, these

[130] Carandini (ed.) 1985; Gualtieri 2003, 134.

[131] Frederiksen 1981, 277; Terrenato 2001a; 2012.

[132] Terrenato 2012, 75.

[133] See in more detail Roselaar 2010, 155–65.

[134] Terrenato 2001a, 13.

[135] Rathbone 2008.

[136] Grelle & Giardina 1993, 70–2, 74. Compatangelo-Soussignan 1999, 12 calls Hellenistic farmsteads 'predecessors of Catonian farms', but this is overly teleological; most Hellenistic farms did not develop into Catonian farms.

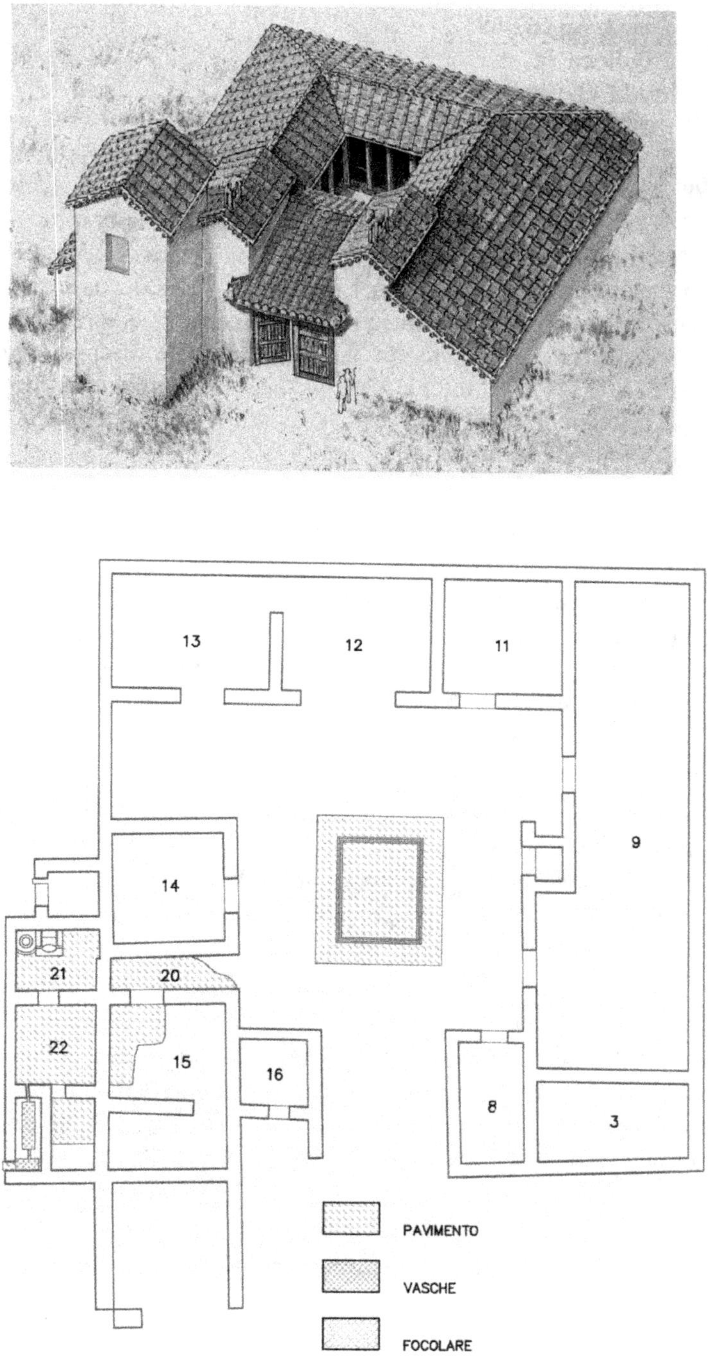

Fig. 3.1. Moltone di Tolve, phase 2.

From: *Da Leukania a Lucania: la Lucania centro-orientale fra Pirro e i Giulio-Claudii.* Istituto poligrafico e Zecca dello Stato, 1992; p. 40.

are the only locations where the export products of Italy could have been produced. Many such farms dating to the third and early second centuries show evidence of commercial production of wine and olives, as attested by the presence of amphorae, *dolia*, and wine and olive presses. It is likely, therefore, that commercial production did not take place on large *villae*, as Cato's description would have it, but on such smaller farms.[137] In this work, I use the term *villa* for any farm that shows evidence of production for the market; the term, in this definition, does not carry with it connotations about the size of the building, its level of decoration, or the crops that were grown.

In order to determine the involvement of Italians in commercial activities, ideally we would be able to identify individual farm owners. Unfortunately, it is difficult to identify the owners of commercial production sites. Some evidence suggests that Italians were involved in commercial production. In Civita di Tricarico in Lucania, an atrium house was built in the mid-second century, with production sites nearby. The excavators suggest that this house had a Roman owner, since it resembles houses in Rome at the time.[138] However, as we will see in chapter 4, atrium houses were by no means an exclusively Roman phenomenon, and appeared in many areas of Italy earlier than in Rome. In Lucania, it is likely that local landowners either continued to work their land, or were allowed to work Roman *ager publicus*. Given the location of the site, there is no reason to assume that the owners were Roman citizens, since land distributions by the Roman state to its citizens did not take place in the area until the Gracchan period.[139] In fact, a tile stamped with the Oscan name of its producer, 'Arronties', was found at Civita di Tricarico.[140] Perhaps the owner of the house, like the producer of the tile, was an Oscan speaker, although we cannot be sure. The tile does show, however, that Italians were involved in supplying commercial farms and thus in the economic networks of Italy.

Like the *villa* at Civita di Tricarico, other second-century commercial production sites were located in areas that did not have Roman citizenship nor were Roman *ager publicus*—for example the *villae* at San Vito in Salapia in Apulia, and Vittimose, S. Giovanni in Ruoti, and Termitito in Lucania. Of course, Romans could have owned farms on allied land, but there is no reason why these farms could not have been in the hands of local Italians. The new economic opportunities in the second century offered many Italian elites the chance to accumulate more land. In ancient Italy, wealth was based mostly on land. Trade was always closely connected to agriculture: products that were traded were mostly agricultural, such as wine and olive oil, while the production of pottery and storage vessels required ownership of clay beds. Money was usually invested in land, while loans were often

[137] See also Roselaar 2010, 158–64.
[138] Battiloro & Osanna 2015, 177. See, on the history of the atrium house, Wallace-Hadrill 1997.
[139] Gualtieri & Fracchia 2001, 126; Volpe 2001, 323; Roselaar 2010.
[140] *Imagines* Potentia 44=Rix tLu 1. See Terrenato 2001a, 28.

secured with landed property. It was therefore virtually impossible to become rich without owning land, at least until the first century. This applied to the Italian as well as the Roman elites. Therefore, it is almost inevitable that most Italian elites were landowners. An example is Lucanians attested in leading positions in the early second century, such as the Acerronii, Babullii, Vaonii, and Epidii.[141] These are all local names, attested in this period only in Lucania. This suggests that local elites had remained in power after the Roman conquest and retained their land, i.e. their economic power base. Even if we cannot determine who exactly owned Italian land, the fact that local elites remained in power strongly suggests that they were landowners. This does not mean, of course, that they accumulated land in large contiguous estates: Roscius from Ameria in the Tiber valley, defended by Cicero, possessed thirteen separate farms.[142] This was most likely the prevalent pattern of landholding among the Italian elites.

The same period saw some important technical innovations, both in Roman and allied areas. Some were introduced in shipping, such as the bilge pump. In agriculture, this period saw the introduction of better irrigation and drainage techniques, such as the bucket chain and water mills, and improvements to grape and olive presses. There were also developments in the exploitation of marine resources, such as tank systems for fish and shellfish. New strategies for food production were introduced, e.g. ley farming.[143] All this allowed for a great increase in the production of agricultural products and thus possibilities for export from Italy.

However, the production of wine and olive oil were not the only economic activities that Italians engaged in, and which gained some of them large incomes. It is likely, for example, that transhumant pasturing and the processing of wool, leather, and meat were very important sources of income. These activities took place especially in the more mountainous regions of Italy, mainly Umbria, Samnium, and Lucania. Most of these areas did not have Roman citizenship in the second century, and it is therefore likely that such activities were carried out by Italian allies. It is possible that many of the impressive rural sanctuaries in Samnium built at this time were partially financed from transhumant pasturing,[144] although in some cases we know that overseas trade was the main source of income, e.g. at Pietrabbondante. Literary sources attest to the production of wool in many areas, e.g. in Apulia, specifically the allied town Tarentum,[145] and in Campania.[146] Several loom weights with Oscan inscriptions have been found in

[141] Fracchia & Gualtieri 1998–9, 335.

[142] Cic. *Rosc. Am.* 20, 43–4. See Finley 1999, 112; Arthur 1991, 65; Cébeillac-Gervasoni 1998, 145 for Campania; Simelon 1993, 38 for Lucania; Mazzei, Mertens, & Volpe 1990; Torelli 1999, 106 for Apulia.

[143] Kay 2014, 155–60.

[144] Giardina 1981; Dench 1995, 118–25.

[145] Plaut. *Truc.* 3.1.5; Plin. *NH* 7.73, 8.91, 8.190, 35.45; Var. *L.* 9.39; Col. *R.* 7.2.3. See Brunt 1987, 368; Vicari 2001, 24–8.

[146] Plaut. *Pseud.* 145. See Vicari 2001, 30–3. Textile production by Italians is attested by the inscriptions of the *magistri* of the religious *collegia* in Capua, who include a *sagarius* (cloak maker; AE 1982, 173–4=1988, 292).

Lucania, Apulia, and Samnium,[147] indicating the involvement of non-Latin speakers in these activities. Evidence of textile production, such as archaeological remains of fullers' workshops (*fullonicae*), has been found in central Italy. In the Latin colony Fregellae in the early second century, many large houses were turned into *fullonicae*.[148] In various places, both Latin colonies and allied areas, inscriptions mention *fora pecuaria* (cattle markets).[149] Some farms located in allied areas indeed show evidence of animal husbandry, for example, Moltone di Tolve, which has large stables and evidence of wool working, such as loom weights. This farm fell out of use in the early second century, before any Roman settlement occurred in the area, so it was likely owned by a local.[150]

Other Italians made money from manufacture, such as the tile producer Arronties. We have already discussed the involvement of Italians in the production of various types of pottery. Other manufactured items also carry stamps by Italians that may indicate production for the market: Pantusinus, for example, stamped pots in allied Tibur in the late second century. We have already encountered the amphora producer Trebios Loisios (see section 3.2.2.1); the same *gentilicium* is attested in Pompeii on brick stamps from the same period. A bilingual Latin-Oscan inscription on a roof tile from Pietrabbondante (see Fig 3.2), likely dating to the late second or early first century, reads *Hn Sattiieís Detfri/seganatted plavtad/Herenneis Amica signavit qando/ponebamus tegila* (Oscan: '*Detfri* of Herennius Sattius stamped the tile with his/her sole'. Latin: 'Amica of Herennius stamped when we were stacking the tiles').

It is usually assumed that the inscription was set up by two slave women, working for an Oscan master who owned a tile factory.[151] It is quite surprising that an Oscan master owned a Latin-speaking slave, but this tile clearly shows that economic power and slave ownership was not only the prerogative of Latin-speaking Roman citizens. Decorative items were also produced by Italians: production of architectural terracottas, used to embellish temples and other buildings, took place in the mid-second and early first centuries in some Italian towns. For example, in Pompeii a man named Asinius produced terracotta moulds, stamped in Oscan.

Several tiles from Bovianum and Campochiaro in Samnium were marked in Oscan by the local magistrate, the *meddix tuvtiks*.[152] This indicates that local authorities, like the sanctuaries discussed in chapter 2.4, were actively engaged in

[147] *Imagines* Abellinum 3=Rix Hi 10; Larinum 6=Rix Fr 10; Teanum Apulum 3; Teanum Apulum 2=Rix Fr 11; Bovianum 75–6; Terventum 39; Venusia 1–3; Frentani 2; Forentum 1; Metapontum 2.

[148] Coarelli 1998; see Flohr 2013.

[149] Ferentinum: CIL 10.5850; Aeclanum: CIL 9.1143; Falerio: CIL 9.5438; Atina: CIL 1^2 1533=10.5074=ILS 5367=ILLRP 551; Aquileia: CIL 1^2 2197=5.8313=ILLRP 487a=ILS 5366.

[150] Guzzo 1984, 204–6; Isayev 2007, 73–6.

[151] *Imagines* Terventum 25=Rix Sa 35. See Wallace-Hadrill 2008, 90–2. It is not clear whether Detfri is a name, and, if so, whether it is a man or a woman.

[152] *Imagines* Bovianum 2–30=Rix tSa 1–34. See Morel 1991b, 134.

Fig. 3.2. Tile from Pietrabbondante.

By permission of the Ministero dei Beni e delle Attività Culturali e del Turismo (Soprintendenza Archeologia, belle arti e paesaggio del Molise).

economic activities. Most likely these were not produced for commercial purposes, but for the maintenance of local buildings. Indeed, the distribution patterns of commercial items, such as Black Gloss pottery and amphorae, were clearly different from those of more domestic items, such as loom weights, *dolia*, tiles, etc. Most of the latter were distributed only locally, with stamps by individual producers occurring only in very small numbers in one location. On the other hand, Black Gloss and amphorae were distributed throughout the Mediterranean; stamps by individual producers ended up in many different locations (see Appendix).

Many Italians were skilled in metalworking and a variety of other manufacturing activities. When Scipio Africanus went on campaign in Africa in 205, he was assisted by various Etruscan towns, which supplied him with various items: Populonia with iron; Tarquinii with cloth for sails; Volaterrae with timber; Arretium with 3,000 shields and helmets, 50,000 arrows, javelins, spears, axes, spades, sickles, and hand-mills. Perusia, Clusium, and Russellae sent wood to build ships.[153] All these towns were allied at this time, and clearly had specific economic specializations, such as metalworking in Arretium and forestry in the wooded areas.

[153] Liv. 28.45.10–11.

Cato similarly illustrates the wide variety of manufacturing activities undertaken by Italians and the specialization that occurred. He advises that

> iron tools, scythes, spades, mattocks, axes, harness, ornaments, and small chains [should be bought] at Cales and Minturnae; spades at Venafrum; carts and sledges at Suessa and in Lucania; jars and pots at Alba and at Rome; and tiles at Venafrum ... The following cities are the best markets for the articles named: oil mills at Pompeii, and at Rufrius' yard at Nola; nails and bars at Rome; pails, oil-urns, water-pitchers, wine-urns, other copper vessels at Capua and at Nola; Campanian baskets from Capua will be found useful; pulley ropes and all sorts of cordage at Capua; Roman baskets at Suessa and Casinum ... Lucius Tunnius of Casinum and Gaius Mennius ... of Venafrum make the best press-ropes.[154]

The locations that Cato mentions enjoyed a variety of different civic statuses: Casinum and Venafrum had *civitas sine suffragio*, while Cales and Suessa were Latin colonies, Minturnae a Roman colony, and Lucania, Capua, and Nola were allied.

The level of skill in bronze working in Italy was high, as shown for example by the Arringatore statue from Perusia, dating to the late second or early first century. The Cista Ficoroni is another good example of Italian metalworking skill. It was made by an artist with a typically Oscan *praenomen*, Novios, although the inscription mentions he worked in Rome.[155] The buyer had a typically Praenestine name, Dindia Macolnia. Praeneste itself was also famous for its metalwork; one speciality was strigils, some of which carry names with an Oscan origin.[156]

A final activity that Italians engaged in was moneylending. Their involvement can be deduced from the names on surviving *tesserae nummulariae*. These were small tags attached to bags of coins, naming the person who had sealed the bag in order to certify that the coinage had not been tampered with. Such *tesserae* record a large variety of names, many of them with an Italian origin. Unfortunately, most of these date from the first century and were found in Rome, so that few conclusions can be drawn about Italian activities before the Social War,[157] but a few may indicate involvement of people of Italian descent in moneylending before the Social War.[158]

[154] Cato *Agr*. 135.

[155] CIL 1.561=ILLRP 1197=ILS 8562: DINDIA MACOLNIA FILEAI DEDIT/NOVIOS PLAUTIOS MED ROMAI FECID ('Dindia Macolnia gave me to her daughter / Novius Plautius made me in Rome').

[156] Gatti & Onorati 1992, 190–1.

[157] Andreau 1999, 87–9; he notes that the *tesserae* system only worked if the people involved in the handling of large sums of cash knew each other's reputation, so that only a relatively small group would be involved. He therefore argues they belonged to the legally recognized companies of *publicani*, who could only be Roman citizens. However, *publicani* were closely connected to others, e.g. bankers and merchants. The network of people who knew each other's reputation may therefore have been larger than Andreau assumes, and could have included Italians, who could not become *publicani*. See, on moneylending, Cic. *Att*. 12.3; 12.12, 12.46; *Leg. Man*. 17–20. See Nicolet 1989, 633–4; Harris 2006, 19.

[158] Abius (Terracina, dated 93) and Ru(brius) Sab(idius) from Minturnae, dated before 96 (ILLRP 990).

It is clear from this short overview that Italians were involved in a variety of agricultural and manufacturing activities on a commercial scale between the fourth and first centuries. In contrast to what is often assumed, Roman citizens did not drive out Italians from these profitable activities. As we have seen, Italians with different civic statuses profited from new economic opportunities for commercial agricultural production and trade in the third and second centuries. Of course, these opportunities were largely created by the expansion of Roman dominance in the Mediterranean, leading to the opening up of new markets in overseas areas and the creation of military and legal protection for Italians overseas. However, this does not mean that Romans monopolized commercial enterprises. In the third and second centuries, not many Romans were as yet very wealthy; the size of houses and levels of luxury in Rome had not yet reached the level they would reach in the first century and the Imperial period. This suggests that the Roman elites did not monopolize commercial activities. On the contrary, many towns in Italy already in the late third and early second centuries show considerable levels of wealth and luxury, which often exceeded those in Rome (see chapter 4.3). Therefore, it is quite possible that some Italians were wealthier than the Roman elites. It is unlikely that this wealth was accumulated by agricultural production for the Italian market, since this market was still relatively small.[159] It therefore stands to reason that other profitable enterprises—the export of agricultural products and manufactured goods—were among the main sources of Italian income. However, before we investigate the connections between commercial activities and the changing landscape of Italy in chapter 4, we must take a closer look at economic developments in Italy.

3.3. Economic Developments in Italy

It is often assumed that the Roman conquest had an enormous, and mostly negative, impact on the economy of Italy. This is most strongly expressed in the case of the southern part of the peninsula: it is assumed that wealthy Romans confiscated large tracts of land as *ager publicus*, on which they established large slave-staffed estates, producing wine and olive oil for the market, as well as 'ranches' for large-scale transhumance. This would have led to depopulation in Italy, especially the south, and the destitution of small farmers.[160] Scholars voicing such ideas often assumed that the free market ruled all economic activity and that communities and individuals who did not participate in it were 'marginal' to the economy as a whole. This supposedly included small farmers, since they are

[159] Rosenstein 2008.

[160] E.g. Toynbee 1965:2, 9–14; Hopkins 1978, 11–13; Carandini 1988; Gabba 1989. See Terrenato 2001b, 62–4 for an overview of older literature.

assumed not to have engaged regularly with the free market. Therefore, small farms were characterized as 'residual'[161] or 'pre-Roman'[162] modes of production. This implies that they were destined to disappear, since they were irrelevant to general developments in Italian economy.

However, it has long been recognized that this picture of economic change in Italy is exaggerated: large, slave-staffed *villae* did not dominate production, nor did small farmers disappear in southern Italy, or anywhere else, during the Republican era. Small farmers cannot be considered 'marginal' in any way, since they played an important role in the economy by producing for their own subsistence and working for wages on larger estates, as we have seen. 'Residual' modes of production, such as small farms, as well as the products they made, such as local types of pottery, played a very important role in local economies, and thus in the economy as a whole. But since they often escape archaeological detection, their importance has been—and sometimes still is—underrated.[163] Moreover, it is now increasingly recognized that not only Roman but also local elites were active in commercial agriculture, animal husbandry, and industrial production, as I have argued in section 3.2.

Recent academic views thus point out the varied and complex economic developments in the Italian peninsula, as well as the degree of agency that lay with Italians, especially the elites. Nevertheless, the role of Rome in these developments should not be underestimated, as will become clear in this section. It cannot be denied that the presence of Rome and its expanding power in Italy and the Mediterranean had a strong influence on the direction taken by the economy of Italy, as Italy started to produce for the market in Rome and for Roman armies overseas. This led to an increase in commercial agriculture in many parts of Italy, although developments varied widely across different regions and even from location to location.[164] Rome's impact was not equally important in all areas of Italy: the city of Rome and the armies overseas were not the only markets available to Italian entrepreneurs, as is shown by the variety of goods traded and the multiple directions this trade took. The enormous involvement of Italians in commercial activities, which we have seen in the previous section, is evidence of the large number of options available to Italians and the vitality of the Italian economy, which functioned largely independently from direct Roman interference.

In this section, I will study four sample areas in more detail, in order to see how their economies developed after the Roman conquest and to determine the importance of Rome in these changes. I will give particular attention to the civic status of each area, since it is often thought that changes in the civic status of an area had a significant effect on the economic impact of Italian regions. It is often

[161] E.g. Lepore 1981: 'modi residui'; see also Giardina 1981.
[162] Rathbone 1983, 161.
[163] Morel 1998, 518.
[164] Roselaar 2008; Stek 2014.

assumed that those who were integrated politically into the Roman state by a grant of citizenship experienced more cultural and/or economic change, and at a quicker pace, than those who remained allied.[165] Some scholars even assume that specific areas held a certain civic status, e.g. *civitas sine suffragio*, because they displayed specific cultural or economic characteristics.[166] As it is not possible to survey economic developments throughout Italy, I have chosen four regions as test cases: Latium, Campania, Apulia, and Lucania and Bruttium.[167] These regions were chosen because they display a wide variety of civic statuses—Latium and Campania had many communities with full or partial citizenship, while southern Italy had some Latin colonies, some *ager publicus*, and many allied communities. These regions also played very different roles within the economic networks of Italy. Within each region, I will look at communities and areas with different statuses in sequence, in order to see whether the civic status of a community had any consequences for its economic developments. Of course, it is impossible to discuss all communities in each region. The sample sites were chosen because they have been the subject of recent archaeological research, and comprehensive publications were easily accessible.

At the same time, this section will describe general economic developments in Italy, in order to study the impact of the political integration of Italy under Roman rule. It will become clear throughout this section that the regions of Italy became more closely connected to each other and to other parts of the Mediterranean as a result of the expansion of Roman power. Thus, to some degree Italy and the Mediterranean became more integrated economically. On the other hand, this integration was mostly relevant for commercial goods, such as wine, olive oil, and some local specialities, as well as products transported to the city of Rome. The local economies of most towns and villages in Italy were focused on their immediate hinterland, where staple crops were produced. They did not interact to a great degree with far-away areas, within or outside of Italy. Thus, the Roman conquest of Italy led to some degree of economic integration, but this had widely varying consequences in each specific location.

[165] Sherwin-White 1973, 98, for example, thinks that the Latin status became 'the path to Roman citizenship, and almost a secondary form of the *civitas* itself'. See Humbert 1978, 207.

[166] Morel 1991b, 130 assumes that Trebula Mutuesca was a site of viritane settlement, because it imported and imitated pottery from Rome. See Torelli 1999, 122.

[167] It should be noted that these regions did not *a priori* have a coherent regional identity; it was only in the Augustan period that these regions were given exact boundaries and a regional identity could develop. Most people in the Republican period still identified with their town first and foremost, and possibly with an ethnic group, but not with a geographical region; see Bourdin 2012; Roth 2012.

3.3.1. Latium

Latium had been closely connected to Rome since the archaic period. During the fifth and fourth centuries, Rome and Latium were united in the Latin League, suggesting that social and economic relations were close.[168] After the Latin War of 341–338, Rome imposed its authority on the Latins by unilaterally deciding the civic status of each Latin community, and thus the relationship of each to the city of Rome. Some towns became Roman citizens, others became colonies, while some, such as Praeneste and Tibur, retained the allied status, although it is unclear what this entailed in the later Republic. Fundi and Formiae were given *civitas sine suffragio*.[169] Thus a great variety of civic statuses was created. In this section, we will survey a selection of communities in Latium and describe economic developments in each.

We will start with areas that received full citizenship. Most of these towns were located close to Rome; they mostly displayed similar economic developments during the Republican period. Around Gabii, for example, settlement was mostly in villages during the fourth century. In the third century, the settlement pattern changed: sites became more regularly spread out over the territory. In the second century, *villae* appeared on the lower hill slopes. At first these were relatively small, but they gradually became larger, especially after the mid-first century.[170] Similar developments took place in other towns with full citizenship. Tusculum had already been assigned Roman citizenship in 381.[171] In the fourth and third centuries, settlement consisted mostly of small farms on the hills; in the later third and second centuries these developed into *villae*. The area mostly produced fruit, flowers, wine, and grain for the market in Rome. In the late second century, it became the most important area for luxury *villae* of Roman elites, together with Tibur.[172]

The Ager Pontinus has been the subject of intensive research. After the Latin War, Roman viritane settlements were established here. Some previously existing towns lost importance after the Roman conquest, e.g. the important centre of Satricum, while others remained. These were especially towns that were well connected to the Via Appia and the coast. Smaller rural sites also show much continuity; there is little evidence of a transition to larger *villae* in the Republican period. The Pontine plain itself was difficult to cultivate because of its marshy nature, so that the only settlement of importance took place near the Via Appia itself. On the other hand, the coastal plain, which was secured by the Roman

[168] Humbert 1978, 71; Cornell 1995, 302.

[169] Liv. 8.14. Many other towns not mentioned by Livy at some point received full Roman citizenship; we have no evidence of when this happened, but it is assumed that they received this right in 338; see Toynbee 1965:1, 135; Humbert 1978, 172; Roselaar 2010, 301.

[170] Musco & Zaccagni 1985, 90–5.

[171] Cic. *Planc.* 8.19.

[172] Plin. *NH* 13.5, 21.16, 21.20–7. See Brun 2000, 290; Valenti 2003, 27, 55–6.

colonies of Antium and Circeii, became a favoured location for luxurious *villae* belonging to the Roman elite.[173] The Monti Lepini to the north of the Ager Pontinus formed the home region of the Volsci, with whom the Romans had been in continuous war in the fifth and fourth centuries. They emphasized their conquests by the establishment of Roman citizen colonies along the edge of the Monti Lepini. This turned the area into a densely populated and cultivated landscape, as shown by the rise in the number of rural settlements here. On the slopes of the Monti Lepini, from the second half of the fourth century a great increase in agricultural exploitation occurred and many larger farms appeared. Their number increased further in the third and second centuries. Most of these were located around the colonies Cora and Setia. Around the colony Norba, settlement was much less dense. Thus, even though all these towns had been founded as colonies after 338, they experienced different developments.[174]

Arpinum, Formiae, and Fundi received the *civitas sine suffragio* in 338 and full citizenship in 188.[175] Arpinum seems to have experienced rapid economic growth in the early second century; this was probably stimulated by textile production, since a large number of *fullonicae* has been found.[176] Fundi produced wine and olive oil for the market at Rome in the later second and first centuries, as shown by the large number of Dressel 1 amphorae found here. Important for Formiae's economic development was the building of a road in the early second century, which connected Fundi to the harbours at Terracina and Formiae. Along this road, a number of *villae* emerged around this time.[177]

Anagnia in the Sacco valley was assigned *civitas sine suffragio* in 306; it is not clear when full citizenship was imposed.[178] The valley of the Sacco river was an important route for transhumance. It shows evidence for small farms with a mixed economy in the plains, olive oil and wine production on the hill slopes, and animal husbandry in upland areas. From the late fourth century, an increase of defensible small farms appears; some of these were abandoned in the second century. At this time, more luxurious *villae* appeared on the plains and in the hills, although many smaller farms remained.[179]

We will now turn to Latin colonies. After 338, several Latin colonies were established in Latium. Fregellae, in southern Latium, was one of the first colonies, founded in 328. It experienced great economic prosperity during the Republic.[180] Fregellae owed this in part to its location on the crossing of a number of important roads, including transhumance routes; *fora pecuaria* (cattle markets) are attested

[173] Attema, Burgers, & Van Leusen 2010, 32–58.
[174] Andreussi 1981, 354; Attema & De Haas 2005.
[175] Liv. 38.36.7–9. See Di Fazio 2006, 21.
[176] CIL 10.5628. See Cic. *Leg.* 2.1–6; Plu. *Cic.* 1.1; Dio 46.4–5. See Coarelli 1991, 185; 1998, 37–8.
[177] Di Fazio 2006.
[178] Humbert 1978, 38; Tan forthcoming.
[179] Andreussi 1981, 349–50, 354.
[180] Pesando 1997, 177; Coarelli 1998, 35–7.

in several locations near Fregellae.[181] In the early second century, several public building projects took place in the town (see chapter 4.3). At the same time, a large number of *fullonicae* was created in the town, as well as workshops for metal-working.[182] Livy reports that by 187, many Samnites and Paeligni had moved to Fregellae;[183] Coarelli suggests this migration caused the depopulation of Samnium in this period,[184] but other possibilities must be taken into consideration, such as good economic prospects in the colonies—Fregellae was clearly producing manufactured items on a large scale in this period.

The Latin colony Interamna Lirenas was founded in 312, but seems to have played a much less important role in the regional economy than Fregellae. At first, the inhabitants may have lived in villages, since some rather large settlement clusters have been identified.[185] A large increase in the number of sites is visible in the second century. *Villae* also appeared here in the second century, but these were mostly small, with an economy based on polyculture rather than specialized commercial production. The town had no impressive public buildings. Its limited importance was possibly caused by the fact that the Via Latina, the major road though the area, did not pass directly through the town, so that it was isolated from major road networks.[186]

The only towns in Latium that retained the allied status until the Social War were Tibur and Praeneste. This probably meant that they were now equal to other allied towns in Italy; there is no evidence that they held similar privileges to the Latin colonies. Livy states that both were deprived of some of their territory in 338,[187] but despite this, both towns experienced continuous prosperity during the Republic. In the area south of the Anio river, *villae* already appeared in the fourth century; north of the Anio, the economy was based mostly on forestry and animal breeding in the Monti Tiburtini. Larger *villae* appeared in the late second and first centuries, for both commercial production and leisure, although there were still many small and medium-sized farms with mixed agriculture.[188]

As we have seen in section 3.2, many inhabitants of Praeneste were very active in international trade, much more so than those of Tibur. Praeneste was also famous for its metalworking, although the production of mirrors and metal items in Praeneste declined in the third century and had completely disappeared by the early second.[189] It seems that some Praenestine families moved their

[181] CIL 10.5074, 5850; Coarelli 1998, 62; Morel 2007, 501.

[182] Coarelli 1991, 184; 1998, 45; Pesando 1997, 282.

[183] Liv. 41.8.6.

[184] Coarelli 1998, 36.

[185] Pelgrom 2008, 347–9.

[186] Wightman & Hayes 1995, 34–6.

[187] Liv. 8.14.9.

[188] Andreussi 1981, 354.

[189] Coarelli 1992, 257–60, ascribes this decline to the 'proletarianization' of the middle classes, due to the confiscation of land by Rome. This supposed proletarianization is, according to him, proved by the fact that only a very small group of elite families held local magistracies. However, there is no reason why the confiscation of *ager publicus* in the fourth century would have such effects in the later third century. Moreover, many local families are in fact attested in the second century, so that the existence of a small, closed elite is unlikely.

metalworking enterprises elsewhere, as better sources of metal became available: the Dindii set up business in Aquileia in the second century, using metal from the Alps.[190] Black Gloss pottery was produced by various members of the Samiarii.[191] Praeneste also produced perfume,[192] wine, onions, roses, and nuts.[193] Animal husbandry also played a role, as attested by an inscription recording a *collegium* of cattle merchants.[194]

We may conclude that remarkable variety occurred in the economy of Latium. Developments varied greatly, even among cities with the same civic status, and also between neighbouring towns. Some towns engaged in commercial agriculture already in the early and middle Republic, especially those close to Rome, while others only engaged in commercial production from the second century onwards. For its food supply, Rome was dependent on Italy, and especially Latium, for most of the Republican period, as import of staple crops from abroad was rare.[195] According to early forms of location theory, such as Von Thünen's nineteenth-century model,[196] production near a city should focus on perishable goods, such as fruit and vegetables; further away, the production of grain, wine, and olive oil should occur. This matches Cato's advice on building a farm: he states that a farm owner should adapt the crops he grows to the distance to the (urban) market. He advises that 'near a town it is well to have a garden planted with all manner of vegetables, and all manner of flowers for garlands'.[197] This division of production areas also partially matches the distribution of production near Rome. In nearby towns like Praeneste and Tibur, flowers and vegetables were produced. However, wine and olive oil production were very common at all sites suitable for such crops, at whatever distance from the market at Rome, as the discovery of wine and oil presses in many sites in Latium indicates. These were located on both large sites and smaller farms.[198] Of course, Rome was not the only market for Italian goods at any point during the Republic: all towns served as central places in their own regional economic networks.[199]

It is important to emphasize that there seems to be little difference in economic developments between areas with different civic statuses. No matter whether an area had full or partial citizenship, or was a colony or allied town, in most cases production took place in small or medium farms in the fourth and third centuries; only in areas very close to Rome did *villae* appear before the second century. In the later second century, relatively small *villae* appeared almost everywhere; again, the status of each area was not relevant in this development. Only towns

[190] Strazzulla Rusconi 1982. [191] Gatti & Onorati 1992, 206–31.
[192] Plin. *NH* 13.5, 21.16, 21.20–7. See Brun 2000, 290.
[193] Athen. 1.26F; Plin. *NH* 15.90, 17.96, 19.97, 21.16, 20; Cato *Agr.* 133.
[194] CIL 1^2 1450=14.2878=ILLRP 106. [195] Morley 1996, 113–14; Jongman 2003.
[196] Morley 1996, 59–62, 170–4.
[197] Cato *Agr.* 8.2. See Var. *R.* 1.16.3; Col. *R.* 7.3.13, 7.9.4, 8.5.9, 8.7.
[198] Marzano 2013, 88–95. [199] Morley 1996, 170–4.

with very little opportunity for commercial production saw no emergence of larger sites in the second century. Clearly, some fundamental economic changes were taking place in Latium at this time—but in other areas as well, as we will now explore.

3.3.2. Campania

The history of Campania has been influenced by many peoples: the Etruscans, who settled here in the seventh to fifth centuries, the Greek colonies on the coast founded between the eighth and fifth centuries, and the Samnites, who conquered much of the territory in the fourth century. It is important to be aware of all these influences, so as not to ascribe any cultural change or development occurring after the Roman conquest in the late fourth century to the influence of Rome. Campania already enjoyed a flourishing economy before the Roman conquest, so it would be wrong to consider all economic developments after the conquest as a result of Roman dominance. As we have seen, it was the most important region in Italy for the production and export of wine, olive oil, and pottery for overseas markets. We will briefly explore economic developments of Campania in the fourth to first centuries, in order to investigate how these may be related to the expansion of Roman hegemony.

There were not many Latin colonies in Campania. Cales, founded in 334, had only limited influence on the economy of the surrounding area. Although trade between Cales and the nearby allied town of Teanum Sidicinum occurred, pottery from Cales was in the minority here compared to items from Magna Graecia and Greece. Cultural exchange was also limited: Teanum continued to use the Oscan language until the Social War.[200]

In contrast, there were many colonies with the Roman status. Minturnae, on the border between Latium and Campania, was founded as a colony with full Roman citizenship in 296. It functioned as a harbour for the export of products from the Liris Valley, such as wine, as well as metal goods from Fregellae.[201] This economic prosperity led to immigration, as we have seen (chapter 2). A number of *villae* emerged in the territory in the second century.[202]

Sinuessa was also founded in 296 as a Roman citizen colony. It served as an export harbour for the products of northern Campania and the Ager Falernus, including the famous Falernian wine.[203] In the third century, several *villae* were already present in the territory, although these were quite small. The *villae* were all located close to the colony and surrounding villages, which provided suitable

200 Morel 1991b, 136–9; Pedroni 2001.

201 Rauh 1986b, 205; Guidobaldi & Pesando 1989, 44–5; Hesnard et al. 1989, 26.

202 Broadhead 2002, 65.

203 Morley 1996, 174; Olcese 2004, 174–5, 181–3; 2005/6, 65.

markets; thus, not all of them produced for export. Others were located along the Via Appia, in locations with easy transport to the harbour.[204]

Puteoli was founded as a colony with Roman status in 194 and quickly became the most important harbour of Campania, also serving the city of Rome: ships from abroad were unloaded here, after which the goods were taken to Rome by smaller ships or overland.[205] Even before its foundation as a colony it had been a major port, as attested by the creation of *portoria* (harbour taxes) in 199; around 126/5 it was described by Lucilius as a *Delus minor* ('small Delos').[206]

Not all Roman colonies experienced the same level of growth: Volturnum was also founded in 194, but experienced very different economic developments. The sites in its territory were mostly small or medium farms. Some *villae* for commercial agriculture appeared in the second century, but on a much smaller scale than, for example, near Pompeii, which had allied status.[207]

Capua and its territory, the Ager Campanus, were assigned *civitas sine suffragio* after the Roman conquest. However, when the town chose Hannibal's side during the Second Punic War, it was deprived of this status and remained an allied town until the Social War. It is difficult to gauge the effects of this decision, but since the local farmers were left in place to work the land, the punishment seems to have affected mostly the local elites. In general, Capua seems to have flourished, despite its demotion.[208] The literary evidence attests to the fertility of the area; according to many, Hannibal's army was weakened by luxurious living in Capua.[209] The town had been an important centre of bronze-working from the fifth century onwards and metal tools remained an important element of its economy: Cato recommends the town for buying various bronze items, as well as ropes and baskets.[210] Textiles were also an important export product, attested by the presence of a *lintio* (linen producer), *vestiarius* (trader in textiles), and *purpurarius* (purple dye producer) among the magistrates of the religious colleges in the town. Perfumes were also produced at Capua: L. Novius Dionysius, an *unguentarius* (perfume producer) from Capua, is attested at Delos.[211]

Of the allied towns in Campania, Pompeii is by far the best known. It remained an allied town until the Social War; in the second century, it became the second most important harbour in the area after Puteoli.[212] Production in the hinterland itself took place mostly for local and regional markets. Many *villae* for wine

[204] Curti, Dench, & Patterson 1996, 176; Crimaco 2002, 94.

[205] Musti 1980, 206.

[206] Lucil. 3.123 Marx; 3.124 Krenkel (Festus 109L); see Plb. 3.91.2–4; Liv. 23.7.3; Cic. *Verr.* 2.5.154.

[207] Crimaco 2002.

[208] Liv. 26.16.8. See Morley 1996, 181.

[209] Liv. 7.38.5–8, 23.4.4, 23.18.11–14, 27.3.2; Plb. 7.1; Diod. 26.11; App. *Hann.* 43.

[210] Cato *Agr.* 135.2. See Plin. *NH* 34.95. Other professions attested in the inscriptions of the Capuan religious *magistri* are an *aerarius* (goldsmith), a *gla(diarius)* (swordmaker), a *scutarius* (shield maker), and *aurifices* (workers in gold). See Frederiksen 1959, 110; Morel 1991a, 202.

[211] CIL 1^2 1594. See Frederiksen 1959, 110–11.

[212] Pesando 1997, 276.

production emerged along the Sarno river and to the south and east of the town, closest to the market. In the plains, settlement consisted mostly of small farms; this area was mostly used for grain production, while cattle breeding and wool production took place in the hills further away.[213] Amphorae and *dolia* were produced by many Pompeian workshops, partially for the storage and export of agricultural products from the hinterland; tiles were produced for the various building projects that took place in the second century.[214] Many workshops and shops (*tabernae*) were built in the late second century. A variety of industries was carried out in these workshops, such as salting fish and tanning.[215] In general, Pompeii was a prosperous town, with continuous investments in production and manufacture aimed at maximizing profits. Its prosperity was due mainly to the interconnectedness of its economy, with Vesuvian wine exported through the main harbour at Puteoli. This meant that a large part of the population enjoyed a varied diet and luxury consumer goods, including rather large houses.[216]

In conclusion, it is clear that Campania was a very fertile and prosperous region throughout the Republican period, with a high settlement density of small and medium farms in most areas. As in the case of Latium, there seems to have been little difference between towns with colonial status and allied towns: each could profit from the economic opportunities offered by the expansion of Rome into the Mediterranean. The prosperity of the region is reflected in the public and private buildings that were erected in many Campanian towns during the second century (see chapter 4.3). However, there were great differences between individual sites within Campania. Areas that were less well connected to the new economic networks, such as Volturnum, show continued occupation by small farms, with less development of *villae*. Clearly, civic status did not play an important role: Latin and Roman colonies were not always very influential or prosperous, while many allied towns flourished. Transportation possibilities played a great role in determining the economic prosperity of individual towns: the transport of wine and other export goods from more distant farms to the coast was simply too expensive to be profitable.[217]

More and larger farms for commercial production appeared in many areas of Campania in the second century, as they did in Latium.[218] At the end of the second century, larger *villae* emerged, but only after the Social War—especially during the Sullan period—did these become very large, with the accumulation of great amounts of land by single individuals.[219] It is clear that the growth of Rome as the central market for the peninsula had a large impact on the economy of Campania, which started to produce for the market at Rome, as well as for export overseas. However, as we have seen, many Campanian products, especially wine and olive oil, were

[213] Jongman 1988, 132–4, 142–5, 159–61.
[214] Strazzulla 1981, 193. [215] Ellis 2011. [216] Flohr 2017, 80–1.
[217] Kay 2014, 171–3. [218] Arthur 1991, 64–5. [219] Frederiksen 1981, 269–72, 277–8.

exported not to Rome, but to other parts of the Mediterranean. Rome did not interfere directly in the trade carried out by Campanian businessmen abroad.

3.3.3. Apulia

Apulia was conquered by the Romans during the Samnite Wars and the Pyrrhic War of 280–275, with further operations in 268. Considerable amounts of land were taken as *ager publicus*, some of which was used for the foundation of Latin colonies: Luceria in 314, Venusia in 291, and Brundisium between 246 and 243. Other *ager publicus* remained in the hands of existing Italian landholders.[220] The remaining territory remained in the hands of the local population, who now became allies of Rome. Economic developments in the Latin colonies in Apulia were varied, as we will see in this section.

As discussed in chapter 2, Brundisium quickly developed into the most important centre of Apulia. It profited greatly from its role in the supply of Roman armies in the East. For example, in 169 'the praetor . . . put out a bid for the transport of 6,000 togas, 30,000 tunics, and 200 horses to Macedonia'.[221] These items were in all likelihood shipped from Brundisium, and it therefore makes sense that they were produced by the surrounding Apulian population. The area also engaged in wine production for export; as we saw in section 3.2.2, amphorae were produced on many sites around the town. It is clear that the prosperity of the city greatly stimulated the economic growth of the surrounding area; near the city, wine and olive oil were produced, while the hills were used for grain and the mountains for animal breeding, especially for the production of leather and wool for the army.[222] Its foundation had important consequences for the surrounding allied area, as we will see on page 105–106.

The foundation of the Latin colony Venusia in 291 is clearly visible in the landscape, with many small farms, spread out over the territory, suddenly appearing; former local centres, such as Bantia, declined in size. Venusia fulfilled a very different role in the economy than Brundisium, however. Farms throughout the Republic were small; only in the mid-first century did more *villae* appear. The town was connected to the economy of central Italy: in the second century, imports of pottery from Campania were common. Grain, oil, and wine were produced for the local market. Wool production was another important aspect of the economy, but seems to have been conducted mainly at subsistence level.[223]

Many allied towns were deprived of some land when the area was conquered in the third century or after their disloyalty during the Second Punic War. This land

[220] Roselaar 2010, 305, 311–12, 319.
[221] Liv. 44.16.4. [222] Burgers 1998, 267–87.
[223] Marchi & Sabbatini 1996, 103–17, 123–8; Sabbatini 2001, 58–71, 80–1, 128; Marchi 2010.

was declared *ager publicus*; it used to be argued that in the second century this land was appropriated by the Roman elite, who used the land for pastoralism and extensive grain production. This would have led to a decline in the local population.[224] However, in most cases, *ager publicus* remained in the hands of locals until the Gracchan land reform; economic developments on this land during the second century varied widely.[225] Herdonia, for example, remained allied after the conquest, but lost much of its land as *ager publicus* after the Second Punic War.[226] Before the war, it had profited from its position on a crossing of three important roads, as well as various *tratturi*.[227] A variety of coinage, mostly from other towns in Apulia, has been found in third-century Herdonia, attesting to its central position in the regional economy.[228] Farms usually remained fairly small in the second century; from the late second century, more commercial farms for the production of olive oil appeared.[229] This development might be connected to the influx of new settlers after the remaining *ager publicus* was distributed in the Gracchan period, although we cannot determine who owned these farms.

Canusium also lost much of its land as *ager publicus*. It had been a prosperous town before the Roman conquest, and this prosperity continued throughout the third and second centuries. After the Second Punic War, some goods were produced for long-distance trade—wine and olives grown on the coast, animals and grain from the hinterland. These were produced on small and medium-sized farms.[230] The wide-ranging economic connections of Canusium are attested by the fact that some Canusians are attested as traders on Delos and elsewhere in the East in the third and second centuries (see section 3.2.1). As in Herdonia, there is little evidence that the confiscation of land as *ager publicus* affected the local economy. Most sites remained in use; many even increased in size, showing the wealth of the local elites. Only after the Gracchan land reform were some old sites abandoned and replaced by new *villae*.[231] However, these *villae* probably did not appear as a direct result of the Gracchan land distributions that took place here, since these benefited mainly small farmers.

Most areas of Apulia remained allied and did not lose any land as *ager publicus*. In allied territory, similar economic developments are visible across different towns and regions. The Roman conquest in the early third century does not seem to have had immediate effects. Only from the late third to mid-second century did some significant changes in settlement patterns in allied territory occur. Many sites declined in size or were abandoned altogether, some as the direct result of Roman aggression or events during the Second Punic War. Others

[224] Gabba 1977, 277; Torelli 1990, 89, 109–12; 1999, 142–3; Grelle & Giardina 1993, 65–7, 76–80; Pareti 1997, 438–41.

[225] Roselaar 2010, 79–84.

[226] Liv. 27.1.14.

[227] Strab. 6.3.7.

[228] Scheers 1995, 327–31.

[229] Volpe & Mertens 1995, 307–13.

[230] D'Andria 1979, 307–10; Grelle 1981; Grelle & Giardina 1993, 70–2, 74.

[231] Goffredo 2010, 25.

disappeared for reasons that are now unclear to us. However, sites still in existence grew, a development also visible in other parts of Italy, so that overall population decline is unlikely.[232]

Evidence for commercial production is clear in some areas. At Vagnari, a site that had been abandoned in the late third century, settlement reappeared in the late second century, but now centred around a *villa*. Its most important product was wool: over 500 loom weights have been found. It was located on the Via Appia and the road to Tarentum, an important wool market. It has been suggested that the land had become *ager publicus* and the *villa* was owned by a Roman,[233] but there is no evidence for this. A similar development occurred at Gravina, which had functioned as a central market for the region in the early third century. In the later third century, the size of the town and the number of settlements in the surrounding area declined. In the mid-second century, a new site layout appeared. The largest building was now a luxurious *villa*. Sheep and goats, raised for wool, became the most important product.[234]

The Salento isthmus, between Tarentum and Brundisium, has been the subject of long-term research. The developments of two well-studied centres, Valesio and Oria, illustrate the changes caused by the Roman conquest and the establishment of Brundisium. Valesio, some 10 kilometres south of Brundisium, experienced significant economic changes after the settlement of the colony: after a large increase in sites in the third and early second centuries, a sharp decline occurred after the mid-second century. Eventually the site disappeared almost completely. It may be that many of its inhabitants moved to Brundisium, which at this time was very prosperous. *Villae* appeared in the second century and there is evidence for the production of Greco-Italic amphorae for wine and olive oil. Since Valesio was close to Brundisium, it made sense to produce agricultural goods here, but the town was no longer needed as a centre for settlement or services.[235]

Oria, on the Via Appia between Tarentum and Brundisium, flourished throughout the Republican period. As in Valesio, the number of sites at Oria diminished in the second century, but the sites that remained became much larger. This suggests that specialized agriculture took place at Oria. Grave goods from the territory of Oria attest to the survival of local elites (see chapter 4.4).[236] The establishment of Brundisium clearly stimulated local trade; pre-Roman settlement mostly continued on the line Oria–Brundisium, along the Via Appia. In contrast

[232] Grelle & Giardina 1993, 65–7, 76–80; Gallone 2007, 26–7.

[233] Small 2014.

[234] Small 1992, 16–18; Whitehouse, Wilkins, & Herring 2000, 305–7. Small explains the *villa* as the result of the Gracchan land reforms; however, such *villae* could also be owned by locals. In any case, the Gracchi distributed land mostly to small farmers, rather than to large landholders, so it is not clear why a *villa* would have appeared as a result of their reforms.

[235] Boersma & Yntema 1987, 94–5; Yntema 2006, 105; Compatangelo-Soussignan 1999, 99–100, 105.

[236] Fracchia 2013, 195.

to Valesio, Oria was still needed as a local centre, since it was further from Brundisium. Other settlements, which were less well connected to the road network and therefore to the market, declined or even disappeared.[237] Thus, the fate of individual settlements was related to a change in the role of specific sites in the regional economy, as well as the economy of the peninsula as a whole.

Other towns in Apulia also display significant change after the Roman conquest. The allied town of Arpi in northern Apulia had long maintained trade contacts with areas overseas, for example, Delos, Delphi, and Corcyra. It declined in size in the second century. A likely reason is the development of the Latin colony Luceria into an important centre in the region, even though its influence on the regional economy was limited.[238]

The southern part of the Salento, ancient Messapia, also remained allied. Some land was taken as *ager publicus* after the Roman conquest, but this remained in local hands until the Gracchan land distributions. Most evidence for trade points to contacts with the eastern Mediterranean rather than with Italy. Some local elites were clearly very wealthy in the pre-Roman period: graves contained Eastern glass, Greek pottery, etc.[239] In Ugentum, until the mid-third century most amphorae were imported from Corinth and Corcyra, as well as Crete, Sicily, and the Aeolian islands.[240] Coinage attests to trading links with Tarentum, Velia, Neapolis, Corinth, north-western Greece, Syracuse, and Carthage. Not much change occurred immediately after the Roman conquest; in the third and second centuries, many items were still imported from Asia, Alexandria, and Greece, such as amphorae from Rhodes and Knidos,[241] as well as coins from Sicily, Egypt, and Asia. In the second century, there was an increase in olive oil and wine production in the area, mostly on medium farms. Messapia became an important area for the production of amphorae, used to transport wine from the hinterland, as we have seen in section 3.2.2.[242]

The Greek colonies in Magna Graecia also remained allied after the Roman conquest. Tarentum had been the most important export harbour for crops from middle and southern Apulia, such as grain, wine, fish, timber, and weapons, which were traded with Greece and Carthage.[243] From the late third century, it lost much of its role as an export harbour, after the rise of Brundisium. In the Second Punic War, the town was destroyed and its inhabitants slaughtered.[244] Still, Tarentum retained some commercial activities in the second and first centuries: in the first

[237] Burgers 1998, 291–2; Attema & Burgers 2012, 115.

[238] Mazzei 1991, 113; Grelle & Giardina 1993, 27. Luceria resembled Venusia: most sites were small, with a mixed economy of livestock and vineyards; see Grelle 2008, 370.

[239] See Yntema 2006, 110–12; 2009; Colivicchi 2011, 119–20.

[240] Desy & De Paepe 1990, 188, 216, 231.

[241] Lippolis 1997, 22–3.

[242] Compatangelo-Soussignan 1999, 17, 98.

[243] Plb. 10.1.3–5.

[244] Plb. 1.83.7–10, 10.1.4–9, 23.9.12; 17.3, 34.11.1, Plin. *NH* 14.8.69. See Càssola 1970–1, 324; Marasco 1986, 60–2; Desy 1993, 92–3; Lomas 1993, 89–90; Yntema 1993, 177; Isayev 2007, 165–70.

half of the second century, many Rhodian amphorae were imported into Tarentum, while from the mid-second to mid-first century it exported wine.[245] Furthermore, it was the most important location in Italy for the production of purple dye and the famous Tarentine wool.[246]

The traditional picture of the pre-Roman Apulian economy insists on a predominance of animal husbandry and transhumance. It is often assumed that wine and olive oil only started to be produced after the Roman conquest,[247] which in some cases is considered as detrimental to 'traditional economic activity', leading to economic upheaval and a decline in population.[248] In fact, agricultural activity had been very important throughout the history of Apulia. Grain was an important product of Apulia and was sometimes exported to central Italy or Greece. An example may be the Messapian Bouzos Orteiras, active at Delos in the second half of the third century. Around 234 a famine was raging at Delos, so Bouzos may have made his fortune selling grain in Greece.[249] On the other hand, it is clear that the production and export of wine and olive oil increased in the second century; most likely this was the result of new markets opening up after the expansion of Roman hegemony in the Mediterranean.

As in the case of Latium and Campania, it is important to keep in mind the differences within Apulia as a whole. Most cities show a similar pattern of production, with farms producing for subsistence, as well as some larger farmers that also produced for the market. As in other regions of Italy, the number of rural sites declined after the Roman conquest and especially in the early second century, but the sizes of those that remained increased.[250] In some cases, we have seen that older settlements were replaced by *villae*, such as at Gravina and Vagnari. Thus, although indeed many pre-Roman sites declined or disappeared, this does not mean that the population as a whole declined. Rather, this development reflects a new settlement hierarchy: those better placed to profit from new economic opportunities grew, while more isolated sites declined.[251] It has been argued that 'Catonian' *villae* appeared in Apulia from the Gracchan period onwards, as a result of the influx of Roman settlers.[252] However, as discussed in section 3.2.3, third- and second-century 'Hellenistic' farms also functioned as commercial farms; these did not necessarily have Roman owners. Larger *villae* only appeared in the late second and first centuries, as in most areas of Italy and

[245] Strab. 6.3.1. See D'Andria 1979, 277–85; Cordano 2008, 70. Guzzo 1991, 84 thinks that most of the land of Tarentum was used for animal husbandry after the Second Punic War, but this is exaggerated.

[246] Plin. *NH* 9.137; Hor. *Ep.* 2.1.207; Var. *R.* 2.2.18; Col. 7.2.3. See Marzano 2013, 154–9.

[247] Desy 1993, 185–7; Lamboley 1996, 398.

[248] E.g. Compatangelo 1989, 81–2.

[249] See Liv. 22.23–4, 22.40; Plb. 3.107.1–4; Strab. 6.3.9; Var. *R.* 1.57.3, 2.1.16; Col. 3.8.4 on agriculture in Apulia. See Morel 1991a, 200–1; Mele 1993, 286–91; Small 1994, 553; Yntema 2009.

[250] Gallone 2007, 27–9.

[251] Yntema 2006, 117.

[252] Grelle & Giardina 1993, 70–2.

the Mediterranean.[253] Even such larger *villae* may very well have been owned by local elites, rather than by Romans.[254]

Economic change after the Second Punic War, therefore, was mostly a continuation of processes that had already started earlier. Trade overseas, which was already taking place in the fourth century, continued and grew in the third and second. Apulia clearly fulfilled a different role in the economic system of Italy as a whole than the regions discussed above: its economy continued to focus less on the market at Rome itself, as in the case of Latium and Campania, and more on trade with the Greek world, as had been the case before the Roman conquest. We may conclude, therefore, that the economy of Apulia underwent significant changes between the fourth and first centuries as a result of the economic changes that occurred in the Mediterranean at large when Roman dominance expanded. However, most of these economic changes cannot be attributed directly to the activities of Romans in Apulia itself, but rather to the local inhabitants taking up opportunities that presented themselves.

3.3.4. Lucania and Bruttium

Lucania and Bruttium are often represented as the backwater of Italy, with little to offer economically. Especially after the Roman conquest, the area is thought to have declined in prosperity and population. However, the picture is not quite so bleak. Rome conquered Lucania and Bruttium in the third century, after which some land was taken as *ager publicus*, specifically the Sila forest and the Tanager valley. After the Second Punic War, more land was expropriated; some colonies were immediately established on this land, while another part remained in the hands of the previous Italian owners until it was distributed by the Gracchi.[255]

Paestum was the first Latin colony established in the area, in 273. It was located at the northern edge of Lucania, near Campania, with which it had traditionally interacted most. It had been established as a Greek colony, but had seen a gradual influx of Oscan speakers, probably of Lucanian descent, in the fourth century. The economy was based on grain production in the plains and specialized agriculture in the hills, as well as the town's role as a major harbour in the region.[256] Changes in the settlement pattern occurred in the territory after the Roman conquest; the number of sites declined strongly. The town remained prosperous for a while after the colony's foundation, as monumental building here attests (see chapter 4). In the later second century, however, the economy declined and the town's

253 Mele 1993, 286–7, 289–91; Roselaar 2010, 161–4; Terrenato 2012, 73–4.

254 Mazzei, Mertens, & Volpe 1990, 180–2.

255 Roselaar 2010, 316–17, 321–2.

256 Gasparri 1994, 152–5.

importance as a regional centre dwindled. This may have been caused especially by the silting of the harbour; furthermore, the town experienced rising competition from Puteoli, which developed into one of the most important harbours of Italy at this time. Larger commercial farms, which emerged in almost every part of Italy in the second century, did not appear in Paestum. The new Via Popilia, built in 133, bypassed Paestum;[257] this was a sign of the declining importance of Paestum, and contributed further to its decline.

Various colonies were settled in southern Lucania after the Second Punic War: Thurii Copia, founded in 192 in a former Greek colony, had Latin rights. The economy was based mostly on animal husbandry and the exploitation of the Sila forest; the town seems to have had little impact beyond the local area.[258] In the late second and early first centuries, many small *villae* appeared in the valleys, while the number of small farms declined.[259] In this case, this may indeed be a sign of depopulation of the area, as there were few economic opportunities here.

Several colonies with Roman rights were founded shortly after the Second Punic War. Croton was founded in 194, also in a former Greek colony, but seems to have experienced economic difficulties immediately after its foundation: its size decreased, and there are no references to public buildings or temples. Only the harbour ensured that the city survived at all; it served as a point of export for products from the hinterland, such as copper, sulphur, and wood and pitch from the Sila forest.[260]

Buxentum, founded as a Roman colony in 194, was the only important centre in western Lucania in the second century. Its start was not very promising: eight years after its foundation, Buxentum had been abandoned by the settlers.[261] At this time, there were certainly more attractive options for settlement in Italy: many colonies were refounded after the Second Punic War, because they had suffered population decline during the war. Nevertheless, Buxentum was repopulated and became moderately successful. Wine was exported from the second century onwards, although *villae* did not appear until the late first century. Despite its relatively small economic role, the town had a large impact on the surrounding territory. In the fourth and third centuries, settlement had focused on the hill fort of Roccagloriosa, 15 kilometres to the north, with many small farms spread out around the fort. This fort disappeared in the second century; the number of settlement sites in the area grew, but they were now located in the vicinity of Buxentum rather than near Roccagloriosa. This attests to Buxentum's role as a regional centre.[262]

[257] Pedley 1990; Lomas 1993, 91, 116–17.

[258] Smurra 1989, 120.

[259] Sangineto 1994, 563–4, 579–80. [260] Mele 1993, 286–91. [261] Liv. 39.23.3–4.

[262] Gualtieri & Fracchia 2001, 79, 117; Gualtieri 2003, 156–9; Isayev 2007, 122.

Much of the land in Lucania and Bruttium was confiscated as *ager publicus*, but in the third and early second centuries, the Roman state did not use this land. It most likely remained in the hands of locals until the Gracchan land reform.[263] The Tanager valley (Val di Diano) was the most important area of *ager publicus* in northern Lucania. This area had traditionally interacted much with Tarentum and the other Greek colonies on the Ionian Sea. When their economy took a downturn after the establishment of Brundisium, the Tanager valley became a more important centre in the local economy. The Gracchi distributed great amounts of land here, leading to the immigration of Roman citizens. At the same time, various *villae* appeared here in the second half of the second century, such as Vittimose.[264] It measured 1,170 m^2 and had a large yard with *dolia*.[265] The residential section was modest, but had a small bathhouse. Many loom weights have been found; textiles were probably produced for household needs, but may have been sold on the market.[266]

Some scholars assume that the confiscation of land as *ager publicus* must have caused these changes; they identify these *villae* as 'Catonian',[267] with slave workers and absentee Roman landowners. However, these farms did not closely match Cato's description. Strikingly, *dolia* at Vittimose were stamped with the name Numerius Hercleidius, son of Paccius, clearly a local.[268] He may have been the owner of the *villa* or the producer of the *dolia*; in any case, as we have seen for other *villae*, local inhabitants were clearly connected to commercial production sites. As noted in the previous section, the Gracchi distributed land to small farmers, so that it is not easy to explain how the influx of these settlers led to the creation of *villae*.[269] However, an influx of Gracchan settlers obviously formed an attractive market for local producers, which may have led to an increase in wealth for local elites, such as Numerius Hercleidius.[270] Still, it seems as if the best agricultural land ended up in the hands of Gracchan settlers, while continuity of settlement is attested mostly near the earlier sanctuaries and hill forts.[271] This may have been an important reason for Italian discontent in the region in the

[263] Roselaar 2010, 71–84. [264] Isayev 2007, 175–83.

[265] Small & Buck 1994, 39; Gualtieri 2003, 140–1. For other larger farms appearing in the third and second centuries, see Gualtieri 2003, 136–69; Fracchia & Gualtieri 2011.

[266] Dyson 1992, 142.

[267] Pareti 1997, 429. See Kay 2014, 150 for S. Pietro di Tolve, which he calls 'a prototype of a Catonian villa'.

[268] Gualtieri 2003, 141. Coarelli 1981, 224–5 thinks he was the producer of the *dolium* rather than the *villa* owner, but his only argument is that it is more likely that a Roman was the *villa* owner, which makes little sense. See Gualtieri 2003, 141. See De Gennaro & Santoriello 2003, 50–3 on the local nobility.

[269] It is possible that the Gracchi granted Italians security of tenure on land up to a maximum of 500 *iugera* (Roselaar 2010, 248–9). The fact that the land was now held in private ownership may have encouraged investments in commercial agriculture.

[270] La Greca 2006, 34–5. [271] Isayev 2007, 181–3.

late second century—the inaccessibility of prime agricultural land limited their economic prospects.

In land that remained allied, significant economic changes were visible already in the late fourth and third centuries. Settlement in the fourth and third centuries had mostly been in hill forts and isolated farmsteads,[272] but many of these disappeared in the course of the third century or after the Second Punic War, as did the first phase of the farm at Civita di Tricarico.[273] This may in some cases have been caused by military action during the war, but for other locations, their disappearance seems to have been part of a wider development in settlement patterns throughout southern Italy. Rural sanctuaries, which appeared from the late fourth century onwards, also played a role as central places. Most of these again disappeared in the late third and early second centuries, although some remained in use until the first century.[274]

In allied areas, some agricultural sites developed into larger farms already in the late fourth or early third centuries, such as Masseria Ciccotti, Moltone di Tolve, and Mancamasone (Montelupino) in northern Lucania.[275] Moltone's first phase dates to the mid-fourth century; in the late fourth century, it was enlarged to 660 m^2. It was now fairly luxurious, with plastered walls and roof decorations of animals. This architectural phase resembles farms at Delos and elsewhere in Greece; it also had a bath similar to Greek and Sicilian examples.[276] Some argue that this layout mirrors Roman houses, suggesting that the house was therefore owned by a Roman,[277] but there is no evidence that this was the case. In fact, we have already seen that the house could very well have been owned by a local, as were other farms of this type.[278] As we have seen, medium and larger farms appeared in many parts of Italy around this time,[279] and it would be unwise to assume Roman ownership for all of these. Indeed, no Roman settlement in Lucania is attested in the fourth to early second centuries, so that locals could very well have owned these *villae*. Moltone was again enlarged in the early third century, but now with a larger focus on manufacture rather than luxury; it was finally abandoned in the early second century.[280]

The former Greek colonies in Lucania and Bruttium all remained allied until the Social War. Some Greek towns disappeared almost completely in the third and second centuries, such as Petelia, Laos, and Terina.[281] The reasons for this are

[272] De Cazanove 2004, 771–3.

[273] Isayev 2017, 163.

[274] Isayev 2007, 170–4; De Cazanove 2004, 776–7, 794–8; Senatore 2004, 305. On the sanctuary at Rossano, see Gualtieri 2008, 206.

[275] Fracchia & Gualtieri 1998–9, 298–304; Gualtieri 2003, 136, 169; Goffredo 2008, 289.

[276] Tocco 1990, 96; Small & Buck 1994, 38; Isayev 2007, 73–6; Goffredo 2008, 289.

[277] Tocco 1990, 95. She calls this a typical 'Catonian' villa, which appeared as the result of 'Romanization' (p. 98).

[278] Compatangelo-Soussignan 1999, 12. For other farms owned by locals, see De Lachenal 1993, 41; Morel 2009, 72.

[279] Terrenato 2007, 19.

[280] Isayev 2007, 75–6.

[281] Sartori 1975, 99, 103, 114.

difficult to identify: they may have suffered from Hannibal's depredations during the war, rather than from the Roman conquest.[282] Metapontum is often presented as the worst case: the late third century saw a sharp decline in the number of inhabited sites. Pottery finds from this period are also rarer. It is possible that this part of Lucania became less prosperous in general after the Roman conquest, since the most important land routes, especially the Via Appia, bypassed it in favour of a direct road from Venusia to Brundisium.[283] From the mid-second century, *villae* appeared in the area; it is likely that these were owned mostly by the local elite, as no Roman involvement is recorded in the area.[284] Regium, on the other hand, remained relatively prosperous; it was the most important harbour in southern Bruttium, close to Sicily, and therefore very important to the Romans. The nearby Sila forest, which was *ager publicus*, supplied timber and pitch for shipbuilding. Other important elements of its economy were fishing, wine production, and manufacturing.[285] In the third and second centuries, both the size of the town and the number of sites in the countryside grew.[286] Imported artefacts, such as vases, jewellery, and lamps, came from Alexandria and Asia Minor, but there was also local production, mostly copies of Eastern artefacts.[287]

In general, the economy of Lucania experienced some developments that were similar to many other areas in Italy, regardless of their civic status. Changes in settlement patterns were already underway when the Romans appeared on the scene: more fortified sites were built in the late fourth and early third centuries, as occurred in Apulia. Many of these were then abandoned in the later third century; the same goes for rural sanctuaries. The abandonment of hill forts may have been stimulated by new economic opportunities. In the pre-Roman period, there was less need for settlement close to rivers and the sea, because there was as yet not much opportunity for commercial production for the market. Now that new markets had opened up, and trade within Italy had become safer due to the pacification of the peninsula, Italians took the chance to profit from these opportunities and built new sites that were better connected to other parts of Italy.[288]

Animal husbandry played an important role in the economy of Lucania at all times and grew in importance in the second century. Horses, cows, pigs, and sheep were kept for milk, meat, wool, and leather.[289] It has been argued that this development took place mostly on *ager publicus* and was carried out by wealthy Romans. It has also been thought that the shepherds were mostly slaves, leading to

[282] Liv. 23.30-1-8. See La Torre 1997, 29.
[283] Giannotta 1980, 48–9; Desy 1993, 93; Lomas 1993, 91; Carter 2005, 243–8.
[284] Lomas 1993, 120.
[285] Plb. 24.2–3, Strab. 1.15–17. See Castrizio 1995, 53–4.
[286] Nucera 2008, 14, 26. [287] Castrizio 1995, 79–86. [288] Facella 2001, 60–1, 79.
[289] Simelon 1993, 46, although agriculture, e.g. wine and olive oil production, was also practised (pp. 49–57).

a decline in the free population. An important piece of evidence for this stance is the *Elogium Pollae*, dating to the late second century (see section 3.2.1), which describes how a Roman magistrate drove shepherds off their land and replaced them with farmers. This has been seen as evidence for large-scale displacement of agriculture by animal husbandry in Lucania, carried out by Roman elites and local landowners.[290] However, as discussed above, it is more likely that the inscription refers to the situation in Sicily, not in Lucania. Furthermore, we have seen that in some areas of Lucania, new *villae* for commercial production of crops—not just animals—appeared in the second century, as happened in most areas of Italy in this period. *Villae* along the western coast of Lucania produced wine, olive oil, and grain, some of which was exported by sea to Rome, while the those in the mountainous hinterland continued to focus on animal breeding.[291] As elsewhere, the appearance of *villae* in Lucania by no means spelled the end of small farms: many farms remained in use. Furthermore, there is no reason to assume that all or most locals lost their land: much of the land in Lucania remained allied rather than *ager publicus*. Even *ager publicus* was still exploited by locals, at least until the Gracchan period. In many cases, therefore, those investing in animal husbandry could very well have been local Lucanian and Bruttian elites.

3.3.5. Macroeconomic developments in Republican Italy

From this short survey, the most important conclusion is that economic developments varied widely from place to place, even over short distances. It is also clear that communities with the same civic status often experienced widely differing economic and cultural developments, while areas with different statuses often experienced similar developments. For example, some Latin colonies became important trade centres, such as Brundisium; others became production and trade centres on a regional scale, such as Fregellae, whereas others focused mostly on agricultural production for local markets, such as Cales and Venusia. Some, such as Paestum, even suffered economic decline, usually caused by specific local circumstances. Similarly, some Roman colonies fulfilled important economic roles, with some serving as export harbours, such as Minturnae and Puteoli, and to a lesser degree Regium. Others became important production centres, such as Sinuessa. There was not much difference between Latin and Roman colonies: when the circumstances were right, both types of colony could grow into prosperous cities, but both could fail as well. Thus, the colony's connections with Rome did not always lead to prosperity.

[290] Senatore 2004, 311. For *villae* in Bruttium in general, see Guzzo 1984, 234–5; Accardo 2000, 42–3, who both think all *villae* were owned by Romans rather than locals.

[291] De Lachenal 1993, xvii–xx; La Torre 1997, 31.

The presence of a colony could have a large impact on the surrounding territory. Much of the economic developments in central Apulia in the third and second centuries seem to have been caused by the establishment of Brundisium. We have seen that this colony developed into a very important export harbour, and that agricultural and pastoral products of Apulia were transported to Brundisium and from there further into the Mediterranean. This attracted immigration from nearby communities, to the extent that nearby sites declined or even disappeared. Even small colonies could have a significant effect on the local economy, e.g. Buxentum. On the other hand, some colonies hardly influenced the economy of the surrounding territory, such as the Latin colonies Interamna Lirenas and Luceria, and the Roman colony Sipontum.

Developments in allied territory varied as well. In Apulia and Lucania, some common developments throughout the area occurred in the late third and early second centuries. In most areas the third century first saw an increase in the number of sites, including towns, sanctuaries and *villae*. This trend has been identified in many archaeological surveys, both in lowland and upland areas, intermontane basins, and valleys, which suggests that only macroeconomic factors can explain this development.[292] The increase in sites is often associated with intensification of agricultural production. Many sites indeed show evidence of manuring, indicating intensification of production; more marginal areas were brought under intensive cultivation in the third century. More specialization in commercial crops, such as wine and olive oil, is also visible, especially on 'Hellenistic farms'.[293] Similar developments can also be discerned in many parts of Italy which have not been discussed in this book, for example, the Biferno valley in the Molise,[294] the Sangro valley in the Abruzzi,[295] the area around Reate in Sabinum,[296] and the Sinni valley[297] and Basentello valley in Lucania.[298] These developments were in many areas followed by a decline in the size of villages and the abandonment of many sanctuaries and *villae* in the late third and early second centuries. Finally, in the later second and early first centuries, more *villae* for commercial production appeared in most areas, although small farms always remained as well. There was not much difference in economic developments between areas that held Roman citizenship and those that did not. Most areas, whether colonies, *ager publicus*, or allied territory, show an increase in the number of *villae* in the late third and second centuries, which produced wine and olive oil for the market. A further increase in the number of *villae* in many cases occurred in the later second century, often in conjunction with a decline in the number of

[292] Attema, Burgers, & Van Leusen 2010, 161–4, 179.
[293] Attema & Burgers 2012.
[294] Lloyd & Barker 1981. [295] Lloyd, Lock, & Christie 1997.
[296] Coccia & Mattingly 1992. [297] Quilici & Quilici Gigli 2001. [298] Small & Small 2002.

small farms. This, however, cannot be seen as a symptom of economic decline or depopulation.[299]

Instead, these developments should be seen as a sign of expansion and transformation of economic networks, which, instead of focusing on the local and regional economy, now became part of a larger geographic network. This new economic framework was in part created by the Roman state: on the one hand the pacification—although by violent means—of large areas of the Mediterranean and the creation of a system for the settlement of disputes meant that trade between different peoples became easier. On the other hand, new markets were opened up for enterprising Italians, both in the city of Rome and in parts of the Mediterranean conquered by Rome. This offered new opportunities for profitable enterprise for those Italians willing and able to take their chances. Finally, the unification of coinage and legal systems (see chapter 4.2) greatly facilitated trade.

Because trade over longer distances became possible, it was no longer necessary for every region to provide only for its own needs. They could now spend more land and labour on the most profitable crops, while importing staple goods from elsewhere—to a certain degree, as most agricultural production was still focused on subsistence rather than commerce. Thus, the integration of the economy of Italy enabled regional specialization.[300] Each town or region created its own niche in the economic system; the decline in the number of small farms in some areas was a sign not of economic decline, but of the changed role of each area in the economic system of Italy. Thus some fundamental changes took place in the economic system, and only those sites that could become part of the new economic networks remained. The second century was clearly a turning point in the economic history of Italy, in which its economy came to be united more than ever before. This had an impact on all regions of Italy, and thus on all inhabitants of the peninsula, from elites to small farmers.[301] Of course, the extent of these changes should not be overestimated, since subsistence agriculture remained the most common form of agriculture throughout Italy. Still, the creation of new economic networks significantly affected both subsistence and commercial producers.

The city of Rome grew over time, and with it its impact on the Italian economy. In the early Republic, Rome did not yet dominate the economy of Italy: it was still relatively small and only a limited part of the Italian territory was needed to supply the city of Rome.[302] As the Roman state expanded, the economy of Italy started to focus more and more on Rome and the market it provided. More surpluses from central Italy were transported to Rome.[303] Therefore, producers in central Italy had excellent opportunities for profit from supplying Rome. However, although

299 Jongman 2003, 106, 112; Terrenato 2007, 19.
300 Morley 1996, 183.
301 Morley 1996, 108–34; Attema, Burgers, & Van Leusen 2010, 167–8.
302 Jongman 2003, 113–14; Rosenstein 2008.
303 Morley 1996, 110–14; Erdkamp 1998, 166–87.

Rome was by far the largest market in Italy, opportunities for Italians to supply this market were limited because of transport difficulties and related costs. Most crops were priced so low that it was not worth transporting them over long distances; only expensive, specialized products could be sold in far-away markets. Possibilities for trade therefore depended on the size of the market: most people lived at or near subsistence level, and although the aggregate demand of the lower classes was large, each individual market was small, and demand met by local production.[304] Areas on the western coast could send goods by ship, and some sent goods downriver to Rome, but for many inland areas of Italy, it was difficult to transport surpluses to Rome.[305] Producers in the north, east, and south of Italy therefore sought other markets, often overseas, as we saw in section 3.2. Furthermore, despite the size of the city of Rome, not everyone could get a share of the market. It is to be expected that Roman senators and *equites* supplied a large part of the goods needed to feed the urban population of Rome, leaving only a small share for Italian suppliers.[306] This means that trade within Italy could not have paid for the wealth displayed in many parts of Italy, strengthening the idea that much wealth was gathered in overseas trade.

As we saw in chapter 1.3, Finley argued that long-distance trade was intermittent and periodic, and involved only those items that could not be produced in the area itself, such as non-essential foodstuffs and luxury items.[307] He is right that most trade focused on such items—although wine and olive oil can hardly be called 'non-essential', given their ubiquity. However, this trade was not intermittent and periodic, but a continuous and regular aspect of the economy of Republican Italy. Contrary to Finley, the Italian economy was not cellular, but rather 'a system of interconnected sub-economies',[308] in which contacts between the different regions of Italy were frequent, even if most regions focused on their own subsistence. Of course, not all social groups were equally integrated into the international market: most farmers produced for subsistence or for the market in the nearest town.[309] Still, many small farmers gained access to some imported goods, as shown by the presence of imported wine amphorae and grave gifts in Samnium and Apulia.[310]

As we have seen in chapter 1, state institutions played a role in the degree of integration: states might influence the economy by taxation, the regulation of currency, price control, direct ownership of economic assets, and the purchase of goods for state purposes. However, the Roman state did not engage in most of these activities. The regulation of currency was haphazard and the state did not enforce price controls (see chapter 4.2.3). Furthermore, Rome did not actively

304 Morley 1996, 63–5.
305 Dyson 1992, 34.
306 Rosenstein 2008.
307 Finley 1999, 158–62.
308 Harris 1993, 29.
309 Bowman & Wilson 2009, 15–16.
310 Scopacasa 2015.

encourage commercial production and mercantile activities on the part of the Italians. It created favourable conditions by the conquest of the Mediterranean, but this was motivated by internal Roman affairs rather than by concerns for the welfare of the Italians. Rome was happy to offer the Italians protection (see chapter 4.7), but played only a limited role in the creation of economic networks. Rome functioned as a market for Italian products, but it was not the only market. Italians were free to find the best market for their products without Roman guidance, and clearly succeeded in doing so. Thus, it seems that opportunities on the free market played the greatest role in the economic integration of Italy. Local and regional fluctuations of supply and demand, leading to fluctuations in prices, were mitigated by activities on the free market, carried out by both Italians and Roman citizens.

As Witcher explains, as Rome's dominion expanded, the developments in the Italian economy can be described as a process of globalization. He lists ten characteristics of the 'global countryside', which indicate the interconnectedness of rural areas to global developments.[311] The most relevant for the Republican period are as follows:

1. *Elongation of commodity chains and increased dependency on imported commodities.* This applied to the Republican situation to a certain degree, since Rome itself became dependent on imported commodities, although these came mostly from Italy itself at this time. Italian towns did not depend on commodities from elsewhere, but often imported luxury items from abroad (as they had done before the Roman conquest).
2. *Externalization of property ownership and investment.* Although it is often argued that the Roman elites increasingly monopolized the use of the Italian countryside, I have argued that this was not the case. Instead, from the first century we see Italian elites owning property elsewhere in the Mediterranean, especially the East.
3. *Social power and economy are monopolized by fewer people and institutions.* This was true to a certain extent, as the Roman state increasingly monopolized political and economic power. As I will argue in chapter 5, the Italian elites succeeded in regaining power by the grant of citizenship after the Social War.
4. *The scaling up of social and political authority beyond local reach.* As we will see in chapter 5.3.1, Rome was increasingly able to demand almost anything from the Italians, and came to be seen as the ultimate arbitrator in Italian affairs. Nevertheless, Roman rule depended for its stability on the successful management of local affairs by local (Italian) leaders, and this remained the case throughout the Republican and Imperial periods.

311 Based on Woods 2007.

5. *Enhanced social polarization, so that the enterprising few have new opportunities to amass wealth but the majority do not.* Among Roman citizens, the second century certainly saw increased polarization, leading eventually to the Gracchan reforms. It is more difficult to establish whether the Italian areas also experienced increased inequality. In some areas this may indeed have occurred,[312] although in other cases, such as Pompeii, there seems to have been a fairly large middle class.[313]
6. *The countryside as a supplier of migrant labour.* As we have seen, mobility in Republican Italy was large, especially because of pull factors, such as seasonal wage labour and economic opportunities in the expanding towns of Italy.

An important characteristic of the global countryside is its diversity: towns and rural areas react to globalization in different ways. In each location, an 'ongoing dialogue between local and global' takes place, which leads to 'micropolitics of negotiation and hybridity'—in other words, a process of 'glocalization' (see chapter 1.5). Thus, not all areas or all social groups profit from increased globalization, although it does provide new economic and social opportunities for many.[314] This is indeed what happened in Italy in the Republican period: many areas profited, but to a varying degree in each location, while some did not profit at all, as discussed in sections 3.3.1–3.3.4.

3.4. Conclusion

Throughout this chapter, we have seen that Italians without Roman citizenship were involved in all kinds of economic activity in and outside of Italy. Trade relations between various Italian regions and between Italy and areas abroad had already existed in the pre-Roman period and continued after the Roman conquest. We find Italians active in the production and trade of wine and olive oil, pottery, and many other products that were exported to the western Mediterranean and the Greek East. All regions of Italy were involved in this trade, not just central Italy, but also the Adriatic coast, Apulia, and to a lesser degree Lucania and Bruttium. Each region had its own focus with regard to the markets it approached: people from western Italy traded mostly with Gaul, Iberia, Sicily, and Africa, while those on the Adriatic coast traded with Illyria and Greece. This brought the Italians considerable wealth, which was invested in public building in many locations in Italy, as we will see in chapter 4.3. The Roman state in general was content to leave the Italians to pursue their activities; in fact, the Romans contributed in some ways directly to the welfare of the Italians (see chapter 4.7).

[312] See Yntema 2006, 121–3 for parts of Apulia.
[313] Flohr & Wilson 2017, 15–16.
[314] Witcher 2017, 32–6; quotes p. 36.

Civic status was not directly relevant to economic developments: anyone, whether Roman citizen, Latin, or Italian ally, could profit from the economic opportunities created by the expansion of Roman dominance in the Mediterranean and the new markets that opened up. The Italian elites exploited these opportunities eagerly; although Finley argued that ancient economies were limited in their development by the lack of interest among the elites to pursue profitable activities,[315] this was certainly not the case for the Italian elites.[316] This led to a gradual integration of the Italian and Mediterranean economy, as the economies of these areas became increasingly globalized through Roman dominance.

Of course, not all Italians benefited in the same way from the new economic networks, as the changes in these networks caused changes in the role of individual towns and villages. Some regions specialized in production for the market, sometimes even in specific products.[317] Areas that could not find a meaningful way of participating in the economic network experienced economic decline or a decline in population. However, this does not mean that the Italian population overall declined. Changes in settlement patterns should rather be explained by migration, which occurred because of new opportunities elsewhere. Those who wanted to take part in the new economic network migrated to areas where they could find work, as shown by the fact that many towns grew in the second and first centuries. Not just Rome, but other Italian towns as well were targets for immigration.

The Romans sometimes contributed to economic developments directly—as in the case of Tarentum, where they slaughtered the population during the Second Punic War—or indirectly, by building roads and founding colonies. Most developments, however, were caused by the general development of Italian and Mediterranean economy under Roman rule. We might therefore speak of 'economic Romanization': Rome's conquest created a new economic system and thus influenced the peoples under its control, as well as the Mediterranean at large. However, economic developments did not depend just on Rome's actions or even on Rome as the largest market in the peninsula. Many areas traded abroad more often than with Rome itself, such as Apulia. Roman armies overseas formed a large market for Apulian products, and the Roman conquest of the Mediterranean made overseas trade easier and safer. However, it was the Apulians themselves who took the initiative to profit from these opportunities—not Roman elites arriving in Apulia from central Italy. Furthermore, Apulians traded not only with Rome's armies, but with many other partners in the Illyrian Sea and eastern Mediterranean.

All this does not mean that the Italians necessarily engaged with Romans in other ways, such as socially or politically. Italian elites did not view themselves as

[315] Finley 1999, 51–9.
[316] Andreau 1999; 2000; Rauh 1986b, 7–12; Kay 2014, 133–5.
[317] Morley 1996, 148–53.

Romans—as we will see, they considered themselves the social equals of the Roman elites, but they did not identify with Rome in the cultural sense. In fact, we will see (chapter 4.6) that at this time a common Italian identity emerged, which could be opposed to that of Rome. The same applies to small farmers: the disappearance of hill forts and sanctuaries and the appearance of larger commercial farms naturally affected these farmers' daily lives, but they may not have recognized these events as the result of the Roman conquest. Instead, they might have considered such developments as the result of developments in their own local and regional communities and the actions of their local leaders. They would have no reason to identify with Rome, since their lives remained focused on the local economy and local cultural events. Therefore, even if economic 'Romanization' occurred, this does not mean that cultural Romanization occurred as well, as we will see in chapter 4. On the contrary, the Italians eventually noticed that they did not receive the full benefits of the Roman conquest, which led them to take up arms against Rome, as we will see in chapter 5.

4
Consequences of Interaction
Institutional and Cultural Change

4.1. Introduction

So far, this book has focused on the various interactions that occurred between Romans and Italians and on the economic activities of the Italians. We have seen that Italians were very active in trade throughout the Mediterranean and profited from the new economic opportunities that came their way. At this point, we must look at the consequences of these activities for the integration of Italy in the Republican period. Although the degree of interaction between Romans and Italians, and between different Italic peoples, certainly increased, this does not necessarily mean that integration occurred in the cultural sense.

The first section of this chapter will look at institutional changes. We have seen (chapter 1.3) that institutions play an important role in either stimulating or limiting the economic possibilities of any state, and this was no different in the Republican period. The Roman state gradually developed several instruments that facilitated trade between Romans and Italians. At the same time, the Italian peoples experienced some changes in their own institutions, which seem to have been influenced in some ways by Roman practice. We will first investigate the role of laws regarding trade. Commercial relations between people of different states were hindered by the fact that the peoples of Italy did not have the same laws: the Italian allies were citizens of their own respective states, so that they were considered aliens with regard to Roman law. Specifically, Italians could not make use of the Roman *ius civile*, which was only accessible to Roman citizens. This meant that conflicts concerning trade between peoples of different states were difficult to solve, unless there was an efficient system of international legislation.

Commercial relations were also limited by the fact that Romans and Italians did not use the same currency. Many Italian towns minted their own coins—over sixty have been identified as striking coinage, in widely varying quantities. The economic unification of Italy is clearly visible through changes in Italian currency: as the Roman conquest of Italy progressed, many Italian towns adapted their coinage to that of the Romans. Eventually Roman coinage came to dominate Italy, while independent Italian currencies disappeared completely. In this chapter, we will review these changes in order to see whether coinage was an important instrument

Italy's Economic Revolution. Saskia T. Roselaar, Oxford University Press (2019). © Saskia T. Roselaar.
DOI: 10.1093/oso/9780198829447.001.0001

for the economic unification of Italy in the third to first centuries. Furthermore, the existence of reliable weights and measures is extremely important. Making sure that an exchange used correct measurements took time and effort, raising transaction costs. Many different units of weight and measurements were in use in Italy, which slowed down economic transactions. As with coinage, these units became more uniform as time progressed; in many cases, however, this occurred rather late, in the first century.

In section 4.3, we will investigate how the profits of the various economic activities described in chapter 3 were invested by the Italians. Some profits were probably invested in agriculture and manufacture, which both increased in scale, as we have seen. Furthermore, profits were spent on conspicuous consumption, attested by public and private building projects. We will analyse who paid for this and whether there is any connection between economic activities and investment in Italy. Thus we will be able to discern the effects of the economic activities pursued by the Italians, as described in the previous chapter.

Sections 4.4 and 4.5 will briefly trace the cultural and linguistic integration of Italy. It is to be expected that the frequency and intensity of contacts with Rome, as described in chapter 2, affected the integration of Italy into the Roman framework; areas that interacted often with Rome might be expected to have experienced more cultural change and at a quicker pace. In chapter 3, we investigated whether areas with specific civic statuses—that is, varying levels of political integration—experienced different economic developments than areas that were less 'Romanized' politically. However, cultural change in Italy was complex and proceeded at different speeds in different areas. These sections will therefore re-evaluate commonly held ideas about 'Romanization', especially the idea that all cultural change occurring in Italy after the Roman conquest should be explained by the impact of Rome.

As we saw in chapter 1, 'Romanization' was not a conscious aim of the Roman state; Italians did not necessarily feel 'Roman' because they were now parts of Rome's dominion. Rather than a 'Roman' identity, the Italians came to share a common identity between them. Section 4.6 will investigate changes in identity as expressed by the Italians in the middle and late Republican period. As time progressed, the idea of 'Italia' as a geographical unit, and its people as 'Italians', slowly emerged. Although this development was not coordinated by Rome, we will see that Rome's activities directly affected the way the Italians saw themselves, and the identity they chose to adopt. Thus, a clearer Roman-Italian dichotomy slowly emerged, as became fully clear at the start of the Social War in 91.

Finally, the last section of this chapter will discuss the active engagement of the Roman state in the economic well-being of the allies. Rome realized that it was important to ensure the economic well-being of the allies. On the one hand, the allies needed to have sufficient wealth to outfit the soldiers they sent to Rome's armies. On the other hand, the allies needed to feel that their association with

Rome was worthwhile, otherwise they might revolt. Therefore, the state protected its allies when they traded overseas. Furthermore, Rome sometimes included its allies in the benefits of empire, e.g. by imposing favourable tax regulations. We will investigate how much of these efforts by the Romans were the result of a concerted policy, and how effective they were.

Thus, this chapter will show that the consequences of the Roman conquest of Italy were significant, but also that they varied widely between the different peoples of Italy. This chapter will therefore allow us to reconsider the concept of 'Romanization' and suggest possible alternatives for viewing the developments in Italy in this period.

4.2. Legal and Institutional Instruments for Interaction

4.2.1. Legal developments

As interaction between the peoples of Italy became more common and occurred on a larger scale than before, this had an important impact on the legal and institutional instruments that the Italic peoples used to maintain commercial relations. The fact that the Italian states remained independent and therefore used their own laws meant that the institutions prevailing in Italy were not immediately suited to stimulate trade. Therefore, the Romans, as well as the Italians, needed to deal with the fact that their citizens carried out commercial relations with people from other states.

Roman law of the early Republic was inadequate to deal with disputes between Romans and *peregrini*: the latter had no access to the *ius civile*, which permitted the use of the *legis actiones*. These were highly formalized methods to solve disputes, in which exact formulae of speech and gesture had to be observed in order for the trial to be valid. There were several types of *actiones*, each dealing with a specific problem or crime; if the case did not fit any of the *actiones*, a trial was not allowed. Many issues could not be solved by the *legis actiones* and therefore were not permissible in court at all. Most importantly, *peregrini* were not admitted to these instruments, so that the Roman legal system could not accommodate disputes involving *peregrini*.[1]

From the fourth century, when Rome's conquests in Italy expanded the territory under its control, new legal instruments were gradually developed. The large number of innovations in legal instruments, which gradually became more and more inclusive, indicates that there was sufficient contact between citizens and non-citizens—and therefore more disputes involving *peregrini*—to make provisions to facilitate them. The most important change was the gradual adoption of

[1] Gaius 4.11–31. See Kaser 1996, 44–60, 64–81; Metzger 2013, 17–18; Tellegen-Couperus 2002, 21–4.

the formulary system. In some ways this resembled the *legis actiones*, specifically in the fact that lawsuits still proceeded in two phases: in the first phase the praetor decided whether to allow the case to go ahead, and if so, which formula would be used. In the second phase, the facts of the case were heard by the judge (*iudex*). At the start of the year, the praetor issued an edict in which he announced which types of disputes he would allow in his court and which instruments he would use to solve these. He also provided templates for model clauses for the actions and defences to be used, which resulted in the *formula*: a short instruction to the judge, setting out the main issue under dispute and under what circumstances the judge should find in favour of the plaintiff.[2]

In the formulary system, the praetor—first created in 366—was especially important in creating new formulae. If there was no suitable existing *formula*, the praetor could create a new one. This could happen through the so-called *actiones utiles*, which adapted an existing *formula*, or through *actiones in factum*, which created a new *formula* based on the facts of the case. When a *formula* had been used successfully, it could then be added to the praetor's edict in the following year, establishing it as a legitimate *formula*. Thus, the *ius civile* eventually was supplemented by the *ius honorarium*, the body of law created by the magistrates of the Roman state, especially the praetor.[3] If the *ius civile* could not be applied, the praetor could issue an *actio ficticia*. This ordered the judge to proceed as if something were the case, although it was not. In some cases, it was possible to proceed as if a *peregrinus* were a Roman citizen.[4] The fiction allowing for the treatment of *peregrini* as citizens is usually thought to have been introduced in the second century, probably under the influence of treaties of mutual assistance concluded with Greek states in this period.[5]

A second praetor was added in 241. The senior praetor now became known as the *praetor urbanus* ('city praetor'), while the junior one was called *praetor peregrinus* or *praetor inter peregrinos* ('foreign praetor' or 'praetor over foreigners').[6] This addition of a second praetor does not necessarily point to a change in the law; we cannot assume that *peregrini* only now started to receive assistance from the praetor. It is more likely that the second praetor was introduced because the number of disputes had become so large that a single praetor could no longer manage them. Before the creation of the *praetor peregrinus*, *peregrini* could approach the single praetor.[7] Much debate has centred around the issue of who had access to the *praetor peregrinus*. Some scholars argue that the praetor created in 241 only adjudicated cases between foreigners, and that cases between a Roman

[2] Gaius 4.30–187. See Kaser 1996, 220–382; Tellegen-Couperus 2002, 21–4; Metzger 2013, 21–5.

[3] Tellegen-Couperus 2002, 48–59; Metzger 2013, 22–3.

[4] Gaius 4.37.

[5] Sotty 1977; Vicente Jordá 1999, 225–56; Coşkun 2009a, 49–50; Winkel 2013; Ando 2015.

[6] Joh. Lydus, *De Magistr.* 1.38, 45; Liv. *Per.* 19; *Dig.* 1.2.2.27–8. See Daube 1951.

[7] Brennan 2000, 85–9.

and a foreigner were settled by the *praetor urbanus*.[8] However, it seems unlikely that the second praetor was assigned to judge cases between *peregrini* only. The Roman state was first and foremost concerned with the interests of its citizens, so that there was no need to cater especially to disputes between foreigners.[9] The earliest epigraphic evidence for the title is the *lex repetundarum* of 123–122, which mentions the *pr(aetor) quei inter peregrinos ious deicet* ('praetor who judges between foreigners').[10] Livy uses the phrase *ius inter peregrinos dicere* for the year 189,[11] but in other instances he says *praetor inter cives ac peregrinos* ('between citizens and foreigners').[12] It is likely that the word *inter* should be read as 'having authority over', rather than the more intuitive 'between', in analogy with the *quaestio inter sicarios et veneficiis* ('court to judge murderers and poisoners'), established in the 140s.[13] The *praetor peregrinus* in that case was authorized to judge lawsuits involving foreigners, but it is unlikely that this function was created to cater to foreigners only. I believe therefore that the *praetor peregrinus* mainly judged cases between Romans and *peregrini*, but could also be called upon to judge between two *peregrini*.[14]

Over time, other new instruments of law were developed. For example, because the *ius civile* offered very limited possibilities for transferring property and the *legis actiones* were not accessible to *peregrini*, more and simpler ways of transferring property were created, which were also available to *peregrini*. *Traditio* was the easiest and was already used in the archaic period. This simply consisted of handing over the item to the buyer. This was joined, perhaps already in the fifth century, by *stipulatio*.[15] This was originally only permissible to citizens, because it required a specific Latin formulation, but it soon became possible to give a *stipulatio* in other languages than Latin, as long as both parties understood one another. A *stipulatio* could be used to enter into all kinds of contract, such as buying and selling, lease, credit, etc.[16]

Especially in the third and second centuries, many new legal instruments appeared. The *bonae fidei iudicia* ('judgements of good faith') were created in the second century. These instruments gave the judge full power to decide the matter if both parties had acted in good faith. They protected the contracts of *emptio-venditio* (buying and selling), *locatio-conductio* (leasing and hiring), *societas* (partnership), and *mandatum* (performance of services). The contract of *emptio-venditio* was probably the earliest of these, and had emerged by *c.*200, *locatio-conductio* in the mid-second century, and *mandatum* by 123.[17] Such contracts were also accessible to *peregrini*; they were simple agreements between two people, who required no special status.

[8] Daube 1951, 67. [9] Brennan 2000, 85–9. [10] *Lex repetundarum* l. 12.
[11] Liv. 37.51.6. [12] Liv. 35.41.6, 39.8.2, 39.38.2, 45.12.13.
[13] Dig. 48.8; Cic. *Clu.* 21, 144. [14] Raggi 2010.
[15] Gaius 3.93, 116–20. See Terpstra 2013, 60. [16] Chiusi 2011, 32–3.
[17] Watson 1961, 12–13; Wegner 1969, 61–4.

The *actiones adiecticiae qualitatis* should likely also be dated to the second century. The *actio exercitoria* made a father or master responsible for the actions of his son or slave who engaged independently in business matters. The *actio institoria* made fathers and masters responsible for sons or slaves appointed as managers of estates or shops. These *actiones* were clearly intended to facilitate commerce, and responded to situations that had become increasingly common in economic reality.[18] Thus, they reflect the increased complexity of commercial arrangements in this period, as well as the willingness of Roman lawmakers to take into account the interests of commerce. As we will see in section 4.2.3, a similar awareness of market developments was visible in the developments of Roman currency.

Peregrini were also protected against disruption of their possession by the possessory interdicts. The *interdictum uti possidetis* protected a person who was in actual possession of an item, provided he had not obtained it 'by violence, stealth, or on sufferance' (*vi*, *clam*, or *precario*) from the other party. The burden of proof was thus laid on the plaintiff rather than the defendant. Through an *interdictum utrubi*, the possession of a movable thing was declared to belong to the party who had held it for the greatest part of the past year. The *interdictum unde vi* protected someone who had been driven by force from his possession. The praetor could grant such an interdict to the plaintiff, without the need for a full lawsuit. These interdicts probably existed since the late third or early second century and could be granted also to *peregrini*.[19]

Many scholars assume that the most important instrument by which *peregrini* could receive the right to trade with Roman citizens was the *commercium* or *ius commercii*, translated as 'right to trade'.[20] It is usually assumed that *commercium* was a right that could be granted to non-citizens, and permitted them the use of Roman legal instruments pertaining to trade, such as *mancipatio*, which were otherwise only available to citizens. Many scholars believe that *commercium* was essential for trade between Romans and *peregrini*, since it enabled *peregrini* to conclude contracts with Romans that could be upheld in Roman courts of law.[21] A common follow-up assumption is that trade between Romans and *peregrini* was rare, because *peregrini* either were not allowed to trade with Romans, or did not want to run risks due to their inferior legal position;[22] or conversely, that

[18] Kaser 1960; Watson 1961, 5–6; Harris 2000, 285.

[19] Festus 260-2L mentions Aelius Gallus (*fl.* 170–150) as the oldest authority; see Gaius 4.160. In Ter. *Eun.* 319–20, written *c.*161, one of the characters says: 'obtain her for me either by force, stealth, or entreaty.' This seems a clear reference to the *interdictum uti possidetis*. Plaut. *Stich.* 696 refers to the *interdictum utrubi*. The *interdictum unde vi* is mentioned in the *Lex agraria* of 111, ll. 18–19; see also Cic. *Leg. Agr.* 3.11. See Brunt 1987, 553; Crawford 1996, 164; Kaser 1996, 408–21; Metzger 2013, 15–16.

[20] For *commercium* and *conubium* in more detail, see Roselaar 2013a; 2013b.

[21] Sherwin-White 1973, 125; Bispham 2007, 74.

[22] Mouritsen 1998, 92.

commercium was common among Latin and/or Italian allies, since a great amount of trade between Romans and Italians occurred.[23]

However, in this discussion it is essential to distinguish between *res mancipi* and *res nec mancipi*. *Res mancipi* were certain items, namely *Ager Romanus* (land owned by Roman citizens or the Roman state), buildings on *Ager Romanus*, slaves, horses, mules, cattle, and certain rustic servitutes. These items could only be transferred through *mancipatio*, also called *per aes et libram*. This was a ceremonial sale, carried out according to ancient ritual.[24] Only Roman citizens could transfer property by this method. If a foreigner wanted to transfer such items, it is usually assumed that he needed the right to participate in the transfer of *res mancipi*. This could be achieved by either gaining citizenship or the *ius commercii*.[25] The idea that *commercium* was necessary for trade in all items is therefore, in my view, incorrect. The only limitations on trade concerned *res mancipi*.[26]

It is indeed likely that some legal restrictions existed concerning trade in *res mancipi*: trade in *res mancipi* between a Roman and a *peregrinus* without official access to *mancipatio* did not enjoy the protection of Roman law courts.[27] However, *peregrini* could certainly trade *res mancipi* with Romans, if one party was unable to participate in *mancipatio*; in such cases, ownership could be transferred by *traditio*.[28] *Peregrini* who traded *res mancipi* without *mancipatio* were not automatically protected in the case of a dispute. Therefore, those who had the right to trade in *res mancipi* had a much stronger position when a dispute arose, because the onus of proof was on the person challenging the ownership, rather than on the apparent owner.

However, as we have seen, the praetor played an important role in protecting *peregrini* dealing with Romans. By means of an *actio ficticia*, the praetor could treat the plaintiff as a Roman citizen, when in fact he was not.[29] This means that *peregrini* who disputed a *res mancipi*, even if they did not have the right to participate in *mancipatio*, might have been able to gain recognition in a Roman court of law. On the other hand, protection was not certain, as the praetor did not automatically apply such fictions. Therefore, not having the right to access the *ius civile* was still a problem for a *peregrinus*: he could never be certain that his ownership would be protected by the praetor.[30] Having the right to participate in *mancipatio*, which brought protection in the courts, remained an important privilege.

[23] Salmon 1967, 315; Ilari 1974, 13–29; Galsterer 1976, 103; Keaveney 1987, 48–9.

[24] Gaius 1.119–20. See Kaser 1960, 107.

[25] A separate *ius mancipii* is postulated by some scholars (Kaser 1953, 140–4; Kremer 2006, 13–14), but its existence cannot be proved, see Coşkun 2009a, 42–5; Roselaar 2013a.

[26] Ilari 1974, 13 n. 30; Coşkun 2009a, 39–47.

[27] Bernardi 1973, 84; Kremer 2006, 11; 2014, 229.

[28] Kaser 1953, 151–2; Vicente Jordá 1999, 196–209; Mayer-Maly 2003, 6.

[29] Vicente Jordá 1999, 225–56; Coşkun 2009a, 49–50; Chiusi 2011, 33; Ando 2015.

[30] Kaser 1953, 137.

Further limitations on economic relations may have been created by the lack of *conubium*, the right that allowed *peregrini* to marry Roman citizens.[31] A lack of *conubium* could have serious consequences for inheritances within families that included people of different civic statuses. For example, if a Roman father had a *peregrinus* son, the son could not inherit from his father, which would severely damage his economic opportunities. The possession of *commercium* and *conubium* was strongly connected to a third privilege, *ius migrationis*, as we will discuss next.

In discussing the economic relations of the Italian allies (who were *peregrini*) with Roman citizens, it is important to distinguish between Latins and other allies. Within the group of Latins, it is necessary to distinguish further between ethnic Latins—that is, people from Latium—and people living in colonies with so-called Latin rights. It is often thought that the ethnic Latins collectively had been granted *conubium*, *commercium*, and *ius migrationis* by the *Foedus Cassianum* of 493 and retained this after the Latin War, ending in 338.[32] However, the evidence for this is weak. In my view, the only evidence for the existence of these three rights applies to those who lived in Latin colonies.

A passage from Livy dating to 177 has often been interpreted as evidence for the existence of *commercium* and *ius migrationis* for Latin colonists. It discusses the various (fraudulent) ways in which Latin colonists attempted to gain Roman citizenship:

> By law Latin allies were entitled to become Roman citizens as long as they left a son of their own at home. In abusing this law some men committed an injustice against the allies and some against the Roman people. To avoid the necessity of leaving a son at home, men would hand their sons over (*mancipio dabant*) as slaves to anyone with Roman citizenship, on the condition that the sons would be manumitted; and as freedmen become citizens. Men with no offspring to leave behind adopted sons to become Roman citizens.[33]

The expression *mancipio dabant* suggests that Latins, who handed over their sons as slaves—which were *res mancipi*—to Roman citizens, were allowed to use *mancipatio*, and therefore that they held *commercium*.[34] However, as we have

[31] See in detail Roselaar 2013b.

[32] Sherwin-White 1973, 32–7, 109–16; Humbert 1978, 98–108; Cornell 1995, 295–7; Laffi 1995, 51.

[33] Liv. 41.8.8–10: *Lex sociis nominis Latini, qui stirpem ex sese domi relinquerent, dabat, ut cives Romani fierent. Ea lege male utendo alii sociis, alii populo Romano iniuriam faciebant. Nam et ne stirpem domi relinquerent, liberos suos quibusquibus Romanis in eam condicionem, ut manu mitterentur, mancipio dabant, libertinique cives essent; et quibus stirps deesset, quam relinquerent, ut <...> cives Romani fiebant.* See Laffi 1995.

[34] Galsterer 1976, 103; Laffi 1995, 54; Tarpin 2014, 163. Sirks 2014, 173–4 criticizes my interpretation in Roselaar 2013b, in which I argued that this passage shows that Latin colonists held *commercium*. Sirks argues that the sons were not sold as slaves, but given as free men to a Roman citizen, who then, through *usucapio* of one year, acquired *mancipium* over the son. The Roman could then free the son from his *mancipium*, after which he was free to move to Rome. This is indeed a more likely

seen, *res mancipi* were also transferable by *traditio*. This passage therefore does not prove that all Latin colonists possessed *commercium*. It does shed light on the *ius migrationis*, however: the Latins' right to migrate to Rome was subject to a specific condition, namely to leave a son behind in the colony. They could not simply move to Rome without leaving a son behind, nor could sons migrate to Rome at the same time as their fathers. This is shown by a further instance in 187, when the Romans were asked by some Latin colonies to return to them people who had moved to Rome.[35] Rome then ordered these people to return home. However, if all Latins had the right to migrate to Rome, then the Roman state could not expel them—they could only migrate if they left a son behind, as became clear in 177.

Since many Latin colonists were originally from Rome,[36] it makes sense that they were allowed to return to Rome, as long as they left a son behind in their colony. Having an opportunity to return made it more attractive for Roman citizens to join a colony. For the state, this arrangement assured that the colonies, which were strategically important, remained at full strength. A similar concern lay behind the rule that the inhabitants of colonies with Roman citizenship status (the so-called *coloniae maritimae*) were not allowed to spend more than thirty days at a time outside the colony.[37] It makes sense if the requirement to leave a son behind in the colony had been in place since colonies began to be established by Rome on its own, after 338. The law requiring colonists to leave a son behind was thus not cancelled, but rather reinforced in 177.[38] There is no reason why it would not have remained in force and why those who acted within the law would not have been allowed to use their right to migrate. I therefore argue that Latin colonists, both before and after 177, were allowed to become Roman citizens upon moving to Rome, but that they were obliged to leave a son behind in order to ensure that the manpower of the Latin colonies remained at full strength. There is

interpretation, so that the text does not absolutely prove that the Latin colonists held *commercium*. However, I disagree with Sirks' assumption that the text refers to non-colonist Latins, since he assumes Latin colonists held *ius migrationis* and were therefore free to move to Rome—correct, but their sons did not, and the whole point of the Latins' deception was to make it possible for their sons to leave the colony with their fathers. It is likely that the text refers to Latin colonists only, since the Roman state cared little about the population of other Latin towns.

35 Liv. 39.3.4–5.

36 Cornell 1995, 367–8.

37 In the case of Roman citizen colonies, which were intended as coastal garrisons, intricate regulations existed to maintain the colonist contingent at full strength; see Humbert 1978, 115–16; Roselaar 2009. Erdkamp 2011, 124–36 argues that Latin colonists were allowed to migrate wherever they wished. However, the examples he gives, e.g. the abandonment of Sipontum and Buxentum in 186 (which were in fact Roman, not Latin, colonies; see Liv. 39.23.3), show that the Roman state was highly concerned about the manpower of its colonies: it repopulated the colonies immediately. Mouritsen 1998, 94 thinks that a grant of Roman citizenship gave Italians *ius migrationis* and thus allowed them to move, but this makes no sense; Roman citizens, except the inhabitants of *coloniae maritimae*, were free to move wherever they wanted. Italians were in any case free to move, since the Roman state did not regulate the movements of non-citizens; see Isayev 2017, 36–8.

38 *Contra* Humbert 1978, 114; Tarpin 2014, 173.

no reason to assume that ethnic Latins, or any other Italians, were subject to a law that required them to leave a son behind in their town, nor that they had the right to become citizens when moving to Rome. The *ius migrationis* thus only applied to Latin colonists.[39] This indeed matches the assumption that mobility in Republican Italy was large, as is generally accepted in current scholarship.[40] Rome could not, nor did it intend to, impose any limitations on the mobility of Italians, other than Latin colonists.

If we now return to the importance of Livy's passage for the issue of *commercium*, I suggest that Latin colonists were granted *commercium* and *conubium*, together with *ius migrationis*, as a standard package. This may have been laid down in the charters that were set up when the colonies were established, although we have no examples from the middle Republic. Examples from later periods, such as the *lex Irnitana*, offer detailed regulations about changes in civic status; this law also ensures that a change in status would not sever previous family ties.[41] It would make sense if such regulations had also existed for the Latin colonies settled in the Republican period. This would have been necessary especially for reasons of inheritance: if many settlers were of Roman origin, they would have wanted to receive inheritances from or bequeath to their family members who had remained Roman citizens. The possession of *conubium* was closely connected to *commercium*: since inheritances could include *res mancipi*, *peregrini* could not inherit from Romans without being allowed to take part in *mancipatio*. Therefore, if Latin colonists received *commercium* as a privilege, it would make sense that they also received *conubium*. Having *commercium* meant that they were to defend their ownership of *res mancipi* that were included in inheritances in the Roman courts.[42] If Latin colonists were granted the three rights *commercium*, *conubium*, and *ius migrationis* as a standard 'package', this would on the one hand ensure that the manpower of the colonies remained at full strength, and at the same time make joining a colony more attractive, because the colonists could maintain relations with their families in Rome and in other Latin colonies, who would still be able to inherit from and bequeath to them.[43]

As for the Italian allies, there is little evidence that they all possessed *conubium*. A passage in Diodorus has been seen as evidence that some Italian allies enjoyed *conubium*: in a battle during the Social War, soldiers from both parties recognized

[39] Broadhead 2002; Coşkun 2009b, 70–200, esp. 107–10. Kremer's 2014 attempt to argue in favour of the *ius migrationis* as applying to all Latins is unconvincing.

[40] See Isayev 2017 for the most recent overview of mobility in ancient Italy.

[41] Lex Irnitana ch. 21–3.

[42] Sirks 2014, 173 argues that *res mancipi* could be transferred by *traditio*, and that therefore a grant of *commercium* or *conubium* was not necessary for Latin colonists to receive *res mancipi* through inheritance. However, if someone who was not permitted to use *mancipatio* received a *res mancipi* through *traditio*, his legal status in the case of a dispute was weak.

[43] Bernardi 1973, 68 argues that there was no *conubium* between the colonists of different colonies, but this is unlikely, since members of the same family might go to different colonies.

each other as 'men whom the law governing intermarriage had united in this kind of friendly tie'.[44] Some scholars argue on the basis of this passage that all *socii* possessed *conubium*,[45] but this is very unlikely; some of the Italian rebels were Latins, such as those from the Latin colony Venusia. Furthermore, there were *socii* fighting on both sides, so it is more likely that people from different allied states had married each other, which was certainly allowed (see chapter 2). In any case, we cannot draw conclusions from this statement, which mostly aimed for rhetorical effect by indicating how closely the two sides were related.

A separate group were the *cives sine suffragio*. Since they were *cives*, it could be assumed that they were subject to Roman *ius civile* and therefore had *conubium* with Romans.[46] The Campanians, who received this status as a reward in 338, indeed married Romans, as shown by their considerations before they joined Hannibal in the Second Punic War: 'the only circumstances which prevented them from immediately revolting were the old established right of intermarriage (*conubium vetustum*) which had led to many of their illustrious and powerful families becoming connected with Rome and the fact that several citizens were serving with the Romans.'[47] After Rome recaptured Capua in 211, its leaders were punished with the loss of their *civitas*. They appealed to the Romans, stating that 'they were for the most part Roman citizens, connected with Roman families by ancient ties of marriage (*conubio vetusto*)'.[48] There is indeed some evidence for marriage between Romans and Campanians: Pacuvius Calavius, leader of Capua in the Second Punic War, had married a daughter of Appius Claudius (*cos* 212), and Calavius' daughter had married M. Livius (*cos.* 219, 207).[49] Other *cives sine suffragio* most likely enjoyed the same rights of marriage and trade with Romans.

In short, I argue that *commercium*, *conubium*, and *ius migrationis* were not widespread among the Italian allies. *Conubium*, *commercium*, and *ius migrationis* formed clearly defined instruments of Roman hegemony, which were used to maintain the strength of the Latin colonies. Thus they served a military purpose; military duties were the most important duties that the allies fulfilled, in the eyes of Rome. The Roman state was not eager to grant these rights to anyone else, including Italian allies; the three rights—separately or together—could be granted as rewards for loyalty, whether to individuals or to towns or peoples, but the recorded number of such grants is limited. As we will see in chapter 5, the Roman state was not usually willing to share the privileges of its citizenship with others.[50]

[44] Diod. 37.15.2.

[45] Galsterer 1976, 103; *contra* Bernardi 1973, 83; Coşkun 2009a, 38 n. 78.

[46] Sherwin-White 1973, 125.

[47] Liv. 23.4.7.

[48] Liv. 26.33.3. See Liv. 31.31.11: 'we had forged links with [the Campanians] first by a treaty, subsequently by marriage and family ties (*conubio atque cognationibus*)...'

[49] Liv. 23.2.6.

[50] Coşkun 2009b.

The Latin status, far from being an integrative force in the peninsula under Roman rule,[51] in fact served to separate Latins from Romans and Latins from other allies. It is possible that the Latin status became more 'integrative' from the late second century, when the introduction of the *civitas per magistratum* (see chapter 5.4) contributed to the integration of the elites of Latin towns into the Roman state.

So far we have seen, therefore, that it was perfectly possible for Romans and Italians to trade with each other. In chapter 3, we have seen that many Italians were involved in trade with Rome, and that many regions were connected with each other through commercial relations. Most trade occurred in *res nec mancipi*, especially foodstuffs, but also pottery and luxury items. The only *res mancipi* that can be assumed to have played an important role in trade were land and slaves. That trade in slaves took place between Romans and Italians may be assumed from the composition of the population of Delos: this island, a central node in the slave trade, attracted both Roman citizens and Italians. However, legal barriers, which in theory were still in place, seem to have been of very little importance in these activities.

4.2.2. Italian administration and institutions

All Italian allies were part of their own independent states with their own government. In many cases, they were organized as city-states, although in some cases the Italians may have been organized in leagues or other structures.[52] Each Italian state had its own laws, but unfortunately, there is very little evidence for Italian laws. The main sources are three long inscriptions—the *tabula Bantina (TB)* and the *cippus Abellanus (CA)* in Oscan, and the *tabulae Iguvinae (TI)* in Umbrian—as well as some shorter inscriptions, all dating to the relatively late period, the second and early first centuries. These sources show that legal and administrative concepts in Italy were influenced by Roman law, especially by the use of Latin terms for administrative concepts and institutions. This may suggest that the frequency of relations between Rome and Italy was increasing, and that the Italians applied useful concepts in Roman law and administration to their own states.

As regards the administration of towns, the sources show a large degree of influence from Roman titles for magistrates. For example, the Roman terms quaestor, aedile, censor, senate, legate, *praefectus*, *imperator*, *civis*, and *comitia* all appear in Oscan texts: *kvaísstur* or *kvestur*, *aídil*, *censtur* or *keenzstur*, *senateís*, *lígatúís*, *praefucus*, *embratur*, *ceus*, and *comono*. These texts come from widely

[51] As assumed, for example, by Sherwin-White 1973, 98.

[52] It is not always clear how the Italian states were structured; for example, it is often thought that the Samnites were organized in a league (Salmon 1967, 80–7), but this is not clearly attested. See Stek 2009, 546–54; Isayev 2017, 335–6.

varying locations in Italy, before the grant of citizenship.[53] However, not all these magistracies appear regularly: censors, aediles, quaestors, and *tribuni plebis* are rare. Thus, local magistracies could take different configurations depending on local needs, whether or not they were derived from Roman examples in name or in function.

The adoption of Latin titles in the epigraphic evidence does not necessarily mean that Italian states adopted the administrative systems of Rome. In some cases, Italians may have indeed adopted new administrative systems, based on the example of Rome. The *tabula Bantina*, for example, is a charter for the village of Bantia in Lucania, written in both a Latin and Oscan version. There is much controversy about the date of the Oscan text, which is assumed to be later than the Latin. Whether the Oscan version was written before or after the Social War cannot be determined. It is likely that the Bantians used a Roman model for their text, perhaps from the nearby Latin colony Venusia. The Oscan text may have been written to symbolize independence from Rome and could therefore have been written during the Social War. In this case, Venusia would be an especially suitable example, since it, as the only Latin colony, revolted against Rome. As we will see, other elements of the administrative structures set up by the Italian rebels were also heavily influenced by Roman practice, such as coinage. In any case, the *lex Osca tabulae Bantinae* cannot date to a much later period, since, as the editors of the text argue, some elements in the text are incompatible with the municipal structure established in first-century Italy.[54]

The *tabula Bantina* is thus not a representative example of the use of Latin in Italian administration, since it was written under rather peculiar circumstances and at a relatively late date. In the other texts that have survived, it seems that Italian towns did not change their pre-existing administrative structures, but only changed the titles of magistrates to their Latin equivalents.[55] For example, many towns already had a local council of elders and now adopted the title *senatus* for this body. Although it makes sense to suppose that such Latinized titles were only used in inscriptions aimed at a Roman audience, their origins speak against this. The *cippus Abellanus*, for example, was a treaty between the towns of Nola and Abella, and was not aimed at a Roman audience. In fact, it uses not only the titles

[53] Porzio Gernia 1970, 98–100. In *tabula Bantina* l. 2, *q* appears as an abbreviation of quaestor, showing that even the Latin habit of abbreviating terms was adopted. Another inscription from Bantia records a *tr(ibunus) pl(ebis)* (Torelli 1995, 133). A *keenzstur* at Pietrabbondante appears in *Imagines* Terventum 8=Rix Sa 4; a Marsian *cetur* in *Imagines* Antinum 1=Rix VM 3. There are a senate, praetors, aediles, and quaestors at Falerii (CIE 8036–41), aediles and quaestors at Pompeii (*Imagines* Pompei 8–9, 13, 24=Rix Po 1, 3, 5–6), a senate, quaestors, and legates at Abella (*Imagines* Abella 1=Rix Cm 1), quaestors, a censor, and a senate at Rossano di Vaglio (*Imagines* Potentia 1, 3, 9–10=Rix Lu 5–8, 10), aediles in Alfedena (*Imagines* Atina 1=Rix Sa 14), and quaestors in the Frentani area (*Imagines* Histonium 1=Rix Fr 1). In the *tabulae Iguvinae*, a *kvestur* appears (TI Va l. 23, Vb l. 2), but only with cultic functions.

[54] Crawford & Coleman 1996, 274–6; see Bispham 2007, 142–51; Wallace-Hadrill 2008, 94–5.

[55] Campanile & Letta 1979, 38; Dench 1995, 159.

senate, quaestors, and legates, but also the Oscan title of *meddix*. Other texts mentioned in note 53 were not aimed at Roman audiences either. A text from Pietrabbondante mentions not only a censor, but also a *meddix*.[56] Therefore, it seems that the use of these Latinized titles was as a sign of influence from Rome on the administrative structure of the Italian states. However, this does not mean that these people experienced influence from Rome in other ways, such as cultural.[57] The adoption of Latin titles for magistrates has been ascribed to 'admiration for Rome',[58] but Roman models were adopted because they answered specific Italian needs.[59]

In allied areas, much variation existed for the name of the leading magistrates: some towns had a *meddix* as their leading magistrate, others a dictator or praetor, while others had two praetors, or two or more aediles. The title consul, interestingly, is never used; this shows that the Italian states did not adopt the Roman title for leading magistrates. After the Roman conquest we still find *meddices*, e.g. at Capua during the Second Punic War and in various inscriptions from Pietrabbondante and Campochiaro.[60] Evidently pre-Roman government systems survived, even though local titles could be adapted if these suited local purposes. Even when Italians were granted citizenship, the Roman state did not order Italian states to change the titles of their magistrates: the *civitas sine suffragio* Velitrae, for example, had two *meddices* in the third century.[61] It was only after the grant of citizenship to the Italians in the Social War that the whole of Italy was municipalized, i.e. a Roman-type administration with *duoviri* as leading magistrates was introduced in most towns. Even in this period, however, there were still local variations: Arpinum still had three aediles in the first century.[62]

Not only the titles of magistrates, but also many technical phrases from Roman law and government were adopted in Italy. Often these local terms were simply translations of Latin. A few Oscan examples are:

- *publica esto* ('shall belong to the state')—*toutico estud*[63]
- *improbe factus esto* ('shall be judged unlawful')—*amprufid facus estud*[64]

[56] *Imagines* Terventum 8=Rix Sa 4.

[57] E.g. *Imagines* Atina Lucana 1=Rix Lu 2 refers to a building set up *[sena]teis tanginod* (de *senatus sententia*). This is a sign of 'romanizzazione delle istituzioni amministrative' (Fraschetti 1981, 205), but does not mean that 'Romanization' in any other sense took place. The culture of Atina shows little influence from Rome; see Coarelli 1981.

[58] Campanile & Letta 1979, 41: 'cultural superiority of Rome'; see Brunt 1965, 100; 1988, 118.

[59] Salmon 1967, 88; Mouritsen 1998, 77.

[60] Liv. 23.35.13, 24.19.2, 26.6.13; TB 1.12; *Imagines* Bovianum 20=Rix tSa 19; *Imagines* Nola 2=Rix Cm 7.

[61] *Imagines* Velitrae 1=Rix VM 2.

[62] Cic. *Fam.* 15.15.1; ILLRP 546–7, 595–7, 601–4. See Campanile & Letta 1979, 42; on the municipalization of Italy, see Bispham 2007.

[63] TB 23.

[64] TB 23, 30. See Porzio Gernia 1970, 118–19.

- *sciens sine dolo malo* ('consciously and without wrongful deceit')—*sipus perum dolom mallom*[65]
- *iuret dolo malo* ('he swears with wrongful deceit')—*deivaid docud malud*[66]
- *manum asserere earum rerum* ('to lay claim to these items')—*manim aserum eizazunc egmazum.*[67]

Even whole sentences were literally translated into Oscan, such as the phrase in the tabula *Bantina: maimas carneis senateis tanginud amp[ert nei mins pam] XL osins pon ioc egmo com{.}parascuster* ('in accordance with a decree of the majority of the senate, provided that [no less than] 40 were present when the matter was being discussed').[68] Another example is the phrase *kúmbennieís tanginud úpsannam deded ísídem prúfatted,* from an inscription from Pompeii in the late second century, a direct translation of the Latin formula *de conventus sententia faciendam dedit, idem probavit* ('gave and approved (this building) according the assembly's decision'), following the exact word order of the Latin.[69]

Grammatical constructions also show close connections to Latin, e.g. the possibility of indicating a command with a future imperative, as in the *tabula Bantina*: *iurato—deivatud* ('he should swear').[70] The use of prepositions and conjunctive clauses was also paralleled: *facito ut... sententiam decant* was translated as *factus pous... tanginom deicans* ('let it be so... that they give judgement').[71] However, it is important to keep in mind that it is not always clear whether there is a direct influence from Latin.[72] In fact, the same constructions also appear in the Umbrian *tabulae Iguvinae*, so it may be that these similarities were caused by linguistic relations between the languages, or shared legal traditions that occurred in several parts of Italy.[73] Direct influence of Latin may be assumed for the position of numerals in the *tabula Bantina*. Here, the numeral is placed in the middle, e.g. *zicolois X nesimois* ('for the next ten days'). This order is unknown from other Oscan texts, but very common in Latin, including in the Latin text published on the reverse of the Oscan *tabula Bantina.*[74]

It is unlikely that Oscan could not have formulated another way to convey the same meaning, instead of exactly translating the Latin. It is difficult to explain these close parallels, unless we assume that there were also close parallels in actual practice. For example, if Oscan-speaking areas adopted the Roman process for contracting out public buildings, as well as approving them when they were finished, it made sense also to adopt the Latin phrase to describe this process.

[65] TB 5, 11, 14, 20, 21. See Adams 2003, 138; Decorte 2015.
[66] TB 9, 113.
[67] TB 24. It is interesting that the TB uses the Latin verb *asserere*, which means 'lay hands on', i.e. 'arrest', while the Latin phrase for 'lay claim to' was actually *manum iniecere*. Apparently, some misunderstanding of Latin legal phrases took place. See Decorte 2015, 280.
[68] TB 3–4. See Decorte 2015, 281.
[69] *Imagines* Pompei 24=Rix Po 3. See Adams 2003, 137; Wallace-Hadrill 2008, 89.
[70] TB 5. See Porzio Gernia 1970, 128–9.
[71] TB 9.
[72] Porzio Gernia 1970, 141–2.
[73] Decorte 2015, 286.
[74] TBL l. 14, 23. See Decorte 2015, 289–90.

A phrase like *sciens sine dolo malo* has a very specific meaning in Roman law; it is unlikely that the people of Bantia possessed the same exact legal concept, and that this happened to have a perfect Latin equivalent. It seems therefore that some Roman legal concepts and their accompanying terminology were introduced into the Italian communities under Roman influence. Even if Italians did indeed adopt some legal practice from Rome, as appears from the Pompeian building inscriptions, this does not mean that Italians adopted Roman law and all its instruments as a whole. They did so only if they thought that Roman law offered aspects that were of use in local public life, or adopted phrases that were helpful to express existing Italian legal concepts.

Interestingly, there were also differences between Latin and the Italian languages. For example, Latin used the verb *operari* for 'making a sacrifice', while Oscan used the same word to mean *facere* ('build'), for example, in constructing buildings.[75] There were also differences between the various Italian languages; in contrast to Oscan, Umbrian used *facere* with the meaning 'sacrifice', as in Latin, so that *tre buf fetu* in the Iguvine Tables parallels the Latin *tres boves facito* ('three oxen should be sacrificed').[76] Other differences between Latin and Italian languages concerned grammar: for a prohibition, Latin used *ne* + future imperative, while Oscan used *ne* + conjunctive perfect.[77] Oscan used the locative much more often than Latin, so that *in comitio* ('in a public meeting') was rendered as *comenei*,[78] while *sub consulato* ('during the consulate of') had Italian parallels in *meddikkiaí*,[79] *kvestretie*,[80] or *maronatei*,[81] depending on the local eponymous magistrates.

Influence was not completely one-directional from Latin to Italian. The construction for a prohibition in Oscan, with *ne* + conjunctive perfect, was taken over in some Latin texts, especially those written in areas near Oscan-speaking territory. This is shown by a law from the Latin colony Luceria from the early third century, using the phrase *stercus ne [qu]is fundatid* ('no one may depose dung').[82] Some writing habits were also influenced by Oscan practice. Curse tablets (*defixiones*) appeared earlier in Oscan than in Latin; the earliest Latin examples come from Oscan-speaking areas, e.g. Cumae and Pompeii, and contain phrases directly paralleling those in Oscan texts.[83]

In short, Italian legal and administrative texts from the second and first centuries experienced much influence from Rome, in both language and content.

[75] TB 11–12, 20–1. See Porzio Gernia 1970, 122.

[76] TI I a 3. See Porzio Gernia 1970, 118.

[77] E.g. *ne sternito* in the Twelve Tables (Gell. *NA* 20.1.25) and *nei facito* in the *Lex repetundarum* l. 69, while Oscan examples are *ni hipid* (= *ne habuerit*, TB 7) and *ne pruhipid* (= *ne prohibuerit*, TB 25). See Porzio Gernia 1970, 131.

[78] TB 5. [79] *Imagines* Capua 25–28=Rix Cp 27–30. [80] TI Ib 45, TI IIa 44.

[81] *Imagines* Asisium 1=Rix Um 10. See, for the locative, Porzio Gernia 1970, 137–40.

[82] ILLRP 504=CIL 1^2 401. See Porzio Gernia 1970, 132.

[83] Oscan examples from the fourth and third centuries are *Imagines* Capua 24=Rix Cp 37 and *Imagines* Cumae 8=Rix Cm 14. Early Latin examples are CIL 1^2 2541=ILLRP 1147; CIL 1^2 3128–9. See Adams 2003, 139.

It is unfortunately very difficult to reconstruct the laws of the various Italian states, as they were in force before the Roman conquest. All our evidence dates from the second and first centuries, when the Italians had been under Roman dominance for at least a century and often much longer. The fact that in this period Italian legal and administrative texts show a high level of adaptation to Roman practice is interesting, since it shows an interest among Italian states to conduct business with Rome, in both an administrative and a commercial sense. The Roman state did not force Italians to adopt the language of Roman law and certainly did not oblige Italian towns to adopt Roman laws. An example of this appears in Cicero's works: in 115, a debate arose in Arpinum between M. Tullius, the grandfather of Cicero, and M. Gratidius, a local magistrate who had proposed a law about the voting procedure at Arpinum. Although several laws about the voting procedure had been passed in Rome in the preceding decades, these had not been imposed by Rome on Arpinum—a town with full Roman citizenship—and local magistrates were free to propose laws regarding the subject. Clearly Arpinum, despite its proximity to Rome and the citizenship it shared with Rome, still enjoyed a lively and independent civic life.[84]

Cicero explains, with regard to the laws of Rome:

> When the Roman people had ordered anything, if the allied peoples and the Latins had adopted and ratified it, and if the law which we had among ourselves was in this manner established among some people on a firm footing, then that people should be bound by the obligations of that law; not in such a manner as to detract in the least from our privileges, but that those nations might enjoy either that law which was established among us, or some other advantage and benefit. The Latins have adopted whatever of them they have chosen; even by the *lex Iulia* itself, by which the rights of citizenship were given to the allies and to the Latins, it was decreed that those people who did not ratify the law should not receive Roman citizenship... When the Roman people has enacted anything, if it be a matter of that sort, that it appears it may be granted also to some other nations, whether joined to us by a treaty, or free to decide themselves which law they prefer using, not about our affairs, but about their own; then it seems necessary to inquire whether they have adopted and ratified our law, or not; but the senate never intended that those peoples should have the power of ratifying or declining to ratify measures which concern our republic, our empire, our wars, our victory, and our safety.[85]

[84] See Nicolet 1967.

[85] Cic. *Balb.* 20–2: *Quid enim potuit dici imperitius quam foederatos populos fieri fundos oportere? Nam id non magis est proprium foederatorum quam omnium liberorum. Sed totum hoc, iudices, in ea fuit positum semper ratione atque sententia ut, cum iussisset populus Romanus aliquid, si id adscivissent socii populi ac Latini, et si ea lex, quam nos haberemus, eadem in populo aliquo tamquam in fundo resedisset, ut tum lege eadem is populus teneretur, non ut de nostro iure aliquid deminueretur, sed ut illi populi aut iure eo quod a nobis esset constitutum aut aliquo commodo aut beneficio uterentur ... Quas Latini voluerunt, adsciverunt; ipsa denique Iulia, qua lege civitas est sociis et Latinis data, qui fundi populi facti non essent civitatem non haberent ... Cum aliquid populus Romanus iussit, id si est eius modi ut quibusdam populis, sive foederatis sive liberis, permittendum esse videatur ut statuant ipsi non de nostris sed de suis rebus, quo iure uti velint, tum utrum fundi facti sint an non quaerendum esse*

It appears that any allied state, whether Latin or Italian, was free to adopt the laws of the Roman state, but was not forced to do so. This process is often called *fundus fieri* in modern scholarship, after the first sentence of Cicero's text, *quam foederatos populos fieri fundos oportere*. From the last sentence, it appears that only laws regarding external politics and the *maiestas* of the Roman state were imposed upon the allies directly.[86] This also meant that allies were free to accept Roman citizenship or not after the Social War, as Cicero indeed states. Some communities were deeply divided about this issue (see chapter 5.6).

With regard to administrative procedures imposed by Rome, such as the census, the allies were again free to arrange them in any way they saw fit (see chapter 1.6). When the Roman state ordered a census, as long as the Italian states organized a census and communicated the results to Rome, the Senate was satisfied. The *tabula Bantina*, for example, states that 'whoever shall have been a citizen of Bantia is to be listed, himself and his property, under whatever condition those (local) censors may have pronounced for the census'.[87] Only in extraordinary circumstances did the Roman state impose specific regulations on the Italians. In 204, the Senate imposed strict rules on how to conduct the census on twelve Latin colonies, which had refused to deliver soldiers five years earlier, ordering that 'a census should be taken in those colonies, according to a formula appointed by the Roman censors, which should be the same which was employed in the case of the Roman people'.[88] Other towns were still free to conduct the local census as they wished.[89]

We may conclude that the Italians enjoyed considerable leeway in conducting their internal legal and administrative affairs. The Roman state had no interest in imposing specific regulations on them, except when it perceived Rome's power to be under threat, as in the case of the disobedient Latin colonies. In any case, the Romans did not have the capacity to control every aspect of the Italians' life, and therefore left them to make their own decisions. A similar laissez-faire attitude is displayed in the Roman treatment of Italian coinage, as we will now see.

4.2.3. Italian and Roman coinage

An important issue with regard to trade between Rome and the Italians, and between various Italic peoples, was the use of coinage. Although it is possible to trade using non-monetary systems, such as barter, transaction costs are lower when all trading parties use an efficient monetary system.[90] During most of the Republican period, a variety of currencies was in use within the Italian peninsula. The city-states of Magna Graecia used one system of coinage, based on the

videatur; de nostra vero re publica, de nostro imperio, de nostris bellis, de victoria, de salute fundos populos fieri noluerunt.

[86] Humbert 1978, 298–308. [87] TB 19–20. See Crawford & Coleman 1996, 275.
[88] Liv. 29.15.9–10. [89] *Contra* Tarpin 2014, 165. [90] Heady 2005.

drachma. Some southern Italian towns also produced their own coinage, based on the same drachma system. Rome appeared relatively late as a coin-producing centre. Its coins were gradually adopted by the Italic peoples, but this occurred rather late in the Republican period: only in the second century did Roman money definitively oust Italian coinage as the common method of exchange. In this section, I will examine the changes that occurred in Italian and Roman coinage as Italy came under increasing Roman influence.

We will first investigate briefly the developments in Italian coinage after the Roman conquest of Italy. Italian towns had started minting coins long before Rome. Some Greek colonies in Magna Graecia started minting in the sixth century. Most Italians at this time did not produce their own coinage, but used the coins of Greek colonies, which have been found in many indigenous areas of Italy. Rome started to produce its own coinage relatively late. Much debate surrounds the date of this first Roman coinage; most scholars now accept a date shortly after the treaty with Neapolis in 326.[91] Interestingly, the earliest Roman coins were minted not at Rome itself, but in Neapolis. The first bronze issue used designs and weight standards that copied those of Neapolis and were stamped in Greek letters ROMAIOON.[92] The next issue, the first silver, was a didrachm on the Neapolitan weight standard, showing the head of Mars on the obverse and a horse's head with the Latin legend ROMANO on the reverse. This is usually dated to *c*.285–0.[93]

The earliest Romano-Campanian issues, made in Neapolis, may be interpreted as a cultural phenomenon, under the influence of Greek culture that gained popularity in Rome around 300.[94] However, the volume of Roman coin production suddenly increased in the Pyrrhic War; this phenomenon must surely be connected to the needs of the war. Other Italian towns involved in the war also produced large volumes of coins in the same period to finance their contribution to the war effort. The increase in the production of coinage by Rome and other Italian towns should therefore be connected to the need to furnish the soldiers with pay and/or distribute spoils.[95]

The connection between war and the production or coinage became clear again during the First Punic War, when a large number of Italian towns started to produce coinage for the first time; soon after the war, many of these mints disappeared again. It is likely that the most important reason for the production of these coins was the fact that many Italians now served in the Roman army and that the introduction of money made it easier to share the spoils of war.[96] This

[91] Thomsen 1961:3, 79–81; Burnett 1978, 128; but see 1995.

[92] Burnett 1989, 37; Crawford 1985, 29–30; Marchetti 1993, 43; Catalli 1995, 132; Taliercio Mensitieri 1998, 58–63.

[93] Thomsen 1961:3, 82, 153–4.

[94] Morel 2007, 502; Burnett 2012, 310–11.

[95] Marchetti 1993, 59–61, 65; Taliercio Mensitieri 1998, 126–7; Erdkamp 2007, 106.

[96] Crawford 1985, 32–5; Marchetti 1993, 59–61, 65; Catalli 1995, 123; Taliercio Mensitieri 1998, 126–7; Rutter 2001, 8.

shows that the primary function of coinage at this time was to accommodate large state expenditures, especially related to warfare, rather than to facilitate economic interaction. This is shown by their designs: various towns produced issues depicting Victory, an excellent design for coins that were distributed as spoils, since it reminded the soldiers of the victory they had achieved and thus the achievements they could reach under Roman command.[97] The First Punic War formed an integrative event in the history of Italian coinage: more communities produced coinage and the coinages became more uniform, both in weight and in type.[98] It must be noted, however, that the Romans did not compel their allies to produce coinage. Even at Rome itself, coinage was only a recent innovation, and Rome's government and war effort could have been maintained without the use of currency for most of the third century.

The Second Punic War again illustrated the impact of war on the economy of the Italian towns. Many towns again started to mint coins for Rome; some of these had never produced coinage before, while others had also minted during the First Punic War and now resumed their activities.[99] The wars of Rome were therefore an important factor in the changing monetary behaviour of the Italians, but Rome was not directly responsible for decisions regarding coin production in the Italian towns. Although the increase in coinage production was connected to the Roman conquest, many Italian towns still minted coins on the Greek model.[100] The influence of Neapolis on Italian coin production was especially large. Bronze coins similar to those of Neapolis were minted by various Latin colonies, as well as by many allied towns in Campania.[101] Tarentum was the other Greek town with a major influence on Italian coin production. In the fourth century, many Apulian mints started to produce silver coinage that resembled that of Tarentum.[102] Neapolis and Tarentum had long-standing commercial relations with Italic peoples, so that it is natural that Italian coinage was adapted from Greek examples available to the Italians.

Various weight standards were used in Italy in the fourth and third centuries. The Roman system was based on the bronze *as*, which had weighed one Roman pound when Roman coinage was first introduced. This was subdivided into twelve *unciae*. Throughout the Republic, various reductions of the *as* took place, as the Roman state did not have enough precious metal to maintain the standard. The Greek towns employed various weight standards; most important were the Neapolitan and the Tarentine didrachms.[103] Other weight standards were in use in specific regions of Italy. This variety in weight standards continued after the Roman conquest of Italy. Many mints were only active in the Second Punic

[97] Ercolani Cocchi 2000, 39.
[98] Termeer 2015; forthcoming.
[99] Crawford 1985, 58, 69–70.
[100] Crawford 1985, 34–5, 37; Rutter 2001, 8–9, 17.
[101] Crawford 1985, 47–8; 2011, 20; Marchetti 1993, 52–4; Taliercio Mensitieri 1998, 101; Rutter 2001, 7.
[102] Crawford 1985, 64; Catalli 1995, 134.
[103] Catalli 1995, 132; Rutter 2001, 8.

War, presumably under direct orders from Rome; these produced coins exactly like Rome's. Among the towns that produced coins in Rome's name were not only towns with Roman citizen status, but also Latin colonies or allied towns. Those towns that had already minted before the war were allowed to continue using their own weight standards. Most likely the Roman state had no capacity to supervise all monetary activities of its allies and colonies, and just told individual military commanders or towns to produce as many coins as possible.[104]

Interestingly, civic status mattered little in regard to the standard that was used. For example, many communities on the Adriatic, some of which were Latin colonies, while others were allies, shared a single standard. They used an *as* of 350–400 grams, heavier than the Roman unit, which was divided into ten *unciae* instead of twelve.[105] Some communities in Apulia, both Latin and allied, also used the division into ten instead of twelve, but with a lower unit of weight.[106] Even colonies were quite independent in their choice of weights, as well as coin designs. The Latin colonies in the third century mostly followed Roman standards and reductions,[107] but this was not always the case. Especially with bronze coinage, local moneyers were quite independent.[108] The independence of the Latin colonies becomes very clear when looking at the production of Brundisium during the Second Punic War. At this time, coinage in Rome was subject to rapid devaluation, until the introduction of the new *denarius* system. However, the Brundisian coins did not follow the developments in Rome, but held on to the older weight standard. Furthermore, the designs resembled those of nearby Tarentum, with a dolphin on the reverse.[109]

As stated above, most Italian towns minted only intermittently, mostly during wars. Furthermore, most coins circulated only in small area near their location of production. This goes for both allied towns and Latin and Roman colonies.[110] Bronze coins in particular circulated only locally, so that the difference in weight standards did not confuse users elsewhere. Only a few mints produced coins with a wider distribution: the coins of some Latin colonies were used in larger areas, as well as those of some allied towns in Campania.[111] Trade over longer distances most likely made use of these coins issued, which were known throughout Italy. In this way, the coins of towns such as Neapolis, Tarentum, and later Rome itself, as well as important colonies such as Brundisium, played a crucial role in the economic network of Italy, and their coins served to provide currency for larger parts of Italy. This matches what we have seen in chapter 2: some towns were

[104] Crawford 1974, 599–620, 633–94. [105] Robinson 1964, 39; Crawford 1985, 43–6.
[106] Crawford 1974, 31. [107] Burnett 1991, 30–2.
[108] Stazio 1970, 86; Crawford 1985, 185.
[109] Crawford 1985, 66, although he states that it was 'purely Roman'; see Stazio 1970, 80–1; Catalli 1995, 125, 132–3.
[110] Stazio 1970, 62–3; Catalli 1995, 99, 104. For coins minted by colonies, see Termeer 2015, 387–98.
[111] Termeer 2015, 399–407.

more important in the overall economy of Italy. Yet whether they were Roman, Latin, or allied made little difference regarding the distribution of their coinage in the third century.

Roman money at first played only a small role in the economy of Italy. Even though Rome in the third century was in complete control of the Italian peninsula, local coinage was still dominant in many areas. Eventually all Italian towns stopped minting, but it took a long time before all towns had stopped their coinage production. Most towns stopped minting silver relatively quickly, but continued minting bronze for longer periods. This pattern fits what occurred in the provinces, e.g. Iberia and the East, after the Roman conquest: silver disappeared quickly, to be replaced by Roman coinage, but bronze continued for another century or so.[112] The disappearance of local Italian silver currency cannot be explained by a takeover by Roman coins, because at this time Rome did not supply all Italy with enough coins to replace earlier currencies. In fact, Roman coinage permeated Italy only very slowly. This can partially be explained by the fact that Rome simply could not produce enough money to supply all of Italy with coinage. Only after the defeat of Carthage, which brought in large amounts of spoils, and the conquest of the Bruttian silver mines in the mid-third century, was Rome able to produce enough coinage for the whole peninsula.[113] Even then, its distribution was patchy and slow. Many areas of Italy, such as Apulia, were hardly reached by Roman coinage until the mid- or late second century.[114]

After the Second Punic War, many Italian towns stopped minting. Some towns continued to mint coins, but adapted these to Roman standards. For example, the decimal unit used in eastern Italy, as mentioned above, disappeared in the second century in favour of the Roman duodecimal standard.[115] By the late second century, most Italians towns had stopped minting altogether. Only Uxentum, Velia, and Vibo sporadically issued coins until the Caesarian period, and Paestum until Tiberius.[116] The only coins still produced were small bronzes; in most cases, these issues were too small to serve as an actually functioning coinage system. Paestum, for example, minted small coins, which were distributed during holidays. The minting magistrates were most likely benefactors, rather than magistrates in charge of regular coin issues, as is shown from the fact that a woman, Mineia, sponsored an issue in Paestum.[117] The fact that Roman currency only slowly became predominant in Italy suggests that coinage was not essential for daily economic transactions, or in other words that the monetization of the Italian economy was relatively low. In line with the suggestion that most coinage was produced for state expenditures, the decline in coinage outside of Rome may indicate a decline in state expenditures by the Italian states. Especially after the

[112] Burnett 2006. [113] Crawford 1991, 135. [114] Stazio 1970, 75; Travaglini 1982, 232.
[115] Catalli 1995, 98. [116] Crawford 1985, 71–2; Catalli 1995, 154.
[117] Burnett 1982, 128–9; Catalli 1995, 154.

Second Punic War, the Italians only fought together with Rome and therefore did not need to produce coinage for independent military expenditure.

A secondary but important function of coinage was to communicate messages to a wide audience. Indeed, Italian towns saw coinage as an important way to emphasize local identity, especially within the wider Hellenistic world. Coins from Nuceria, of the first half of the third century, carry the Oscan legend (S)ARNSNEI, with or without an image of the Dioscuri; this has been interpreted as an allusion to the Sarrasti, a legendary people from the Peloponnese.[118] Thus these towns claimed a connection with Greek history and mythology, and defined their place in the network of states that surrounded them. Coin designs often refer to a variety of cultures: Larinum minted coins that were modelled on Campanian and Apulian designs, but depicted people wearing helmets of local design.[119] Coins were usually marked with the name of the town or people that produced them. These legends, by their choice of language, identified the ethnic orientation of the people minting them. Some coins minted in Messapia had Messapian legends, e.g. Oria (ORRA) and Valesio (BALETHAS), although these used the Greek alphabet; others used Greek legends, e.g. Arpi (ARPANOON, 'of the Arpians').[120]

Latin legends were used mostly by Latin colonies, but also by allied towns.[121] Some scholars assume that the language used by a people reflects their civic status; for example, it has been suggested that coins from the Vestini should be dated after the Roman conquest in 301, since they used the Latin legend VES.[122] However, in many cases the language used did not match the political status of the area; many Oscan towns continued to use Oscan after the Roman conquest. Nevertheless, as we have seen, many Italian towns started to mint coins during the Pyrrhic or First Punic War. Therefore, Scheu argues, 'the use of Oscan legends about the time of the First Punic War is an expression of pro-Roman Italian nationalism'.[123] At this time, the idea of 'Italy' as a unified whole gradually emerged (see section 4.6), and the First Punic War could be presented as the fight of all Italian peoples against a foreign oppressor. It is fascinating that pro-Roman 'nationalism' could be expressed in the local language; again we see that, as long as the Italians remained loyal to Rome, the Romans were not concerned about the way in which this loyalty was expressed.

Coins could be an excellent mechanism to proclaim political allegiance. In the third century, some allies indicated loyalty to Rome on their coinage. A remarkable coin comes from Locri around the time of the Pyrrhic War: it minted coins with the goddess Roma, crowned by Pistis (Faith). This should be

[118] Cantilena 1996. This interpretation is not certain; *Imagines* Nuceria Alfaterna 1 suggests it is the name of the location or building where the coins were minted.

[119] Cantilena 1991, 141, 147. See, for Arpi and Salapia, Stazio 1970, 85–7; Travaglini 1990, 249–50.

[120] Stazio 1970, 85–7; Boersma & Yntema 1987, 71.

[121] Catalli 1995, 130; see 116–17 for Larinum.

[122] Catalli 1995, 104, 109.

[123] Scheu 1964, 66.

interpreted as a recognition of the fact that Rome had assisted in liberating the southern Italian towns from Pyrrhus. Locri now also started to follow Rome's weight standard.[124] Coins from the Greek colony Velia of the late fourth or early third century often depict Athena wearing a Phrygian cap. This is usually seen as a symbol of a connection with Troy, and it is possible that Velia wanted to show its connections with Rome by alluding to the shared Trojan history of both cities.[125]

Thus, from 200 the coinage used in Italy was mostly Roman,[126] but the changeover was gradual and happened at different speeds throughout Italy. The causes of the slow but steady expansion of Roman coinage were diverse. It has been suggested that the accumulation of wealth in Italy (see chapter 3) served to spread Roman coinage through Italy, because Italians were trading with Romans on a more regular basis.[127] Some scholars even assume that Rome after the Second Punic War adopted an aggressive policy towards the coinage of the Italian states and forbade them to produce coins, and that Rome took active steps to remove Italian coinage from circulation.[128] However, many Italian towns were still nominally independent at this time and such a far-reaching intervention in Italy's affairs would have been impossible. Moreover, Italian coins remained in circulation during the second century, first accompanied and then replaced by Roman coins. Hoards from the second and first centuries usually contain a mix of Roman and Italian coins.[129] The Italian decision to stop coin production and adopt Roman coinage was therefore made by individual Italian towns, who, in light of the advantages of sharing the same currency as Rome, concluded that it was more practical to adopt Roman coinage.

This overview shows that remarkable changes took place in Italy between the early third and early second centuries. Within the space of a century, the impact of Rome had caused a number of developments to occur in many Italian towns: first, many of them started to produce coinage, probably due to the demands of war; after the Second Punic War, most towns stopped minting for good. Although Rome was an important factor in the Italian decision whether or not to produce coinage, the weights and designs of the coinage and the amount of coins produced were decided by the towns themselves. Many adhered to weight standards that were not Roman, but had been used previously by the Greek or indigenous towns, and adapted their designs to local needs. Even Latin colonies, despite their close relationship with Rome, were mostly independent in deciding when and how to mint. Coin production was therefore an issue on which Rome adopted a laissez-faire policy, as in many other fields.

The same cannot be said, however, of the monetary policy of Rome itself. From the earliest creation of Roman coinage, Rome showed an awareness of other

[124] Crawford 1974, 48; 1985, 33; Catalli 1995, 150. [125] Greco 2004, 631–2.
[126] Burnett 2012, 308. [127] Crawford 1991, 136. [128] Burnett 1982, 126.
[129] Crawford 1969.

people in the peninsula. At first, many Roman coins matched the existing coinage of the Italic peoples. The silver coinage of Rome matched the weight of the didrachm, so that it was interchangeable with coins already in circulation.[130] In the Second Punic War, Rome introduced a new currency system, based on the *denarius*.[131] Even though Rome was by now the undisputed master of Italy, the *denarius* system still accommodated non-Roman currencies. For example, it introduced the *victoriatus*, which did not quite fit in with the rest of the system, since it was worth three quarters of a *denarius*. However, it looked very much like the drachm used in Magna Graecia. Indeed, early *victoriati* have been found mostly in Magna Graecia and Hellenized areas of Campania, Apulia, and northern Lucania. They even show messages intended for a Greek audience, such as Nike crowning a trophy. In Campania and Greek-speaking parts of Italy, the diobol still survived as a unit of reckoning and was considered an equivalent of the *sestertius*, because it had the same silver content.[132] Rome also introduced a gold coin with an oath scene on the reverse. This coin would have reminded the Italian allies of the 'strength through cooperation' ideology that the Romans attempted to promote.[133] Thus, when Rome introduced a new currency, it was aware that not all Italy shared the same weight standards, and adapted the new system so that it could be used everywhere.

After the Second Punic War, the production of coinage was concentrated at Rome itself; most of the other mints producing for Rome were no longer active. As Rome became more powerful, the coinage reflected its growing power; less concern was shown for Italian monetary systems. For example, *victoriati* were no longer minted after *c.*170.[134] Some adaptation to local needs occurred, however: the *quinarius*, which was produced very rarely in the second century, became more common when Rome undertook more military action in Gaul in the early first century. It is possible that this was necessary to enable trade between the Roman army and the local population, who used coins that matched the *quinarius* in weight.[135]

Throughout the second century, the majority of coins minted by Rome were bronze, indicating the growing importance of money for small transactions.[136] This growing rate of monetization from the second century onwards is also visible in the way in which the Roman state adapted its coinage to developments in the market. The bronze *as* continued to decline slowly in value, since the Roman state found it difficult to provide enough bronze to maintain the full weight of the *as*. This made it less valuable in the marketplace; people preferred to use the silver *denarius*, which had a more reliable weight and metal content. In 141, therefore,

[130] Crawford 1985, 38–41; Taliercio Mensitieri 1998, 99.

[131] See discussion in Crawford 1974, 3–35; 1985, 55–7; Marchetti 1993, 30–4; Burnett 2012, 305; Woytek 2012, 329–30.

[132] Crawford 1985, 346. [133] Crawford 1974, 46, 715. [134] Woytek 2012, 318–21.

[135] Crawford 1974, 610; 1985, 181–3. [136] Crawford 1974, 625; 1985, 72.

the *denarius* was retariffed at 16 *ases*, whereas it had been worth 10 *ases* at the time of its introduction. This did not mean that the *denarius* suddenly increased in value; rather, its value in the marketplace had gradually risen in the preceding years in relation to the *as*, and the state was forced to acknowledge this.[137] However, the standard of the bronze coinage continued to fluctuate. In 85, the tribunes asked the praetors 'to adopt by joint resolution a standard of value for our currency; for at that time the value of money was so fluctuating that no one could tell how much he was worth'.[138]

It is clear that the Roman state found it difficult to maintain a consistent weight standard throughout the Republican period. Fluctuating weight standards caused problems for trade, since people were unsure how much their money would actually buy.[139] Often the state was forced to follow developments in the marketplace by changing the currency. The state's policy with regard to the provision of bronze coins was haphazard, with many types not being minted for long stretches of time; this has led Crawford to believe that the state 'did not give a damn'.[140] However, it certainly did care: especially in the late second and early first centuries, as we just saw, a number of laws was introduced to remedy the situation, showing that the state did in fact appreciate the importance of a stable and reliable monetary system. This indicates that the Roman state's monetary policy was partially motivated by concerns for the smooth running of trade, as well as providing enough coins for the state's immediate, mostly military, purposes.[141]

We may conclude that Italian towns had started minting coins long before Rome and that Rome started producing its own coinage relatively late. Even then, it was heavily influenced by existing Italian coinage. The start and early growth in the volume of coin production must be connected to the needs of the war, especially the Pyrrhic and First Punic Wars. This applies to both Roman and Italian coinage, since during these wars, many Italian states started to produce for the first time. Although the increase in the production of money was connected to the Roman conquest, many Italian towns still minted coins based on Greek models and continued to use their own weight standards. The takeover of Italy by Roman coinage was slow: many areas were hardly reached by Roman coinage until the mid- to late second century. At the same time, the monetary policy of Rome showed an awareness of the variety existing in the peninsula; many coins were produced to match the existing coinage of the Italic peoples. It was only in the second century, when Rome's dominance of Italy was secured, that Rome

[137] Plin. *NH* 33.45; Festus *s.v. sesterti not[am]*. See Crawford 1974, 612–14; 1985, 145.

[138] Cic. *Off.* 3.80. See *Att.* 12.3; 12.12, 12.46; *Leg. Man.* 17–20.

[139] Andreau 1987; Nicolet 1989, 633–4.

[140] Crawford 1985, 185.

[141] Lo Cascio 1978 assumes that the primary concern of the state was to provide enough money for commerce, but changes in monetary policy were usually connected to exigencies of war; see Andreau 1999, 110.

started to show less consideration for the needs of the Italic peoples—as was the case in many other respects, as we will see in chapter 5.3.1.

4.2.4. Weights and measures

As we have seen, various weight standards were used for coinage, but weights and measures were also important in other aspects of trade. Commerce may have been complicated by the fact that various systems of weights and measures were in use in Italy. This variety called for *mensae ponderariae*, tables set up in the marketplace, at which standard measures were displayed. Such tables have been attested for many towns.[142] Scales, used to measure coins and small valuable items, have been found in many locations.[143] Individual money-changers also used weights and scales to verify the value of money.[144] The lack of unified measures was a transaction cost problem, since it raised the costs of trade; for example, traders had to invest in a set of reliable measures. Therefore, it was cost-effective to use the same weights and measures throughout Italy. However, whereas Roman coinage became dominant in the Italian economy during the second century, local Italian systems of weights and measures remained in place for much longer.

Many different systems of weights and measures were in use, although we are not always able to determine exactly how they worked. For example, the *tabula Cortonensis*, dated to the second century, records various Etruscan surface measures, e.g. the *tenthur* and the *sran*,[145] but we have no idea what area was represented by these units. In Oscan-speaking areas, the terms used for measurements were influenced by Greek; however, the actual measurements were not always equal to Greek ones. At Pompeii in the second century, a set of inscribed standard measures was set up in the town, including a *[hd]ímnúm* (Greek *hemimedimnon*), *díasiís*, *ka[dd]íks* (Greek *kyathos*), *kúíníks* (Greek *choinix*), and *sehsík [s]* (Greek *xestes*). These measures themselves were the equivalents of an amphora, half-metretes, *urna*, *modius*, and *half-modius*. The half-metretes was a Greek measure; the others were Roman.[146] Thus even in the second century, local measures, which formed a curious mix of Oscan and Greek, were still in full use at Pompeii, no matter the increasing influence of Roman language and institutions in Italy.

As with coinage, there seems to have been no Roman control over the activities of its citizens and colonies; in the Latin colonies Cales, Luceria, Paestum, and Suessa, there is evidence for centuriation grids measured in the *vorsus*, rather than

[142] CIL 1^2 1517=10.6466=ILLRP 663 (late third century); CIL 1^2 681=10.379=ILLRP 718 (dated 98); CIL 9.980; 9.3046; 10.145; 11.5695.

[143] CIL 9.1656; 10.793; 10.8067.

[144] See Plaut. *Truc.* 50–2.

[145] Pandolfini Angeletti & Maggiani (eds.) 2002.

[146] *Imagines* Pompei 27=Rix Po 19.

the Roman foot. The Roman standard unit of surface measured 120 by 120 Roman feet, but the *vorsus*, in use in Umbria, Campania, and other Oscan-speaking areas, measured 100 by 100 Oscan feet.[147] The Greek *plethrum* was used in the area between Suessa and Sinuessa and in the Ager Falernus, inhabited by Roman citizen settlers. These centuriations were probably local initiatives, rather than Roman state-organized schemes,[148] but the fact that non-Roman measures were used apparently did not bother the Roman state at all. The Latin colony Fregellae monumentalized its sanctuary in the early second century, using the Oscan foot as a measure; this has led to suggestions that Oscan people had moved into the colony (see chapter 2.2).[149] However, other explanations may be possible—for example, that Oscan labourers were hired to build the sanctuary.

There was no change in Italian weights and measures until relatively late. Adaptation to Roman measures by Italians and others took place voluntarily; an Athenian law of the late second century introduced new standard measures, which matched Roman ones. This may have been caused by the trade at Delos, which reached its zenith in this period. Nominally Delos was under Athenian control, so it makes sense that its magistrates enforced standard measures on the island, which was visited by people from various parts of the Mediterranean. That these measures were Roman emphasizes the importance of Rome for Delian trade.[150] Some Roman terms for measurements were gradually adopted into Oscan: a law found at Roccagloriosa, in Oscan written in Greek letters, refers to weights in *poundioum* (Latin *pondium*).[151] However, it is not clear whether this measurement in fact equalled the Roman pound.

Changes in Italian weights and measures started to occur from the late second century onwards. In 98, a private donor at Capua placed a set of Roman-standard weights in the marketplace,[152] which may have been the first time they were introduced in the town. Various other towns set up new weights and measures in the first century.[153] In Pompeii, this did not happen until about AD 2; at this time, the Oscan names for the measures were crossed out and the holes in the table enlarged to conform to Roman measures.[154] Although we have seen that economic integration in the peninsula was already significant at a much earlier date, this clearly did not mean that a change in measures was deemed necessary. The Augustan period was the era in which weights and measures were finally united. According to Dio, this unification was not yet complete by the start of Augustus' reign: as Dio observes, Maecenas suggested that 'none of the cities should be

[147] Var. *R.* 1.10.1; Frontinus 30L. See Crawford 1985, 14.

[148] Pelgrom 2008, 362–5.

[149] Lesk 1999, 64.

[150] IG 2.2 1013. See Breglia Pulci Doria 1985.

[151] *Imagines* Buxentum 1=Rix Lu 62.

[152] CIL 1^2 681=10.3789=ILS 3609=ILLRP 718. See Heurgon 1952, 116; Adams 2003, 149.

[153] CIL 9.2845; 10.6017; 11.6375. See Cooley 2002, 80.

[154] *Imagines* Pompei 27=Rix Po 19; CIL 10.793. See Crawford 1985, 177; Cooley 2002, 80–2.

allowed to have its own separate coinage or system of weights and measures; they should all be required to use ours'.[155] It is unlikely that Dio made this up; the speech comes from a passage in which he discusses a large number of Augustan innovations, many of which were indeed introduced during Augustus' reign.

It is clear, therefore, that Roman policy with regard to the weights and measures used by the Romans was remarkably laissez-faire, even more so than with regard to currency. The Roman state could not impose the use of one system of weights and measures, since it did not have the manpower to assure compliance. Furthermore, since many Italian states were independent until the Social War, Rome did not, in strictly legal terms, have the authority to impose unity. In any case, it clearly saw no need to impose one unified system, since the cost and effort of policing it would have outweighed any possible benefits of its introduction.

4.2.5. Conclusion

In this section, we have reviewed the institutional changes that occurred in the Roman and Italian states during the Republican period. Throughout the Republican period, Roman and Italian practice converged: Roman law increasingly accommodated for disputes between Romans and Italians, Roman coinage came to dominate Italy, Roman weights and measures were spread through Italy, and Latin administrative and business language influenced Italian practice. However, these developments were limited in scope and mostly occurred in the late Republic; Roman coinage did not become dominant until the second century, while weights and measures remained variable until the late first. We may conclude, then, that such elements of daily life as coinage, weights, measures, and especially language were important for the Italians and formed part of their identity. As long as there was no compelling reason to give them up, or manifest advantages to adapting to Roman practice, the Italians retained their own instruments of law and commerce. The Roman state had little interest in unifying the institutions of the Italic peoples; the optimal running of the Italian economy was not the main concern for Rome. It therefore did not pursue a concerted policy on Italian economic affairs.

From the early second century, the influence of Rome was great: Roman coinage became the main method of exchange in the whole of Italy; Italian law and administration adapted to Roman practice, although the speed and extent of this development differed widely across Italy; and the Latin language became the *lingua franca* of the peninsula. Indeed, it may be argued that, if we can detect 'Romanization' in any aspect of Italian life, it was in the economic and

[155] Dio 52.30.9.

institutional sphere, which transformed much more quickly than cultural aspects of Italian life. This shows the limits to the inclusiveness of the legal instruments created by Rome: although the Italians were free to continue to use their own coinage, weights, measures, and language, business with Romans and other Italians was easier if everyone was using the same instruments. This expedited business, leading to a decrease in transaction costs. It was not necessary to change fundamental elements of their identity and culture, such as language and material culture (see sections 4.4 and 4.5). Therefore, it may be concluded that some Italians did indeed, by their own free will, adapt to Roman institutions.

However, Italians who adapted voluntarily to Roman practice, by doing so, acknowledged the changing power relations in the peninsula: Rome had become the dominant power, and Italians who wanted to profit from the commercial and political instruments created by Rome—law, coinage, administration—had to adapt. But this did not impact a great number of Italians; many, until the late second century, were not interested in Rome and its culture, and therefore showed little inclination to adapt their language, coinage, and measurements to those of Rome. Even those who had shown themselves ready to adapt to Roman practice were denied the possibility to make full use of all Roman legal and commercial institutions, as became clear in the late second century. Therefore, they were unable to profit fully from the new economic opportunities that arose, which eventually led to resentment among many Italians (see chapter 5).

4.3. The Investment of Wealth in Italy

As we have seen, Italians were not passive victims of economic and political change in Italy; they actively negotiated their position in the Mediterranean economy and in their local communities, as well as their relationship with Rome. One way in which such Italian negotiation is visible is through the buildings erected in Italy in the third to first centuries. The remains of these buildings are among the most important sources for economic developments in the Republican period. These buildings give an indication of the level of wealth reached by the Italians, as well as their choices for investment. Of course, other investment also took place, e.g. improvements in agriculture, but these are more difficult to determine. Therefore, this section will focus on public and private buildings set up in Italy. Here we will see how Italians used building to advertise and enhance their own status within their local communities, as well as the status of their community in the region.

It is well known that most regions of Italy show great prosperity in the second century; as discussed in chapter 3, this may be deduced from developments in agriculture and settlement patterns. At the same time, many cities experienced a boom in the construction of public buildings, especially in the late second century.

It has long been maintained that this building boom was financed by Italian commercial activities in the Mediterranean.[156] In order to clarify the relationship between overseas trade and investments, in this section we will take a closer look at the connections between trade and investment. Furthermore, the style of these new public buildings can tell us much about the cultural influences that affected Italy, allowing for a critical re-evaluation of 'cultural Romanization'.

Towns in general experienced constant urban renewal in the fourth to first centuries, but this peaked in different areas in different periods. Especially the early and again the late second century were periods of great change in urban landscapes, as shown by new city layouts and investments in structures such as roads, pavements, shops, fountains, etc. This occurred even in small towns without a prominent role in the economic network of Italy. In Umbria, a region with relatively few economic contacts with the Mediterranean or the rest of Italy, urban reconstruction still took place in many towns at this time, although in most cases these interventions involved small structures, rather than complete overhauls of the cityscape.[157] Latin and Roman colonies took part in this general trend of urban renewal: at Cosa in the early second century, the forum was expanded and utilitarian buildings were built, possibly workshops for pottery or metalworking, as well as shops.[158] Minturnae was enlarged and enclosed in a new wall in the late third or early second century, and several new public buildings were erected.[159]

The connection between commerce and public building is clear in some cases. The temple of Fortuna Primigenia at Praeneste is an especially impressive example of a splendid building sponsored by local elites; it was completely rebuilt in monumental style around 110–100, with the contributions of many families attested in inscriptions on the building.[160] Some of these names, such as the Anicii, Avillii, Magulnii, Orcevii, Rupilii, and Saufeii, were very active merchants. This suggests that these people directly invested their wealth in the embellishment of their town. Many families from Tibur also accumulated wealth in the East, while at the same time several buildings were dedicated in the town by people with the same *gentilicia* as those active abroad.[161] For other cities, however, the connection with overseas trade is not so clear; we can only assume that the donors of buildings were well-off, but cannot identify where their wealth came from. This is the case, for example, with the masters of the slave *magistri* at Minturnae in the first half of the first century. The *magistri* were slaves and freedmen in charge of the religious colleges in Minturnae. The names of the *magistri* have survived in a

[156] Càssola 1970–1, 318; Stek 2009, 44–5; Kay 2014, 222–4.

[157] Sisani 2009, 84–6.

[158] Brown 1980.

[159] Guidobaldi & Pesando 1989, 38; Rauh 1986b, 205; Crimaco 2002, 89–90.

[160] Bodei Giglioni 1977, 73; Gros 1978, 51. The temple had been important for a long time: already in 241 a Roman consul visited it (VM 1.3.2); see Liv. 42.1.6, 45.44.8; Cic. *Div.* 2.87; CIL 14.2929.

[161] Bodei Giglioni 1977, 72–3. See Appendix.

number of inscriptions, recording gifts to the deities that the colleges worshipped. The slaves usually mention their masters; some have standard Roman names, but many of these names are also attested in Oscan. These masters were most likely involved in profitable business, which allowed them to own slaves and to provide the money for such donations. As we have seen, Minturnae was an important harbour and attracted many immigrants (see chapter 2.5), so it is no surprise that the local inhabitants and their slaves were wealthy.

Building activity took place not only in towns, but in the countryside as well. In fact, many sanctuaries in rural areas of Italy had been monumentalized already in the fourth or third century, e.g. Pietrabbondante.[162] Many rural sanctuaries went through a further phase of monumentalization in the second or early first century, attesting to the continued economic prosperity of many southern Italic regions.[163] In Pietrabbondante, Temple A was constructed in the first half of the second century, Temple B in the second half.[164] In this case, the connection with Eastern trade is clear: many inscriptions on the temple record local families, such as the Dekitii, Staii, Statii, and Stenii, who are also attested at Delos.[165] At nearby Schiavi d'Abruzzo, the Papii and Dekitii, who were active in the East, financed the mosaic temple pavement.[166] This shows that some areas of Samnium enjoyed considerable wealth in this period, as we also saw in chapter 3. Of course, the scale of these monumental sanctuaries was not the same everywhere; Pietrabbondante was far larger than all other temples. A more typical sanctuary is the smaller temple at San Giovanni in Galdo (see Fig 4.1); many similar shrines appeared in Samnium in the late second century.[167]

The largest sanctuary in Lucania, Rossano di Vaglio, had been built in a monumental style from its inception in the fourth century, with a paved courtyard surrounded by colonnades, although it was smaller than the temples in nearby Greek colonies on which it was based. At this time, private wealth in Lucania was invested mostly in defensive walls for settlements and private tombs, rather than conspicuous sacred buildings. In the second century, the original layout remained in use, with the addition of Hellenistic-style statues, donated by a member of the local elite, Heirens Pomponis. This building activity indicates new conceptions of elite representation: at the same time that the sanctuary at Rossano di Vaglio was monumentalized, rich graves in the area declined in number, indicating that elites

[162] Masseria & D'Anisi 2001, 127–30; Scopacasa 2015.

[163] E.g. Vastogirardi (mid- to late second century): Morel 1976; Campochiaro (mid-second century): Capini 2003; Iuvanum: Bradley, Fossataro, & Menozzi 2008; Lucus Angitiae: Torelli 1982, 165–8; Lecce nei Marsi: Campanelli 1985, 329–30. In general, see Crawford 1981, 160; Bradley 2005, 1027. For Lucania, see Battiloro 2010, 202–14.

[164] Bodei Giglioni 1977, 68; Gros 1978, 49; Crawford 1981, 159; Dench 1995, 137–40.

[165] Wallace-Hadrill 2008, 137–42.

[166] *Imagines* Terventum 36=Rix Sa 2. La Regina 1976, 237 assumes it was modelled on Roman, Latin, or Campanian examples, but this is not necessarily the case. See Wiseman 1983 for the engagement of local elites with Hellenistic culture.

[167] La Regina 1976, 237–41; for the religious landscape, see Stek 2015.

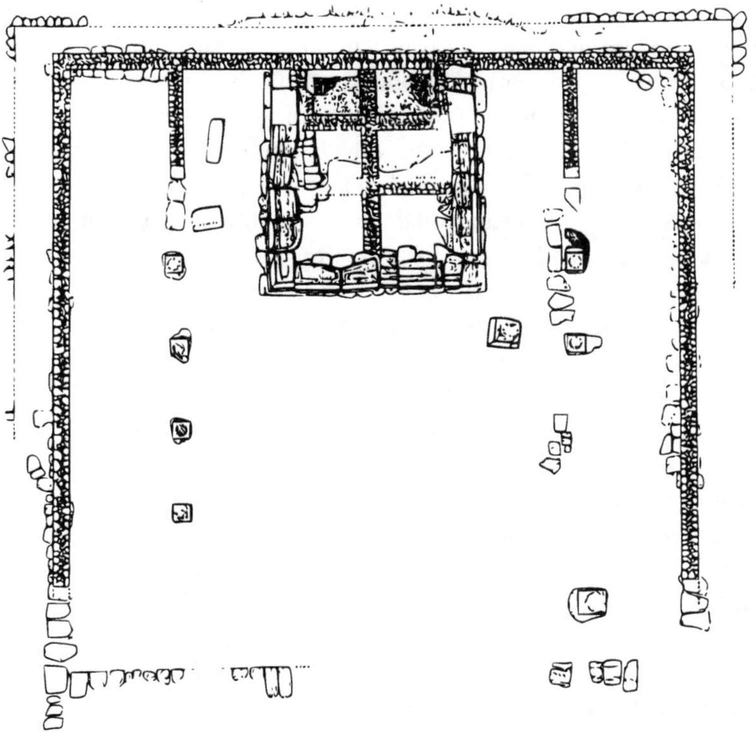

Fig. 4.1. Temple at San Giovanni in Galdo.

Drawing by Benito Di Marco. By permission of the Ministero dei Beni e delle Attività Culturali e del Turismo (Soprintendenza Archeologia, belle arti e paesaggio del Molise).

chose new methods to display their wealth, which more closely matched those in the rest of Italy. Nevertheless, temples in Lucania retained their own regional style; Rossano was very different from temples elsewhere, like Pietrabbondante.[168] This is a clear example of the fact that the expansion of economic networks throughout the Italian peninsula, as well as the growing dominion of Rome, did not eradicate regional cultural identity, as we will also see in the next two sections.

Various lists have been made of all buildings that were erected in Italy in the late third to early first centuries. According to the list compiled by Jouffroy—which is now rather old, but still offers a useful overview of which buildings were the most common—temples formed the largest category of public buildings. The number of new or remodelled temples was the largest in Latium (twenty-nine locations, sixty-four buildings), followed by Campania (ten locations, thirty-six buildings), Samnium (thirteen locations, eighteen buildings), Etruria (nine locations, nineteen buildings), and southern Italy (fourteen locations, seventeen

[168] Isayev 2007, 33–4, 84–5; 2010, 214–17; Andrisani 2009, 119.

buildings). From this overview, it is clear that most public buildings were erected in Latium, but also that many areas in Italy were not far behind.[169] Other large building projects, such as porticoes, fora, pavements, and sewers, is fairly similar: most were built in Latium and Campania (twenty locations), followed by Samnium, Picenum, Umbria, and Etruria, with sixteen locations between them, and the rest in southern Italy. *Macella* and *basilicae* are less common, and are attested mostly in Latium and Campania, while theatre buildings have a wider distribution in Samnium, Etruria, and Umbria.[170] Areas from which many people are attested in commercial activities, e.g. Campania and Samnium, indeed saw a building boom in the later Republican period. It is interesting, however, that Apulia—an area from where we know several merchants were active in the East—saw very little public building at this time.

When looking at building projects in Italy, it is important to establish who paid for them. If we want to determine the level of wealth possessed by Italians, inscriptions recording a donation by a private individual are the most important evidence. Still, if a donation was made from the town's purse or by a collective, this shows that there was money available for the town as a whole, giving some indication of the level of wealth that its people commanded. Unfortunately, for the great majority of surviving buildings we do not know how they were paid for, since no inscriptions have survived that indicate the source of the money.

Private donations (indicated with the term *de sua pecunia*, 'from his own money') occur by far the most frequently in my corpus, namely forty-one times.[171] Famous examples are the gifts of P. Lucilius Gamala in Ostia in the 80s,[172] and L. Betilienus Varus in Aletrium, who donated streets, gates, a sundial, a market building, a *palaestra*, a basilica, seats in the theatre, a bath, and an aqueduct, probably before 90.[173] Private gifts could also be combined with money from other sources; in Capua in 84, a pool was dedicated *Iovei de stipe et de sua pequnia* ('from the treasury of Jupiter and his own money').[174] Money could also be provided by magistrates as a *summa honoraria*, the usual

[169] These building works were facilitated by several inventions of new building techniques. It is often argued that concrete (*opus caementicum*) was invented in the late third century, and from there gradually spread through Italy (Coarelli 1977, 16). However, the latest research (Mogetta 2015) shows that concrete was used in Rome itself only from the late second century, when many new buildings were erected, stimulated by a new interest in Greek architecture among the Roman elites. This means, however, that Italy did not take its inspiration from Rome, since Hellenistic-style buildings had already been erected in Italy before they were built in Rome. Many Italian constructions used cocciopesto rather than concrete, as in Fregellae around 200. In any case, there were great variations between individual towns in the use of building techniques (Torelli 1995, 191–210, 212–45; Wallace-Hadrill 2008, 102).

[170] Jouffroy 1986, 16–58.

[171] It should be noted that the corpus in the Appendix only contains inscriptions in which individuals are named; anonymous inscriptions have not been taken into account. See Jouffroy 1986, 60–1.

[172] CIL 14.375. See Zevi 1973; Cébeillac-Gervasoni 1991, 202–3.

[173] CIL 1^2 1529=10.5807=ILS 5348=ILLRP 189, 528.

[174] CIL 1^2 683=ILS 5734=ILLRP 720.

contribution made by magistrates when entering office.[175] The minimum fee was laid down in local regulations, but could be raised voluntarily by the magistrate.

Towns themselves also had income from various sources, which could be invested in public building. The terms *pecunia publica* or *pecunia commune* were used in inscriptions to indicate that the building was paid for by the public purse of the town.[176] This appears six times in my corpus. In Circeii, a public water system was paid for by the *respublica Circeii* ('community of Circeii').[177] An Oscan inscription from Pietrabbondante records the dedication of a shrine, paid *Buvaianud akdafed* ('from the money of Bovianum').[178] Money from fines imposed by the town provided a good source of income: ten inscriptions record this as a source of money for public buildings. For example, an Oscan inscription from Pompeii records a sundial set up *eituvad multasikad* ('from the money from fines').[179]

Various semi-public bodies are attested as donors for buildings. In Terracina, an *aedicula* (niche to hold a shrine) and *helix* (small column) were set up *de colegi sententia* ('by decision of the college').[180] Since a *collegium* was a private organization, this probably means that the members collected the funds for these buildings from their own money. At Pompeii in the late second century, a building was erected from money donated to the *vereia*, some kind of military institution.[181] Donations could also be made by private associations; this is attested three times, including one by a society of singers[182] and one by a society of carpenters.[183] A collection could also be held among the general public, resulting in a building set up *de conscriptorum sententia* ('by dedication of the subscribers'). This is attested four times in my corpus.

It is important to note that the civic status of a town mattered very little when it came to local building activities: allied towns were just as active, if not more so, in building than colonies and Roman citizen communities. Thus, the presence of public buildings in a fashionable Hellenistic style was not limited to colonies or towns with full Roman citizenship. In allied Pompeii, for example, an impressive number of new public buildings was erected in the late second and early first centuries, such as the Capitolium, the 'Samnite palaestra', and the Stabian baths.[184] The inscriptions of the religious *magistri* from allied Capua also show that an impressive number of other buildings was erected in the late second and early

175 CIL 1² 1635=ILLRP 648=ILS 5707.

176 *Pecunia commune*: ILLRP 606=CIL 1² 1690=10.221; ILS 5665; *pecunia publica*: CIL 1² 1533=10.5074=ILLRP 551=ILS 5367; CIL 10.817, 824, 893=ILS 5726; CIL 1² 1628=10.819=ILLRP 641.

177 CIL 10.6431. See Cébeillac-Gervasoni 1991, 195.

178 *Imagines* Terventum 18=Rix Sa 7.

179 *Imagines* Pompei 21=Rix Po 4.

180 ILLRP 764=CIL 1² 1555. See Flambard 1983, 80.

181 *Imagines* Pompei 24=Rix Po 3. It is unclear what a *vereia* was; most likely it was a military organization (Guzzo 2000, 109; Isayev 2007, 133) or a mercenary company (Tagliamonte 1989–90, 366; Bourdin 2012, 563), but other suggestions are a youth organization (Crawford 2011) or the 'whole people' (Rix 2000).

182 ILLRP 771=CIL 1² 2519.

183 CIL 9.3842.

184 Gros 1978, 45–7; Guzzo 2000; Wallace-Hadrill 2008, 131–7.

first centuries, from a theatre and two porticoes to smaller structures such as pavements, gardens, and fountains.[185] This wealth should most likely be connected to the role of each town in the economic network of Italy, which became more integrated as the second century progressed. As we saw in chapter 3, the function of each town in this network was in no way related to its civic status, so that it makes sense that the wealth of their inhabitants was not dependent on their status either. This activity was part of an Italy-wide trend that introduced new forms of social competition, which focused on investment in public benefactions. This was in marked contrast to previous forms of competition, such as investment in burials. Nevertheless, not all local elites participated in this trend: some Samnite and Apulian elites continued to invest their wealth in funerary display, as had been traditional since the fifth century (see section 4.4). Within general cultural trends, therefore, there was space for individual choice.[186]

This indicated that not only public but also private building occurred on a large scale in the late third to first centuries. Many large houses were built, often with Hellenizing elements. Houses in Pompeii, for example, show the local elite active in conspicuous consumption from the early second century onwards. This is clear in the construction of the Villa of the Mysteries and House of the Faun, dated 180–170. The latter measured 2,940 m^2, which puts it ahead of many Hellenistic palaces of the time. Its mosaic of Alexander's victory over Darius, dated *c.*100, shows the inhabitants' affinity with Greek culture.[187] It is usually assumed that the owner of the House of the Faun was called Satrius, although this not certain.[188] If this is true, he belonged to a family widely attested in the East, where he could have found inspiration for his house. Satrius was a common name in Oscan and is attested in a number of inscriptions on public buildings dating to the same period. An inscription in the floor at the entrance reads HAVE (= *ave*), suggesting that the owner was Latinized to some degree (see section 4.5); however, this certainly does not mean that he was a Roman citizen.[189] Many smaller houses in Pompeii also displayed high levels of luxury: many had *atria*, peristyles, colonnades, and panel paintings.[190] This luxury also permeated the inland areas of Italy, most of which did not have Roman citizenship: a late-second century house in Saepinum in Samnium had a coloured mosaic floor.[191] At the Samnite site of Monte Vairano, the 'house of LN' sported a roof antefix with Hercules and the Nemean lion. Although it is no match in size for the largest houses of Pompeii, it does show the cultural sophistication of the owner.[192]

[185] Frederiksen 1959, 91. [186] Scopacasa 2016.

[187] Gros 1978, 25–7, 45–7; Dyson 1992, 44; Wallace-Hadrill 1999, 307–8; Zevi 2000.

[188] Wallace-Hadrill 1999, 307, but see Zevi 1996, 133.

[189] Zevi 2000, 120. However, he ascribes many aspects of the house to 'Roman influence', e.g. the atrium and floor mosaics.

[190] Flohr 2017, 76–80. [191] Gros 1978, 17–18.

[192] Lloyd & Barker 1981, 301–3; De Benedittis 1990; Dench 1995, 134, 151. Many more luxurious private houses have been found, many of them in areas with the Latin or allied status; see Pesando 1997.

Private consumption of luxury items, often with Hellenistic cultural influence, also increased. For example, grave stelae at Ancona in Picenum show similarities with those from Rheneia, the necropolis of Delos. People from Ancona are attested at Delos and may well have brought these new cultural elements back home. Throughout Italy, a large market for luxury goods gradually developed. A telling example are dining couches, which appeared in many areas of Italy from the early second century, not only in towns like Praeneste, Luceria, and Ancona, but also in more out-of-the-way places, even in the Alps. The Mahdia shipwreck, dated between 110 and 90, contains large numbers of bronze couch legs. The same wreck also contained bronze statues for the market in Italy.[193] Wealth was also displayed in graves; in the Apulian towns Mesagne and Oria, for example, some very rich second-century graves have been found (see section 4.4), which may well have belonged to indigenous elites active in the East. Levels of private wealth can also be deduced from donations to the gods found in temples and votive deposits. Various dedications in Oscan have survived, showing that some Italians were already quite wealthy in the third century. Examples are statues donated in the early third century at Saepinum by Trebis Dekkis and around 250 by Vip[ei]o(s) at San Benedetto dei Marsi.

The question remains as to the source of this wealth. Overseas trade is a possibility; many Italian sanctuaries were greatly influenced by Hellenistic models, which makes sense if their dedicators had encountered this building style on their Eastern ventures. Other important sources of wealth were agricultural production and transhumant pasturing. For example, Samnium has many rich rural sanctuaries and towns located on transhumance routes, such as Saepinum and Monte Vairano.[194]

It is worthwhile to investigate whether we can identify a link between these buildings and the commercial activities of their donators. As we have seen in the cases of Praeneste and Tibur, some people who donated public buildings were also active in trade, or at least people with the same *gentilicia*. An exact match, showing the same individual in Italy and abroad, is unfortunately rare. Possible connections with trade can be found in the case of a *palaestra* with statues, donated at Abella by Statius and Vestricius, both names attested in overseas trade around the same time. At Aletrium, several donations were made by the Betilieni, from a well-known family of traders and amphora producers.[195]

Unfortunately, in most cases we have no indication of the way in which Italians amassed the wealth that paid for these public and private buildings. Several Italian

[193] Wallace-Hadrill 2008, 361–75, 421–31. The most expensive couch legs were made of ivory, but bone imitations catered to less wealthy consumers. This imitation of luxury items in a less expensive way also occurred other items, e.g. pottery and lamps. See, for this 'consumer revolution', Wallace-Hadrill 2008, 315–55; Osborne & Vout 2010.

[194] Dench 1995, 121–3.

[195] ILLRP 528=CIL 1^2 1529=10.5807=ILS 5348; ILLRP 189.

gentes were clearly important and wealthy, as attested from their involvement in public building and local magistracies, but they are not attested outside Italy before the first century. Some notable 'absent' *gentes* are the Caesidii, Cluentii, Digitii, Maii, Papii, Poppaedii, and Tettii; these names occur many times in Italy as local magistrates and benefactors, but are never attested in any kind of commercial activity. Others are only attested overseas from the first century onwards, although they were already important among the local elites of Italy in earlier periods. Of course it is difficult to argue from silence, since inscriptions recording these *gentes* may have been lost. On the other hand, for a few Italian families, e.g. the Aufidii, Cossutii, Gerillani, and Saufeii, we actually have more attestations overseas than in Italy itself, suggesting that commerce was more important for them than for other Italians. If there is no evidence at all for overseas activity of a particular *gens*, we may assume that, even though some evidence of such activity has been lost, it was at least not a very important part of the family's portfolio. The main source of their wealth must therefore have been other activities, such as agriculture or pasturing in Italy.

Of course, Italian elites were not the only people who experienced increased economic prosperity in this period. The attested building activity required a great amount of labour. There is, for this period, no evidence for great numbers of slaves working in building. For the lower classes, seasonal labour, including construction, was a very important source of income (see chapter 2.3). This boom in public and private building activities therefore meant that the lower classes had ample opportunities to find work in construction. It is interesting to note that in the late second century many large building projects took place in many areas of Italy, actually more than in Rome itself. This means that the economic problems experienced by the lower classes in Italy could very well have been less serious than in Rome itself, where the activities of Tiberius Gracchus were motivated by a real process of proletarianization among the urban poor.[196]

We may conclude that commercial activities were an important source of income for Italian elites, and that this wealth was often invested in Italy in public or private building. How this money was spent depended on the region: in Samnium, for example, most monumental buildings were sanctuaries, while the number of expensive private buildings was limited. Despite the economic integration of Italy and the diffusion of Hellenistic culture in most regions, different cultural choices could still be made by the peoples of Italy, as we have seen for Rossano di Vaglio. Thus, cultural developments in Italy varied from region to region, as we will explore in the next section.

[196] Boren 1958; Coarelli 1977, 16–18; Roselaar 2010, 216–17.

4.4. Cultural Developments

In this section, we will explore the cultural changes that occurred in Italy after the Roman conquest of Italy—but whether these changes were a direct result of the conquest remains to be seen. As we have seen in chapter 1, integration is often viewed as a cultural phenomenon, in which a subject population adapts to a dominant society. The situation in Republican Italy was different from that in modern times: in contemporary society, integration is usually experienced by people migrating to a new country. In the Republic, on the other hand, Rome itself 'expanded' into Italy by conquest. The Italians already had their own culture, which was in no way inferior to that of the Romans. Therefore, there was no *a priori* reason for them to change anything after the Roman conquest. Of course, the fact that they were now part of the Roman state meant that they could choose to adopt Roman institutions, as we have seen. It also opened up new possibilities for economic gain, created by Roman power, which Italians eagerly exploited. Finally, as we have seen in chapter 2, new possibilities for interaction with Romans were created, as various new 'points of contact' between Romans and Italians emerged.

Too often, cultural changes in the Republican period are ascribed to the influence of Rome; they are seen as the effect of political 'Romanization', i.e. conquest (chapter 1.5). However, for many Italians there was little reason to interact with Romans; they could meet Romans if they wanted to, but they did not have to. Furthermore, Romans were not the only group with which Italians interacted: many of them were active in the East and encountered Greek culture there. Since for many Italians the Greek East was their main economic and cultural focus, it is difficult to see (all) cultural change in Italy as the effect of 'Romanization'. The only 'Romanization' that we have been able to identify so far occurred in the laws and institutions of the Italians, as well as their engagement in the economic networks created by Rome. These changes were so far-reaching that we might speak of 'institutional' and 'economic' 'Romanization'; however, there is no reason to assume that such developments automatically caused cultural change as well.

It should be emphasized that Italians were not passive recipients of foreign culture, whether Greek or Roman. If they adopted certain new elements of culture, this was because these had a specific use for Italians, i.e. a certain purpose in local society—as we will see throughout this book, local politics and culture remained the focus of life for most Italians. Therefore, cultural expressions were in most cases the result of a conscious choice. For example, institutional change could have important economic advantages: having the same coinage and laws reduced transaction costs and therefore had tangible benefits. Cultural change did not have such direct consequences; it would be helpful for Italians to speak Latin in order to trade with Romans, but this did not exclude speaking other languages (see the next section). Therefore, direct rewards for cultural change were less tangible than for institutional change. At the same time, the cost of abandoning one's culture would be higher in emotional terms than a change in institutions and laws. It is therefore to be expected that cultural change proceeded at a slower pace than institutional and economic change.

In this section, we will briefly describe some cultural developments in Italy in order to determine the motivations behind them and to see what benefits the Italians could have expected to gain from them. I will investigate whether influence from Rome might have motivated these changes and whether other sources of inspiration can be identified. Thus it will be possible to re-evaluate the importance of the Roman conquest for cultural developments in Italy. It is impossible to present a comprehensive analysis of cultural developments in this short space, but some interesting points can be discussed.

Several 'points of contact' have been suggested as the routes through which cultural change occurred. It is often stated that Latin and Roman colonies were important instruments of cultural change. However, as we have seen in chapter 2.2, the amount of interaction between settlers and locals was not always large. Furthermore, there was great variation in the economic development of colonies and therefore in their attraction to Italians. Especially in the first phase of the colony, the settlers often used existing facilities, such as temples. There were, furthermore, great differences between colonies with regard to their city layout, the public buildings erected, the gods that were worshipped, etc. We will briefly examine some examples of cultural change and continuity in colonies, in order to investigate how much cultural impact colonies really had on the surrounding peoples.

At Minturnae, a Roman citizen colony, the extra-urban sanctuary of Marica, originally a goddess of the local Aurunci, remained in use after the colony's foundation. The temple was redecorated in the second century, with palmettes (decorative plaques resembling fan-shaped leaves) similar to those used in the temple of the archaic period.[197] Clearly, the inhabitants of the colony continued to use the pre-existing temple and retained its cultural peculiarities.

Paestum was originally founded as a Greek colony around 600; from the late fifth century, influence from the surrounding Lucanians is visible. Nevertheless, many aspects of Greek culture continued, even after the Latin colony was founded in 273. The colonial foundation did not radically change the town's layout: the Forum was rebuilt, since this was necessary for the government of the colony, but many pre-existing buildings remained, such as the *ekklesiasterion* (assembly building), Asklepieion, and *heroon* (a temple honouring the founder of the town). The extra-urban temples at Foce del Sele and Santa Venera remained in

[197] Livi 2006, 105–13.

use as well. Greek art was still produced and the Greek alphabet remained in use for inscriptions in both Greek and Oscan. Monumental tombs were decorated with paintings in a mix of Hellenistic and local styles. Even after 273, the town's coins were still Greek in design.[198] Extensive building occurred in Paestum only several decades after the foundation of the colony. At this time, the *comitium* was built and the old *bouleuterion* (council building) removed. At the same time, the temples of Fortuna Virilis and Venus Verticordia were erected. It has been argued that this new complex closely resembled the Aventine in Rome,[199] but the resemblance with the Aventine is not very close. In any case, the fact that the new layout included pre-existing buildings shows that the colonists did not set out to eradicate all memory of local culture.[200]

The best-studied allied town is of course Pompeii. In this town, the expression of local identity in public building can be traced in some detail. For example, Corinthian capitals were adopted in the late second or early first century, as well as a new layout for the town and for individual houses. This has been interpreted as 'self-Romanization', since it occurred around the time that Pompeii received citizenship and a colony was settled here by Sulla.[201] However, if these developments occurred before the Social War, there would have been no reason for the Pompeians to 'Romanize'. It is more likely that the local elites adopted cultural elements shared by many Italian towns, and that these elements were not considered 'Roman' at all. It is clear that many Pompeians shared an ideal of what a civilized house should look like, even if most houses did not follow this plan exactly. The atrium and peristyle were part of this social standard; they appear even in fairly small houses. Apparently such elements communicated a specific social message, which would have been relevant especially to the local inhabitants, rather than to Rome.[202]

The foundation of Brundisium as a Latin colony in the 260s had a significant impact on the surrounding allied area. We already saw in chapter 3 that many nearby settlement sites disappeared or declined, showing the impact of the new town on the regional economy. Cultural change also occurred in settlements around the town, such as Oria and Valesio (see chapter 3.3.3): grave gifts became cheaper and simpler than before, for example, simple terracotta lamps, perfume bottles, and coins.[203] These changes may be connected to the economic developments: some sites declined in prosperity, since they were not located in a favourable position to engage with Brundisium, the new centre of the local

[198] Pedley 1990; Crawford 2006; Herring 2007, 11–12. See Greco 2004, 583–97 on the Heraion, which was rebuilt in a style similar to that of sanctuaries in allied Italian territory.

[199] Torelli 1999, 64–77.

[200] Crawford 2006, 66–7, against Curti, Dench, & Patterson 1996, 186, who assume it was a brutal intervention in the local landscape immediately after the colony's foundation. See Greco 1988, 82.

[201] Zevi 1996, 126–4.

[202] Flohr 2017, 76–80.

[203] Burgers 1998, 267–9, 274–7, 282–7; Steingräber 2000, 140–3.

economy. Therefore, their inhabitants could no longer afford expensive grave gifts.[204] Messapia, to the south of Brundisium, had a strong regional identity, with its own language and characteristic pottery. Since the late eighth century, it had been in contact with the Greek settlers in Tarentum and it enjoyed many economic connections with the Greek world. This led to some adoption of Greek cultural elements, such as the names of gods and types of pottery, but Messapia also maintained a specific local culture and language. For example, in graves many Greek objects have been found, but also a local type of pottery, the *trozzella* (see Fig 4.2), which had been placed in female graves from the seventh century onwards, as well as depictions of people in local dress.[205]

Changes in Messapian culture after the foundation of Brundisium were significant, but local culture did not disappear completely. Some elite graves from Mesagne and Oria, for example, show a large degree of cultural continuity: a second-century grave from Mesagne contained an Apulian red-figure krater, which was between 140 and 170 years old when it was buried, as well as Gnathia pottery from the third century. The tomb itself was constructed like traditional Messapian cist graves of the fourth and third centuries. The deceased, or at least those who buried him, clearly wanted to stress his connection with traditional Messapian culture. At the same time, the tomb also contained Black Gloss pottery produced in Brundisium in this period, Rhodian and Knidian amphorae, and a gold funerary crown. The tomb was painted in a style similar to the Pompeian first style. The grave also contained many gifts imported from the East, such as glass and silver vases, jewellery, and bronze and ivory chairs. Another grave from Mesagne and two from Oria held similar grave goods. Thus, these graves showed engagement with new cultural trends, as well as some elements of culture that were typical for the region. Graves with similar goods, apart from the locally specific items, have been found in Arpi and Canusium in northern Apulia and as far north as Ancona. All this indicates the breadth of the cultural community to which the Messapians belonged. Interestingly, the total number of graves decreased in the second century. This indicates either a decline in population, or perhaps increased poverty among the lower classes and greater differences in wealth between the elites and the lower classes.[206]

The individuals buried in such wealthy graves must have belonged to the elite of Brundisium, several of whom we know by name, e.g. Gaius Statorius and Gaius Polfennius (see chapter 3.2.1). These were local men, although their names were Latinized, who all maintained contacts with the Greek world as well as with Romans, in their role of members of the ruling class of the colony. Their engagement with Rome, as leaders of a colony settled by Rome, therefore did

[204] Torelli 1990, 95; Guzzo 1991, 82; Lamboley 1996, 487–90.
[205] Herring 2007, 15–20, 23.
[206] Yntema 2006, 110–13, 120–2; Colivicchi 2011, 119–20.

Fig. 4.2. Trozzella.
Museum of Abrantes, Portugal; photo by author.

not mean that they gave up their Messapian identity.[207] The poet Ennius, from the small town of Rudiae in southern Messapia, wrote in the early second century that he had 'three hearts, because he was proficient in three tongues, Greek, Oscan,

[207] Lamboley 1996, 425–6; Compatangelo 1989, 49; Yntema 2009.

and Latin'.[208] This statement certainly also applied to the men buried in such graves, although their 'third heart' was more likely Messapian, not Oscan. Some names of Messapian origin survived into the Roman period, often in adapted forms, such as Alsinaeus, Dasius, Statorius, and Tutorius, indicating the continued importance of the local elites in the region.

Still, some elements of Messapian culture disappeared in the third or second century, for example, the *trozzella*. It could be argued that the Apulian elites in the second century increasingly adopted a *koine* culture that was visible in many areas of Italy, indicated by the presence in graves of strigils, styluses, game pieces, etc, as well as depictions in graves in civilian dress, rather than the previous depictions of warriors. However, this should be ascribed not directly to 'Romanization', but to 'the increasing integration of Salento into the Hellenistic and Roman world'.[209] The Salento (Messapian peninsula) engaged with this *koine* culture in general, leading to cultural change; however, this was a direct consequence not of increased contacts with Rome, but of contacts with the Greek world and various parts of Italy, especially along the eastern coast. Many of these contacts were the result of increased economic activity, especially as Brundisium became the central harbour for Rome's military activities in Greece. Part of this was the result of Rome's expanding power, but the Apulians and Messapians themselves chose to use these economic networks and interact with the cultural opportunities they brought with them.

The former Greek colonies in southern Italy, which remained allied after the Roman conquest, strongly held on to their cultural identity, often more so than other allied areas. At Tarentum, for example, burial rituals changed more slowly than in the surrounding area. Only when a colony was founded here in 123 did changes take place: cremation rather than inhumation now became the most important way of burial. In graves, expensive terracotta statuettes and precious metal items almost disappeared; the gifts were now cheaper and mostly locally made, including glass bottles, small alabaster amphorae, bronze mirrors, and coins.[210] This matches the difficult economic situation of the town in the second century.

Regium also retained much of its Greek culture: in the second century, it still used Greek terms for its institutions, such as *boule* (council) and *haliasma* (decree of the assembly); Greek was still spoken and the same cults were venerated as before. Only after the Social War did this change quickly.[211] Heraclea also still had magistrates with Greek titles. Only in the first century was an active attempt made by Rome to adapt its institutions to those used in other Italian towns. This is

[208] Gell. *NA* 17.17.1. However, Ennius also stated 'we are Romans who were once Rudians' (fr. 525: *Nos sumus Romani qui fuimus ante Rudini).* Of course, in a political sense the people of Rudiae, or at least their elites, could not deny their connection with Rome; some, like Ennius, even received Roman citizenship. Since he was writing for a Roman audience, he stressed the impact of Rome.

[209] Boersma & Yntema 1987, 93; see Steingräber 2000, 145; Stek 2013a, 348.

[210] Desy 1993, 90–6, 126–7; Crawford 1996, 302–3; Steingräber 2000, 142.

[211] Sartori 1953, 140; Castrizio 1995, 64.

shown by the *tabula Heracleensis*, a law drafted for the town by Caesar; before this time, no intervention by Rome had taken place.[212]

There were differences, however, between the various Greek cities: those in Campania, such as Paestum and Cumae, were more influenced by Oscan language and culture—although this does not apply to Neapolis. At Cumae, for example, few traces of Greek-style buildings or the Greek language remain. Most individuals we know from Cumae have Oscan names. Greek towns that were resettled as Roman colonies in the second century, such as Vibo Valentia and Thurii Copia, no longer had magistrates with Greek titles, nor did they retain many Greek buildings.[213] This matches the cultural changes visible in Tarentum after the foundation of the colony in 123.

As we have seen, already in the third century, many buildings erected in Italy were Hellenistic in style, and their number increased in the late second and early first centuries. In Rome, such buildings often appeared later than in other areas of Italy; Rome, therefore, was generally not the model on which Italians based their public and private buildings. For example, theatres built of stone were already present in many Greek cities in southern Italy in the fourth and third centuries. In the second and early first centuries, many Greek-style theatres in stone were built in a large number of Italian towns, both Latin colonies such as Cales and Alba Fucens, and areas with Roman citizenship like Gabii, Lanuvium, and Nemi, as well as allied towns, e.g. Capua, Pietrabbondante, Pompeii, Teanum Sidicinum, Praeneste, and Tibur.[214] The first stone theatre in Rome was not built until 55, more than a century later than some of the Italian examples.[215] Another example is the double portico complex built at Minturnae between 190 and 174, while in Rome itself such a building was not erected until after the victory over Macedon in 168.[216] Greek influence was strong in some cases: around 175, Fregellae's sanctuary was monumentalized in Hellenistic style, with a winged stoa with Doric columns, covered in stucco with paintings in the so-called First Style.[217] Something like this did not exist in Rome at the time. Statements like '[Rome] became... the cultural leader as well as the political mistress, and it is this that largely accounts for the speed with which Hellenistic civilization penetrated all Italy'[218] can therefore no longer be maintained.

It is difficult to establish exactly which trajectories led to the construction of these temples. The temple-theatre complex at Pietrabbondante in Samnium

[212] Sartori 1953, 98–9. [213] Sartori 1953, 114–15, 128. [214] Johannowsky 1976, 272.

[215] Dyson 1992, 45. An earlier stone theatre, built in 154, was destroyed by the consul Scipio Nasica (VM 1.15.3; App. *BC* 1.28; see North 1992). For cultural change in Rome, see Coarelli 1996; Wallace-Hadrill 2008.

[216] Gros 1978, 25; Guidobaldi & Pesando 1989, 50. [217] Coarelli 1998; Lesk 1999, 63.

[218] Salmon 1982, 100. He argues that this was the case especially in 'Roman or Latin Italy', citing as an example Monterinaldo in Picenum (which cannot be called 'Roman or Latin' in any sense), but also argues that the temple in Pietrabbondante owed much to Rome in style, layout, and decoration (p. 117); see Salmon 1967, 137. See also Keaveney 1987, 25: 'Italians took their cue from Rome.'

(see Fig 4.3) in some ways resembles the theatre at Sarno in Campania, as well as examples from Magna Graecia. The podium of temple B at Pietrabbondante resembles that of the temple at Fondo Patturelli near Capua quite closely,[219] although the Pietrabbondante complex as a whole is not mirrored elsewhere. In

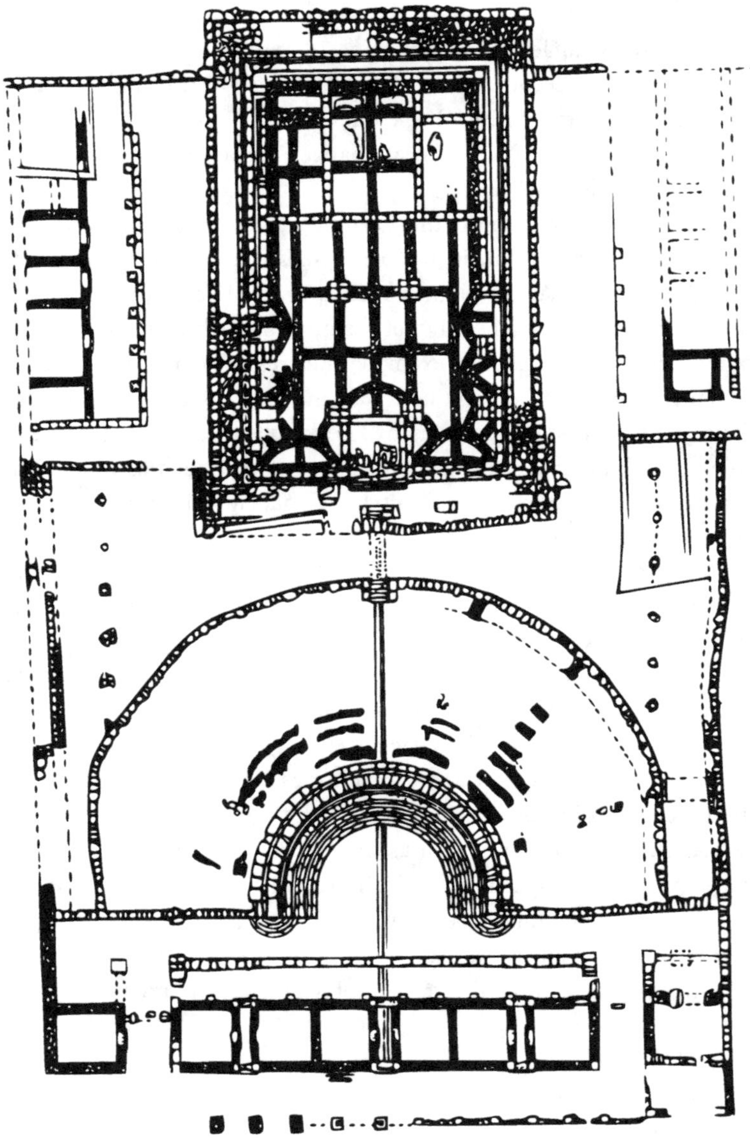

Fig. 4.3. The temple-theatre complex at Pietrabbondante.

Drawing by Benito Di Marco. By permission of the Ministero dei Beni e delle Attività Culturali e del Turismo (Soprintendenza Archeologia, belle arti e paesaggio del Molise).

[219] Lauter 1976, 415–16; Stek 2013b.

the case of Pietrabbondante, the temple may have been inspired by models that local merchants encountered during their travels in the East, or by Campanian models. But it is certain that temples in Rome and nearby Latin colonies were not the main inspiration for these buildings; the temples at Aesernia and Sora, the closest Latin colonies to Pietrabbondante, were smaller and rather old-fashioned in comparison to the large and stylish Hellenistic complex. Whatever the source of inspiration, such buildings could be used to express local feelings of identity. At Pietrabbondante, the temple was built on the same spot as an archaic sanctuary, indicating the importance of continuity of local landscapes.[220] A second-century inscription commemorates the dedication of a temple by a local leader of the *Safinim*, 'the Samnite people'.[221] This has led to the suggestion that Pietrabbondante was the central temple of the Samnite people, but, as we have seen (chapter 1.6), it is unlikely that there was an official institution ruling all Samnite people, with a central temple. In the same period, smaller temples were built in other locations in Samnium, indicating the importance of sacred buildings for the expression of local identity.[222]

It is to be noted that the wholesale acceptance of Greek theatre, both in the style of theatre buildings and in the content of actual performances, was more common in Samnium and Campania, where no pre-existing theatrical culture existed, than in Rome. In inland Italy, theatre was taken over directly from Greece as a religious and civic medium. Romans found Greek-style theatres less useful, because theatrical and other performances already existed in Rome, along with the buildings in which they were performed. Therefore, they only adopted buildings that did not yet exist in Rome, e.g. the Odeion.[223] In other cases as well, Italians engaged more closely with elements of Greek culture than Rome did. Not all elements of Greek culture were adopted in Rome, e.g. gymnastic activities, while in the rest of Italy, many *palaestrae* were built.[224]

As for city layouts, some towns in Italy developed a regular grid-like layout in the third or second century, which is characterized by some scholars as 'Roman'.[225] However, such layouts also existed in Greece and the Greek colonies in southern Italy. There is no reason to assume that a change in city layout was the result of direct Roman influence.[226] It is more likely that these developments were part of a general trend towards urbanization visible in Italy in the second century.[227]

Italian elites also shared a cultural *koine* in private building, which was again mostly derived from Hellenistic examples. We already saw the houses with *atria* and peristyles built in Pompeii; these were common elsewhere too. In Suasa in the Ager Gallicus, a second-century house had an atrium and peristyle and was

[220] Stek 2013b.
[221] *Imagines* Terventum 8=Rix Sa 4. See, for the meaning of this term, Dench 1995, 198–206.
[222] Stek 2015. [223] Lauter 1976, 419–22.
[224] Gros 1978, 43–4; Jouffroy 1986, 39–58; Mouritsen 1998, 74–6; Osborne & Vout 2010, 238.
[225] Gabba 1987, 117. See Salmon 1982, 100, 159. [226] Lomas 1998, 67; Mouritsen 1998, 75.
[227] Jouffroy 1986; Dyson 1992, 44–5.

decorated with mosaics and First-Style paintings. The excavators describe this as an expression of *urbanitas* and *Romanitas*.[228] However, luxurious atrium houses with peristyles appeared in the second century in many Italian towns, but in Rome not until the first century. The atrium house was certainly not a Roman invention, but already existed in Etruria in the fifth century.[229] It is therefore unwise to suppose that all such houses were derived from Roman models or that they expressed a cultural or civic loyalty to Rome, rather than an adherence to a general Italian fashion.

The appearance of such buildings in Italy therefore cannot be ascribed to the 'Romanization' of tastes and culture. Rather, we may speak of 'Hellenization', which occurred in Italy in many locations at roughly the same time.[230] Already by the second century, we can speak of 'a sort of Italic *koine* of luxury consumer goods'.[231] The Italians, as active agents in their own cultural representation, 'triangulated' themselves between Greek, Roman, and local culture.[232] The Hellenization of public and private building spread through Italy without direct influence from the Rome. Furthermore, it is often assumed that colonies played a leading role in these developments (see chapter 2.2), but this is incorrect; they took place in allied towns just the same, and in many cases even earlier than in the colonies.

Although we have not been able to trace cultural change in detail in this short section, it has become clear that the impact of Rome on the cultures of the Italian peoples was fairly limited. We may conclude that it is no longer possible to maintain that 'by *c.* 100 the trend towards Romanization everywhere in Italy was undoubtedly evident and probably irreversible: by then the whole country was manifestly destined to adopt Roman ways sooner or later. The Social War ensured that it happened sooner'.[233] Much of the monumentalization of public and private building was carried out by local elites, in a process sometimes called 'autoromanizzazione'.[234] In many ways, the cultures of the various Italian peoples became more uniform in the last centuries BC, as a *koine* culture appeared, based mostly on Hellenistic elements. However, local agents picked the elements from this *koine* that were the most appropriate for the local situation.[235] The term 'cultural revolution'[236]—or rather 'evolution', as these developments took place over several centuries—can therefore be applied to this phenomenon. Many expressions of local culture disappeared only in the first century BC, although the tempo of these changes varied from place to place (see chapter 5.8). The same applied to changes

[228] Dall'Aglio, De Maria, & Podini 2007, 190. Likewise, Zevi 2000, 119 argues that atrium houses from Pompeii were based on Roman models.

[229] Mouritsen 1998, 74–6; Wallace-Hadrill 1997.

[230] Zanker 1990, 331–8; Cébeillac-Gervasoni 1991, 200, 207; Dench 1995, 7, 112: Stek 2013a, 341.

[231] Wallace-Hadrill 1999, 311. [232] Wallace-Hadrill 2008, 5. [233] Salmon 1982, 159.

[234] See discussion in Cavalieri 2012, 163–73. [235] Versluys 2013, 429–30.

[236] Wallace-Hadrill 2008.

in the languages spoken by the Italian peoples; as language is an important part of identity, we will investigate these changes separately in the next section.

For most of the Republican period, Rome had little direct influence on processes of cultural change. Still, this monumentalization was partially financed by wealth gathered by local elites in commercial activities abroad, which were greatly facilitated by the expansion of the Roman state, so that we cannot completely deny the influence of Roman hegemony.

4.5. Linguistic Developments

Like laws and coinage, the languages of Italy gradually converged. Eventually the Italic languages disappeared and were replaced by Latin, but this process was only complete at the end of the first century. Linguistic change in Italy cannot be fully discussed here, but some interesting changes can be observed.[237] We will survey linguistic change only briefly, in order to investigate how wide Rome's reach was in this respect. As we have seen, in some spheres, such as institutions and coinage, Roman influence was quite large from a relatively early period. As this section will show, developments were very different with regard to linguistic change.

In the Republican period, speaking Latin became a 'social necessity' for Italian elites, since many Italians had social relations with Romans, and with other Italians who spoke a different Italic language. Latin was, from the mid-third century onwards, the most logical choice as a *lingua franca* for all Italian people, since it facilitated contact across Italy. Therefore, 'we find communities voluntarily adopting Latin alongside, or instead of, their own languages, in recognition of changes in their status or in pursuit of the advantages that the use of Latin might bring, politically and commercially'. At Delos for example, Latin was the *lingua franca* among the Italian traders.[238] The traders at Delos quite naturally were bilingual, or in fact perhaps trilingual: Latin and Greek texts are common on the island, written by people with an Oscan background. Speaking the same language brought considerable commercial benefits: it enhanced the chance of a profitable agreement and reduced the chance of being cheated if one business partner did not understand the other. It also eliminated the need for interpreters, which lowered transaction costs.[239]

Changes in language could occur for quite specific reasons in each location. The people of Cumae asked Rome in 180 'to be allowed to speak Latin in public and that the auction masters were allowed to sell in Latin'.[240] Auctions are specifically mentioned: clearly the commercial use of Latin was important. Especially in auctions, more than in private business, the ability to negotiate quickly was

[237] See Adams 2003. [238] Clackson & Horrocks 2011, 81.
[239] Hingley 2005, 99; Clackson & Horrocks 2007, 82–3. [240] Liv. 40.43.1.

essential. Cumae, a town originally founded as a Greek colony, in the second century had a mostly Oscan-speaking population. There were also many Latin colonies in the area, as well as foreign traders visiting the harbour at nearby Puteoli. Cumae therefore needed a common language. Of course, the city could have changed to Latin without asking Rome's permission, but the Cumaeans wanted to let Rome know that they had done this.[241] Thus, the request may have been motivated by considerations of the prestige that Cumae enjoyed in the eyes of the Roman state. On the other hand, regional considerations may also have played an important role in the change of language. Firstly, Cumae and Capua were rivals in the regional political sphere before and during the Second Punic War.[242] It is possible, therefore, that Cumae used its language policy as a way to stay ahead of Capua, by making itself attractive for merchants. Secondly, Puteoli, founded in 194, had become an important rival for the position of most important harbour in Campania, so that Cumae may have been trying to attract people to its own markets instead.

Language can be an important marker of identity; it can show allegiance to the identity of a dominant power, or resistance to it. As we have seen (chapter 1.4), people can display different identities in different situations, and this included the choice of language. Even if Latin was used in public in a specific town, such as in official publications of the town or by individuals communicating in public, as was the case in Cumae, other languages continued to be used in private. For example, people in Etruria often used Etruscan in private, for example, on funerary inscriptions, even though their towns used Latin in public.[243] The Messapian town Uxentum used the Messapian legend OZAN on its coins, even in the first century. Even though Messapian was no longer spoken at this time, its use was still a marker of local identity.[244] The reverse occurred as well: in the entrance to the Casa del Fauno in Pompeii, a Latin inscription reads HAVE (*ave*, i.e. 'welcome'), while Oscan was still the public language of Pompeii when the house was built.[245] Clearly the owner wanted to express his knowledge of the Latin language and the status that it carried in certain circles.

Linguistic change was not the result of Roman pressure: Rome did not try to stamp out other languages.[246] This means that there was much variation in the rate of change between the Italic languages. Some dialects, such as Marsic and Vestinian, already show much Latin influence in the third century. Others, like Paelignian, Etruscan, and Messapian, changed much more slowly;[247] inscriptions in Messapian and Etruscan were still set up in the first century.[248] We must

[241] Adams 2003, 113–14; Clackson & Horrocks 2007, 82.
[242] Fronda 2010, 124–5.
[243] Kaimio 1975.
[244] Stazio 1970, 85–7.
[245] Wallace-Hadrill 1999, 297, 307; Zevi 2000.
[246] Harris 1971, 172.
[247] E.g. ILLRP 7 is an early Latin text from the Marsi area; see Letta & D'Amato 1975. See Crawford 2011 for an overview of the different Italic languages.
[248] De Simone & Marchesini, 2002.

remember that in some cases, a complicated mix of language traditions was already in use. In Lucania, for example, many inscriptions used the Oscan language, but were written in Greek characters, while Latin was used for institutional terms (see section 4.2.2).[249]

Etruscan was the slowest of all Italic languages to disappear, although it experienced different rates of change in different locations. Latin appeared in Etruria in official texts by the late second century and in private texts in the early first century.[250] The earliest changes occurred in the naming system: from the second century, Etruscans started to use both Etruscan and Latin names on grave inscriptions. Sometimes the names were simply Latinized: Ca. Puplece Ma. fel. became C. Publicius *Marci filius*.[251] Others translated their name into Latin, so that Ziχu became Scribonius, from *scribere* (to write), a direct translation of the Etruscan meaning.[252] Sometimes Etruscans chose a completely different Latin name: an Etruscan inscription from Africa records Arnth Unata, who in Latin calls himself Otacilius. It is possible that Unata was a client of the Otacilii and chose this name as a token of respect for his patron.[253] Change was not always one-directional: sometimes parents with Latin names gave their children Etruscan names; it was also possible for brothers to use two different languages.[254] This double onomastic identity enabled Italians to display two different identities at different times. We cannot therefore assume that 'pure' language traditions existed that experienced one-way influence from Latin until indigenous languages had disappeared.

Similar mechanisms were at work in the Sabellic (Osco-Umbrian) language family: in many cases, people simply Latinized their Oscan names, turning Betitis into Betitius and Fuvfdis into Fufidius. The similar structure of the two languages made this quite easy, although some changes were necessary, such as turning *ai* into *ae* and removing or adding vowels (Gnaivs—Gnaeus; Helevis—Helvius; Niumsis—Numerius). Many Oscan *gentilicia* remained in use, in a Latinized form, into the Imperial period; in the *tabulae* of the Sulpicii, dating to first-century AD Pompeii, common names are Castricius, Marius, Suettius, and Stlaccius, which have direct Oscan parallels in the fourth or third century BC.[255] Some Oscan *praenomina* gradually disappeared, especially those that had no close parallels in Latin (Baiz, Bantis, Kluvaz), although some of these were turned into *gentilicia*, such as Bantius and Cluvatius.

Umbrian shows grammatical changes in the second century, with more private texts appearing in Latin, and the Umbrian language increasingly written in the Latin alphabet, as the *tabulae Iguvinae* show.[256] Private inscriptions also show

[249] *Imagines* Atina Lucana 1=Rix Lu 2. See Fraschetti 1981, 205.

[250] Kaimio 1975, 218–21; Benelli 1994; Sisani 2008, 115–16.

[251] TLE 541.

[252] Kaimio 1975, 145; Bakkum 2009, 214.

[253] Benelli 2001, 13.

[254] CIE 1075, 1079, 3057–8. See Kaimio 1975, 209; Benelli 2001, 10.

[255] Lejeune 1976, 127–45; for the *tabulae* of the Sulpicii, see Camodeca 1999, 27.

[256] Sisani 2008, 112–13.

early Latin influence. However, only after the Social War were inscriptions written exclusively in Latin.[257] Such changes were especially noteworthy near the Via Amerina and Via Flaminia, indicating the importance of communication routes in these processes. Towns near these roads quickly adopted elements of the Latin alphabet, and from the late third century onwards they used the Latin language.[258] In some towns, such as Reate, radical linguistic change accompanied the Roman conquest. This was an area of viritane settlement, so it seems that viritane settlers caused the disappearance of local epigraphic testimonies.[259] It is unlikely that viritane settlers from Rome expelled the locals, but as we have seen (chapter 2.3), there was probably much occasion for interaction between settlers and locals in such circumstances, and therefore more linguistic change here than in other areas.

The effect of civic status on language has been debated; as we have seen, for economic developments it mattered very little whether a town or area had Roman citizenship, *civitas sine suffragio*, or Latin or allied status. It might be assumed that people who had Roman citizenship, with or without the vote, experienced more cultural change than those who remained allied. For example, inscriptions from Caere in Etruria—which is assumed to have received *civitas sine suffragio* in 273 (see chapter 1.6)—show that already in the third century there was a change towards the Latin naming system, using the *tria nomina*, although Latin itself was not used until the first century. A sudden change from Etruscan to Latin occurred in the early first century, around the time the city received full citizenship, although we cannot assume a direct causal relation between the two events.[260] Developments in Ateste, a town of the Veneti in Cisalpine Gaul, show that it was not necessary for an area to have citizenship in order for linguistic changes to occur. Linguistic change, especially in the use of names, occurred in Ateste in the second century, when the town was still allied.[261] A Venetian *praenomen* or patronym could be changed into a *gentilicium*, and a *praenomen* added. Thus T. Crumelonius was a Latinized version of the Venetian Krumelons.[262] When a person was given Roman citizenship, the local name became the *cognomen*, e.g. C. Antestius Ambudsuilus.[263]

We may conclude that in some areas with Roman citizenship language change occurred fairly quickly, but this also happened in non-citizen areas, such as those of the Marsi and Vestini. Allied areas, such as Etruria, Messapia, and most Oscan-speaking areas, used their own languages for longer, with most of them disappearing only in the first century. It is also interesting to note that there was no direct

[257] Bradley 2000, 205–14; Benelli 2001, 8–9; Sisani 2008, 103–4.

[258] E.g. Rix ST Um 6, 7, 38 (alphabet); CIL 1^2 2112, 11.5449, 11.8037 (language). See Sisani 2008, 103–5, 109–13.

[259] E.g. Rix Um 37. See Harris 1971, 169–87; Coarelli 1996, 249; Clackson & Horrocks 2011, 83; Nonnis & Sisani 2012, 56–60. That the Umbrians were physically driven out is unlikely.

[260] Harris 1971, 45–7; Kaimio 1975, 195; Benelli 2001, 10. Humbert 1978, 38 dates the grant to 350.

[261] Lejeune 1978, 88–92.

[262] CIL 1^2 818=AE 1997, 584.

[263] CIL 3.4274.

relation between different types of cultural change: Campania, for example, was more urbanized than the Marsic and Samnite areas, but less Latinized than the Marsic region.[264]

Many towns displayed local pride in the late second century, and rightly so, since at the time many Italian cities were at the height of their prosperity and Italian businessmen were known throughout the Mediterranean. This pride was visible in the continued use of their own languages: in the late second and first centuries, some texts seem to consciously avoid Roman influence. The Oscan *tabula Bantina*, for example, has been interpreted as an attempt to strengthen local identity by writing down local laws in the local language. Its creation may have been motivated by the fear that Oscan would disappear, although it certainly was still in use, judging from the many inscriptions written in Oscan at this time. The *tabula Bantina* therefore seems to have been written too early to be part of a 'revival' of Oscan.[265] The *tabulae Iguvinae*—dated to 200–120 for the Umbrian texts and 150–70 for the Latin—may be interpreted similarly as an attempt to save the local language in a changing world. Both these texts were influenced by Rome, in content as well as language. However, this does not make the effort of preserving Italian languages and laws any less significant, as it shows how important language was to the Italians that spoke it.[266]

We may conclude that Mouritsen is at least partially correct in stating that

> no generalised Latinization can be demonstrated in allied Italy... [O]nly in some areas, geographically close to Rome, are there any signs of Latin actually having been used internally... The obvious Romanization encountered in the [Augustan] period contrasts sharply with the barely traceable Roman influence prior to the Social War.[267]

He argues that only in areas close to Rome was Latin used for internal communication, but that in other areas it was limited to communication with Romans. This is not quite true, since areas further away, such as Lucania, also display some impact of Latin, as shown by the *tabula Bantina*. As in other areas of life, such as cultural change, as seen in the previous section, Roman influence on language was fairly limited. Rome did not attempt to eradicate local languages,[268] and had not tried to eradicate Italian coinage or laws either. In most cases, change occurred at the initiative of the Italians themselves. In the case of coinage, the change occurred much more quickly than in the case of language, because using the same coinage brought direct, tangible benefits. With language, there were certainly benefits in being able to communicate with Romans, but it was perfectly possible to use two

[264] Salmon 1982, 21; Keaveney 1987, 23. For language change, see Langslow 2012.

[265] As Crawford & Coleman 1996, 276 do, but see Adams 2003, 115.

[266] Bradley 2000, 206; Bispham 2007, 145.

[267] Mouritsen 1998, 79–84.

[268] As Sisani 2008, 121–3 thinks. This occurred only in specific cases: in Pompeii, Oscan disappeared very quickly after the establishment of the Sullan colony in 82; see Crawford 2011, 39.

languages in different contexts, so that a quick change in language was not necessary.

As this section has shown, the impact of Rome on the languages of Italy was, for a long time, fairly limited. At the same time, however, a gradual change in the identities displayed by the Italians took place. Although many people still spoke their own language, and, as we have seen, there were still many cultural differences between the various Italian peoples, it also became possible to identify oneself as an Italian. Thus, a common identity for all inhabitants of the Italian peninsula appeared, as we will now see.

4.6. The Concept of Italia and Italian Identity

We have seen that many Italians were active in overseas trade and other profitable enterprises outside of Italy. During these activities they made great profits, but also gained status: Italians received honours from Greek towns, such as free hospitality with local elites (proxeny), local citizenship, and *ateleia* (tax emptions). Many Italian settlers in Delos and elsewhere in Greece became closely associated with local society, for example, by acquiring land, participating in local government and religion, and marrying into local families.[269] Their overseas activities ensured that throughout the Mediterranean, Italians enjoyed a reputation as successful businessmen. These experiences overseas significantly affected the way in which the Italians perceived themselves and what they expected from the Roman state.

We have seen that there were many differences within Italy; the Italians belonged to different states and did not share a common culture and language. There was no concept of 'Italian' identity, at least not in the period before the Roman conquest of Italy. Gradually this changed, until in the Social War the Italians could organize collective military action and set up an independent state called Italia, with the capital Italica.[270] It has been argued that the Italian experience in the Mediterranean played an important role in the creation of an 'Italian' identity: through their shared experiences, Italians as a whole came to identify themselves with each other and with the geographical unit called *Italia*, in addition to their continuing ties to their home towns and/or peoples.[271] This is indeed an important factor in the creation of an Italian identity, as I will argue.

Important insights into the Italian view of their identity can be gathered from Greek inscriptions regarding Italians, mostly from Delos. Two expressions often appear in these texts, *Rhomaioi* and *Italikoi*, in Latin *Italici*. The use of these terms is revealing with regard to the identity expressed by those who set up these inscriptions. The term *Rhomaios* was used only in Greek and bilingual

[269] Errington 1988, 149–50; Eberle & Le Quéré 2017.
[270] Strabo 5.4.2.
[271] Gabba 1989, 224.

inscriptions, written by Greek speakers and intended for a Greek audience. At first, the Greeks seem to have been unfamiliar with Roman naming conventions. For example, Roman officials are indicated with just a *praenomen* followed by Rhomaios, e.g. Titus Rhomaios, none other than T. Quinctius Flamininus, consul of 198.[272] Later, the term Rhomaios came to be used by Latin speakers as well. In the early second century, Rhomaios came to be used as part of someone's name, either in the location where a *gentilicium* or *cognomen* would normally stand, or after a *cognomen*, e.g. Lucius Acilius Rhomaios or Lucius Aufidius Bassus Rhomaios. It seems to have served as a marker of origin, that is, an indication that the person was from Rome or was associated with the Roman state. It was normal Greek practice to indicate a person's home town: people from Magna Graecia called themselves, for example, 'Herakleitos, son of Nikodemos, from Tarentum'.[273]

It is not clear whether people called Rhomaios were always Roman citizens, as some scholars suggest.[274] In some cases, it seems that a person named Rhomaios was an Italian, who possibly did not hold Roman citizenship. This is the case, for example, with Maraius Gerillanus Rhomaios at Delos around 100. Maras or Maraios was an Oscan *praenomen*, attested in Italy in Pompeii, Neapolis, and Bruttium, all allied areas. On the other hand, D. Cossutius Rhomaios, working as an architect at Athens in 174, was a Roman citizen, despite his name, which is attested in Capua and Tarentum.[275] The number of Rhomaioi with clearly Italian names is low; most people have common names, which also occur among Roman elites. The term was not applied to people of a specific social standing: of the 221 attested Rhomaioi, eighty-eight were freeborn, ninety-five freedmen, and forty-eight slaves.[276] Of course, slaves were not citizens, so the term was not strictly a designation of civic status—the theory that people of Italian origin used the term *Rhomaios* to show that they were Roman citizens cannot be supported, therefore.

It is thus difficult to find a connecting element in the use of the term *Rhomaios*; some people described in this way were Roman officials, while others were people with some kind of connection to Rome or Italy. We cannot be certain that the term refers to the city of Rome specifically or that it indicates possession of Roman citizenship. For Greeks, it was difficult in any case to determine whether someone was a Roman citizen; therefore, when Greeks addressed Italians, or Romans and Italians together, they used the term *Rhomaioi*. We may only conclude that *Rhomaios* served as an identifier for people who had something to do with

[272] E.g. ID 439, a, 76–77; 448, B, 6–7.

[273] IG 12.9, 187, B, l. 2.

[274] Solin 1982, 113 thinks they were either Roman citizens or inhabitants of Rome itself (free or slaves); Nocita 2012, 166 argues that the use of the term *Rhomaios* declined when all Italians had received citizenship, but in fact it was used until the late first century. See Adams 2003, 651–84.

[275] Vitr. 7.pr.15.

[276] Hatzfeld 1919, 247–8. See Brunt 1987, 212–13; Rauh 1993, 33 n. 70; Adams 2003, 644.

Rome, and that it was intended to distinguish them from other people by the fact that they were connected to Rome.

The term *Italikoi*/*Italici* is much less frequent; it appears only in the plural and is used for groups who described themselves in this way or were described as such by others. Again, the use of the term *Italici* reveals much about the way those who used it thought about themselves. The term was used in Latin, Greek, and bilingual texts, in contrast to Rhomaios. When *Italici* appears in the nominative, i.e. when the *Italici* were the dedicators of an inscription, they used Latin or bilingual texts. Often, Italians call themselves 'the Italians who are in . . . ', e.g. 'the Italians who are in Alexandria' (*Italici qui fuere Alexandriae*),[277] or 'the Italians who trade in . . . ', e.g. 'the Italians who trade in Agrigentum' (*Italicei qui Agrigenti negotiantur*).[278]

The most impressive building at Delos was the Agora of the Italians, built around 110. This was indicated in Greek by the term *Italike pa[—]*.[279] Clearly, the building was associated with the Italians as a group and served as a symbol of their wealth and, most importantly, their common identity as Italians. It must be noted that among the financial contributors to the building, who recorded their names on its façade, many people from non-Roman parts of Italy are mentioned, e.g. Gerillanus, Novius, Paconius, and Vibius. The use of the adjective *Italike* shows that the level of identification with Italy was increasing among Italians in the late second century. Other buildings were also associated with Italians: L. Orbius Diphilos in the early first century set up a statue and a bath house for the *Italici* at Delos. The Italians did not actively separate themselves from Romans, however; the Italian Agora saw donations from many people with Roman names too, as well as Greeks and people from further abroad, such as Philostratus of Ascalon.[280] In many towns in the Mediterranean, Italians joined Roman citizens in associations (*conventus*) or religious groups (*collegia*).

As we have seen, language is often an important marker of identity. The Latin language was indeed used as a marker of an Italian identity: when *Italici* made a joint dedication with Greeks, Latin was always one of the languages. The religious *collegia* at Delos, consisting of Italians and Romans only, set up Latin inscriptions, unless the inscription was intended expressly for a Greek audience; for example, honorific inscriptions addressed to Greeks were written in Greek. When dealing with Roman officials, Italians were careful to project a connection with Rome, by erecting Latin or bilingual inscriptions; Roman officials were never addressed in Greek only by *Italici*. Thus, 'Italians in potentially hostile environments sought to

[277] ILLRP 343. [278] CIL 1^2 2710=6.40903=ILLRP 380.

[279] Unfortunately, the term used to describe the type of building is fragmentary, so its function is unclear; it may have been a gymnastic space, since the building is called a *palaestra* in a Latin inscription (*ID* 1743). Others suggest that it was a market for the slave trade (Coarelli 1983) or a multifunctional space (Rauh 1993, 355–8).

[280] *ID* 1717.

use linguistic strategies to underline their connection with the Roman state'.[281] Indeed, if the main advantages of association with Rome were protection and the award of economic benefits (see section 4.7), the Romans would not appreciate it if the Italians consciously took their distance from Rome.[282]

We may conclude that there was a difference in meaning between the terms *Rhomaios* and *Italikos*, contrary to the opinion of some scholars, who assume they were interchangeable.[283] This is shown by the inscription set up by A. Novius Rhomaios, who made a dedication to the 'Apolloniastes and Italikoi'.[284] The use of the terms *Rhomaios* and *Italikoi* in the same inscription suggests that there was a clear difference in meaning, and that the meaning of each was clear to those reading the text.

Italians at Delos also announced their association with Rome in other ways. For example, some families relatively quickly abandoned specific names that marked them as Italians. Some *praenomina* used at Delos were Oscan, such as Minatos and Maraios, but many were Roman, even when combined with a typically Italian *gentilicium*. Gaius Staius, for example, used a Latin *praenomen*, although the Staii in Italy in the same period used Oscan *praenomina*. The most common Oscan names at Delos are those that had a Latin equivalent: Lucius/Lúvkis, Vibius/Vibis, Gnaeus/Gnaivs, Numerius/Niumsis, Decimus/Dekis, and Marcus/Mamereks. This allowed people to display different identities in specific Roman or Italian settings, as discussed in chapter 1. This may be construed as evidence for the 'Romanization' of Italian *praenomina*;[285] however, the fact that Italians preferred names that had both a Roman and Italian form suggests that they were not ready to give up their Italian identity completely, but chose options that could be used in multiple settings.

The fact that it was possible for Italians to use the term *Italikos* shows that Italy itself had become a united whole. The term *Italia* was used, from the third century onwards, to identify a specific geographical area. From a Roman point of view, Italy formed a single geographical unit, which should naturally be under Rome's control. Polybius describes how, after the Pyrrhic War, the Romans 'now for the first time attacked the rest of Italy not as if it were a foreign country, but as if it rightfully belonged to them'.[286] In 268, a depiction of Italy may have been painted in the temple of Tellus (Earth) at Rome; perhaps this was the first attempt to associate Italy with the idea of the earth, or a privileged part thereof.[287] In Polybius'

[281] Adams 2003, 646–69, quote p. 657. [282] Gabba 1976, 229; Keaveney 1987, 8–10.

[283] E.g. Badian 1958, 229 n. 111–12; Galsterer 1976, 39–40; Kendall 2013, 120. Badian 1970–1, 401 suggests that *Rhomaios* was used in the East and *Italikos* in the West, but this is incorrect.

[284] CIL 3, sup. 1, 7213; *ID* 1690, 1691. [285] Poccetti 1984, 655–6.

[286] Plb. 1.6.6. See Serv. *Aen.* 9.52. See Bispham 2007, 55.

[287] Var. R. 1.2.1. The temple of Tellus was dedicated in 268, but it is not clear whether this 'map' was painted at that time. See Bispham 2007, 56; Roth 2007b for pictorial depictions of Italy in the third century; see Isayev 2017, 383–4 for what this 'map' may have looked like. For the concept of *Italia*, see Dench 2005, 162–73. It is clear that for Greeks, Italy was a geographical unit; Greek speakers described themselves, for example, as 'Herakleios ap Italias' ('from Heraclea in Italy'); see Nocita 2012.

account of the Mamertine affair in 264, Italy also appears as a unit: if Messina, a city in Sicily just across from Italy, were to be taken by the Carthaginians, it would form a bridgehead for their further progression into Italy.[288] The Romans therefore wanted to help the Mamertines, an Oscan group that controlled Messina, because they were 'a people from Italy'.[289] The nascent idea that the Mamertines were closely related to the Romans served to unite the peoples of Italy against the external threat of Carthage.[290] The Gallic invasion of 225, which, as Polybius emphasizes, was a threat to Italy as the common homeland of all Italians, also served to strengthen the idea of Italy as a unified whole, as did the invasion of Hannibal.[291] However, even if Italy was a united whole, Rome was the most important power in Italy and therefore its leader, so that 'pan-Italianism was Rome's creation'.[292] In other words, the various Italic peoples would never have been united in one geographical unit called Italia if Rome had not unified them under its hegemony.

By the late third century, the geographical idea of Italy had been clearly established. Those who had survived the battle of Cannae were, as punishment, shipped off to Sicily and forbidden to 'be brought back into Italy' as long as the war lasted.[293] Inhabitants of maritime colonies were not to spend more than thirty days outside their colonies 'as long as the enemy was Italy'.[294] In all these passages, the only logical meaning of *Italia* is the whole of peninsular Italy.[295] Livy, in his account of the Bacchanalian affair of 186, cites the Senatus Consultum on the Bacchic cult, which uses the phrase 'any of them, who were at that time outside the land of Italy...'.[296] Livy is likely echoing the official text of the Senatus Consultum, although the surviving inscription of the Senate's decree does not mention the term Italy.

At this time, Cisalpine Gaul did not form part of Italy, so it is most likely that the official term *Italia* referred to the area south of the Rubicon-Arno line, although a clear border may not have been established at this time. However, Cisalpine Gaul was already in the process of becoming part of Italia. Cato's *Origines* aimed to 'record the origins of each community of Italy',[297] and included Gaul, Liguria, and Venetia. Cato describes the Alps as 'the wall that protects Italy'.[298] However, not all Italians were considered equal, at least by Cato: he describes the Gallic people as warlike intruders and the Ligurians as untrustworthy and ignorant. The Veneti had a mythical Trojan origin and could thus

[288] Plb. 1.10–11. In 3.26.3 he mentions a treaty between Rome and Carthage dating to the First Punic War, as reported by Philinus (FrGH 174 F1), in which the Carthaginians were obliged to stay out of 'the whole of Italy'. See App. *Hann.* 7.59; Liv. 23.33.4, 27.51.13; 30.20.

[289] VM 2.7.4; see Dio fr. 43.1–4; Zon. 8.8–1: 'a nation of kindred blood' with the Romans.

[290] Göhler 1939, 32; Russo 2012.

[291] Plb. 2.23.12. See Harris 1971, 130–1; 2007, 307–8.

[292] Keaveney 1987, 28.

[293] Liv. 25.5.10.

[294] Liv. 25.7.4, 27.38.5. See Roselaar 2009.

[295] Bispham 2007, 60–8. See Bleicken 1990, 112–20.

[296] Liv. 39.17.3: *extra terram Italiam.* He also says that the Bacchanalia were celebrated 'in all of Italy' (39.14.7) and that edicts were sent 'throughout the whole of Italy' (39.15.6). See Plb. 30.19.8.

[297] Nepos *Cat.* 3.3.

[298] Cato FRH 150; see Liv. 21.35.8, 21.41.15, 39.54.12. See Williams 2001, 129.

form part of the Hellenized cultural *koine* of Italy, but not all Gauls enjoyed this advantage.[299] Thus, to be part of Italy required a certain degree of civilization, which most Italians had attained, in contrast to the Gauls of Cisalpina.

Some scholars have argued that Italia in official documents referred not to the whole of Italy, but only to the *ager Romanus*, i.e. land inhabited by Roman citizens. In the epigraphic *lex agraria* of 111 and *lex repetundarum* of 123, the terms *in terra Italia* and *in Italia* are employed. The *lex repetundarum* states that inspectors will be sent to *Italia*, but especially to *fora* and *conciliabula*, when there is no other jurisdiction. *Fora* and *conciliabula* also appear in Livy's description of the Bacchanalian affair, where 'those who presided over these mysteries were to be sought out . . . everywhere where people were in the habit of assembling (*per omnia fora et conciliabula*)'.[300] Since there were no local magistrates here, officials were sent out from Rome to investigate. Since Rome did not have any official authority over the allies, it is often assumed that *Italia* in these texts referred only to *ager Romanus* and the Roman citizens living there.[301] However, the text of the *SC de Bacchanalibus* clearly distinguishes between 'Rome' and 'Italy', which are the only two geographical units mentioned. A geographical meaning fits the text of the edict as recorded in Livy and would make eminent sense. The same applies to the *lex repetundarum*. If *Italia* had a technical meaning, i.e. referred to the *ager Romanus*, we would expect this to be stated explicitly, especially since *Italia* in many other texts of the same period (e.g. Cato's *Origines*) refers to the geographical unit. It therefore makes more sense if the term *Italia* always referred to the whole of Italy.[302] In any case, in the second century Rome hardly cared about the official limits of its jurisdiction, as we will see in chapter 5.3.1. That *Italia* was a geographical concept in the late second and early first centuries is clear from the *lex Plautia Papiria* of 90, which gave citizenship to those Italian allies who had not rebelled (see chapter 5.6). One of the conditions for gaining citizenship during the Social War was that the Italians 'be domiciled in Italy' (*in Italia domicilium habuissent*).[303] This clearly meant in the geographical area of Italy, as it would make no sense if *Italia* in this case referred to Roman citizens.

It is clear, then, that the term *Italia* indicated a united geographical whole from the third century onwards; the term *Italikos*/*Italicus* therefore included both Roman citizens and Italians without citizenship. The Italians abroad thus acted as a group, in a way they had not done in Italy itself. They were continuously addressed as a coherent group by Greeks, and used one blanket term to indicate

[299] Cato FRH 33–4; see Plb. 2.14.6–7. See Dench 1995, 18–20; Bispham 2007, 57; Isayev 2017, 289–95.

[300] Liv. 39.14.7.

[301] Galsterer 1976, 37; Bleicken 1990, 112–19; Solin 1982, 116–17; Mouritsen 1998, 46–56; Bispham 2007, 93–5, 117–23.

[302] Göhler 1939, 76–8; Pailler 1988, 330–2; Roselaar 2010, 243–51.

[303] Cic. *Arch.* 7; Schol. Bob. p. 175 St.

themselves. This indicates that for Greeks and others, it was difficult to see the difference between those with Roman citizenship and those without. For example, when Mithridates carried out his attack on the Italians and Romans in the East, he did not distinguish between Italians and Romans.[304] And why should he, since Italians had gained great wealth from their association with Rome? The Italians had moved remarkably quickly from being conquered and exploited by the Romans to assisting in conquering and exploiting the rest of the Mediterranean.[305] Thus, as we have seen in chapter 3.2.1, when Cirta was attacked during the Jugurthine War, 'the Italians on whose valour the defence of the town depended, were confident that in the event of surrender they would escape injury because of the prestige of Rome'.[306] However, they were slaughtered together with the Romans.

The similarity between Romans and Italians, as it was experienced abroad, had important consequences for the way the Italians felt about their relationship with Rome. Apparently they were so similar to Romans in the eyes of provincials that they were often seen as part of the conquering Roman state, and treated accordingly. Their common identity is likely to have increased dissatisfaction among Italians about their political position. If outsiders could not see the difference between Italians and the Romans, and if Italians were allowed to associate with and even identify themselves with Romans while abroad, why should there be any practical and legal difference in Italy itself? If they were being taken for Romans in any case, then the least the Roman state could do was offer the Italians the same legal and political protection as Roman citizens enjoyed, either by giving Italians citizenship or by creating other means of protection (see chapter 5). Thus the activities of Italians overseas contributed in important ways to the creation of a common Italian identity, which, in the early first century, was mobilized against Rome.

4.7. Roman Protection of its Allies

As we have seen, many Italian allies were active in trade throughout the Mediterranean. It stands to reason that Rome would protect her allies while they were trading outside Italy.[307] The Romans had to take the economic welfare of her allies seriously, since the Italian allies were liable to contribute to the military

[304] App. *Mith.* 23. See Keaveney 1987, 9; Isayev 2017, 49–56. On the other hand, Hannibal clearly distinguished between Italians and Romans, as he freed his Italian prisoners of war in order to gain their allegiance, but did not free the Romans; see Plb. 3.77.3–7, 3.85.

[305] Hatzfeld 1919, 243–4.

[306] Sall. *Iug.* 26.1. Depending on the circumstances, the association with Rome could also be seen in a negative way; Philopoemen, leader of the Achaian league, called Sicily and Capua 'the acknowledged slaves of Rome' (Plb. 24.13.4).

[307] See, in more detail, Roselaar 2012.

contingents of their towns (see chapter 2.6.1), as well as paying any local taxes that applied. The political stability of the Italian towns therefore depended on their citizens' ability to contribute financially. Furthermore, the number of soldiers that could be supplied by the allies depended on their economic welfare. But Roman protection of allies was also used for Rome's own gain: an attack on an ally was an attack on Rome, and therefore could be used as a pretext for war.

In this section, I will review the motivations for Rome's support of Italian allies, especially in overseas trade. I will investigate whether such intervention was motivated by a Roman ideology that dictated a duty to assist its allies, or whether a more practical reason can be detected, namely to protect Roman economic or strategic interests by assisting its allies. However, this did not mean that Rome saw the Italians as equals, or that Italians identified with Rome: the obligation to protect allies was normal in ancient societies and did not mean that treaty partners shared the same culture or otherwise integrated. Furthermore, there were limits to the amount of protection the Romans were willing and able to offer their Italian allies, as we will see.

There was a strong tendency in Roman literary works to emphasize the benefits of Roman rule for her citizens and allies. In general, the Roman state felt an obligation towards its allies to protect them against attacks from third parties. Cicero states:

> Wars were waged in the interest of our allies or to safeguard our supremacy; … the senate was a haven of refuge for kings, tribes, and nations; and the highest ambition of our magistrates and generals was to defend our provinces and allies with justice and honour. And so our government could be called more accurately a protectorate of the world than a dominion.[308]

This obligation to protect allies was taken seriously when Rome's allies were attacked. In 268, for example, the Gallic Senones attacked the Etruscan city of Clusium. The Romans intervened on behalf of their allies and sent ambassadors to protest.[309] Usually an embassy was sent out first; when this had no effect, military action was undertaken against the offender. If allied interests were harmed, this could be seen as a justification for war, i.e. the cause of a *bellum iustum*.[310]

In some cases, Rome reacted to threats against allies that were not of a military nature, but could be termed 'economic'. Cicero indicates that threats to merchants were sufficient cause to declare war: 'How many wars, and what serious ones, do you think that our ancestors undertook, because Roman citizens were said to have been ill-treated, or Roman vessels detained, or Roman merchants plundered?'[311] Although he refers only to Roman citizens, Rome also assisted Italian allies for

[308] Cic. *Off.* 2.26–7. See *Off.* 1.22, 35–6; *Rep.* 3.34–5, *Verr.* 2.5.166–7; DH 2.72, 1.5.; Liv. 9.20.10.

[309] Florus 1.13.6. See Liv. 9.2.5, 31.2.5. This attitude also benefited allies overseas; see Liv. 31.9.1–4, 31.11.9–10.

[310] See Albert 1989, 17; Keller 2007, 47.

[311] Cic. *Verr.* 2.5.149.

economic reasons. When the Numidian War broke out, one of the immediate causes was the murder by Jugurtha of Italian traders in Cirta (chapter 3.2.1).[312] The fact that Sallust mentions the Italians shows that the attack against them was seen as a factor in the outbreak of the war. Thus, protection of economic interests could also lead to a *bellum iustum*.

Several wars may have been started at least partially with economic considerations in mind. From an early period, it is clear that economic as well as political motivations could play a role in the decision to assist an ally. In 343, Rome's ally Capua requested Roman aid against the Samnites, who were also allied with Rome: 'Many [senators] realised how the largest and richest city in Italy, with a very productive territory near the sea, could become the granary of Rome, and supply every variety of provision. Still, loyalty to treaties outweighed even these great advantages.' Because the Romans had concluded treaties with the Samnites, the Senate refused to fight them, but sent ambassadors to solve the tension between the Samnites and Capua.[313] This passage shows that the obligation to assist allies was important, but also that economic motivations played a role in Roman external policy. In this case, the economic interests of Rome were overshadowed by the pre-existing treaty with the Samnites, which could not be broken without offending the gods.

It is possible that one of the motivations for the First Punic War was the threat posed to Italian and Greek trade by growing Carthaginian power. Rome was allied with several Greek states, but if Rome could not protect them, the Greeks might instead ask Carthage for help in protecting their commercial interests. To preserve their reputation and maintain their claim for dominance in the Mediterranean, the Romans had to act against the Carthaginian threat.[314] Thus both economic and political motivations were in play: the proven capability of Rome to protect the economic interests of her allies increased Rome's political prestige among the allies. Although the First Punic War ended in a victory for Rome, the Carthaginians still harassed Italian merchants, for example, in 238:

> The Carthaginians, when they captured at sea traders coming from Italy to Libya with supplies for the enemy, brought them into Carthage, and there were now in their prisons as many as five hundred such. The Romans were annoyed at this, but when, on sending an embassy, they recovered all the prisoners by diplomatic means, they were so much gratified, that in return they gave back to the Carthaginians all the remaining prisoners from the Sicilian war... They gave

[312] Sall. *Iug.* 26.1–27.3.

[313] Liv. 7.31.1. Other fourth-century actions to protect trade are described in Diod. 16.5.3 (359/8); Liv. 10.2.4 (302); Plu. *Pyrr.* 9.2 (290–87), 15.2; Paus. 1.12.1, 4.35.5–7. Already in 273, Rome maintained diplomatic relations with Egypt, especially to protect trade: Plb. 30.5.6. See Marasco 1986, 41, 77–9, 86.

[314] Thiel 1954, 132.

> permission to their merchants to export all requirements for Carthage, but not for the enemy.[315]

In this case, the Romans were ready to defend the interests of their Italian allies, first by freeing the prisoners, then by allowing them to continue to trade with Carthage, as long as they did not trade with those directly fighting Rome.

A much-debated case is the First Illyrian War, which started in 229. Polybius emphasizes Illyrian attacks on Italian merchants as a cause for the war:

> The Illyrians ... for a long time previously had been in the habit of maltreating vessels sailing from Italy, and now while they were at Phoenice, a number of them detached themselves from the fleet and robbed or killed many Italian traders, capturing and carrying off no small number of prisoners. The Romans had hitherto turned a deaf ear to the complaints made against the Illyrians, but now when a number of persons approached the Senate on the subject, they appointed two envoys, Gaius and Lucius Coruncanius, to proceed to Illyria, and investigate the matter.[316]

Dio and Appian state that the island of Issa (modern Vis) asked for Roman aid. This indicates that economic interests were indeed important, since Issa functioned as a hub for trade between Italy and the East. Dio specifies that the merchants had been using Brundisium as their base.[317] Thus, they may have been Roman citizens, Latin colonists, or Italian allies from southern Italy. There was an obvious political message to Rome's intervention: Polybius states that by protecting her allies, Rome would 'get the reputation of aiding such as joined their cause'. This improved the standing of Rome and made those who considered attacking her think twice. Clearly the Roman aim was to show that it was now the main power in the Adriatic. Nevertheless, the fact that Polybius presents complaints by Italian merchants as a valid cause for Roman intervention shows that the economic welfare of Rome's allies could be a legitimate reason for intervention by the Roman state.

Unfortunately, the Roman state was often unable to assist when Italians or Romans got caught up in wars; thus many Italians and Romans ended up in slavery. For example, in 189

> 'it was said that a large number of Roman and Italian prisoners were enslaved throughout [Crete] ... Fabius ... sent messengers around the cities: ... each state was to search out and restore prisoners from its respective towns and country

[315] Plb. 1.83.7–10; see 3.28.3. Zonar. 8.18 states that the Romans 'secured Sardinia from the Carthaginians ... by charging them with injuring Roman shipping'; see App. *Lib.* 5; VM 5.1.1a; Eutr. 2.27. Gruen 1984, 310 n. 115 argues that these merchants were probably Italians; see Càssola 1962, 51–2. Derow 2003, 53 suggests that the merchants were from the 'coastal colonies of Italy'; however, they were not necessarily from colonial towns. See Vollmer 1990, 50; Andreau 2000, 233.

[316] Plb. 2.8.1–3. See Zoumbaki 1998, 112; De Souza 1999, 76–80; Eckstein 2008, 33.

[317] Dio fr. 12.49.2; App. *Ill.* See Eckstein 2008, 33–4.

areas ... According to Valerius Antias, 4000 prisoners were restored from the island.[318]

It is not clear why there were Roman and Italian prisoners on Crete; they may have been traders who had been captured by slavers, or been made prisoners of war in the Second Punic War and sold into slavery.[319]

The most important threat to commerce in the Mediterranean was piracy. When pirates captured ships, they often sold those aboard as slaves. A stock theme of both Greek and Latin comedy is an abducted person returning home after being captured by pirates, as in Plautus' *Miles Gloriosus* and *Menaechmi*.[320] The Romans undertook many attempts to limit piracy, often mobilizing their allies against this threat. In 190, for example, 'the praetor despatched two vessels belonging to the Italian allies and two Rhodian ships ... to the Strait of Cephallenia. This sea was infested by pirates ... and supplies from Italy were cut off'.[321] In this case, the action against the pirates was undertaken by allies of the Romans, both Italians and Greeks, at the command of the Roman praetor. Trade outside Italy became increasingly important for many Italians in the late third and second centuries. Therefore, if Rome was actively concerned about the economic situation of her Italian allies, it had to take an active stance in fighting piracy and other threats to Italian affairs. It has been argued that the Romans expended little effort to contain the pirate threat.[322] For example, among the slaves on Delos whose ethnicities we know, there were Romans, Samnites, Lucanians, Messapians, Bruttians, and 'Italians'.[323] It is possible that these people were the victims of piracy, but there is no record of Roman attempts to stop the sale of Italian slaves on Delos. Nevertheless, Rome repeatedly attempted to stop pirates, even though these actions were usually aimed at small sections of the Mediterranean. For example, around 122, action was undertaken against the inhabitants of the Balearic Islands by Metellus, earning him the cognomen Balearicus. This period saw an increase in shipping between Italy and southern Gaul, so it was necessary to keep this part of the Mediterranean safe for commerce.[324] In 102, Rome took direct action against pirates in the eastern Mediterranean, at a time when Roman and Italian trade in the East were at an unprecedented level. This suggests that commercial interests in

[318] Liv. 37.60.3–6.

[319] See Liv. 34.50.4–7; Diod. 28.13; VM 5.2.6; Plu. *Flam*. 13.6–9 on the freeing of Roman slaves in Greece by Flamininus in 198. Diodorus calls them *Italiotai*, suggesting that not only Roman citizens, but also Italians had been enslaved. This is certainly possible considering the amount of travel between the Greek towns of Italy and the Greek mainland; see Nocita 2012.

[320] Isayev 2017, 222.

[321] Liv. 37.13.11–14.1. See Marasco 1986, 45; De Souza 1999, 88–90. Already in the mid-third century, Rome asked Rhodes for help against pirates (Syll.^{3} 1225). See Marasco 1986, 89.

[322] Morstein Kallet-Marx 1995, 306. See Lampela 1998, 211–12.

[323] SGDI II. 1800, 1960, 1985, 2000, 2042–3, 2045, 2116, 2227, all dating from the early second century. See Vollmer 1990, 23–4.

[324] Strab. 3.5.1; Liv. *Per*. 60.9; Florus 1.43.1–3; Oros. 5.13.1. See De Souza 1999, 92–6.

fact played an important role in the decisions of the Senate.[325] Several treaties and laws of the late second and early first centuries, furthermore, show a concern with safeguarding the allies from the actions of pirates. The *lex de provinciis praetoriis* (dated 100) states: 'The Roman people <will have> care that the citizens of Rome and the allies and the Latins, and those of the foreign nations who are in a relationship of friendship with the Roman people, may sail in safety.'[326] Thus, the Romans tried several times to end pirate threats, but this was often not very successful,[327] until in 67 Pompey took decisive action.[328]

Some wars were started with economic interests in mind, but for the benefit of Romans rather than allies. The Mithridatic War, for example, began as result of commercial activity: Roman officials had restored Nicomedes of Bithynia to his throne in return for a hefty fee, and he had borrowed from Roman moneylenders in order to pay. Roman ambassadors and moneylenders were now pressuring him into attacking Mithridates, hoping for a profitable war, even though Nicomedes did not want to do so; being in debt to the Romans put him in an inferior position, and he had to obey their wishes.[329] Rome in this case was clearly more concerned with its own profits than with the interests of its ally Nicomedes.

The Roman state sometimes made decisions that immediately benefited the interests of the Italian allies. Already in the fourth-century treaty with Carthage, for example, it was stipulated that there would be peace between Rome and its allies on the one hand, and Carthage and its allies on the other.[330] When making treaties with defeated enemies, Rome often stipulated tax exemptions, in which Latins and/or Italians were sometimes included as beneficiaries. A *Senatus Consultum* of 187 stated: 'The Ambracians should have all their property restored to them; they should be free to live under their own laws; they should impose such harbour dues and other imposts by land and sea as they desired, provided that the Romans and the Latins and allies were exempt.'[331] On the other hand, Rome could also make decisions that had a negative impact on the Italians, but the Italians had no way in which to influence Rome's policies (see chapter 5.3.2).

Momigliano argued that

> the *motive force* behind Rome's unending wars in the third and second centuries BC was the necessity of keeping the Italian allies busy, the claim being that they could not have been expected to remain loyal if they had not been given very

[325] Gabba 1954, 75; 1976, 83.

[326] Knidos copy, col. II, l. 1–11, see col. III, l. 29–35=SEG 3.378. See Nicolet 1978, 901; Morstein Kallet-Marx 1995, 227–39 (who calls it *lex de Cilicia Macedoniaque provinciis*); Crawford et al. 1996; De Souza 1999, 108–15.

[327] Càssola 1962, 33–4.

[328] Plu. *Pomp.* 24, 26. See Morstein Kallet-Marx 1995, 306–11.

[329] Just. 38.3.4–4.4; App. *Mith.* 11; Gell. 7.11.2. See Gabba 1954, 76.

[330] Plb. 3.24.1. See Isayev 2017, 269–70.

[331] Liv. 38.44.3: *in libertate essent ac legibus suis uterentur; portoria, quae vellent, terra marique caperent, dum eorum immunes Romani ac socii nominis Latini essent* (see chapter 3.2.1 on the phrase *socii nominis Latini*). See Wilson 1966, 91; Càssola 1962, 63; Gruen 1984, 310–11; Zoumbaki 1998, 151.

> regular opportunities to acquire glory and plunder and the economic benefits of overseas conquest.[332]

Thus, the allies played an important role in Rome's economic policy;[333] this was, as Càssola argues, 'aperta e intelligente', because 'l'arricchimento degli alleati era vantaggioso anche per Roma e per gli uomini d'affari romani'.[334] Harris points out that the actual benefits for allied states of the association with Rome were small: they did not receive part of the spoils or indemnities paid by defeated states, or of provincial taxation, and they continued to contribute financially to their own states. Only individual allied soldiers received spoils of war (chapters 2.6.1 and 5.3.2). However, even though the direct benefits of Roman conquest did not accrue to the Italians, they undoubtedly profited from their association with Rome.[335] As seen above, most areas in Italy show unprecedented economic prosperity in the second century. Many individual Italian allies were active in overseas trade; this meant that local elites became wealthier and invested their wealth in Italy on a scale never seen before.[336]

It is clear that the Roman state had the interests of its Italian and overseas allies in mind in formulating its foreign policy. There was no coherent, long-term policy, since the Romans were mostly reactionary in their defence of their own and their allies' economic interests, but defending its allies was a general aim of Roman rule.[337] The Roman state in many cases took the interests of its Italian allies seriously, and an attack on them could be used as a valid reason for war, even without an official request for intervention by the allies. By protecting the Italian allies in this way, the Romans created a bond between them and the allies. The Italians appreciated Roman assistance and even counted on the fact that their association with Rome would protect them, e.g. in the Jugurthine War. But this does not mean that they saw themselves as part of the same polity as Rome: their contacts with Rome were regulated by treaties, which enacted mutual protection, as was normal in treaties between friendly states in Antiquity. These treaties could be adjusted or terminated at any time. Although relations between Rome and the Italians moved towards more cooperation as time progressed, there was no intention, at least on the part of the Italians, to give up their own state structures and subsume themselves into the Roman state.

[332] Momigliano 1975, 46 (author's emphasis), paraphrased in Harris 1984, 91; see David 2006, 99.

[333] *Contra* Badian 1952, 73–5.

[334] Càssola 1962, 63–4, 70–1, quote p. 64.

[335] Harris 1984, 97–100.

[336] Càssola 1970–1, 318; Harris 1984, 100; Wallace-Hadrill 2008, 84–5, 448.

[337] The Roman state did not pursue a commercial policy as such; its aims were strategic and political. Amassing wealth was not the main reason for Rome's expansionist policy; see Andreau 2000, 230–2, 236–7. On the other hand, as Harris 2000, 288 argues, it is difficult to separate commercial from strategic aims.

We may conclude that Roman actions often had great impact, whether positive or negative, on the economic well-being of their allies.[338] The increasing importance of all allies in Roman economic and foreign policy was conducive to the economic and political integration of Italians into the Roman framework. Allies of Rome enjoyed considerable benefits—not only direct protection by the Roman army, but also increased opportunities for material gain from successful wars and in access to the Roman mediation and (military) protection. Rome depended for the stability of its alliance on the cooperation of the local elites. It was therefore a common approach of Rome to win the support of local elites by safeguarding their economic well-being.[339] Local leaders valued their autonomy, but also knew that, if the need arose, they could approach the Romans for help, for example in disputes between two independent states (see chapter 5.3.1). Thus they were encouraged to remain loyal and to exert themselves to maintain and increase Roman rule. The allies benefited from their association with the Roman state, as is clear from the economic prosperity of many Italian towns.

Of course, there were limits to this, as we have seen in Rome's lack of success in protecting its allies against piracy. The Roman state, furthermore, did not hesitate to renege on its promises to allies, if it suited its interests.[340] Overall, the system of alliances that the Romans created—a small group of Roman citizens, with a much larger group of allies, who were disadvantaged in their dealings with Romans, but profited from their association with Rome in the outside world—only worked as long as the benefits the allies drew from it outweighed the disadvantages of being subject to Rome. However, in the second century, Rome was increasingly abusing its power. Instead of protecting its allies' interests, Rome gradually came to exploit its network of allies for its own interests. This eventually contributed to the dissatisfaction of the Italians with their status as allies of Rome, as we will discuss in chapter 5.

4.8. Conclusion

In this chapter, we have investigated some of the consequences of the Roman conquest of Italy and the interactions between Roman and Italian that this caused.

[338] Curti, Dench, & Patterson 1996, 187 describe the Romans as 'controllers' or 'engineers' of the market, but this is too strong; Rome did not have sufficient control over the economy to engineer all its aspects.

[339] This is evident, for example, in a letter of T. Quinctius Flamininus to the Chyretienses in Thessaly, around 197–4 (IG 9.2.338=Sherk no. 33), where he states that 'all landed property and buildings belonging to the public domain of the Roman state which are still in its possession we give to your city, so that in this too you may learn our character and the fact that we are determined to seek absolutely no financial profit'. Thus the Romans aimed to become the *patroni* of local elites.

[340] For example, the Romans refused to honour the treaty concluded with the Samnites after the defeat at the Caudine Forks; Liv. 9.8.6–8.

First, we have seen that throughout the Republican period, Roman and Italian institutions and administrative habits converged: Roman law accommodated for disputes between Romans and Italians, Roman coinage came to dominate Italy, and Roman weights and measures were spread through Italy. However, these developments mostly occurred in the late Republic; Roman coinage did not become dominant until the second century, while weights and measures remained variable until the late first. We may conclude, then, that such elements of daily life as coinage, weights, measures, and especially language were important for the Italians and formed part of their identity. As long as there was no compelling reason to give them up, or manifest advantages to adapting to Roman practice, Italians retained their own instruments of law and commerce.

Furthermore, we have seen that many areas in Italy experienced cultural and linguistic change as well. Like economic changes, cultural change cannot be simply attributed to 'Romanization': many of the cultural developments taking place in Italy were derived from Greek culture. Since economic interaction between Italians and Greeks continued throughout the Republican period, Italians often encountered Hellenistic culture in Magna Graecia and abroad. This inspired building projects in Italy, as well as other cultural expressions, such as paintings, mosaics, grave gifts, etc. Thus, cultural change in Italy was not stimulated by Rome; in many cases, new cultural developments appeared earlier in Italy than in the city of Rome itself. Nor did Latin colonies have much impact on the culture of the surrounding areas: again, they were often rather late in adopting elements of Hellenistic culture. All in all, the Italian elites had plenty of reason to feel that they were up to date with the latest fashion in building and decoration; moreover, many of them were wealthy and respected individuals in their communities.

The identity of the Italians gradually changed over time. Italians active in the Mediterranean were often identified with Romans by others. This strengthened the idea that Italians were in all respects equal to Romans, except for the fact that they were not recognized as such by Rome. Eventually the lack of recognition of their elevated status by Rome was one of the grievances that led to Italian dissatisfaction in the late second century. Furthermore, Italians abroad often acted in a united group, putting up inscriptions in the name of all *Italici*. This contributed to a new-found feeling of connection between the peoples of Italy, who had previously only identified with their own home towns and regions. This new Italian identity was one of the factors allowing the Italians to act in concert against Rome in the late second and early first centuries.

Furthermore, this chapter has shown that, since Rome did not have the military might to control Italy on its own, the loyalty of the Italians was very important: if the Italians stopped supplying Rome with soldiers, it could not continue its expansion, and if the Italians took up arms against Rome, they might be able to threaten the very existence of the Roman state, as became clear in the Second Punic War. Therefore, it was important that Rome offered the Italians incentives to remain loyal. Some of the benefits accruing to the Italians were a share in the spoils of successful wars and the creation of new markets in the Mediterranean. A further advantage for the Italians was the military protection offered by the Romans to its allies against third parties, as well as economic gains that were arranged for them.

The combined benefits of association with the Roman state—new economic opportunities, military protection, shares in the profits of war—for a long time were sufficient to keep the Italians satisfied, even though they did not enjoy Roman citizenship. This lack was not a major disadvantage, since the Italians could easily continue their economic activities without it, as they had done for centuries. However, in the late second century, many Italians gradually began to feel dissatisfied with their position vis-à-vis the Roman state. In the next chapter, we will explore why this happened in this period and how the Italians eventually became Roman citizens—though not yet, in many respects, Romans. As this chapter has shown, Italy was in some respects fairly integrated, but in others not at all. In 91, many Italians were able to cooperate in a revolt against Rome, which would have been impossible two centuries earlier. Still, this did not mean that their civic integration into the Roman state and their social integration into Roman society were inevitable, as we will see in chapter 5.

5

From Economic to Political Integration

5.1. Introduction

This final chapter will bring together the various developments we have traced in the previous sections. Economic, social, political, and administrative relations between Rome and the Italic peoples had gradually intensified throughout the third and second centuries, as we have seen. The cultures and languages of Italy had changed as a result of these intensive contacts with the Roman state, even if we cannot speak about these developments in terms of straightforward 'Romanization'. The level of change was different in each region of Italy and was often limited to specific elements of life, such as the administration of Italian towns. In this chapter, we will investigate how economic contacts, as we have encountered in the previous chapters, contributed to the civic integration of the Italians into the Roman state. As we will see, Italians suffered some disadvantages in economic opportunities, because they were not Roman citizens. This may have contributed to their wish to gain citizenship, which became stronger in the late second century. As the Romans were reluctant to grant citizenship to them, the Italians eventually revolted in the Social War of 91–88. This war finally gained the Italians full political integration into the Roman state by a grant of Roman citizenship. However, the acceptance of Italians as full citizens was not welcomed by Rome: in practice the Roman state tried to limit the influence of the Italians on Roman politics until later in the first century. Furthermore, as we will see, political integration did not mean that the Italians now felt themselves to be Romans and presented themselves as such culturally.

The first part of this chapter will investigate to what extent economic considerations played a role in the Italian desire for citizenship: were Italians really limited in their economic development because they did not have citizenship? Or were other considerations, such as the desire to share in the prestige of citizenship or to gain political office in Rome, more important? And did all Italians in fact desire citizenship? Firstly, we will explore whether Romans held prejudice against Italians and whether this may have prevented Italians from participating in economic relations with them. Secondly, we will study the changing position of the Italians in the second century. Many Italians were wealthy and participated in cross-cultural exchange throughout the Mediterranean, but they were not full citizens of the Roman state. Therefore, they could not follow up on their increasing economic prosperity with participation in the ruling of the state, which had

Italy's Economic Revolution. Saskia T. Roselaar, Oxford University Press (2019). © Saskia T. Roselaar.
DOI: 10.1093/oso/9780198829447.001.0001

now gained absolute power in the Mediterranean. In fact, in the second century Italians were treated more often as subjects rather than as equals by the Roman state, although their economic and social position within their own states and in the Mediterranean did not warrant this.

Finally, by not having Roman citizenship, the Italians missed out on lucrative economic opportunities, especially the chance to become *publicani*. In fact, they were at risk of losing their assets, especially land, when the Roman state introduced land distribution schemes in the 130s. They were also subject to other economic disadvantages that the Romans did not experience, such as the requirement to pay local taxes and the impossibility of inheriting from Roman citizens. We will explore whether these problems increased in scope in the second century and whether this could have led to a demand for Roman citizenship, which Italians had not desired in earlier periods.

Eventually some—but not all—Italians revolted against the Roman state. The reasons for the outbreak of this war have been much debated, as have the exact demands of the Italians. The war ended with a grant of citizenship to all Italians, which was sufficient to make most of them lay down their weapons. This suggests that, even if they had not explicitly desired citizenship, they were happy to accept it as a solution to the problems that had led them to revolt in the first place. We will further explore the motivations for the war and the solution offered by the Romans.

Next, we will investigate whether the Italians gained any economic benefits from the grant achievement of citizenship. Were they indeed able to profit from new economic opportunities that became available to them? Some who had been active as traders before the war also became active in Roman politics. Others continued their commercial activities, now protected by the most valuable asset of all: citizenship of Rome. Finally, we will explore briefly how the civic integration of the Italians created further opportunities for cultural change. Civic integration—that is, gaining citizenship—was by no means the conclusion of all processes of integration between Romans and Italians; on the contrary, it created new incentives and possibilities for social, economic, and cultural change.

5.2. Cultural Prejudice against Italians

It is often thought that Romans enjoyed feelings of superiority towards Italians. If this was indeed the case, this may have had consequences for Roman willingness to trade with Italians: if Romans thought that Italians were lazy or unreliable, this might have stopped them from doing business with them. Such prejudice might also have hindered Italian access to Roman citizenship: if the Romans thought Italians were backward country bumpkins, they would not have wanted to share the citizenship with them. However, as we have seen, many Italian cities were very prosperous in the second century and had public buildings that outmatched those in Rome. We may suspect that some Roman prejudice was the result of feelings of insecurity—although the Romans were certainly the strongest military power, they were not so sure of their cultural superiority.

The Italic peoples enjoyed various reputations in Roman minds. On the one hand, they could be presented as the source of all Roman virtues, especially frugality and diligence.[1] On the other hand, Italians could be portrayed as country bumpkins who were not quite up to scratch with Roman culture. This ambiguity is visible in the literary sources from the late third century onwards. At this time, many Romans felt that true 'Roman' identity was under threat, especially by Greek culture, which became more popular at the time, leading to the erection of many buildings in Hellenistic style in Rome. Nevertheless, even when Greek culture was already popular among the Roman nobility, many still objected to it, arguing that it damaged traditional virtues, such as frugality and simplicity. Many literary works, especially those of Cato the Elder, deplored the negative effects of Greek influence. He argued that Romans should make pragmatic use of Greek examples, but not lose track of the values of Roman national culture, the *mos maiorum*. Nevertheless, Greek culture was clearly popular in Rome itself, so Cato's views should not be seen as representative of all members of the Roman elite. This identity 'crisis', with Greek culture being on the one hand popular, but on the other feared for its negative effects, was not fully resolved until the Augustan period (see section 5.8).[2]

The Italic peoples were less worried about Greek influence; we have seen that they adopted many aspects of Greek culture. Many Italic peoples even claimed a Greek origin: the Sabines and Tarentines claimed descent from the Spartans, while many southern Italian towns claimed a connection with Diomedes. Most of these legends were not second- or first-century inventions (although some were), but originated in the fourth century, at the zenith of Greek power.[3] Although many Italian towns engaged more with Greek culture than Rome did, they were often presented as primitive and barbarian by Romans. Some were simply presented as boorish, such as the Apulians,[4] but in many cases some ambiguity is clear regarding Rome's position vis-à-vis its Italian neighbours. This Roman ambiguity was obvious, for example, in the case of Praeneste, which could be presented as backward, but also as arrogant. As we have seen, Praeneste was very wealthy in the second century, so that a degree of pride among its inhabitants made sense. Due to its anomalous civic status—the town had remained allied, so that Rome had no power over it—and its close distance to Rome, Romans could easily feel

[1] On racism and prejudice in Antiquity, see Isaac 2004; on the Rome-Italy dichotomy, see Dench 1995, 103.

[2] Wallace-Hadrill 2008, 447–50. On the ambiguous relationship of Rome with Greek culture, see Gruen 1990; Dench 1995, 46–69; Adams 2003, 11–12.

[3] Dench 1995, 44–53, 183–93; Farney 2007, 199–206.

[4] Plaut. *Mil.* 648.

apprehensive at its power. In Plautus' plays, Praeneste appears several times as a byword for arrogance. In the *Bacchides* a character asks his slave about another man: 'Of what country did he seem to you?', to which the slave replies: 'I think he is of Praeneste; he was such a boaster.'[5] In the case of Praeneste, these jokes may actually 'reflect real anxiety about a potential cultural and political threat to Rome, and seek to "cut her down to size"'.[6] The Roman elite could feel threatened by the Greek fashions of the Italian elites, rather than confidently outshining them.[7] By making fun of the Praenestines, Romans could make themselves believe that the threat was not so great.

The people of Capua were also seen as arrogant. Cicero points out that many Capuan institutions reflect those of Rome: '[It] was almost more than one could endure, to see the countenance of Considius;... when we saw him at Capua with Campanian haughtiness and royal pride, we seemed to be looking at the Magii, Blossii, and Vibelii.'[8] Cicero is talking about the colony in Capua founded in 83, led by Considius and Saltius. Considius, as Cicero represents him, saw Capua as his own little kingdom and behaved with the arrogance of the previous Capuan leaders, the Campanian Blossii, Magii, and Vibellii. At the same time, Capua had the reputation of being wealthy and therefore weak. Hannibal spent the winter here, which allegedly weakened his army: 'Those who are fighting are enervated by the luxury of Capua and have worn themselves out through a whole winter's indulgence in wine and women and every kind of debauchery.'[9]

While the Praenestines and Capuans were seen as arrogant, Etruscans were often regarded as effeminate. Plautus refers to their love of sexual pleasures: 'This is not a place where in the Etruscan way you are disgracefully to earn a dowry for yourself by prostitution of your person.'[10] The Etruscan knowledge of divination, although it was of ancient standing and important in Roman politics, could also be ridiculed. Cicero recounts how in 163 the *haruspices* tried to stop the elections because of a bad omen, but the consul said angrily: 'Shall you, who are Etruscans and barbarians, pretend that you have authority over the Roman *auspicia*, and a right to give judgment in matters respecting the formality of our assemblies?'[11] Clearly he was of the opinion that Etruscan soothsayers should stay out of Roman business. In the late Republic, when many Roman politicians prided themselves

[5] Plaut. *Bacch.* 11–13. See also *Capt.* 880–90; Hor. *Sat.* 1.7.
[6] Dench 1995, 76.
[7] Wallace-Hadrill 1999, 308.
[8] Cic. *Agr.* 2.93. See Schol. Bob. *Planc.* 153S for the arrogance of the Tusculans.
[9] Liv. 23.45.2. See Cic. *Agr.* 2.95.
[10] Plaut. *Cist.* 562–3. See Farney 2007, 127–40.
[11] Cic. *Nat. D.* 2.10–11. Eventually the consul realized that the *haruspices* had been right in their interpretation of the omen. However, rather than admitting this, he made up a new omen, without acknowledging the Etruscan *haruspices*. Other Roman leaders as well were unhappy about the Etruscan influence on Roman politics, or perhaps about the importance of religious omens for politics in general. Cic. *Div.* 2.51 mentions a joke by Cato the Elder: 'I wonder that a *haruspex* does not laugh when he sees another *haruspex*.' The Marsi also had certain mystic powers, such as snake-charming and divination. Already in the second century this was frowned upon, e.g. by Ennius; see Cic. *Div.* 1.132.

on their Italian heritage (see section 5.8), not many new men claimed to have Etruscan ancestors, perhaps because of the negative associations with Etruria.

On the other hand, there were many legends about the frugality and honesty of Italic peoples. Many Roman virtues had allegedly been brought to Rome by Italians. Especially the Sabines, who had been instrumental in the creation of Roman state from the start, came to embody the moral virtue of the Romans. Cato says about himself that 'from my earliest days I kept myself away for the whole of my youth in frugality, hardship, and hard work, by tending the land, the Sabine rocks'.[12] This hard upbringing instilled in him the essential virtues of frugality, manliness, and toughness, which were the mainstays of Roman society. Many Italic peoples could be ascribed such virtues, often in contrast to the Greek luxury that had invaded Rome. The Samnites, for example, were presented as simple and primitive: 'The Samnites, . . . living the free open-air life of mountaineers themselves, despised the less hardy cultivators of the plains who, as often happens, had developed a character in harmony with their surroundings.'[13] This primitivism became a positive trait: rural Italians had retained many values that the city-dwelling Romans had lost.[14] Although Livy describes the Samnites as poor, frugal mountain dwellers, a few chapters later he states that they were in fact very rich: 'There were two divisions; one had their shields plated with gold, the other with silver.'[15] Archaeological evidence has shown that many Samnites were indeed not poor at all: many tombs have yielded finds of gold, silver jewellery, and other precious items, made of alabaster, ivory, and amber, as well as imported Etruscan, Campanian, Apulian, and Greek pottery.[16] Clearly there was some awareness of this wealth in Roman minds, but Roman works could emphasize either Samnite luxury or poverty, as required.

It seems, therefore, that indeed some prejudice of Italians existed among Romans. Part of this was born from fear about the wealth and power of Italians, since many of them were in fact wealthier and more au fait with Greek culture than Rome. By the third century, Rome dictated power relations within Italy and the Mediterranean, so that it could present the Italians as rustic barbarians, who needed Rome to guide them. Rome had to explain to its citizens and Italian subjects why it deserved to be the ruling state. On the other hand, it was also necessary to explain that the Italians had many valuable contributions to make to the Roman state, since the Italians would not accept being brushed aside. As we have seen, their loyalty to Rome could never be completely taken for granted, so

[12] Cato *Against Thermus* (Festus 350L). See Serv. *Aen.* 8.638. Cato *Agr.* pr. 4 states that the countryside produces the best soldiers: 'It is from the farming class that the bravest men and the sturdiest soldiers come.'

[13] Liv. 9.13.7.

[14] Already by the late second century, Roman and Sabine together could be opposed to Greek, as Lucilius 881–91M does: 'You preferred to be called a Greek, Albucius, rather than a Roman and Sabine.'

[15] Liv. 9.40.2.

[16] Scopacasa 2014.

that the importance of their contribution to Rome's expanding power had to be acknowledged and rewarded both materially and in literature. Therefore, already in the early second century Roman works such as Cato the Elder's *Origines* emphasized the contribution that the Italians had made to the development of the Roman state, as well as the worthiness of their character.

Overall, the amount of prejudice against Italians seems to have been fairly limited; it remained confined to certain general preconceptions about the character of the various peoples in Italy. There is no indication that these ideas had any impact on economic relations between Romans and Italians. As we have seen, commerce between Romans and Italians was widespread. For example, Romans traded wine with Capua and imported metal objects and pottery from Praeneste. Thus, material benefits, including the accumulation of money, trumped cultural prejudice. Nevertheless, the fact that the Romans expressed such ideas about the Italians may have had negative consequences for the process of social and cultural integration: the more often such ideas were repeated in Rome, the more Roman audiences started to believe that they were better than the Italians. This could have led to Italians being treated as inferior, giving the Romans free rein in exploiting the Italians for their own benefits. In fact, it seems that this was happening in the second century, as we will now explore.

5.3. The Position of Italians in the Late Second Century

We have seen that many Italians were wealthy and well versed in Greek culture, but that the Romans could represent them as arrogant and uncivilized. This ambiguity was reflected in their civic status: on the one hand they were respected businessmen who traded throughout the Mediterranean, but on the other they were disrespected by many Romans. This could obviously be a reason for resentment among Italians, who felt that their high social and economic status in their own communities and abroad was not acknowledged by the Romans. However, we must remember that in many cases, Rome was not the focus of life in Italy at all. There was no *a priori* reason why Italians would want to be acknowledged by Rome; many were happy to be leading men in their home towns, which were often richer and more Hellenized than Rome itself.

Especially in the third and early second centuries, many Italians preferred to stay in their home towns. An example is M. Anicius of Praeneste, who commanded a contingent of his townsmen during the Second Punic War. He received numerous honours in his home town, including a statue in the forum of Praeneste and three in the temple of Fortune. This was one of the highest honours that a citizen of Praeneste could achieve. The Roman Senate also wanted to show its gratitude and decreed that 'double pay and an exemption for five years from further service should be granted to the Praenestine troops. They were also offered the full Roman citizenship, but they preferred not to change their status as citizens of Praeneste'.[17] Praeneste at this time enjoyed great prestige in Italy and beyond, so there was no reason why its inhabitants might have preferred to change their civic status. In Praeneste, these men were famous because of their exploits, while in Rome they would have been nobodies in comparison to members of the Roman elite. And even if they remained in Praeneste, to accept Roman citizenship would signal to their fellow Praenestines that their town's citizenship was worth less than that of Rome. Even after the Social War, not all Italians desired to become Roman citizens: in Heraclea and Neapolis, heated debate focused on the question of whether or not to accept Roman citizenship.[18]

Considering the fact that many Italians in the third and second centuries preferred local citizenship to the Roman status, Roman prejudice might not have bothered the Italians much, as long as they suffered no practical disadvantages because of the way they were treated by Romans. But in the second century, this was exactly what happened, as we will explore now.

5.3.1. Roman and Italian power relations

It has often been argued that the behaviour of Romans towards Italians became more tyrannical during the second century. Various cases are indeed reported of petty, random abuse against Italians by Roman magistrates. The Italians could not tolerate this, because they considered themselves to be socially, culturally, and economically equal to Romans. To investigate whether a general change occurred in the character of Roman rule, we must analyse these cases in more detail; it may be that a common motivation for Rome's behaviour can be discerned.

There was no general strategy that formulated the way in which allies were treated. Rome only cared whether the allies fulfilled their duties as laid down in their treaties with Rome. When allies reneged on these duties, Rome acted without hesitation. For example, during the Second Punic War the Romans were desperate to maintain their allies' loyalty and did not hesitate to punish those who disobeyed. This included the Latin colonies, as discussed in chapter 1.6. Whereas the colonies had previously been fully independent in internal affairs, they were now to follow Roman procedures for census and tax collection. One of the main assets of the Italian towns, namely their independence in local affairs, was thus taken away. In the context of the Second Punic War, this was understandable; the Romans had already lost the loyalty of many allies and therefore needed to make sure that the remaining allies did not desert. That these colonies held Latin rights, and might therefore have been considered closely connected with Rome, made no

[17] Liv. 23.19–20.

[18] App. *BC* 1.49–50; see Cic. *Balb.* 21. See Sartori 1953, 45.

difference; an example had to be set to prevent further disloyalty. The punishment of Capua in the Second Punic War (chapter 2.3) was part of the same tendency,[19] as were the confiscations of land from disloyal allies.[20] All these actions of Rome were motivated by the desire to prevent further disloyalty from the allies. However, there was no set way in which disloyal allies were punished; in each case the measures taken were different, in line with the transgression that the ally in question had perpetrated.

It seems that after the Second Punic War, the Romans found it difficult to restore the previous character of their relationship with the Italians, which had previously been fairly equal. Rome was now the undisputed mistress of Italy; it had shown it could neutralize any threat and felt entitled to mobilize the manpower of Italy for its own goals. Rome had also shown that any disloyalty would be severely punished. It was therefore unavoidable that the Italians looked to Rome more often for guidance, as they were eager to avoid any semblance of disobedience.

As the second century progressed, the Italians felt Rome's grip tighten slowly, with more and more intervention in allied affairs. The Bacchanalian affair of 186 was the first time the Romans intervened on a large scale in the internal activities of their allies. The epigraphic *Senatus Consultum de Bacchanalibus*, found in the Ager Teuranus in Bruttium—which was *ager publicus*, although copies of the decree were most likely distributed throughout Italy—was addressed to *Bacanalibus quei foideratei esent*, 'the Bacchants who are allies'.[21] Much debate has focused on the term *foideratei*. Many scholars argue that the Romans had no formal authority over their allies, and therefore the decree applied only to Roman citizens.[22] However, the decree then goes on to command that 'no man is to be a Bacchant, neither a Roman citizen, nor one of the Latin name, nor any of our allies unless they come to the *praetor urbanus*'.[23] It is therefore quite clear that the edict was aimed at allies and Latins, as well as citizens. The fact that Rome officially had no authority over the allies was irrelevant; so soon after the Second Punic War, when the Romans had been the victim of an Italy-wide 'conspiracy', it was reasonable for them to take steps to prevent this from ever happening again. Although the Bacchanalian rituals were strictly religious, they could develop into political meetings and thus into sedition.[24] This is the first example of Roman interference in the business of the Italians in peacetime, although it had already been foreshadowed by Rome's actions during the Second Punic War. Another example is the order by Rome in 171, at the start of the Macedonian War, that the Macedonian envoys 'and all other Macedonian residents should leave Rome

[19] Liv. 26.13–16. [20] Roselaar 2010, 320–4. [21] CIL 1[2] 581; see Liv. 39.18–19.

[22] Galsterer 1976, 169; Rich 2008, 65–6.

[23] Ll. 7–8: *Bacchas vir nequis adiisse vellet civis Romanus neve nominis Latini neve sociorum quisquam, nisi pr(aetorem) urbanum adiissent.*

[24] Pailler 1988, 103; Gruen 1990, 37, 43–4; De Cazanove 2000.

immediately and Italy within thirty days'.[25] Most Italian states at this time were still allied, and Rome therefore had no authority to decide who was admitted as a resident or visitor to an Italian state. However, the Italians were expected to follow Rome's lead in matters of international politics, which the Macedonian War clearly was. Most likely the order was aimed especially at Macedonian elites living in exile in Italy (and Rome specifically), since it is unlikely that Rome could keep track of all Macedonians who may have lived in Italy, such as merchants.

In this case, it could be argued that the Romans had a legitimate reason to intervene, since their authority was under threat from the Bacchanalian meetings. However, many random acts of violence were perpetrated by Roman officials against Italians during the second century. In 173, Q. Fulvius Flaccus despoiled the temple of Juno Lacinia in Croton:

> Q. Fulvius Flaccus, the censor, was building the temple of Fortuna Equestris (in Rome)... The beauty of the temple would be enhanced, he thought, if it were roofed with marble tiles, and with this object he went down to Bruttium and stripped off half the roof from the temple of Juno Lacinia.

Representatives of the town came to the Senate to protest; the censor was severely criticized, because 'even in the case of private buildings such conduct would be thought disgraceful, but he [was] demolishing the temples of the immortal gods'. The Senate ordered that the tiles should be brought back and that expiatory sacrifices should be offered to Juno. In the event, however, the Crotonians could not be fully satisfied, because 'the contractors reported that, since there was no one who understood how to replace the tiles, they had been left in the precinct of the temple'.[26] This sad affair knew only victims, including the censor, who committed suicide the next year, his mind 'overwhelmed by grief and fear' for Juno's wrath.[27]

The year 173 was not a good one for Roman–Italian relations. The consul Postumius displayed high-handed behaviour with regard to the Praenestines:

> Postumius was angry with the Praenestines, because when he had gone there in a private capacity to offer a sacrifice in the temple of Fortune, he had not received any marks of honour, either publicly or privately. So before he left Rome he sent a message to Praeneste ordering the chief magistrate to go out and meet him, to have a place prepared by the municipality where he could stay, and to see that pack animals were ready to carry his luggage when he left. No one before this consul had ever been a burden or expense to the allies.

[25] Plb. 27.6.3; Liv. 42.48–14; App. *Mac.* 1.9. See Isayev 2017, 243–4.

[26] Liv. 42.3. See Jaeger 2006.

[27] Liv. 42.28.10–12. In 205, the propraetor Pleminius had plundered the town of Locri and taken its temple treasury as punishment for the lack of assistance that Locri had provided Rome during the war. The Locrians presented themselves to the Senate to complain. Eventually Pleminius was sent into exile and the goods, as far as possible, were returned (Liv. 29.16, 31.12.1–4, 32.1.7–8). In this case, the Roman state could claim that it acted legitimately, since the war was still going on and any reluctance to help Rome should be punished, but Pleminius' actions were certainly excessive.

Livy then states that

> the vindictiveness of the consul, even if justifiable, ought not in any case to have appeared while he was in office. The Praenestines, unfortunately, whether through modesty or timidity, allowed the matter to pass without protest, and this silence furnished the magistrates with a legal colouring, as though following an unquestioned precedent, to demands which became continuously more burdensome.[28]

Surprisingly, the Praenestines did not protest against their treatment by the consul. Livy suggests that Postumius' behaviour was 'justifiable', since he was entitled to some show of honour, even when he visited Praeneste in a private capacity. On the other hand, Livy deplores the fact that the lack of protest by the Praenestines created a precedent: from this time onwards, more such unreasonable demands were made by Roman officials.

Another example of Roman imperious behaviour in 173 concerned the Ligurian Statellati, who were defeated by Rome and made an unconditional surrender (*deditio*), 'in the hope that the consul M. Popilius would not treat them with greater severity than former generals had done. However, he deprived them all of their arms, sacked their town and sold them and their property'. Again, the Senate did not approve, especially since *deditio* meant that the Statellati had entrusted themselves to the good faith of the Roman people. This breach of good faith by the consul was both a moral and a religious offence. Therefore, the Senate determined that 'Popilius should restore the Ligurians to liberty and return the purchase-money (of their slavery), and see that as much of their property as could be recovered should be given back to them; their arms also were to be restored'.[29] Indeed, the next year the Ligurians received land, even if it was not the land that had been taken from them, but elsewhere in Transpadane Gaul. Despite the Senate's anger at the abuse of the Ligurians, M. Popillius had his command extended in the following year; his brother, who had served with him, was elected consul for that year. Both later managed to escape prosecution for their crimes, despite universal odium.[30]

The Italian allies were not the only group to experience abuse in the same period; in 171, a deputation from the Spanish provinces

> complained of the rapacity and oppression of the Roman magistrates, and falling on their knees, begged the senate not to suffer the allies of Rome to be robbed and ill-treated in a more shameful manner than even their enemies were treated. There were other indignities that they complained of, but the evidence bore chiefly upon the illegal seizure of money.[31]

[28] Liv. 42.1.6–12. See Fronda 2011, 232.
[29] Liv. 42.8.4–8.
[30] Liv. 42.22.5–6. See Harris 1991, 270–1; Pina Polo 2006, 189–90.
[31] Liv. 43.2.1–2. See also complaints from Chalkis in Greece, Liv. 43.7–8.

Again the Senate took action against the perpetrators: the two main actors went into voluntary exile and, although the Spaniards were not compensated for their losses, measures were issued to avoid further abuse.[32]

Thus, in the period around 170 various events took place that emphasized Rome's power over the affairs of its allies, both in Italy and outside. Some of these were motivated by genuine fear of disloyalty among its allies, but others were instigated by individual magistrates who acted like this simply because they could. Excessive action during battle might be explained by the universal pressure on magistrates to enhance their reputation in battle and gain a triumph, but the arrogance of Postumius in Praeneste seems to have been motivated by simple arrogance.

Praeneste's neighbour and fellow allied town in Latium, Tibur, also felt the power of the Roman Senate. Some time before 159, a letter from the Roman Senate was sent to the town, which has survived in a fragmentary state. It appears that Tibur had committed an unknown act of a religious nature against the Roman people. The Tiburtes were worried that they would be punished, and had tried to avoid any blame by sending an embassy to the Senate to absolve themselves. The Senate's letter acknowledged that the people of Tibur had not committed the error on purpose and cleared them of any wrongdoing.[33] The fact that Tibur went through such effort to defend itself shows that harsh treatment by the Senate was not unthinkable. One of the arguments that the Senate used to establish the innocence of the Tiburtes was that 'it was not advantageous for you or your state to do (this)'.[34] The Roman state recognized, therefore, that Tibur was an independent state that could make decisions that opposed Rome, but believed that it would not so do, because there was no gain in a revolt against Rome. The main point is that Tibur was completely in Rome's power; severe punishment was a serious possibility and Tibur took all possible steps to prevent getting into Rome's bad books.

Unfortunately we have fewer sources for the latter part of the century, but it appears that further cases of abuse occurred, both in Italy and in the provinces. Some time before 123, an unnamed consul visited the allied town Teanum Sidicinum, where his wife wanted to bathe in the men's baths. The consul then 'ordered Marcus Marius, the quaestor of Sidicinum, to send away the bathers'. The wife complained that it took too long and the baths were not clean, after which Marius, 'the most illustrious man of his city', was publicly whipped in the forum. Other towns were treated similarly: 'At Ferentinum, for the same reason, our praetor ordered the quaestors to be arrested; one threw himself from the wall, the other was caught and beaten with rods.' At Cales, a Latin colony, the people took the precaution to forbid anyone to use the public baths when a Roman magistrate

[32] Liv. 43.2.

[33] CIL 1^2 586=ILLRP 512. See Bispham 2007, 131–2.

[34] Line 8-9.

was in town.[35] These anecdotes of abuse of power by Roman magistrates seem rather insignificant in themselves, but they show that abuse of Italians—both allies and Latins—was possible for any reason. Italian towns had to protect themselves by agreeing with all Roman demands, no matter how small.

Flogging in particular became a hot topic in the late second century. Roman citizens could not be subjected to bodily punishment, but allies could, as the magistrate of Teanum experienced. Being flogged could signify a loss of citizenship: the censors of 138 publicly flogged deserters, to show that they had lost their Roman citizenship.[36] Latins were increasingly placed on the same level as allies: in 123, a Roman magistrate proposed that 'any Latin should be chastised with rods even during military service', a punishment from which Latins had formerly been exempt.[37] That this indeed occurred is clear from the case of the Latin Turpilius. During the Jugurthine War, he had commanded the garrison of Vaga, which was treacherously taken by the Numidians. Only Turpilius escaped; he was court martialled as a deserter, and 'being unable to justify himself, he was condemned to be scourged and put to death; for he was only a Latin'.[38] The fact that Latins could now be flogged and executed was a step down from their previous status and could therefore easily have created dissent.[39] Physical abuse remained one of the main grievances of Italians against Rome in the period until the Social War. The war broke out in Asculum in Picenum in 91 during a theatrical performance. There were many Roman spectators in town, who lynched an actor for performing badly. A Latin comedian, Saunio, was then put on stage to appease the public, but the Picentes wanted to kill him as well. Hoping to avoid this fate, Saunio stated: 'I am not a Roman, but, like you, am likely to be subjected to the floggings of Roman magistrates'. Fortunately, the crowd was persuaded by this argument.[40]

Roman magistrates in the provinces continued to be equally dictatorial in this period. As proconsul in Iberia in 150, L. Licinius Lucullus, 'being greedy of fame and needing money, . . . invaded the territory of the Vaccaei, . . . against whom war had not been declared by the Senate, nor had they ever attacked the Romans, or offended Lucullus himself'.[41] Lucullus was a *homo novus* who, as such, was especially desperate to make his name in politics; even those new to Roman politics quickly adopted the same behaviour as the established aristocracy. The Senate did nothing to interfere in this instance. In 136, the Vaccaei were again the victim of unwarranted violence, when M. Aemilius Lepidus attacked them. In this case, the Senate ordered Lepidus to desist, but he refused.[42] The Senate could do

[35] Gell. *NA* 10.3. See Salmon 1962; Dart 2014, 56–9. [36] Liv. *Per*. 55.
[37] Plu. *CG* 9.3. See Dyson 1992, 54. [38] Sall. *Iug*. 69.3; Plu. *Mar*. 8.
[39] Kendall 2013, 111–13. [40] Diod. 37.12. See Brunt 1988, 128; Dart 2014, 92.
[41] App. *Hisp*. 53.
[42] App. *Hisp*. 80–1. An example later in the second century (110) was the quaestor L. Licinius Crassus: he was 'angry with the Athenians, because they would not repeat the mysteries, for which he had come two days late' (Cic. *De Or*. 3.75). For Roman–Greek relations, see Gruen 1990; Eckstein 2008.

very little to stop a rampant governor. Soon after, in 123, the state attempted to limit damages to allies by issuing the *lex Acilia repetundarum* (see section 5.4).

The fact that Rome was undisputed master of Italy thus in many ways caused a deterioration in the position of the allies. On the other hand, it also offered a way to solve disputes between Italian towns, as Rome often served as the supreme arbiter in conflicts. In the fourth and third centuries, Italian politics had often been characterized by conflict between various groups of the local elite (leading, for example, to disputes regarding whether or not they should choose Hannibal's side) and violent conflict and competition between neighbouring towns.[43] Rome came to be seen as an impartial power that could judge such conflicts and prevent violence; it could also offer assistance against external attacks or in financial matters. Many issues that at first sight could have been easily handled by the towns themselves were relegated to Roman decision. In many cases, these disputes had to do with boundaries between towns, so that a decision would have an impact on the economic position of the towns involved. For example, in 168 the Senate sent a committee to investigate a dispute between Luna and Pisae.[44] But mediation could be risky: in the first half of the second century, Q. Fabius Labeo was sent to arbitrate a land dispute between Nola and Neapolis; when agreement could not be reached, he decided to add the disputed land to the Roman *ager publicus*, thus depriving both towns of its use.[45]

Rome assisted the Italians in all kinds of matters throughout Italy, such as a civil war in Patavium in 174, a slave uprising in Etruria and Umbria in 196, and a plague of locusts in Apulia in 182.[46] Rome also regularly became an arbiter in international affairs: Livy's chapter 45.13, dated 167, records embassies from Antiochus III, the Ptolemies of Egypt, and Masinissa. Thus, it seems that in the second century the Roman state interfered more often than before in the internal affairs of the Italian allies, as well as overseas allies. Gradually, the allies lost independence in many issues: minting, the freedom to coordinate actions against brigandage, public unrest and slave revolts, and the independent solution of boundary and trade disputes. Rome did not explicitly forbid the Italians to make their own decisions in such affairs. In the case of minting, the Italians simply stopped producing coins because it was more convenient to use Roman coinage. In cases of internal unrest, they approached Rome because it was an impartial mediator, and, possibly, to avoid any suspicion of armed violence against Rome.

Rome's policy was essentially reactionary: it only acted when the allies requested them to intervene. Nevertheless, the fact that Rome became more

[43] Fronda 2010.

[44] Liv. 45.13.10–11. See also CIL 1^2 636=ILLRP 477 (a dispute between Vicetia and Ateste in 136); see CIL I^2 584=ILS 5946=ILLRP 517 for a conflict between Genua and the Veturii Langenses, resulting in the *Sententia Minuciorum* of 117.

[45] Val. Max. 7.3.4a; Cic. *Off.* 1.33, who condemns this action.

[46] Liv. 33.36.1–3, 39.29.8, 42.10.6, 45.13.9–11.

involved in Italian affairs shows that the Italian leaders felt themselves unable to solve their own problems, or that they feared Roman punishment if they acted too independently. This growing exhibition of Roman power imposed a sense of uncertainty on the Italians; they could never be sure that Rome would treat them fairly, as the case of Tibur shows. Sometimes Romans displayed munificence towards Italian towns, such as donations of public buildings in Italian towns. For example, Lucius Mummius in 146 set up statues in various parts of Italy, indicating that the Italians shared in the spoils of his war in Greece.[47] This nevertheless undermined Italian independence: it emphasized the presence of Rome and diminished the importance and prestige of local leaders. Thus the Italian nobility became less important as time went on; the more powerful Rome became, the less important the Italian elites became, at least outside their own communities.[48] We have seen that many Italians were wealthy and influential outside Italy, but within Italy they had no official power. Their only course of action in order to influence Roman policy was to approach Roman friends or patrons and ask them to intercede for them.

The loss of political independence had no direct consequences for the economic development of the Italians: trade continued and grew in the second century as never before. However, some of the episodes discussed here had potentially devastating effects on those Italians at the receiving end: the Ligurians lost their land and liberty, while the Praenestines and others had to spend money on entertaining Roman magistrates. In boundary conflicts, the Italians could never be sure of a positive decision and even ran the risk of losing the land. Furthermore, Italians could never be sure that any benefits of Roman conquest would be shared with them. Sometimes, as discussed in chapter 4.7, they received benefits such as tax exemptions and a share in spoils, but in many cases they received nothing, or less than Roman citizens. It was this uncertainty that probably annoyed the Italians the most: they were completely at the mercy of Rome and could therefore never be certain that they would profit from Rome's conquests. We will now explore in more detail what economic disadvantages the Italians feared.

5.3.2. Lack of Roman citizenship and its negative effects for economic activities

Many analyses of the causes of the Social War focus on the civic disabilities of the Italians. Lack of citizenship meant that possibilities for a political career were limited and that Italians were therefore unable to gain the same prestige and power as Romans. Furthermore, they were not protected against random abuse, as

[47] Zevi 1996, 128. [48] Keaveney 1987, 16.

described in the previous section. While the Italians most likely resented these issues, there is no *a priori* reason why Roman citizenship was desirable to them. After all, they had managed for centuries without it; some who had been offered it had rejected it, as we have seen. In theory, the Italians could continue as before, engaging in their own economic and political activities without Roman interference. Although they were unhappy with the growing abuse of Roman power, they did not need citizenship in order to protect themselves. Yet, when the Italians were offered citizenship during and after the Social War, they accepted it. We must therefore explore whether the Italians really wanted the citizenship and, if so, what their motivations for this desire could have been. Of course, Italian sentiments developed over time; not all of them wanted the same thing at the same time. While in the mid-second century most Italians only wanted some way to protect themselves against Roman abuse, a more general desire for Roman citizenship may gradually have evolved.

In this section, I will review the negative impact of the lack of citizenship on the economic welfare of the Italians. We will see that the economic opportunities of the Italians were limited because of their lack of citizenship. Therefore, economic motivations must be considered among the prime reasons for the demand for Roman citizenship and the Social War. The connection between Italian commercial activities and the desire for citizenship has been pointed out before,[49] but most recent works on the Social War focus on other aspects of the Italians' motivations.[50] I will argue that threats to Italian economic prosperity and limitations on the opportunity to exploit the expanding Roman territory in the Mediterranean played an important role in the development of the Italian desire to gain citizenship.

It is likely that problems surrounding the distribution of *ager publicus* were the most important economic concern of the Italians in the late second century.[51] This land was in theory only accessible for Roman citizens, so that Italians had no legal right to use this land. I have dealt extensively with *ager publicus* elsewhere, and have argued that many Italians had continued to work their lands after they had been officially confiscated. When the Gracchan land commission started its work in 133, the distribution of the land worked by Italians, although legal from the Roman point of view, caused much opposition among its Italian holders. Italian allies most likely did not receive any share of the land that was distributed to small farmers, but I have argued that Italian users of *ager publicus* were given ownership of 500 *iugera* of *ager publicus*, plus some for their children, as were Roman users.[52]

[49] E.g. Gabba 1954; 1989, 224; 1994, 225–6; Nagle 1973; Marshall 1976, 99–100; Rauh 1993, 232.
[50] E.g. Kendall 2013, 142–66; Dart 2014.
[51] Nagle 1973; Mouritsen 1998, 142–51. See also Kendall 2013, 142–66; Dart 2014, 51–2.
[52] Roselaar 2010, 243–51.

It is in the context of the debate about *ager publicus* in the 120s that we hear for the first time about the idea of granting citizenship to Italians. It was suggested that the Italians would be more willing to give up their land if they received citizenship in exchange.[53] The proposal to give citizenship came from a Roman politician, not from the Italians, although some were willing to accept it. This at first sight looks odd: the possession of land clearly brought in large profits, while the economic benefits of gaining citizenship were harder to predict. Why did Italians then prefer Roman citizenship over the possession of land? Of course Appian, our most important source, wrote two centuries after the events, so he may have overestimated the desire for citizenship among the Italians. However, I think that there were tangible material benefits to having citizenship, which the Italians may have rated equally high as using *ager publicus*.

The main reason to accept citizenship in exchange for land may have been the desire for security. The Italians had used Roman *ager publicus* for a long time, never considering that it could be taken away from them, but suddenly the possession of this land became insecure. The secure ownership of 500 *iugera* of land, which I argue the Italians received, was preferable to the insecure possession of, say, 1,000 *iugera*. Moreover, the Italians suffered from the fact that measurements made by the land commission were done very quickly, and not always very accurately, as Appian states:

> Not all owners had preserved their contracts, or their allotment titles, and even those that were found were often ambiguous... In fact, the land having originally been spoils, the survey had never been carefully done. As the original proclamation authorized anybody to work the undistributed land who wished to do so, many had been prompted to cultivate the parts immediately adjoining their own, till the line of demarcation between public and private had faded from view. The progress of time also made many changes... So there was nothing but a general turn-about, all parties being moved out of their own places and settling down in other people's. All this then, and the haste with which judgments were given on these disputes, was more than the Italians could bear.

The Italians approached Scipio Aemilianus to act as a spokesman on their behalf in the Roman Senate, but this had no effect.[54]

It seems, therefore, that Italians were suffering more than Roman citizens from incorrect measurements, since the land had never been assigned to them officially.

[53] App. *BC* 1.21: 'The Italians were ready to accept this, because they preferred Roman citizenship to possession of the land.' See VM 9.5.1; see Sherwin-White 1973, 135. Nagle 1973, 368 and Brunt 1988, 126–7 find Italian willingness to accept citizenship in exchange for land strange. Mouritsen 1998, 110–18 suggests that Flaccus proposed to give citizenship only to the Latins, not to all allies. However, there is nothing in the sources to suggest that this was the case, so that we must assume that all allies were intended. This is indeed more likely, since undistributed *ager publicus* was located mostly in allied rather than Latin territory; see Roselaar 2010, 31–64.

[54] App. *BC* 1.18–19.

In some cases, their privately-owned land was even taken by the Roman state. It must be noted that acquiring citizenship would not give the Italians the right to continue occupying *ager publicus*. Legally, nobody had this right, since its possession was always precarious and the land could be taken away at any time by the Roman state, whether its users were citizens or not.[55] But the citizenship would protect the Italians against confiscation of their private land during land distribution schemes. Rather than having to approach an individual Roman senator to gain redress, which in this case proved ineffective, citizens had access to the Roman courts to protect their titles to privately-owned land. Thus, the protection of privately-owned lands, when threatened by land distribution schemes, was, I argue, an important motivation for the Italians to desire citizenship.

There were other direct economic advantages to the citizenship. An important grievance was that Italians were still contributing to the upkeep and payment of the contingents that they sent to the Roman army, either through taxation by their towns or by supplying their own weapons and armour (see chapter 2.6.1). The Romans had not been paying any direct taxes since the abolition of the *tributum* in 167. Therefore, the financial burdens of the allies were larger than those of the Romans. Especially if they did not always receive the same amount of spoils as the Roman citizens, as discussed in chapter 2, allies were worse off financially than citizens.

Furthermore, a very profitable business, which was only open to Romans, was tax-farming in the provinces and bidding for public contracts let out by the state, such as for building projects. We have seen that Italians could only become involved in tax-farming and other public contacts indirectly, by entering into a partnership with a Roman. This was not as profitable, however, as being a *publicanus* in one's own right. Opportunities for profit grew quickly after the province of Asia was created in 129–126.[56] It is therefore likely that Italians in the late second century wanted to gain direct access to the profitable business of the Roman state.[57] Badian argues that Italians started to bid for public contracts very quickly after gaining citizenship,[58] indicating that some of them had been eager to do so already before

[55] Roselaar 2010, 241–51, 281–2; 2011, for distributions of land. Sherwin-White 1973, 142 thinks that there were no agrarian problems between 125 and 91, so that this played no role in the Italian protests of the 90s; but in fact there were several proposals for land distribution (Cic. *Off.* 2.21.73, *Or.* 2.11.48; App. *BC* 1.29; Dio 27.25.4; VM 8.1.damn.3; Obs. 46).

[56] The situation in Asia was complex; Gaius Gracchus subjected the cities of Asia to taxation by the *lex Sempronia de provincia Asia* of 123 or 122 (Vell. 2.6.3), but other areas may have been taxed earlier, as appears from App. *BC* 5.4. See Gruen 1984, 592–610; Mitchell 1999; Jordan forthcoming.

[57] Salmon 1962, 112–13; Badian 1972, 57–8, 97; Keaveney 1987, 7–8; Kendall 2013, 121–2. Mouritsen 1998, 92–3 with nn. 19, 21 does not believe that commercial activities of the Italians contributed to their demand for citizenship, since the Italians already enjoyed a fairly equal position in the exploitation of the provinces, and having citizenship did not mean the Italians would be able to gain new contracts, since Romans already held the concessions. However, existing public contracts were re-issued every five years by the censors, who also gave out many new contracts. There is no reason why an Italian with citizenship would not be able to win these concessions if he made a better offer than an old Roman citizen.

[58] Badian 1958; 1972, 96–7.

the Social War. This is difficult to corroborate, since the sources—mostly Cicero—do not record the origins of the new *publicani*. Among the known *publicani* in the first century, only two were certainly newly enfranchised: P. Ventidius Bassus and P. Caesius.[59] Nevertheless, Cicero emphasizes the close bond between the *equites*, the *publicani*, and the local elites (*domi nobiles*) of Italian towns. In his speech for Plancius, the son of a *publicanus* from Atina, Cicero on the one hand highlights the support he received from his home town, and at the same time praises the *publicani* in general—and thus the *publicani* with an Italian background as well: 'For the flower of the Roman knights, the ornament of the state, the great bulwark of the republic is all comprehended in the order of the *publicani*.'[60]

The desire to partake in Roman politics is often seen as the most important reason for the Italian desire to become citizens. However, politics was not disconnected from economic interests.[61] Italians may have wanted a voice in overseas policy, since this was important for them as merchants. In the last decades of the second century, many decisions had been taken by the Roman state that influenced trade in the Mediterranean. Many of these had been favourable for Italians, but others had not. The Italians may have wanted to influence which areas were conquered by Rome, so that they could then join in the exploitation of these areas. However, there was no way in which the Italians could influence the decisions made by the Roman government.[62] It makes eminent sense that Italians wanted some influence on Roman decisions regarding warfare. Political influence could lead to decisions that were in the interests of the Italians, and would stop them losing money and lives in wars that they had no say in.[63]

In connection to this, Roman *equites* became more and more powerful in legal affairs in the late second century, at the possible expense of the Italian elites. It is likely that many Italians were worried by Gaius Gracchus' judiciary law, which gave control of the *quaestio de repetundis* (see section 5.4) to the *equites*. This allowed the *equites* unlimited control over the exploitation of the provinces, in which the Italians were heavily involved. If the *equites* were in control of the courts, Italians would have no means of redress against abuse that they suffered at the hands of these same *equites*. Furthermore, the *equites* thus gained more influence over the business that went on in the provinces, in which the Italians played an important role.[64] Gaining Roman citizenship would give the Italians more influence over what happened in the provinces: since many Italian elites were wealthy enough to qualify for the equestrian status, they could become judges in the *repetundae* courts once they were granted citizenship.[65]

[59] Brunt 1988, 126–7. [60] Cic. *Planc.* 23.

[61] Brunt 1965, 104; 1988, 126–7 argues that the primary motive of the Italians to demand citizenship was gaining political influence and that commercial motives were not important; however, political influence was directly related to economic opportunities.

[62] Gabba 1954. [63] Salmon 1962, 109–12; Keaveney 1987, 5. [64] Keller 2007, 53.

[65] Salmon 1962, 111–14; Brunt 1988, 100.

Another disadvantage of not having citizenship was the limitations that were created on trading in *res mancipi*, as discussed in chapter 4.2.1. In such transactions, the legal position of the Italian party was worse than that of the Roman party. Furthermore, as we have seen, it was impossible for Italians to inherit from or make bequests to Romans, if they did not possess *conubium*. This meant that they were not fully free to decide on the best possible strategy to manage their property.

Given these economic disadvantages, which had serious negative consequences for the economic opportunities of the Italians, we would expect Italians with commercial interests to have taken the initiative in the Social War. However, the connection between economic activities and the Social War itself is difficult to demonstrate. The centre of the revolt was located in the Samnite region and among the Marsi, Paeligni, Vestini, Marrucini, Picentes, Frentani, and Hirpini; they were later joined by the Lucanians, Apulians, 'Iapyges' (probably Messapians), the people of Pompeii and Venusia, and subsequently the Etruscans and Umbrians.[66] Not all of these groups were equally interested in commercial activity; as we have seen, the most active traders in the Mediterranean were Latins, Campanians, Apulians, and people from Magna Graecia. Some prime areas for commercial production, such as most of Latium and parts of Campania, already held citizenship before the Social War. Many scholars therefore think that economic interests were not important for the insurgents. Keaveney, for example, thinks that businessmen had little influence in their local communities and therefore were not important in leading the Social War.[67]

Nevertheless, some areas where many active merchants lived did take part in the war. Many Apulians were active traders, and the Apulian towns Venusia and Canusium were among the main instigators of the war. Many Canusians are attested at Delos. Samnium was among the main areas that revolted, while many Samnites are known from Delos. Other areas were more divided: Campania, with its many traders, saw some cities joining quickly, such as Nola and Nuceria, while others joined later, such as Herculaneum and Pompeii. The connection with *ager publicus* is not entirely clear: some who had lost *ager publicus* in the Gracchan distributions were afraid to lose more if they did not stand up for their rights—for example, the Lucanians and Apulians—and therefore joined the revolt. On the other hand, Etruria and Umbria were reluctant; perhaps this should be connected to the fact that there was still *ager publicus* in these areas, which had not been touched by the Gracchi. Perhaps the Etrurians and Umbrians feared that this would be taken away if they revolted. It is clear that not all those active in commerce joined the rebellion. Thus, even those who held *ager publicus* did not all react in the same way, indicating the variety of motives behind Italian discontent. Furthermore, some may have feared that revolting against Rome would hurt

[66] App. *BC* 1.39, 49; see Oros. 5.18.8; Liv. *Per.* 72, 74. See Dart 2014, 101–2.

[67] Keaveney 1987, 10–11; see Salmon 1958, 166–9; Brunt 1965, 104.

their financial interests; of course, the war would cost a lot of money. And whatever the result, a revolt would cause a serious decline in relations with Rome, so that Rome would no longer protect the Italians as it had done before.

All in all, it seems that both landed nobility and merchants had reasons to be dissatisfied with their economic position in the late second century. Of course, motivations varied between the Italic peoples and even between individuals. There may also have been different motivations between different classes: some elite Italians, who were either important local leaders or wealthy businessmen, may have wanted to profit from the political and economic advantages that came with the citizenship. As indicated in chapter 1.3, average economic growth equalled about 0.1 per cent per year from 200 BC to AD 100, raising the living standards of most Romans and Italians.[68] The question remains, therefore, whether the economic position of the Italians in absolute terms had in fact deteriorated; it may be the case that in fact many Italians were richer than ever before, but felt undervalued because wealth in Rome had increased even more or because some economic opportunities were passing them by. These motivations would have been less important for lower-class Italians, but the elites needed to convince those of lower status, in order to recruit soldiers to fight against Rome. It would have been easy to persuade them with emotional arguments, such as the fact that Italians were abused by Rome.

Furthermore, it is unclear whether all Italians profited equally from the new opportunities that arose; unfortunately, social and economic inequality is too large a topic to explore here. Certainly, not all Italians had profited equally from the economic transformation in the third and second centuries, as we have seen. It has been argued that in the second century, the process of assimilation between local and Roman elites led to proletarianization among the middle classes, who lost access to land and could not profit from increasing opportunities for trade.[69] This is of course an exaggeration, since many people of the 'middle class' (if we can use such terms for the Roman period) also profited from the new economic opportunities. Those, however, who had lost their land and incomes may have been willing to fight, since they had nothing to lose. On the other hand, it may well have been the lower classes who persuaded their local leaders to take up arms, motivated by feelings of resentment caused, for example, by high casualty figures in war (see chapter 2.6.1). Some local elites may have been reluctant to fight against Rome. Some, who were active in trade, probably had much to lose and were afraid to antagonize their social and economic relations with the Roman state and Roman friends. It cannot be denied, however, that economic considerations

[68] Morris, Saller, & Scheidel 2007, 5–6.

[69] Osanna & Sica 2005, 52. See Roselaar 2010, 215 for the sale of land by small landowners—perhaps including Italians—to commercial producers, which may have led to accumulation of land in fewer hands.

were very important: the economic welfare of the allies would certainly be improved by gaining citizenship. On the other hand, political and social issues also played a role, and to these we must now turn.

5.3.3. Other causes of resentment

In the late second century, there were many disadvantages for Italians, some in the economic sphere, some in the civic and legal sphere, and some simply in the fact that they did not always enjoy the same respect as Romans. In this section, I will review some of these reasons, in order to investigate their importance in the growing demand for citizenship in the late second century.

Firstly, there were limited political possibilities for ambitious men. Careers in local politics only went so far, as there were few positions available. People who wished to achieve more might have desired a political career in Rome. By being elected as magistrates in Rome, Italians would have been able to influence Rome's policies on matters that involved all Italians, as discussed in the previous section. However, political positions in Rome were only open to those with Roman citizenship. By the early first century, parts of Latium, Sabinum, and Etruria had Roman citizenship. Some new men had managed to be elected in Rome, for example, the consuls Cato and Marius, as well as some lower-level magistrates. People from other regions mostly did not have citizenship and were therefore disadvantaged when it came to political opportunities in Rome.

Again it must be emphasized that not all Italian elites desired a career in Roman politics; indeed, there is no evidence for a massive intake of Italian senators after the Social War (see section 5.7). In fact, many Italians preferred to be leaders in their own towns rather than backbench senators in Rome, for example, Cicero's grandfather. He remained at Arpinum, even though Aemilius Scaurus, the leader of the Senate (*princeps senatus*), stated: 'if only M. Cicero would have applied that mind and spirit to our republic rather than to municipal affairs!'[70] Some evidence suggests that Italians were eager to participate in politics: in Oscan areas, the number of *meddices* and other local magistrates per town increased over the course of the second century, so that more people could hold local office.[71] This may have happened because there were few opportunities in Rome itself, so that Italians created alternative careers at home. We have also seen that some towns adopted the names of Roman institutions. In some cases, this may have led to the creation of new offices, which had not existed before. In either case, the influence

[70] Cic. *Leg.* 3.36: *'Utinam,' inquit, 'M. Cicero isto animo atque virtute in summa re publica nobiscum versari quam in municipali maluisses!'* See Nicolet 1967 on this affair; Keller 2007, 47–50 for the continued interest of Italians in local politics.

[71] Campanile & Letta 1979, 25–6.

of Rome made itself felt, but we can also conclude that for many Italians, a career in local government was sufficient.

Citizenship opened up the chance not only to become active in Roman politics, but also to vote for elections and legislation. It is sometimes argued that gaining voting rights in Rome was not very important for Italians, since extra-urban voters did not often attend the elections. If Italian voters did not show up, this meant that Italian elites had little chance of being elected as Roman magistrates.[72] However, in the first century it seems that Italian towns could often make the difference in elections. It is striking, for example, that the *Commentariolum petitionis*, a first-century handbook on campaigning for office, singles out the Italians as an important group for a candidate to approach. The writer emphasizes the candidate's support among many people: 'all the *publicani*, nearly the whole equestrian order, many municipal towns specially devoted to you, many persons who have been defended by you, men of every order, many *collegia* . . . '.[73] Of course there is some overlap between these groups: many *equites* were also *publicani*, and many people from *municipia*, i.e. Italian towns that had gained citizenship after the Social War, were also *equites*. It was important in a campaign to gain support from the *municipia*, especially because acquaintances of the candidate could mobilize their fellow townsmen to vote for him as well. Cicero gives a good example of this in the *Pro Plancio* of 54, emphasizing the support that Plancius received from the people of his home town, Atina: all of Atina came to Rome to support Plancius, just like Arpinum had supported Cicero.[74] As the first man from his home town to gain office in Rome, Plancius enjoyed great support from his fellow townsmen, who were proud of his achievements. Thus many extra-urban voters did make the effort to come to Rome and vote; not all extra-urban votes were worthless.

Another grievance that the Italians held against Rome related to military demands, as we saw in chapter 2.6.1. Velleius, in his discussion of the outbreak of the Social War, emphasizes the military role of the allies, stating that

> the fortune of the Italians was as cruel as their cause was just; for they were seeking citizenship in the state whose power they were defending by their arms; every year and in every war they were furnishing a double number of men, both of cavalry and of infantry, and yet were not admitted to the rights of citizens in the state which, through their efforts, had reached so high a position that it could look down upon men of the same race and blood as foreigners and aliens.[75]

Although the available figures suggest that the allies did not in fact always supply twice as many soldiers as the Romans, they furnished more than Rome did.[76] After Marius' first conscripted volunteers in 107, it became easier for Romans to avoid

[72] Mouritsen 1998, 95–7. [73] *Com. Pet.* 3.

[74] Cic. *Planc.* 19–22. See also Cic. *Clu.* 197; *Cael.* 5. [75] Vell. 2.15.2.

[76] Some think that Velleius' assessment is accurate, e.g. Brunt 1987, 686; Salmon 1982, 306; Kendall 2013, 104.

service altogether; if there were enough volunteers, no one else had to serve. The Italians, however, did not change their recruitment system, so that Italians who were reluctant to serve could not easily avoid being drafted.[77]

Moreover, as discussed in chapter 2.6.1, allies usually served longer and suffered more casualties than Romans.[78] The Italians were, on the other hand, unable to reap the full benefits from Rome's wars: they received a share in the spoils of successful wars and could, in some cases, participate in land distributions, but these rewards were not guaranteed. Especially in the second half of the second century there was very little to look forward to: after 168, no more land distributions took place, while the wars fought in this period were not very rewarding. The wars in Iberia at this time were less profitable than the earlier Greek conquests, leading to high levels of desertion.[79] Furthermore, between 133 and 91, seven serious defeats occurred, in which many Italians were killed.[80] Italian elites were most likely frustrated by the fact that they had little influence on army strategy: their soldiers were dying in large numbers, but despite the fact that many Italian elites had extensive military experience, Roman generals often refused to listen to their recommendations. The slaughter at Arausio in 105 had occurred, in fact, because the proconsul Q. Servilius Caepio, from one of the most important families in Rome, refused to cooperate with the consul, who was a *homo novus*.[81] The Italians' military ability was fully displayed by their achievements in the Social War, when they inflicted many serious defeats on very experienced Roman commanders.[82] It is likely therefore that the Italians wanted to have more influence on decisions regarding war, especially since the demands made by Rome could no longer be offset by the rewards that the Italians gained. They will have asked themselves whether the cost justified the profits, and in the late second century, they concluded that it did not. Moreover, if Italians would be allowed to command armies themselves, they could gain personal military glory, just as Marius had done.

Finally, we must look again at the impact of cultural change in Italy and Rome. As we have seen, many areas of Italy were culturally sophisticated in the second century, as shown by stone theatres and monumental temple complexes in a Hellenistic style. Italy was often ahead of Rome in these developments, creating buildings and artworks that in Rome had not yet been introduced. Italian elites were rightly proud of these achievements: 'The men who commissioned these buildings knew what they were doing and knew that they were doing things Rome had not done.'[83] However, as we have seen, the Romans could depict the Italians as backward, arrogant, and uncivilized. This clearly did not match the image that Italians held

[77] Kendall 2013, 105–8. [78] Badian 1958; Gabba 1976, 9; Kendall 2013, 93–4.

[79] Plb. 35.4.4–5; Liv. *Per.* 48.17; App. *Hisp.* 49, 84; Lucil. 15.509–10. See Harris 1984, 99; Roselaar 2010, 217.

[80] Kendall 2013, 287–397. [81] Liv. *Per.* 67.3. [82] Dart 2014, 103–4.

[83] Crawford 1981, 159; see Terrenato 2001a, 3.

about themselves, of sophisticated and civilized people engaged in a Mediterranean-wide cultural exchange. This disregard among Romans for Italian achievements must have grated. As Roman citizens, Italians would enjoy greater social prestige in the eyes of existing citizens—although Italian new men would always suffer some stigma—and in the eyes of provincials, who would see them as part of the ruling power (although, as we have seen, many Italians were already seen as such before they actually gained citizenship). Velleius indicates that the Italians felt that they were seen as 'foreigners and aliens' by the Romans, although they should be seen as closely related. Thus, the Italians wanted a share of the prestige that Romans enjoyed, and wished to see their achievements recognized by the Romans.

We may conclude that the grievances of the Italians were mostly based on practical reasons: they suffered economic disadvantages as a result of not being Roman citizens, most importantly the loss of *ager publicus* and private land, and the fact that they could not share in exploiting the provinces. This meant that in the later second century they did not gain sufficient material rewards from wars fought for Rome, nor were they able to influence Roman policy in economic and military matters; furthermore, they were subject to abuse by Romans. Most of these reasons were connected to the economic welfare of the allies; all can be subsumed under the heading of 'not being rewarded for their share in Rome's conquests', as Velleius states. Even the desire to become magistrates in Rome was partially motivated by material reasons, since this would allow the allies to influence Roman policy. The motivation of wanting to share in the prestige of Rome's power seems less tangible, but in fact comes down to the wish that the achievements of the Italians were acknowledged by giving them a share in ruling the state.

However, this does not necessarily mean that the allies wanted to become Roman citizens: all these problems could have been solved by other means, such as a more equal distribution of spoils of war, possibilities to share in the exploitation of the provinces, and protection against random abuse and the expropriation of land by Romans. In the late second and early first centuries, the Italians were proudly independent; many of them were wealthy. There is no reason to assume that the Italians wanted to abandon their local citizenship and become Romans. However, eventually this was exactly what happened: the Italians, after rising in revolt against Rome, were given citizenship and were content with this. We must therefore look in more detail at the events of this period to explain why Italian grievances, which could have been solved without a grant of citizenship, eventually led to the Social War and the grant of Roman citizenship to all Italians.

5.4. Demands for Citizenship in the Late Second Century

The issues discussed above were sufficient to cause discontent among the Italian allies. In the late second century, a demand for citizenship gradually emerged, but this demand appeared only relatively late, and it did not arise among all Italians at the same time. Brunt's statement that 'the desire for citizenship was almost universal in Italy' is certainly inaccurate.[84] It should not be assumed that all Italian elites welcomed a universal grant of citizenship to all Italians, both the wealthy and the poor: this would place all Italians on an equal legal footing, and give the lower classes a chance for social mobility through the new economic and political opportunities that came with the citizenship, thus threatening the social status of the existing elites.[85]

The literary sources, which were of course mostly written by Romans, make much of the legendary inclusiveness on which many Romans prided themselves. According to legend, Romulus was the first to include people from other towns into the Roman elite,[86] and this custom continued throughout Roman history, as Cicero claims:

> The thing which has above all others increased the renown of the Roman name, that that first man, the creator of this city, Romulus, taught by the treaty which he made with the Sabines, that it was expedient to increase the population of this city by the adoption of even enemies as citizens.[87]

Indeed, in the early Republic the Romans had often granted citizenship to allies—although this was not always a reward, as the main obligation of citizens was to pay taxes to Rome.[88] However, after the Latin War (341–338), Rome became less generous with its citizenship. There were isolated instances of awards, as with the attempted gift to the Praenestines in 216, but large-scale grants are not recorded. In fact, between 188, when Fundi, Formiae, and Arpinum received *civitas optimo iure*, and the citizenship grants of Marius (see page 220), no grants are known. This reluctance may be connected to an increasing xenophobia visible in the second century, as we have seen with regard to Greek culture. This resulted in the expulsion of Greek philosophers and rhetoricians from Rome in 161, and the destruction of the first stone theatre in Rome in 154 by the consul Scipio Nasica (see chapter 4.4).[89] Italians did not present the same dangers to Roman culture as Greek culture did; they possessed many admirable qualities and were closely intermarried with Romans, as we have seen. Nevertheless, they could never be 'real Romans of Rome'. This position was caused partially by feelings of superiority among Romans, but also by a real fear that Italians would take over power in Rome if they were given citizenship—after all, they outnumbered Romans four to one.

Already by the early second century, the Romans were reluctant to share the citizenship, and its attendant privileges, with anyone. They symbol of the citizen

[84] Brunt 1965, 93. [85] Bancalari Molina 1987, 431.
[86] Liv. 1.8.4–7, 1.30.1–2, 1.33.1–3, 2.16.3–6; see Sall. *Cat.* 6.1–3. See Dench 2005, 2–3; Coşkun 2009b.
[87] Cic. *Balb.* 31. [88] Tan forthcoming.
[89] For the philosophers, see Gell. *NA* 15.11.1; Suet. *Rhet.* 1.2.

was the toga;[90] if the right to wear it were to be granted to newcomers, this would be an insult to 'real' citizens. The resentment of the Italians was most exacerbated by the fact that freedmen, most of whom were of Eastern descent, were rewarded with the citizenship, while Italians, who were more closely related to Romans, were not. A telling story appears in Velleius. Scipio Aemilianus was booed by the crowds at a public assembly, to which he replied: 'How can I, who have so many times heard the battle shout of the enemy without feeling fear, be disturbed by the shouts of men like you, to whom Italy is only a stepmother?'[91] The assemblies were often attended by freedmen, but clearly Aemilianus clearly found their opinion worthless, since they had never fought for Rome. Whether he would have taken the Italians more seriously cannot be determined. The Italians may have thought so, since they approached him for assistance to protest the distributions by the Gracchan land committee (see section 5.3.2).

There are several reasons why the Romans were reluctant to give the allies citizenship. Many of their objections were quite real in an economic and political sense. For example, it may be that the Romans feared that it would be more difficult to recruit enough numbers of soldiers for the army; citizens could not be obliged to serve in the same way that allies could. If Italians became citizens, they would have to receive equal shares of land and other spoils after successful wars. Moreover, the Romans had to supply citizen soldiers with equipment and food, which had until now been supplied by the allied states. Since citizens did not pay direct taxes, all this would be very expensive for the state.[92] Citizens were also entitled to grain distributions at below-market prices, as instituted by Gaius Gracchus. Italians-turned-citizens were, furthermore, able to influence elections and votes for new laws in Rome, and since they were in the majority, the power of old citizens would be reduced. Roman *publicani* may have feared competition in bidding for public contracts from Italian merchants. Finally, whichever Roman politician successfully proposed a law to give allies citizenship would gain an enormous clientele and thus political power.[93] All these considerations posed serious threats to the Roman state, especially in the financial sphere: giving citizenship to allies would be extremely expensive. It would also cause upheaval in the established political system of the state.

Lower-class citizens of Rome considered the citizenship a jealously guarded asset, which was not given out lightly;[94] they understood that if land and grain distributions had to be shared with large numbers of new citizens, there would be

[90] Ennius fr. 486. [91] Vell. 2.4.4.

[92] Nicolet 1978; Brunt 1988, 120–1. Indeed, when the allies eventually became citizens and stopped paying taxes, the Roman treasury immediately faced problems in providing for its troops. See Wiedemann 2003, 20–1.

[93] See Kendall 2013, 269–84 for an analysis of all possible motivations of the Romans against giving the Italians citizenship. See Dart 2014, 67 for the political power of the man who would gain citizenship for them.

[94] Coşkun 2009a; 2009b.

less for everyone. Their votes would be less important in the assemblies, and they would receive fewer bribes and handouts, which were normally distributed during festivals and elections. In 126, the tribune Fannius encouraged the people to expel non-citizens from Rome, saying, 'Were you to grant citizenship to the Latins, I think, do you imagine that you would still, as is now the case, find a place in an assembly or take part in the games and festivals?'[95] There was also the intangible status and prestige of being a Roman citizen; if more people became citizens, the status of the citizenship would diminish. At this point in the second century, both Roman and Italian elites, as well as the common people, knew what was at stake.

In the early second, indications had appeared for the first time that some Italians wanted to become citizens. Already in 177, action had to be taken against inhabitants of Latin colonies who had tried to gain citizenship illegally: they had tried to circumvent the law by fraudulent methods that obliged them to leave a son in the colony, in order to gain citizenship for both themselves and their sons, as we have seen (chapter 4.2.1). The people involved were only Latins, not all Italians, but something had clearly changed in the attitude of some allies.[96]

In fact, in the late second century the Romans recognized the validity of the Italians' grievances, as well as the importance of keeping their allies happy. One way to do this was to take action against magistrates who abused their powers. In most cases, as we saw in section 5.3.1, the Senate only acted when it received a complaint from an ally; in some cases it punished a rampaging official, but in many cases no action was taken at all. In order to establish a more systematic approach to such complaints, in 149 the first permanent court to judge cases of *repetundae*, the *quaestio de repetundis*, was established by the *lex Calpurnia*. Literally, *repetundae* means 'ask back': the law offered provincials the possibility to ask for the restitution of goods and money unjustly taken by Roman magistrates. This permanent court was only available to allies from the provinces; allies from Italy had no access to it, nor to any other mode of redress.[97]

In 123, the *lex Acilia repetundarum* was passed on the instigation of Gaius Gracchus, which described a detailed procedure for the prosecution of extortionate officials. It is worth citing the passage in full:

> [He (the claimant) is to be a lawful Roman citizen and the sons born to him, when] he shall become a Roman citizen according to this statute, and his grandsons provided they are born to that son, are to be lawful Roman citizens [and] are to cast [their vote in the tribe of the person, who shall have been condemned according to this statute,] and they are to register (them) in that tribe, and they are to have

[95] ORF no. 32, 3.

[96] Dart 2014, 47–51 assumes that all Latins desired Roman citizenship, although this is not certain.

[97] Cic. *Off.* 2.21, *Brut.* 27; *Fin.* 2.16. Richardson 1987 argues that it was available only to Roman citizens, while provincials were dealt with on an ad-hoc basis, but, as Eilers 1991, 170 argues, this is unlikely.

> exemption from military service... If any of those, who [??? shall not wish to become a Roman citizens according to this statute, whoever of them in a Latin state???] shall not have been [??? duumvir, consul, dictator???,] praetor or aedile, shall have power of investigation? according to this statute, [and if the other person shall have been condemned in that trial under this statute, then whoever shall have been prosecuted him, by the agency of whichever of them he shall have been chiefly condemned, he (the claimant) is to have *provocatio* and exemption and] the judge (the president of the court) is then to see that his [exemption] from military service and public compulsory service (*munera*) [be published] in his [own] community.[98]

In short, this law offered citizenship to any ally who had not yet been a magistrate in his own town (see page 219), and who had successfully prosecuted a Roman magistrate.

Thus, the law rewarded successful prosecutions with citizenship—an indication that Italians may have desired the citizenship at this time. At the same time, the Roman state recognized that not all allies might want to become citizens and offered freedom from military service and public services (*munera*) in his home town as an alternative reward, as well as *provocatio*. The latter offered protection against abuse by magistrates; normally a magistrate had the power to imprison, fine, flog, enslave, and banish citizens and allies, to confiscate property, and to mandate pledges and oaths from them. The right of *provocatio*, which all citizens held, allowed them to appeal these rulings at the *concilium plebis*.[99] Thus, if allies were granted this right as well, they would have been able to appeal any magisterial decision of this type. The Roman state thus acknowledged that not all Italians wanted to become citizens, and that abuse by Roman magistrates was an important grievance to them.[100]

The *lex Acilia* offered a new way of making Roman magistrates adhere to the rules, which might have satisfied the Italians. Unfortunately, it was not very effective. Most of the prosecuted magistrates were acquitted. The only people recorded as receiving citizenship after a prosecution are L. Cossinius and T. Coponius, both from Tibur.[101] Although this law acknowledged that Italians may have wanted to become citizens, it did not, in fact, lead to citizenship for many Italians. The Italians therefore had to find other ways to solve their grievances.

[98] Ll. 76–9. It is likely that by this time the *civitas sine suffragio* no longer existed; the towns known to have held it had been granted full citizenship; see Badian 1970–1, 381; Brunt 1988, 136–9. However, Mouritsen 2006 argues that it did in fact still exist. However, if it did, we would expect it to have been recorded in the epigraphic *lex agraria* and *lex repetundarum*, which offer very detailed descriptions of the rights of various groups of people.

[99] Lintott 1999, 99. See *OCD, s.v. lex Valeria de provocatione.*

[100] Sherwin-White 1973, 135. Keaveney 1987, 68 suggests that around 125, only the 'least sophisticated' of the Italians desired *provocatio*, while all others wanted full citizenship. However, it is not clear why a desire for *provocatio* was 'less sophisticated'; many Italians were proud of their heritage and, even after the Social War, some were in doubt as to whether to accept citizenship.

[101] Cic. *Balb.* 53–4. David 2006, 105 wrongly says that no prosecutions were successful.

In order to alleviate discontent among the allies, various new ways of gaining citizenship were created in the late second century. One way in which allies, although most likely only Latins, could receive citizenship was through the *ius adipiscendi civitatem Romanum per magistratum*, that is, the 'right to receive Roman citizenship through holding a magistracy', also termed *civitas per magistratum* in modern scholarship. Unfortunately, very little is certain about this right. It is usually assumed that this right allowed ex-magistrates of an Italian town to become Roman citizens after their tenure of office had ended. As we just saw, the *lex Acilia repetundarum* awarded successful prosecutors either the Roman citizenship or *provocatio*. The law states that this option was given to '[whoever of them . . .] shall not have been [?duumvir, consul, dicta]tor, praetor or aedile'. This suggests that those who had already exercised these local offices had been granted Roman citizenship or *provocatio* because of their service.

It has been suggested that only magistrates of Latin towns could gain these rights, not those of all Italian cities, since dictators only existed in some Latin towns.[102] This argument is not decisive; as Sherwin-White argues, the list apparently intended to 'provide a summary in Latin of every type of civic magistracy existing in Italian communities'.[103] However, the list excludes subordinates like quaestors and *tribuni plebis*, and irregular offices like censors, so that not all magistracies are included. Further evidence that the *civitas per magistratum* most likely only applied to magistrates of Latin colonies is provided by Asconius. He states that Pompeius Strabo, shortly before the Social War, gave some towns in the Po Valley 'Latin rights, so that they would have the same rights as the other Latin colonies, namely to receive citizenship through exercising a local magistracy'.[104] If Asconius means by 'other Latin colonies' those that already existed at the time, i.e. before the Social War, then this shows that the people of these colonies had held this right since before the Social War. This proves that ex-magistrates of colonies with Latin rights were granted the Roman citizenship,[105] but not other Italians. The date of the introduction of the *civitas per magistratum* is debated. Some scholars assume that Latin colonists held this right throughout the Republic,[106] but most believe that it was introduced around 125–124.[107] The latter indeed seems most likely, considering the growing demand for citizenship at this time.

102 Gabba 1994, 105; Crawford 1996, 111; Mouritsen 1998, 99–108.

103 Sherwin-White 1972, 94–5; see Galsterer 1976, 95–6.

104 Asc. 2–3C: *Pompeius enim non novis colonis eas constituit sed veteribus incolis manentibus ius dedit Latii, ut possent habere ius quod ceterae Latinae coloniae, id est ut petendo magistratus civitatem Romanam adipiscerentur.*

105 In 51, the Latins clearly had this right, since the consul in that year flogged a man from Novum Comum, a town with Latin rights, saying that the man was not a citizen since he had not been a magistrate (Cic. *Att.* 5.11.2; App. *BC* 2.26; Plu. *Caes.* 29.1–2).

106 Kremer 2014, 230.

107 Bradeen 1959; Badian 1970–1, 390; Keaveney 1987, 84; Brunt 1988, 97; Dyson 1992, 60; Coşkun 2010, 35; Dart 2014, 60–1. Sherwin-White 1973, 112 argues that it was created in the early first century. Kendall 2013, 716–21 doubts its creation in the 120s.

Thus, the *civitas per magistratum* offered another way in which the Roman state tried to assuage the grievances of its allies, at least the Latin colonists. The desire to become citizens was probably larger among this group than among other allies: as we have seen, many Latin colonists had been recruited from Roman citizens and had been granted an extensive package of rights that made it possible for them to maintain relations with their Roman families. We must assume that the possibility to become a citizen after holding a magistracy was still combined with the requirement to leave a son behind in the colony, so that the colonies' population would not be reduced.

Another way in which people in the late second century could become citizens was by an individual grant from a Roman general. Marius repeatedly made use of this opportunity: the *lex Appuleia* of 103 gave him the right to grant citizenship to a certain number of settlers in his veteran colonies.[108] However, his political enemies used the heated debate on citizenship to attack Marius and question his decisions: one of the settlers, T. Matrinius from Spoletium, was accused of not being a citizen, because the colony in which he was supposed to be settled was in fact never established.[109] In another instance, when Marius 'had bestowed citizenship upon as many as a thousand men of Camerinum for conspicuous bravery in the war, the act was held to be illegal and was impeached by some; to which he replied that the clash of arms had prevented his hearing the voice of the law'.[110] The debate surrounding Marius' citizenship grants was partially due to opposition from his political enemies, who grasped at every chance to harass him. Still, citizenship was central to political debates, indicating that it was a real issue in Roman politics around 100. The laws for land distribution proposed by Appuleius Saturninus, Marius' ally, caused much opposition, because they allegedly gave more land to Italians than to Romans.[111] Even if this was not true, Marius' position as a new man and his supposedly favourable treatment of allies could be used as political weapons against him. Still, Marius was not the only general who gave citizenship to allies: Pompeius Strabo gave it to P. Caesius of Ravenna 'after he had performed mighty achievements in the [Social] war'. Several other grants by generals to individuals or groups of Italians are attested.[112]

In conclusion, these new possibilities to gain citizenship indicate that the Romans were aware of the discontent among their allies and some of the main causes for it. They did not consider it feasible to give all allies citizenship, but tried to dispel some of the allied grievances by other methods. This could not solve all problems: the economic disadvantages that the allies suffered could not be taken away except by a grant of citizenship, which the Romans were not prepared to

[108] Cic. *Balb.* 48 mentions three people per colony; Badian 1958, 206 assumes that all settlers became citizens.

[109] Cic. *Balb.* 48–9.

[110] Plu. *Mar.* 28.2; see VM 5.2.8; Cic. *Balb.* 46.

[111] Plu. *Mar.* 38–9.

[112] Caesius and other instances: Cic. *Balb.* 50–1; *Arch.* 24.

make. Other problems that the allies suffered could be solved by the new options created by Rome. However, these were only available to a small number of Italians: the *civitas per magistratum* most likely was only available to Latins, so that options for Italian allies were limited.

Some scholars have seen the political integration of Italy after the Social War as inevitable, something that was bound to happen. Badian, for example, speaks of a 'gradual process of enfranchisement'.[113] Some even assume that Romans and Italians were by this time so culturally unified that they wanted citizenship and, in the eyes of the Romans, deserved it for being civilized.[114] However, the option to accept *provocatio* shows that not all Italians were equally willing to accept citizenship. Furthermore, the cultural unification of Italy was not very advanced by this time, as we have seen in chapter 4.4. Some scholars have therefore emphasized the political unification of Italy: they argue that Rome in the second century intervened more and more in Italian politics and showed itself able to govern a larger territory, so that Italian elites willingly gave up their authority to Rome. The Romans would have been willing to share citizenship with the Italians because of the close political and social bonds between them. Sherwin-White, for example, states that 'the penetration of Roman authority [was] so thorough, and the performance of military *munera* so customary, that the Italian allies were not only justified in their demands, but fitted, from a Roman point of view, to receive the citizenship'.[115]

However, we have seen in section 5.3.1 that Rome, at least in theory, did not have the authority to intervene in Italy, nor did it have the manpower to supervise the whole of Italy. Rome usually only responded to requests from the Italians, or intervened when this was necessary for the protection of Roman interests.[116] Of course the Italians performed military service for the Romans, but they had been doing so since the fourth century. Furthermore, as we have seen, in the late second century the Italians had many reasons to be dissatisfied with military service, so that it was not necessarily an integrative mechanism. Contrary to Sherwin-White's assumption, the Romans certainly did not think that the Italian allies were 'fitted to receive the citizenship'—on the contrary, cultural differences between Rome and the Italic peoples were still great. The Romans were, for financial and ideological reasons, unwilling to share the privileges of citizenship with the Italians. Therefore, although some Italians profited from the newly created methods of gaining Roman citizenship, there was no reason why all Italians would be eager to accept it at this time, nor were the Romans willing to grant it to them.

113 Badian 1970–1, 381–3.

114 Göhler 1939, 98; Gabba 1989, 207–12, 225–32. Brunt 1988, 112–20 and Kendall 2013, 131–2 suggest close cultural association with Rome by the late second century, e.g. in fighting style, language, titles of magistrates, and dress habits. Although this is true, as we have seen, many other aspects of Italian culture were still very different from those in Rome.

115 Sherwin-White 1973, 129; see Bernardi 1973, 67; D'Andria 1979, 285; Salmon 1982, 125.

116 Mouritsen 1998, 40–2.

5.5. The Outbreak of the Social War

The Italian elites for a long time had derived benefits from their association with the Roman state, but by the late second century, the disadvantages outweighed the benefits. The problems of the Italians were not resolved during the second century; on the contrary, the Romans continued to take the hard line. New measures that could have solved the problems of the Italians were not very successful. The *lex Acilia* led to just a few convictions, while grants of citizenship by individual Roman commanders were often questioned. It is interesting to note that the issue of citizenship had become a tool for Roman politicians to use against their enemies: Marius was often attacked for his lenient stance towards the Italians.

It is understandable that the Italian elites became more and more aggrieved by the treatment they received. This became clear when the *lex Licinia Mucia* was passed in 95. It appeared that during the previous decades, many Italians had infiltrated the Roman census lists by claiming they were citizens. The censors had apparently not checked these claims and had entered them as citizens.[117] The *lex Licinia Mucia* arranged to purge the census rolls of false citizens, expel them from Rome, and make them return to their home towns. Encroachment on the census lists was now treated as a crime, as those who refused to re-register in their home towns could be prosecuted.[118] There were precedents for the expulsion of Latins and allies from Rome, for example, in 187 and 177 (see chapter 4.2.1), and the Roman state was within its rights to enforce the law. Nevertheless, this law was harsher than previous legislation, since it was passed at the instigation of the Roman state, rather than at the request of the Latin towns, as in 177.[119] The Italians were incensed at the passing of the law. Asconius cites Cicero's view on the law:

> 'I see that everyone is agreed that the Licinian-Mucian law concerning the return to one's own citizenship . . . was not only useless but very destructive of the public good.' . . . For the Italic peoples were gripped by a great desire for the Roman citizenship . . . The feelings of the leaders of the Italic peoples were so alienated by this law that it was even the main reason for the *bellum Italicum* that broke out three years later.[120]

It is certainly correct that the law was one of the main reasons for the Social War, although perhaps not the most important one, as Asconius suggests. After all, the war broke out four years after the law was passed, rather than immediately. We do

[117] Diod. 37.13. Badian 1970–1, 405–7 and Keaveney 1987, 81–3 argue that the censors of 97/6 were friends of Marius and therefore of the Italians, and that they turned a blind eye to Italian encroachment onto the lists.

[118] Cic. *Off.* 3.47, *Balb.* 48–9, *Sest.* 30, *Brut.* 63, *De Or.* 2.257; Schol. Bob. *Sest.* 30. See Tweedie 2012; Kendall 2013, 208–10, 235–6. Some, e.g. Brunt 1988, 99, assume that according to the *ius migrationis* it was lawful for Italians to gain Roman citizenship in this way, but as I have argued (chapter 4.2.1), this is unlikely.

[119] Coşkun 2009b; Dart 2014, 62–4.

[120] Asc. *Corn.* 67–8C.

not know how many people were prosecuted under this law, but some certainly were. The censors of 92 did not include allies as citizens, contrary to those of 97/6, and indeed made sure that those who had registered on the lists before 95 were subjected to judicial scrutiny. Thus, the *lex Licinia Mucia* seems to have been strictly executed. By 91, the Italians knew that the law was not an empty threat, and that actual action was taken against Italian encroachment on the census lists. Asconius states that the Italians greatly desired the citizenship; his view may have been coloured by later events, especially the fact that the Italians were eventually satisfied by a grant of citizenship. In 95, however, it is certainly not clear that all allies wanted the same; those who had illegally entered the census lists clearly wanted citizenship, but they were not representative of all allies.

That the Social War broke out in 91, and not earlier or later, was due to the specific events in that year.[121] The Italians by this time had serious reasons for resentment. Since the Gracchan period, when they had first felt aggrieved because of the land distributions, the Italians had gained more reasons for discontent, such as military defeats. They had found out that measures supposed to assuage their grievances, such as the *lex Acilia*, were not very successful. The *lex Licinia Mucia* had treated them as unwanted strangers. They had noted that their complaints were not taken seriously by the Roman Senate, which instead waged personal and political battles over the heads of the Italians. By 91, it might have seemed to them that a grant of full citizenship was the only way finally to solve the problems that they were facing. However, this does not mean that it was the passionate desire of all Italians to become Roman citizens: they had simply experienced that other ways of solving their problems were unsuccessful. They saw the citizenship as a means to an end, namely to improve their political and economic position.

The failure of the various methods to address Italian grievances had made clear that only a well-designed proposal by a Roman politician would have a chance of success.[122] This chance seemed to come in 91, when the tribune of the plebs M. Livius Drusus made another attempt to give citizenship to the allies. One of his proposals involved new land distributions for Roman citizens, for which *ager publicus* would be taken away from Italians who were still holding it. To make them willing to give up their land, he proposed to give them citizenship, under the assumption that they were willing to accept loss of land in return for becoming citizens. Drusus' proposal must therefore have been aimed mainly at Italians, not Latins, since most *ager publicus* was located in allied areas.[123] Again, it was

[121] Two monographs on the Social War were published recently, Kendall 2013 and Dart 2014; unfortunately, neither takes into account the other's work, and both ignore some important recent works by others, so that neither can be considered the definitive work on the war. Kendall's book is very detailed, while Dart's gives a good overview in a smaller number of pages.

[122] Tweedie 2012, 137–8.

[123] Roselaar 2010, 31–64. Mouritsen 1998, 121–2 argues that the proposal was intended only for Latins, but Vell. 2.14.1, Liv. *Per.* 71, and Flor. 2.5.17–18 state that Drusus wanted to give citizenship to all Italians.

assumed that the Italians were willing to accept citizenship in exchange for land. If Italians held Roman state-owned land, they would be obliged to give it up, whether they were citizens or not. It may be that they were afraid, as before, to lose private land due to incorrect measurements, and hoped to protect themselves against this by gaining citizenship. Appian indeed suggests that fear of losing land that was rightfully theirs made the Italians afraid:

> Even the Italians, in whose especial interest Drusus was devising these plans, were apprehensive about the law providing for the colonies, because they thought that the Roman public domain (which was still undivided and which they were cultivating, some by force and others clandestinely) would at once be taken away from them, and that in many cases they might even be disturbed in their private holdings.[124]

Epigraphic evidence shows that two laws for land distribution were passed. A commission was set up to distribute land, but colonies, to which Appian refers, are not mentioned elsewhere.[125]

The desire for citizenship among the Italians seems to have been stronger in 91 than ever before. Drusus was a personal friend of Q. Poppaedius Silo, a leader of the Marsi and later an allied commander in the war, so he must have known what Italians thought about this issue.[126] Appian even says that Drusus proposed his laws 'at the urgent request' of the Italians. This was quite a change from thirty years before, when it had been Roman politicians who had suggested that citizenship might be a worthwhile exchange for land.[127] At some point in 91, Poppaedius brought together 10,000 men 'who had occasion to fear judicial investigations' under the *lex Licinia Mucia*, and marched on Rome. Gnaeus Domitius, the censor of 92, was sent to stop them, but Silo said that he went to Rome 'to get citizenship at the summons of the tribunes'—that is, Drusus. Domitius replied that 'he would obtain the citizenship with less risk and more honourably if he approached the Senate in a manner that was less warlike; the Senate, he said, was in favour of granting this favour to the allies not under compulsion but by petition'.[128] Although some scholars dismiss this story,[129] it gives a fascinating insight into the desperation of the allies to obtain citizenship, and their attempts to negotiate with Rome in order to gain the citizenship in a peaceful manner.[130] But despite

[124] App. *BC* 1.35–6.

[125] An epigraphic elogium (CIL 1^2, 1, p. 199) for Drusus calls him *xvir a(gris) d(andis) a(dsignandis) lege sua et eodem anno v vir a(gris) d(andis) a(dsignandis) lege Saufeia* ('one of ten men to divide and assign land according to his own law and in the same year one of five men to divide and assign land according to the law of Saufeius'). See Dart 2014, 74–5, 83–5.

[126] Plu. *Cat. Min.* 1–2; Diod. 37.15.3; VM 3.1.2; *Vir. Ill.* 80.11. He was also a friend of Marius. See Marshall 1976, 95; Dart 2014, 76–9.

[127] Diod. 37.13; *Vir. Ill.* 81; VM 3.1.2a; App. *BC* 1.35.

[128] Diod. 37.13.

[129] Bancalari Molina 1987, 424; Mouritsen 1998, 125 n. 51.

[130] Kendall 2013, 237–9; Dart 2014, 86–8.

the peaceful language of Domitius, the Senate refused to negotiate with the allied leaders.[131]

The sources suggest that Drusus' law regarding land distributions was passed first: 'Drusus... appealed to the allies and Italian nations and made them hope for the Roman citizenship; with their help, he carried by force laws on the distribution of land and grain.'[132] As Livy's epitomator states, the Italians assisted Drusus in getting these laws passed, with the express promise that in return he would introduce a law regarding citizenship. However, the Italians in the end did not receive the citizenship, since Drusus was murdered before his proposal for citizenship could be passed into law. By the time the revolt started, all Drusus' laws had probably already been cancelled by the Senate, most likely including the land law.[133] Thus, although the Italian allies no longer had to fear the immediate loss of their lands, they had, once again, experienced the fickle nature of Roman politics and the degree to which they were subject to the whims of the Senate. Thus, there was a very real danger that another politician would try to take away their landholdings in the future. At this point, they therefore saw no other option than to revolt in earnest. This is presented in most sources as the direct reason for the Italian revolt.[134] As Appian states:

> [The Italians] considered it no longer tolerable that those who were labouring for their political advancement (i.e. Drusus) should suffer such outrages, and as they saw no other means of acquiring citizenship, they decided to revolt from the Romans altogether, and to make war against them with might and main.[135]

The war broke out at Asculum in Picenum. The revolt started when two Roman magistrates were killed in a riot. Appian recounts:

> [when] the Romans... heard what was going on [i.e. the Italian conspiracy], they sent men round to the towns, choosing those who were best acquainted with each, to collect information quietly. One of these agents saw a young man who was being taken as a hostage from the town of Asculum to another town, and informed Servilius, the praetor, who was in the area. Servilius hastened to Asculum and indulged in very menacing language to the people, who were celebrating a festival, and they, supposing that the plot was discovered, put him to death. They also killed Fonteius, his legate. After these were slain, none of the other Romans in Asculum were spared. The inhabitants fell upon them, slaughtered them all, and plundered their goods.[136]

[131] This harsh position continued when the war had already started. In the winter of 91/90, an Italian embassy was sent to negotiate with the Senate, but it answered that 'if they repented of what they had done, they could send ambassadors, but otherwise not' (App. *BC* 1.39). See Dart 2014, 107.

[132] Liv. *Per.* 71.1–2.

[133] Cic. *Dom.* 16; Asc. *Corn.* 69A. See Dart 2014, 89–94.

[134] Vell. 2.15; Florus 2.6.4; Plin. *NH* 25.52. See Mouritsen 1998, 129; Keaveney 1987, 99; Roselaar 2010, 248–9; Kendall 2013, 219; Dart 2014, 93–7.

[135] App. *BC* 1.38.

[136] App. *BC* 1.38.

There are some interesting points to this story. Firstly, the revolt had been prepared for some time by the Italians, who had even exchanged hostages to ensure each other's good faith. Furthermore, the Roman approach to deal with the rumours of Italian discontent was to send individual Romans to the Italian towns with which they had personal connections, again attesting the importance of social relationships between Romans and Italians. Finally, assuming that the festival mentioned here is the same at which the Latin actor Saunio appeared (see section 5.3.1), Romans and Italians were visiting the theatre together. It seems that many Roman citizens were present in Asculum, either living there or visiting, attesting to high levels of mobility in Italy. Nevertheless, the local people knew exactly who the Romans were and did not hesitate to kill them.

After the riot in Asculum, the war broke out in earnest, with many Italians joining in concerted military action against Rome. It must be kept in mind that not all allies were willing to fight for citizenship: many did not join the revolt.[137] Of the Latin colonies, only Venusia joined the war, but the others were apparently happy with their situation. Possibly they considered options such as *civitas per magistratum* to be sufficient, since this already allowed their elites to become citizens. The threat of land distributions was an important consideration for many allies, as is shown by the fact that many of those who revolted had undistributed *ager publicus* in their territories, or had been subjected to distributions during the Gracchan reforms. The Apulians and Lucanians, for example, had seen much of their land taken and distributed by the Gracchi.[138] In Samnium and surrounding areas, where the Marsi and other Italian groups lived, the available *ager publicus* was most likely *ager scripturarius*, public pasture land, which was not suitable for distribution. Still, these peoples may have been afraid that the Romans would introduce tighter controls on the use of this land. In Picenum there was not much public land left at this time, so that the Picentes probably had different reasons to rebel. Thus, the motivations to join the revolt were not the same for all Italians.

Most scholars assume that the Italians now fought to gain Roman citizenship, since this is emphasized by many ancient sources. Cicero, for example, states that 'the allies were not seeking to deprive us of our citizenship, but to be admitted to it themselves'.[139] Velleius, in the passage quoted above, states the allies were unhappy about being denied the citizenship of the state for which they had fought for so long. The epitome of Trogus states that 'the Marsic War erupted, not for liberty, but for participation in empire and citizenship'.[140] And Florus states that the term 'Social' or 'Allied' War was incorrect, because 'if we are truthful, it was a war against citizens'.[141] Similarly, the account of Appian clearly draws a connection between the failure of Drusus' citizenship legislation and the outbreak of the war. Italian ambassadors were sent to Rome to 'complain that although they had

[137] *Contra* Brunt 1965, 93. [138] App. *BC* 1.36. See Roselaar 2010, 321–4.
[139] Cic. *Phil.* 12.27. [140] Justin. 38.4.13. [141] Flor. 2.18.1.

co-operated in all ways with the Romans in building up the empire, the latter had not been willing to admit their helpers to citizenship'.[142] All these passages have led scholars to assume that gaining citizenship of the Roman state was the most important aim of the Italian insurgents.

However, for a long time there was no reason why the Italians should have felt this way. As we have seen, there was no *a priori* reason why Italians would want the Roman citizenship. Mouritsen therefore, in an important revision of existing scholarly ideas, argued that the Italians wanted independence. He explains the statements in the ancient sources by suggesting that there were two historical traditions, one emphasizing citizenship, the other independence. Because of the eventual outcome of the war, the tradition that focused on independence disappeared from most of the sources.[143] Indeed, only a few sources mention independence or liberty as an aim of the Italians. Ovid, for example, mentions 'the Paelignian people, whose liberty compelled to honest arms'.[144] Eutropius states that the allies, 'who for many years had obeyed the Roman people, then began to claim equal freedom for themselves'.[145] Strabo writes that 'begging for freedom and political rights without getting them, they revolted and kindled what is called the Marsic War'.[146]

However, these two aims—citizenship and independence—are not incompatible, as Strabo already suggests, stating that the Italians desired 'freedom and political rights', while Eutropius says the aim was 'equal freedom' (*libertatem aequam*). The term *libertas*, used by some sources, did not necessarily refer to independence from Rome. *Libertas* essentially meant freedom from 'arbitrary coercion and punishment by magistrates, and some degree of participation in political power'.[147] It included the unobstructed exercise of the political rights that went with citizenship, such as the right to vote and *provocatio*.[148] The Italians would achieve freedom by gaining equality with Romans—that is, by acquiring citizenship. Even sources that mention *libertas*, therefore, can refer to Roman citizenship, rather than complete independence from Rome.

In this light, Kendall offers a new explanation of the motivation of the allies: he suggests that the war started out as a *secessio*.[149] The tactic of seceding from the Roman state until demands were met had been applied successfully by the Roman plebeians in the early Republic, in order to achieve concessions from the patricians.[150] As Kendall rightly points out, independence would not have brought the Italians the same opportunities and advantages as the citizenship. Citizenship would have offered them more material and immaterial benefits, which might

[142] See Dart 2014, 27–40 on the different motives described in the sources.

[143] Mouritsen 1998, esp. 5–12, 124–5, 139–40; see also Sherwin-White 1973, 139–49; Keaveney 1987, 34.

[144] Ovid. *Am.* 3.15.8–9. [145] Eutr. 5.3.1. [146] Strabo 5.4.2. [147] Brunt 1988, 297.

[148] Arena 2012, 47–56. See Brunt 1988, 297; Kendall 2013, 72–3.

[149] Kendall 2013, 229–43. [150] Liv. 2.32–3, 3.55; DH 6.49–94.

collectively be termed 'the profits of empire'. Independence would have very different economic, political, and social effects than a grant of citizenship; most importantly, the Italians would lose any chance of profiting from Rome's expanding hegemony. It is therefore reasonable that the Italians wanted citizenship, as indeed many sources state.

It is unlikely that the continued Roman refusal to grant the Italians citizenship would suddenly have caused a complete reversal in the Italian aims, i.e. that instead of gaining the citizenship they would suddenly have decided to become independent. There is no reason why the Italians would have chosen independence only because they were, for the moment, unable to become citizens. A *secessio*, on the other hand, may have forced the Romans to give in to Italian demands. Of course, the Italians could not be sure that a *secessio* would gain them the desired result; even after a long war, the Romans might still refuse the citizenship. The allies therefore had to plan for every eventuality, including the possibility that the Romans would accept Italian independence in order to avoid a war. The rebels therefore created their own Senate in their own capital and minted their own coins. If the Romans would continue to refuse the citizenship, the possibility of creating an independent state was not beyond Italian capabilities.[151]

The Social War was the first time that various Italic peoples had cooperated on such a scale and so effectively. Although the concept of *Italia* had existed since the third century (chapter 4.6), there was no united Italian identity until the Social War. Serious internal conflicts within Italian cities were brought to light during the Second Punic War, for example; in many cases, rivalries within and between cities determined their course of action.[152] The Social War was the first time that an 'Italian' identity was advertised, rather than a local one. *Italia* could serve as a rallying cry for the Italians, who had previously not shared any common symbols. The Italian rebels established a new capital at Corfinium, which they named Italica.[153] Of course, this Italian identity had been achieved under the influence of Rome. If Rome had not united the Italic peoples under its political power, they would not have been able to create this unity in the first place.

Coinage was an important instrument to display the identity of the Italians during the Social War, as had been the case in previous centuries (see chapter 4.2.3). Rebel coins advertised an Italian identity, by using both Latin and Oscan legends. Some depicted a bull, the symbol of *Italia*, goring the Roman wolf, while others showed an oath scene, symbolizing the mutual support between the rebels. A common legend was ITALIA, sometimes written in Oscan, VITELIU.[154] Language thus

[151] App. *BC* 1.40; Vell. 2.16.1. Diod. 37.2.4–7 suggests that their state was strictly organized; this is followed by Salmon 1958, 169–77; Gabba 1994, 118–19; Keaveney 1987, 215–19. Others have argued that the Italians only installed a war council; see Kendall 2013, 258–67; Dart 2014, 108–13.

[152] Fronda 2010.

[153] Strabo 5.4.2. See Isayev 2017, 320–6.

[154] *Imagines* 1.67–74; see Burnett 1998, 167. A lead slingshot found at Asculum carries the text ITAL (CIL 1^2, p. 560–3).

played an important role in creating or communicating a shared identity, separate from the Romans.[155] A small number of coins, minted by C. Papius Mutilus, leader of the Pentri, carry the legend SAFINIM. The term 'Safinus' could have multiple meanings; usually it referred to Samnium or parts of it.[156] These legends were relevant for a small group only, since not all Italian rebels were Samnites or spoke the Oscan language. It is likely that this coin was struck by the small group of rebels, led by Papius, who continued the fight after the others had given up in 88.[157] It is striking that when the rest of the Italians had abandoned the fight, the Safini reverted to a more local rallying cry. The unification of Italy by Rome had brought the Italians closer together and made it possible for them to create a common identity, but local and regional markers of identity continued to be advertised, as this coin issue shows.

Despite their anti-Roman message, the coins struck by the allies were closely modelled on Roman coins in design (including an oath scene, as depicted on Roman coins of the Second Punic War) and weight standard. By the early first century, the Italians had used Roman coinage for so long that they were unable to disassociate themselves completely from Rome. Compared to the third century, when many local standards and designs had been in use, Italians had quickly become dependent on the Roman currency system. From die studies, it seems that the Italians actually minted very little money, far less than needed to run a fully functional currency system to compete with that of Rome. Most likely, the coinage served as a propaganda tool, rather than as a practical instrument of commerce.[158]

In this section, we have seen that the most important desire among the Italians was a solution to their problems: protection against abuse, access to new economic opportunities, and a say in the economic and military policy of the Roman state.[159] Many of these desires could have been achieved without a grant of citizenship, but in the period between the Gracchi and 91, the various solutions proposed by the Roman state had proved to be ineffective. The only alternative solution to their problems was a grant of full citizenship.[160] The image painted by the sources, especially Appian, that the allies had been working for several decades to gain citizenship, is at least partially incorrect: they wanted a solution to their problems, but this did not require citizenship. By 91, however, it was clear that none of the mechanisms offered by the Romans to alleviate the problems of the Italians had been successful. Therefore, the Italians now desired to gain the Roman citizenship,

155 Dench 1995, 214; Burnett 1998, 166–70.

156 Dench 1995, 198–206.

157 Crawford 1985, 181; Dench 1995, 210; 1997, 47–9; Burnett 1998, 166–70.

158 Brunt 1965; 1988; Keaveney 1987, 13–16; *contra* Dart 2014, 113.

159 Kendall 2013, 135.

160 Dart 2014, 38. Galsterer 1976, 165–6 similarly concludes that for most of the Republic, local and regional self-control, combined with the benefits of belonging to the Roman Empire, were enough for the allies. Only when this was challenged during the Gracchan land reform did they start to feel threatened, because the loss of land might result in them losing their local leading positions. I would go even further and suggest that the desire for citizenship did not emerge until it had become clear that possible alternative solutions, as had been proposed in the last decades of the second century, would be unsuccessful.

and fought for this in the Social War. The citizenship was not an end in itself, but only the means to an end, namely to gain access to the practical benefits that Roman citizens enjoyed. The actions of the Italians in the civil wars of 87–82 clearly show that once they had won the citizenship, they wanted to enjoy all the rights connected to it, as we will see in section 5.7.

5.6. The Grant of Citizenship to the Italians

After some heavy defeats at the hands of the insurgents, the Romans decided to grant citizenship to the Italians.[161] The *lex Iulia* of late 90 offered full citizenship to all Latin and Italian communities that had not revolted:

> The Senate voted that those Italians who had adhered to their alliance should be admitted to citizenship, which was the one thing they all desired most. They sent this decree around among the Etruscans, who gladly accepted the citizenship. By this favour the Senate made the faithful more faithful, confirmed the wavering, and mollified their enemies by the hope of similar treatment.[162]

The direct motivation for the grant may have been the threat of an uprising in Etruria and Umbria, as Appian suggests. Indeed, some special measures were taken: a fragment of Sisenna states that Tuder in Umbria was given citizenship by a decree of the Senate.[163] The law offered citizenship to whole communities, not to individuals, so that each individual community had to accept the law, turning all its inhabitants into Roman citizens. Cicero describes it as 'a law by which citizenship was given to the allies and Latins'. He also explains that the law should be ratified by each individual town or people.[164] However, not all allied towns jumped at the opportunity to gain citizenship. At Heraclea and Neapolis, heated debate surrounded the issue.[165] Cicero's *Pro Archia* explains the details of the law. It seems that Italians could become Roman citizens based on the records of the allied towns; most likely the local authorities simply brought their census records to Rome, which were then transcribed into the Roman records.[166] Archias, originally from Antioch, had been granted citizenship of Heraclea. When Archias registered as a citizen in Rome in 89, he stated that since Heraclea had accepted Rome's offer of citizenship, he therefore was a Roman citizen.[167] Unfortunately, because the records of Heraclea had been destroyed, Archias could not prove his

[161] On the events during the war, see Kendall 2013, 223–418.

[162] App. *BC* 1.49; see Dart 2014, 145–6.

[163] FRH 78: *Tudertibus senati consulto et populi iusso dat civitatem.*

[164] Cic. *Balb.* 21: *qua lege civitas et socii et Latinis data, qui fundi populi facti non essent civitatem non haberent.* See Vell. 2.16.4.

[165] Cic. *Balb.* 21; Gell. *NA* 4.4.3. See Sartori 1953, 45. For a general discussion of the enfranchisement laws, see Bispham 2007, 161–204; Kendall 2013, 353; Dart 2014, 171–87.

[166] Thomas 1996, 109–18.

[167] Cic. *Arch.* 7–10.

citizenship of this town, and therefore was unable to prove that he was entitled to Roman citizenship.

The *lex Iulia* apparently also gave Roman commanders the right to grant citizenship to worthy soldiers under their command. An inscription set up by Pompeius Strabo dated to 89 gives citizenship to Spanish auxiliaries who served with him, and stated that he did so according to the *lex Iulia*.[168] Thus, not only Italian allies, but even those from outside Italy could be given the citizenship if they were deemed worthy. On the other hand, we must note again that Roman citizenship was not universally desired, even at this time: a Cretan archer refused citizenship when it was offered to him by L. Caesar.[169] A further law, the *lex Calpurnia*, is mentioned by Sisenna as authorizing commanders to award citizenship for bravery.[170] When this law was passed is unclear; Pompeius Strabo does not mention it. This could mean the *lex Calpurnia* was passed after the *lex Iulia*. Alternatively, the *lex Iulia* could have incorporated elements of earlier laws, including the *lex Calpurnia*.[171] A *lex Pompeia*, passed in 89, furthermore gave citizenship to communities in Cisalpine Gaul south of the Po, and Latin rights to those north of the river.[172]

Contrary to what is often argued, the *lex Iulia* was not the most important law in the expansion of the Roman citizenship, with other laws being 'supplementary'.[173] The *lex Iulia* only covered a small part of all Italian allies, namely those who had not yet revolted. Unfortunately, it is not exactly clear when and how the remaining Italians received Roman citizenship. It is usually assumed that a further law, the *lex Plautia Papiria* of 89, allowed Italians registered as citizens of an Italian town to obtain Roman citizenship by presenting themselves to a Roman praetor within sixty days after the passing of the law. Some scholars assume that this was the law that eventually gave all allies citizenship.[174] However, most see this law as only an addition to the *lex Iulia*.[175] It is often assumed that most people had been automatically enfranchised when their communities were given citizenship by the *lex Iulia* and that the *lex Plautia Papiria* covered only those who were domiciled in another state than the one in which they were registered, and therefore had not yet been granted citizenship.[176] However, it is unclear why such people could not have been enfranchised at the same time as the communities in which they were registered, since they were still officially registered as

[168] ILS 8888. [169] Diod. 37.18. [170] FRH 71.

[171] Coşkun 2004, 104–5 and Kendall 2013, 357 think that the *lex Calpurnia* was passed before the *lex Iulia*, while Brunt 1965, 108–9 and Dart 2014, 180–1 assume that the *lex Iulia* was the earlier law.

[172] Ascon. 3C; Plin. *HN* 3.138. See Sherwin-White 1973, 157–9; Bispham 2007, 173–4; Dart 2014, 182–3.

[173] As Salmon 1982, 133–4 states. [174] Keaveney 1987, 170–1; Gabba 1994, 126.

[175] Sherwin-White 1973, 152–3; Mouritsen 1998, 167; Coşkun 2009a, 147; Dart 2014, 183–5; but see Coşkun 2010, 43–50 on the problems surrounding this law.

[176] Kendall 2013, 816–30. See Coşkun forthcoming.

citizens of these towns and would therefore have been included on the citizen lists of their home towns.

Furthermore, in 89 many Italians were still fighting against Rome; some of these may have abandoned the fight and registered with the praetor as citizens, but others continued the fight and therefore clearly did not register. Other people may simply have been unable to come to Rome to visit the praetor. It is therefore unlikely that all Italians had become citizens by 89, by either the *lex Iulia* or the *lex Plautia Papiria*. Livy's *Periochae* state for the year 87: 'Citizenship was given to the Italian nations by the Senate', suggesting that this was the year in which all remaining Italians were incorporated.[177] As we will see, this may be correct.

Although many allies had now been given citizenship, the Romans were still not happy with the idea. In fact, various tricks were devised to prevent them from exerting any influence.[178] Before the allies could enjoy the privileges of citizenship, they had to be included on the Roman census lists and assigned to a voting *tribus* and a census class, otherwise they could not vote. At first, the Roman state proposed that the new citizens would be placed into a small number of newly created voting tribes, instead of the thirty-five existing ones. Appian explains:

> The Romans did not enrol the new citizens in the 35 existing tribes, lest they should outvote the old ones in the elections, but incorporated them in ten(?) new tribes, which voted last. So it often happened that their vote was useless, since a majority was obtained from the 35 tribes that voted first.[179]

In any case, the census of 89 failed, meaning that the new citizens were not enrolled into *tribus* and census classes. This meant that they were still unable to vote in any of the assemblies, including the *comitia centuriata*. This was especially important for the wealthier Italians, who qualified to join the higher classes of the *comitia centuriata* and thus would have been able to make a real difference.[180]

The Italians obviously perceived that Rome was unwilling to let them enjoy the privileges of their new citizenship. Rome's refusal to allow the Italians to enjoy their hard-fought rights quickly led to the engagement of the Italians in Roman political strife. Several Roman politicians tried to engage the Italians for their cause by promising them the full recognition of their new citizen rights. In 88, the tribune P. Sulpicius Rufus proposed to distribute the new citizens into the existing

[177] Liv. *Per.* 80.1. See Keaveney 1987, 181–2; Coşkun 2004, 117.

[178] App. *BC* 1.49, 53–5; Liv. *Per.* 76–7; Plu. *Sull.* 8; Vell. 2.19.1, 2.20.2. See Lewis 1968; Sherwin-White 1973, 155–7.

[179] App. *BC* 1.49. There is some debate about the proposed number of new tribes. Most scholars (Coşkun 2009b, 151–2; Dart 2014, 177–8, 185–7) assume ten new tribes were set up for the new citizens, since Appian uses the term δεκατεύοντες, which is translated as 'divide into ten groups'. However, Velleius 2.20.2 states that there were eight new tribes, while Sisenna FRH 38 states there were two. Lewis 1968 argues that the verb δεκατεύω simply means 'to divide', without specifying a number; see Kendall 2013, 360–4. In any case there is no independent source recording these new tribes and it is likely that they were never created; see Coşkun 2004, 122.

[180] Cic. *Arch.* 11. See Wiseman 1969, 63–4; Kendall 2013, 539; Dart 2014, 179–80.

voting tribes. He enlisted the assistance of Marius, hoping to gain the people's support for his proposal. However, the consuls, Sulla and Pompeius Rufus, opposed the proposal and ordered a cessation of public business to prevent it from being passed into law. Marius and Sulpicius then created a riot, which forced the consuls to withdraw their order; the assembly passed the proposal into law. Sulla then marched on Rome, killed Sulpicius, and declared his laws void.[181] This telling example shows the central role that the Italians' rights played in Roman politics.

The Italians did not sit idly by while Roman politicians fought among themselves over their heads. An embassy to king Mithridates of Pontus is recorded, consisting of 'Samnites and Sabellians'.[182] What they discussed with him is not recorded—perhaps the Samnites, who at this time were still under arms, asked Mithridates for military support against Rome, in exchange for their assistance in the war against Rome. At this time, it was clear that Rome was aiming for war against Mithridates, but Marius and Sulla were still fighting each other for the command in this war. The command was highly sought after, because the commanding general would be able to get his hands on the considerable wealth of Mithridates. While some Italians may have been ready to join Mithridates against Rome, other Italians attempted to gain full citizenship by gaining the support of one of the Roman generals, by voting to give him the command against Mithridates.

In 87, the consul Cinna took up the Italian cause. He again proposed the distribution of new citizens over the existing tribes, but was deterred by rioting.[183] Livy's epitome, as we saw, records that around 87, all citizens were given citizenship by the Senate.[184] It may be that this grant was approved by the Senate and people, possibly to deter the Italians from joining Cinna's army. Still, many joined Cinna's cause.[185] A grant of citizenship at this time would be a rather dramatic change from the former Roman stance, but since the Romans had now found a way to diminish the influence of the allies—namely to reduce their power of voting by not assigning them to the existing *tribus*—they may have felt it was safe to admit the allies to citizenship after all.[186] Apparently the Samnites, some of whom were still under arms in 87, were also granted citizenship in this year by Cinna:

> The Samnites . . . said that they would not agree to peace except on condition that they and all the deserters should receive the citizenship, and have their property

[181] App. *BC* 1.55–60; Plu. *Sull.* 8.1–3; Liv. *Per.* 77.1. See Swidzinski 2007, 122; Kendall 2013, 431–42, 452–65; Dart 2014, 191–3.

[182] Diod. 37.2.11; Posid. in Athen. 5.213C (F253). See Gabba 1976, 88–9; Dart 2014, 193–5; Isayev 2017, 316.

[183] Cic. *Cat.* 3.24; App. *BC* 1.64; Plu. *Sert.* 4. See Kendall 2013, 487–93.

[184] Hier. *Chron.* 85; Liv. *Per.* 63. See Brunt 1987, 90–3; Swidzinski 2007, 124–7.

[185] App. *BC* 1.65. See Badian 1958, 226; Keaveney 1987, 170–1; Kendall 2013, 494.

[186] Kendall 2013, 409–14.

> returned. The senate refused, wishing to preserve the ancient dignity of the Roman people. When Cinna heard about this, ... he enlisted the Samnites on the terms which they requested.[187]

Given the fragmentary nature of the evidence, the year in which the remaining allies received citizenship, as well as the law by which this occurred, must remain speculative. Still, we know that the allies received citizenship eventually, and it seems that from 87, the focus of the former allies' demands shifted to being allowed the full use of the citizenship rights they had already gained, rather than being admitted to the citizenship in the first place.[188] Kendall therefore rightly considers the events of this year as the 'real end of the Social War', since it meant that the last Italians had received Roman citizenship.[189]

Whatever happened exactly in 87, the allies as yet did not yet enjoy the full benefits of their citizenship. They had not been entered in the census, and therefore they could not exercise their voting rights. For this reason, they continued to attach themselves to Roman politicians who promised to ensure them the full use of their citizenship. The consul Cinna, who supported the power of the Senate against Sulla, assembled an army of thirty legions against Sulla by appealing to the Italians, promising them that he would hold a census and include all new citizens.[190] Indeed a census was held in 86, but the census figure for this year as reported by Jerome is only 463,000,[191] only slightly more than the previous figure of 394,336 in 115/114.[192] This suggests that not all Italians were registered in the tribes in this year. Some have suggested that Jerome's figure has been corrupted and should read 963,000, in which case the new citizens would have been included.[193] However, other explanations are possible: as we have seen, each community held its own census and then reported the results to Rome. Perhaps the Roman censors were free to reject Italian census results if they were not executed according to Roman procedure, or if the censors suspected that the results were falsified.[194] Furthermore, the censors of 86/5 were vehemently opposed to admitting new citizens,[195] so that it is possible that they avoided registering them.

The willingness of the Italians to support Cinna was closely connected to their own interests, but went only so far. They were unwilling, for example, to help him take the fight against Sulla to Asia. Italian soldiers did not want to fight abroad in a war that was not in their interests, as long as they were not sure that Cinna could ensure them the full rights of citizenship.[196] Finally, when Cinna in 84 recruited an

[187] Gran. Lic. 35.20–1; see App. *BC* 1.68.
[188] Dart 2014, 196–8.
[189] Kendall 2013, 516–18, quote p. 501.
[190] App. *BC* 1.65–7; Vell. 2.21–2; Plu. *Sull.* 27.
[191] Jer. *Chron.* 61.173.4. See Wiseman 1969.
[192] Liv. *Per.* 63.2.
[193] Brunt 1987, 92.
[194] De Ligt 2012, 113–15.
[195] VM 9.5.2; Flor. 2.3.17.7–8; *Vir. Ill.* 66.9.
[196] App. *BC* 1.77–8; Plu. *Sull.* 25. See Swidzinski 2007, 127–33.

army to fight against Sulla, it mutinied and killed him. Both Sulla and the Cinnan party then lobbied the Italians for their support; apparently Sulla's army counted 100,000 Italians.[197] It seems that this had some success: in 84, Livy's epitomator states that 'by senatorial decree, the new citizens received the right to vote'.[198] This may refer to their redistribution over the voting tribes. But if the allies were only distributed among the tribes in 84, it was too late for their rights to be recorded in the census, which had ended in 85. This would at least partially explain the low number of citizens recorded. It should be noted that the Italians were granted voting rights by a senatorial decree. After the recent violence by various anti-senatorial warlords, it was to the Senate's advantage to grant the Italians more rights, since this would ensure their loyalty to the Senate and thus to the Roman state.[199]

When Sulla emerged victorious from the civil wars of the 80s, he assured the Italians that they would retain the rights that had just been granted to them. According to Livy's epitomator, Sulla 'concluded a treaty with the Italian nations, which prevented him from being regarded as a threat to their recently obtained citizenship and voting rights (*civitatem et suffragii ius nuper datum*)'. Since the citizenship and voting rights are stated to have been obtained already, it seems that by this time the Italians had already been admitted to the citizenship, perhaps in 87.[200] However, some Italians, notably the Samnites, who had chosen the Senate's side against Sulla, were severely punished after Sulla's victory at the Colline Gate in 82.[201] The Samnites' fight against Sulla has often been interpreted as the result of anti-Roman feeling among the Samnites.[202] Sulla of course had an interest in depicting the civil war as a fight against a foreign invader; his published memoirs may have influenced later accounts.[203] However, the fact that the Samnites fought for the senatorial party shows their involvement in Roman politics. This shows again that the Italians now desired the full rights belonging to the citizenship. They considered the citizenship a solution to their problems, as described in section 5.3.3; if they were not able to use the citizenship to its full extent, their grievances could not be alleviated. Thus, the citizenship was not only of symbolic importance, an indication that the Italians were now 'Romans', but carried tangible advantages which the Italians desired.

However, the Italians would not be able to enjoy their full rights until they had been counted in the census. The next census was not held until 70, in which

[197] App. *BC* 1.79, 82. See Swidzinski 2007, 123 for these numbers.

[198] Liv. *Per.* 84.4. Coşkun 2004, 129 accepts this statement.

[199] Kendall 2013, 578–80.

[200] Liv. *Per.* 86.3. See App. *BC* 1.77, 1.86; see Keaveney 1987, 171–87; Bispham 2007, 175–94; Kendall 2013, 612; Dart 2014, 201–6.

[201] App. *BC* 1.93; Plu. *Sull.* 29–30.

[202] Based on Strab. 5.4.11; App. *BC* 1.93. See Mouritsen 1998, 156, 164–5; Kendall 2013, 670–3.

[203] Plu. *Sull.* 29.

Image by Heritage Auctions, HA.com Image by Heritage Auctions, HA.com

Fig. 5.1. Coin depicting Italia and Roma clasping hands, 70 BC.
Heritage Auctions, HA.com.

900,000 citizens were registered.[204] This meant that many Italians did not enjoy full civic rights until 70.[205] It is significant that coins minted at this time depicted the final peace reached between Rome and Italy, made official by the inclusion of the Italians in the census. The coins depict Roma and Italia clasping hands, with a cornucopia between them (see Fig 5.1). This, the only Roman Republican coin to depict Italia, symbolized the final unification of Italy and the end of the civil wars, which had started in 91.[206]

The Italians thus had finally succeeded in gaining the Roman citizenship and the full rights belonging to it, even though throughout the process, the Romans had been very reluctant to grant these. What is clear from the events of the 80s is the close connection between Roman and Italian politics. Italian support became essential for any general who wished to claim power in Rome. As before, the issue of the Italians' rights could be used as a weapon in Roman politics, but Italians were no longer helpless victims of Roman decisions: they chose a side in the conflicts between different Roman politicians in order to fight for their own interests. We can conclude from their behaviour that what they had wanted from the start of the Social War onwards—but not necessarily earlier!—was Roman citizenship: when it was offered to them, they accepted it, and they did not rest until they had gained all the rights connected to it. This, they hoped, would finally solve the problems that they had suffered in the late second century. We will now explore whether this expectation was fulfilled: did the Italians indeed profit from the new opportunities that citizenship offered them?

[204] Liv. *Per.* 98.2.

[205] Keaveney 1987, 187. De Ligt 2012, 115–16 argues they may have been able to vote in the *comitia tributa*, if they had been assigned to a *tribus* in 84. They certainly could not vote in the *comitia centuriata*, because for this their property had to be recorded in the census.

[206] RRC no. 403. See Farney 2007, 4–5 on this coin.

5.7. Political and Economic Opportunities for Italians after the Social War

In this section, we will review the political and economic opportunities of Italians after the Social War. The new citizens were quick to recognize the benefits of having citizenship, as they had recognized that the problems they experienced in the late second century could be solved by gaining citizenship. The Social War had far-reaching effects not only on Italian politics, but also on the economy of Italy and its inhabitants. Some scholars argue that even if economic motivations had been important at the start of the war, the allies were left severely impoverished by the war effort; Strabo's comment that 'cities have become villages' was in some cases correct.[207] However, this damage was limited to a few regions and mostly temporary; most areas of Italy continued to experience economic growth after the war. As we have seen, the Italians continued to field large armies in the civil wars of the 80s, so their population was probably not much reduced. In fact, new economic and political opportunities had emerged for most Italians.

The fate of Italian families in the first century was closely connected to their political choices. Those who had made the 'right choice' during the Social War profited quickly: Velleius Paterculus relates how his great-grandfather,

> Minatius Magius of Aeclanum, grandson of Decius Magius, leader of the Campanians ... [displayed] such fidelity towards the Romans in this war ... The Romans abundantly repaid his loyal zeal by a special grant of the citizenship to himself, and by making his sons praetors at a time when the number elected was still only six.[208]

The generals in the civil wars also rewarded their supporters by granting them office in Rome. Sulla, for example, rewarded Italians who had been loyal to him when he added 300 new members to the Senate, which had been depleted by the civil wars and proscriptions.[209] Some of these men had family names matching those of merchants active in the East,[210] suggesting that many new senators came from the merchant class. Those who chose the wrong side, on the other hand, were

[207] Str. 5.4.11. See Burnett 1998, 165.

[208] Vell. 2.16.2. See Cic. *De Or.* 3.78, *Nat. D.* 1.15, 79.

[209] There is no evidence that he increased the number from 300 to 600, as is often stated (e.g. Gabba 1976, 10; Cébeillac-Gervasoni 1978, 240). App. *BC* 1.101 states only that Sulla appointed 300 new senators, but since there were perhaps only 150 left at the time, the total did not reach 600; see Santangelo 2006, 21–2; 2009, 100; Kendall 2013, 655–7; Dart 2014, 207–8.

[210] Wiseman 1971, 197–202 provides a list of business activities of known senators from the first century. Some of these were of Italian background, e.g. the *publicani* Plancius (Cic. *Planc.* 32), Vettius (Cic. *Verr.* 3.167–8), and Ventidius (Gell. 15.4.3), as well as merchants such as Cossutius (Cic. *Verr.* 2.3.55, 185), Herennius (Cic. *Verr.* 2.1.14, 2.5.155–6; Plin. *NH* 19.40), Lurius (ILLRP 1052), Roscius (ILLRP 1262), and Sepullius (Wiseman 1971, 199).

punished heavily: at Praeneste, only twenty families out of the 138 attested before the Social War still appeared in local politics, after the punishment meted out by Sulla for the town's disloyalty to him.[211]

The civil wars could also be used to exploit local tensions, many of which revolved around economic assets. For example, the murder case in Larinum in the Frentani area, described in Cicero's *Pro Cluentio*, had an economic aspect: Oppianicus wanted to get his hands on more land and therefore killed several people, arranging to inherit from them. When he was accused by his local opponents from Larinum, Oppianicus used his (alleged) connections with Sulla to get his local rivals proscribed.[212] In Ameria as well, as depicted in the *Pro Roscio*, the conflict focused on landed possessions that the local elites tried to take from each other. It seems that the Italians were quick to make use of the Roman law courts, which were now available to them, and used their connections with Roman orators such as Cicero, who pleaded for them. Nevertheless, their preoccupations were mostly with local politics; Italians did not focus exclusively on Rome, but attempted to gain power within their own towns.

Many Italians continued their commercial activities in the first century. When the Italians finally gained citizenship, many jumped at the economic opportunities created by their change of status. It is striking that many of those who are known as merchants and wealthy individuals in the middle to late first century were from the same towns and even from the same *gentes* as those attested earlier as businessmen or producers of wine and olive oil.[213] After the Social War, a large increase in the number of *equites* occurred. Many Italians already owned more than the threshold before they became citizens; therefore, when they were first registered in the census, they immediately became *equites*.[214] We know that a large percentage of new *equites* from Italian families were traders or commercial producers. Cicero is our most important source for the commercial activities of Italians; he names various *equites* from municipal towns who had a career in trade, for example, 'M. Fulcinius, a native of Tarquinii, who... at Rome had a considerable business as a banker'.[215] Cicero himself relied heavily on the support of the *equites* throughout his career, while he often represented their interests in the Senate. Thus the relationship between the *equites*, many of whom were merchants, and the Roman Senate, which decided on economic policy, was regulated by to some degree by Cicero and other municipal senators who came from the same

[211] Wikander 1989, 209–10; Wallace-Hadrill 2008, 115. See Vell. 2.16.3; CIL1[2] 1230=9.1140. See Santangelo 2009, 71–7 on Sulla's relations with Italian elites.

[212] Cic. *Clu.* 25. See Santangelo 2009, 85–6.

[213] E.g. M. Castricius, from an Oscan-speaking family, attested in Kos and Smyrna (Cic. *Flacc.* 54, 75; *Att.* 2.7.5, 12.28.5, 30.2; *Verr.* 3.185); L. Cossinius from Tibur (Cic. *Fam.* 13.23.1); T. Hordeonius from a Capuan family (Cic. *Att.* 13.46.3); M. Mindius, attested at Elis, a namesake of many merchants at Delos in the second century (Cic. *Fam.* 13.26.2, 13.28).

[214] Badian 1972, 86.

[215] Cic. *Caec.* 10.

background as the *equites*.[216] The engagement of *equites* in business is shown by their complaints when in 60 the *lex Caecilia* abolished *portoria* (customs taxes) in Italy.[217] It may be that many farmers of *portoria* were *equites* from Italian towns, who had long been collecting these taxes; some *portoria* may have existed before the Social War and been collected as local taxes by Italian towns.

As for general economic developments in Italy in the first century, it seems that levels of wealth increased, and that many people, even from smaller towns, experienced great prosperity. After the Social War and civil wars, large private houses were built in many Italian towns, such as the 'Casa degli affreschi' in Luna, and many large houses in Pompeii, Alba Fucens, Paestum, and Fregellae. Unfortunately, it is in most cases impossible to establish who owned these houses and how the owners had made their fortune.[218] Commercial agricultural production in Italy also continued and usually remained under the control of local elites. In Cosa, for example, the Titii, Gavii, and Pacuvii worked as wine and pottery producers.[219] The local L. Sestius was most likely the owner of the extremely large villa at Settefinestre near Cosa, often described as the 'standard model' of a luxurious Roman villa.

Many local Italian elites—at least 15 per cent of those for whom we have evidence—were involved in banking, as attested by *tesserae nummulariae*.[220] Italian moneylenders also appear in many locations in Asia, often involved in lending money to cash-strapped towns. A well-known example is the Cloatii, of Oscan descent, who loaned money to the Greek city Gytheion.[221] Furthermore, in this period we see many Italians settling permanently in the East, participating in local politics and marrying into local families. Indeed, the number of Italians abroad grew ever greater in the first century. By the time of Varro and Cicero, it was normal for elite Romans and Italians to own land in Epirus, Iberia, or Illyria.[222] Some scholars even estimate that as many as 1 million Italians lived permanently outside the peninsula by the Augustan period.[223] However, this seems exaggerated, especially since the population of Italy as a whole may have been only 5–6 million at this time.[224]

As in the earlier period (see chapter 4), the wealth of many Italians made them attractive marriage partners for the Roman elites, especially those who were in need of money—basically everyone who desired a career in Rome. Antony's first marriage was to Fadia, the daughter of a freedman from Arpinum.[225] The wine

[216] Cic. *Planc.* 23, 35, *Att.* 2.1.8, *Fam.* 1.9.26, 13.9.2, *Q.* 1.1.32, 35, *Flac.* 31, *Verr.* 2.2.166, 168, 172–5, 2.5.154, *Pis.* 86, *Imp. Pomp.* 17, *Off.* 3.58. But see Cic. *Flac.* 70–5, *Att.* 7.7.5; Nep. *Att.* 6.2. See Rauh 1986a, 20–1; Berry 2003.

[217] Cic. *Att.* 2.16.1; Dio 37.51.3. See De Laet 1949, 59.

[218] Pesando 1997, 304–5.

[219] Regoli 2002, 148.

[220] Cébeillac-Gervasoni 1978, 237.

[221] SIG 3, 748. See Cic. *Flac.* 86, 89; *Att.* 6.1–3, *Fam.* 13.56.

[222] Cic. *Quinct.* See Errington 1988; Eberle & Le Quéré 2017.

[223] Brunt 1987, 265.

[224] De Ligt 2004, 730 calculates only 265,000 Italians overseas, which seems a more reasonable figure.

[225] Cébeillac-Gervasoni 1978, 236–7.

producer Sestius' son married the daughter of Scipio Asiaticus and became praetor in 54.[226] Marriage between Italians from different peoples also continued: the brothers L. and App. Saufeius, from the famous Praenestine family, were the children of a Caelia from Tusculum. Octavia, the sister of two senators from Forum Clodii in Etruria, married Lucilius Gamala, a wealthy merchant from Ostia.[227]

The civil wars between Caesar and Pompey and the triumvirs further affected the economy, social relations, and politics of Italy. Many new men profited from the civil wars; those who attached themselves to the winning side were rewarded, while those who chose wrongly often disappeared from Roman politics altogether.[228] A typical profiteer was P. Ventidius Bassus, as described by Aulus Gellius:

> He was born in Picenum, of humble background, and he and his mother were captured during the Social War by Pompeius Strabo, when he subdued Asculum; and when he triumphed the boy was led among the others before his chariot; ... and when he grew up, he was involved in the sordid business of renting out mules and vehicles to magistrates who went to their provinces.... In that situation he began to be noted by Caesar, and left with him for Gaul. Then, when he in that province proved himself to satisfaction, in the civil war he was charged with many difficult and dangerous tasks, and gained not only the friendship of Caesar, but even his nearest council. Soon he was made tribune of the plebs and then praetor.[229]

It is clear that anti-Roman views held during the Social War counted for little in the mid-first century, even though only a few decades earlier Ventidius' family had fought against the Romans. Generals in the later first century were only interested in who could serve them best, and rewarded them accordingly. The civil wars thus allowed a large number of Italian *gentes* to gain access to in Roman politics for the first time, although we cannot be sure that this was always directly related to the political situation in Rome.[230] Certainly the volatile situation in Rome opened up new opportunities for people able to manipulate the situation to their advantage.

For many families, we can establish when they first reached the Senate. There are considerable regional differences within Italy; people from some areas were much quicker to reach the Senate than those from other areas. The first senators from Samnium, Picenum, and the Marsic region appeared already before the Caesarian period, but other regions saw their first senator only in the Augustan

[226] Manacorda 1981, 32–8. [227] Coarelli 1992, 267. [228] Farney 2007, 190–1.

[229] Gell. *NA* 15.4.

[230] For example, Plancius from Atina, who was elected aedile in 55, was a new man who was not supported by a member of the Roman elite, instead relying on the support of his townsmen (Cic. *Planc.* 22).

period or even later, such as the Apulians, Bruttii, Lucanians, and Vestini.[231] Furthermore, some Italians brought far more senators to Rome than others: whereas Latium and Campania supplied many new men, other regions had only a few senators or none at all. An inscription dating to the Augustan period records Q. Varius Geminus, *is qui primus omnium Paelignorum senator factus est* ('who was the first of all Paeligni to be made a senator').[232] It is interesting to see that local elites now took pride in their achievements in Rome, and advertised these publicly. Such achievements were a source of pride for the local population. Overall, the number of *homines novi* was much larger in the first century than in the preceding ones, although this was highest among the lower ranks of senators. Of all sixty-one consuls elected between 78 and 49, only one (Cicero) was a real *homo novus*, while three were from senatorial families whose direct ancestors had not held high office. Among the individuals who reached no higher than the praetorship, 22.5 per cent were *homines novi*; among the *pedarii* (senators who never held office), this percentage rises to 49.5 per cent.[233]

Surprisingly, there were also many Italians who never took up office in Rome. This includes many Italian *gentes* who had been active in economic activities since the second century, such as the very wealthy and locally powerful Samiarii, one of the leading families of Praeneste, and the Staii and Statii, who contributed to the sanctuary at Pietrabbondante. Some had close relations with the Roman nobility, such as Drusus' friend Q. Poppaedius Silo, but did not hold Roman office. Of course, for a long time there was no explicit reason to do so: for many, local politics were more important than Roman. Many Italians still had a strong sense of local identity and pride, so that participating in Roman politics was not necessarily more important to them than leading their local communities. Most Italians realized that they would never reach further than a backbencher career in the Senate, and concluded that a leading position in their own communities would bring them more personal satisfaction than entering Roman politics.

It may be concluded that Italians continued the economic activities that they had already pursued before the Social War, both in Italy and overseas. For most of them, having Roman citizenship did not change much in the way they conducted business,

[231] Wiseman 1971, 25; Torelli 1982. Cébeillac-Gervasoni 1978, 230–1 notes that very few local politicians are known to us, mainly from inscriptions on public buildings. For the period 110–30, assuming Italian towns had two leading magistrates per year, we know only about 3 to 7 per cent of these magistrates from towns in Latium (10 per cent for Tibur and 15 per cent for Praeneste). For towns outside Latium, this percentage is even lower. It is therefore very difficult to discern exactly the origins of the Italians who became Roman politicians after the Social War.

[232] CIL 9.3305=ILS 932.

[233] Wiseman 1971, 105; Gruen 1974, 522–3. We know 178 of 240 praetors; forty (22.5 per cent) were *homines novi*. Of forty-eight known aediles out of a total of 120, fourteen (29 per cent) were *homines novi*. Of the 113 known *tribuni plebis*, thirty-eight (33.75 per cent) were *novi*. Of 200 known *pedarii*, ninety-nine (49.5 per cent) were *novi*. For earlier centuries our evidence is more limited, so comparisons are difficult, but from the evidence we have, it is clear that more new men entered the Senate in the first century than before.

although they were quick to use the new instruments of Roman law available to them. In many cases, they used these to further their own economic and political interests and to get rid of their local rivals. The exploitation of the new provinces, especially Asia, drew the attention of many Italians, who jumped at the chance to loan money to Asian cities. They could have done so without having Roman citizenship, of course, but it was much easier now that they were supported by the law and political infrastructure of Rome. The Italians thus continued to profit, in a more direct way than before, from opportunities created by Rome, as they had done in the third and second centuries. Many Italians chose to enter a career in Rome, supported by the wealth that they had gathered through trade overseas and in commercial agriculture. On the other hand, not all Italians tried their luck in Rome; for many there were no benefits to this, since they would at most become backbenchers, while in their own local societies they were among the most important men. Even after the Social War, therefore, Rome was not the focus of life for all Italians; many identified more with their home towns than with Rome, as we will see in the next section.

5.8. Italian Identity after the Social War

Despite the political and civic unification of Italy and the great amount of economic interaction that occurred between the peoples of Italy, they did not yet share the same culture and language, nor did they all identify with Rome or think of themselves as Romans. In this section, I will briefly review how this attitude changed during the first century; there is obviously not enough space to discuss these developments in full, but some interesting aspects may be highlighted here.

As we saw in section 5.4, many scholars assume that the grant of citizenship to the Italians after the Social War was the completion of the process of 'Romanization' that the Italians had experienced. On the contrary, the grant of citizenship should be considered the beginning rather than the end of the process of integration. As we have seen, most Italians did not feel a close connection to Rome before the Social War. It was only now, when they had the chance to participate in Rome's politics and the exploitation of the expanding territory of the Roman state, that they felt a need to identify more closely with Rome. Still, many Italians who enjoyed a career in Roman politics expressed local or regional pride at the same time. As we have seen, some Italian people enjoyed a reputation for honesty and frugality in Roman minds. Italian politicians were eager to emphasize their background, as a claim of Italian origin was a statement of reliability to voters. They advertised their Italian backgrounds through their names, such as M. Octavius Marsus, Mamius Murrius Umber, M. Herennius Picens, and many others.[234]

[234] Farney 2007, 215.

Italians who served as *triumviri monetales*—who designed the coins minted by Rome—referred to their background on their coins; Q. Sicinius and T. Coponius from Tibur, moneyers around 49, issued coins with Hercules Victor of Tibur.[235] Even a patrician, such as A. Postumius Albinus, could call himself a *homo Romanus natus in Latio* ('Roman man born in Latium').[236] Thus, even people who had been citizens for centuries claimed a connection to the virtues of Italy that were lacking in Rome. That some of these claims were fake was well known, as Cicero jokes: 'My *Orator*... I have handed to your Sabine servant. His nationality made me think that he was a proper person to whom to give it, unless he too has availed himself of the licence of candidates and has suddenly adopted this surname.'[237] Thus, Italian heritage had become a tool of propaganda in the Roman political arena.

Italian elites did not have to give up their Italian identity if they became active in Rome. A famous passage from Cicero explains the way these people felt about the complex relationship between Rome and their home towns:

> I do indeed think that all municipal men have two homelands, one by nature and the other by citizenship... So we too regard that place where we were born and that place where we have been enfranchised as our homeland. But it is necessary for the latter to stand first in our affection, to which the name 'Republic' has attached itself to us all. For this we must die, for this we must give ourselves entirely, and for this we must give all of our possessions as though for sacrifice. But that homeland which raised us is not much less sweet than that which has adopted us... In this way every municipal man has two states, but thinks of them as one.[238]

Before the Social War, it had been impossible to be a citizen of two states. Since the allied Italian towns were independent states, one could not be a Roman citizen and retain local citizenship as well; therefore, if someone received Roman citizenship, he had to give up the citizenship of his Italian town. Only a sentimental connection might still exist, as in the case of Cato the Elder, who prided himself on the simple nature of his Sabine upbringing, which brought much-needed frugality back into Roman politics. In the first century, however, one was a citizen both of the Roman state and of one's home town. This made it easier for Italians to unite pride in their home town with pride for their new fatherland, Rome.

Despite the presence of many Italians in Roman politics, their importance in the economy of Italy, the acknowledgement of the moral values of Italic peoples, and their participation in sophisticated 'Hellenistic' culture, Italians were not always seen as equals by the Romans, even though they were now all Roman

[235] Crawford 1974, 726–31; Cébeillac-Gervasoni 1998, 229; Farney 2007, 274–5.

[236] *Ap.* Gell. *NA* 11.8=FRH F1b.

[237] Cic. *Fam.* 15.20.1; see Catul. 10.8. See Farney 2007, 91–4.

[238] Cic. *Leg.* 2.5, transl. Farney 2007, 7.

citizens. Prejudice against Italians continued among Romans, as appears from Cicero's speeches. The ambiguous reputation of the Italian towns is clear: Cicero does not hesitate to present the Italian towns as the sources of all virtue, but can also present them negatively if it suits his purposes. In the speech for Publius Sulla in 62, Cicero takes the opportunity to extol the virtues of his own home town, Arpinum. The following passage shows a number of interesting aspects of the complexity of Roman and Italian identities. Cicero says to the prosecutor:

> You called me Tarquin, and Numa, and the third foreign king of Rome. I won't say any more about the word king; but I should like to know why you called me a foreigner. For, if I am such, then it is not so marvellous that I should be a king,—because, as you say yourself, foreigners have before now been kings at Rome,—as that a foreigner should be a consul at Rome. 'This is what I mean,' says he, 'that you come from a municipal town.' I confess that I do, and I add, that I come from that municipal town from which salvation to this city and empire has more than once proceeded. But I should like exceedingly to know from you, how it is that those men who come from the municipal towns appear to you to be foreigners. For no one ever made that objection to that great man, Marcus Cato the Elder, though he had many enemies, . . . or even to that great hero of our own times, Gaius Marius, through many men envied him. In truth, I am exceedingly delighted that I am a man of such a character that, when you were anxious to find fault with me, you could still find nothing to reproach me with which did not apply also to the greater part of the citizens. And if we seem to you to be foreigners, we whose name and honours have now become familiar topics of conversation and panegyric throughout the city and among all men, how greatly must those competitors of yours seem to be foreigners, who now, having been picked out of all Italy, are contending with you for honour and for every dignity! And yet take care that you do not call one of these a foreigner, lest you should be overwhelmed by the votes of the foreigners . . . And if, O judges, it is fit for me and you to be considered foreigners by the rest of the patricians, still nothing ought to be said about this blot by Torquatus. For he himself is on his mother's side, a citizen of a municipal town; a man of a most honourable and noble family, but still he comes from Asculum. Either let him, then, show that the Picentes alone are not foreigners, or else let him congratulate himself that I do not put my family before his. So do not for the future call me a foreigner, lest you meet with a sterner refutation.[239]

A number of interesting observations can be made from this passage: firstly, Cicero himself was accused by the prosecutor, Torquatus, of being a *peregrinus*. Legally, a *peregrinus* was someone who did not possess Roman citizenship, and

[239] Cic. *Sull.* 22–5. Although the speech was in defence of Publius Sulla, Cicero himself was also under attack for his role in the suppression of the Catilinarian conspiracy. After the events, Cicero was widely attacked for his role in the affair, leading to his exile in 58. Therefore, Cicero is defending his actions, arguing that they were necessary to save the Republic. See Cic. *Planc.* 19–22, *Clu.* 197, *Cael.* 5, *Mur.* 15–17. See detailed analysis in Roselaar 2017.

could therefore not partake in Roman *ius civile* (see chapter 4.2.1). Furthermore, Torquatus suggests that Cicero had been acting as a king when he executed citizens without a trial during the Catilinarian conspiracy. According to Torquatus, Cicero was a *peregrinus* and therefore had no jurisdiction over Roman citizens. But Cicero turns the argument on its head by saying that many of the most famous men in Roman history, including some of the kings, had arrived in Rome from elsewhere; this did not prevent them from performing great deeds for the Roman state. Of course, even though these men were from outside Rome, they were still Roman citizens, otherwise they could not hold public office. Cicero's hometown, Arpinum, had possessed the citizenship since 188, so Cicero and his ancestors were definitely citizens in the legal sense. In the eyes of city-born Romans, however, their Italian origins could be used as an insult to their character and, more importantly, as an indication of their unfitness for public office. In fact, Cicero counters, men from Arpinum had twice saved the Roman Republic: first Gaius Marius, who repelled the Cimbric invaders in 101; then Cicero himself, when he dealt with Catiline's conspiracy.

Furthermore, Cicero refers to new citizens entering the Roman state in recent times. Cicero argues that, if a long-standing citizen town like Arpinum already seems foreign to Torquatus, the more recently enfranchised citizens must seem even more exotic. Cicero suggests that there is a kind of hierarchy among the Italian towns, with those that had held citizenship for longer being seen as less foreign than those recently admitted. As Cicero warns Torquatus, there was a tangible danger to the old citizens: the Roman citizen body had grown from about 250,000 to 900,000 by the addition of the Italians—and all these people had the right to vote and to be elected as magistrates in Rome. Thus, competition for public office had increased enormously in the years between the Social War and this speech. Furthermore, the power of the new Italian citizens to vote threatened to swamp the power of the old Roman citizens. Therefore, Cicero warns Torquatus, he must be careful about whom he calls a foreigner—before he knows it, he may lose out on public office because the 'foreigners' vote against him. The last irony shows in the fact that Torquatus' mother was from Asculum in Picenum, although his father came from an old Roman patrician family. Therefore, Cicero claims that he, being from the town of Arpinum, which had twice saved the Roman state (through Marius and Cicero himself), has in fact a better claim to Roman-ness than Torquatus, since Asculum was the town where the Social War had begun.

In this passage, in short, a number of interesting issues regarding Italians appear. All Italians were now Roman citizens, and therefore all had equal opportunities for entering Roman politics as magistrates or as voters. On the other hand, some towns had a stronger claim to Roman-ness than others, Arpinum not least among them. The fact that someone was from an Italian town could still be a source of criticism, showing that prejudice among Romans had not ended with the grant of Roman citizenship after the Social War.

Marriage with Italians could be used as criticism during the civil wars: Antony criticized the fact that Octavian's mother Atia was married to a man from Aricia. Cicero countered this by asking: 'What insanity is it for [Antony] to say anything about the want of noble birth in men's wives, when his father married Numitoria of Fregellae, the daughter of a traitor, and when he himself has begotten children of the daughter of a freedman?'[240] Cicero argues that the value of a man (or indeed a woman) was dependent not on his background, but on his moral qualities. Numitorius, who had betrayed his home town Fregellae during its revolt against Rome in 125, could not claim to possess moral goodness, even if he had helped Rome by doing so.[241] However, in general Cicero thinks that people from Italian towns possessed moral qualities in equal or higher measure than many people from Rome, so that an Italian background was not a valid reason for criticism.

Rome may have admitted the Italians into its citizenship, albeit grudgingly, but they were not ready to grant this privilege to people from outside Italy. At the same time that the inhabitants of Cisalpine Gaul were granted full citizenship in 49, Cicero vehemently opposed giving the same rights to Sicilians: 'You know how fond I am of the Sicilians, and what an honour I consider it to be their patron. Caesar granted them many privileges with my full approval, though their having the *ius Latinum* was intolerable.'[242] If it was unthinkable to give the Latin rights to the Sicilians, full Roman citizenship was out of the question. Cicero continually shows admiration for Greek culture, using Greek quotations in his works and buying Greek statues, but actual Greeks, in his eyes, were not worthy of becoming citizens.[243] Even the inhabitants of Sicily, which had been a Roman province for two centuries, were not acceptable citizens.

Even though the Italians were now Roman citizens, this did not prevent them from displaying their own identities. The towns of Italy themselves actively engaged in displaying their own messages. Public building continued throughout the first century and is a powerful indicator of the identity that a town wanted to portray. Towns that had not yet engaged with Hellenistic building styles now realized investment in the urban fabric of towns, and in monumental public buildings, it was necessary to adhere to the ideal of *urbanitas* ('city life') in order to participate fully in public life.[244] New structures appeared throughout Italy in the first century. Some of these, such as *basilicae*, *fora*, and *curiae*, were needed by the governments of the new *municipia* (towns that had recently received Roman citizenship) and thus, in a way, the result of the unification of Italy under Rome's rule. Other buildings, such as roads and *macella* (market buildings), became necessary due to the changing economic role of many towns.

[240] Cic. *Phil.* 3.15–17. [241] Cic. *Fin.* 62. [242] Cic. *Att.* 14.12.
[243] Dench 1995, 63. [244] Guidobaldi 2005, 271.

Nevertheless, even if some of these buildings were influenced by the political incorporation of Italians in the Roman state, they were also used for competition between elites of the same town and between different towns, who strived to display their munificence to their towns.[245] Again it should be noted that not all these buildings were necessarily 'Roman' in style; many such buildings were derived from the cultural package of the Hellenistic *koine* that had been present in Italy in previous centuries, although the types and styles of buildings erected were sometimes regionally specific.[246]

Many towns experienced a new wave of public building in first century, especially in the Augustan period. In many cases, these buildings were donated by local elites, who thus invested heavily in building up their local reputation. They wanted to show that they were aware of the newest cultural developments and that they belonged to the cultural elite of the new Empire. Indeed, 'Roman forms of urban life seem to have been adopted voluntarily by the municipal elites as an idiom for expressing civic identity'.[247] Therefore, although material culture had become more uniform, local interests were still foremost in motivating benefactors to invest money. The desire of local elites to participate in this cultural *koine* reached even the smallest towns. For example, at Rubi in Apulia, a local noble named Alsinaeus (a Latinized version of a Messapian name) erected a city wall with towers. A theatre was sponsored in Canusium by another man with a local name, Dasimius.[248] This tendency not only was visible in cities, but also benefited rural areas: the sanctuary at Rossano di Vaglio in Lucania was rebuilt in the mid to late first century, in a fashion that more closely matched trends elsewhere, contrasting with the earlier local tradition. Apparently, ideas about elite representation had changed, leading the elites to adhere to a more general idea of style, rather than to local traditions.[249]

Many people of lower social status, such as freedmen, tried to emulate the higher classes in order to assert their social status. Social status was more important than ethnic identity: the audience for the message was mainly local, and local competition was more important than possible connections with Rome. People did not intend to express that they were 'Roman', but that they understood the message of the leading classes and emulated it. They used it as a method for distinction from other social classes; this sometimes made elite culture seem 'kitsch', which caused the top of society to look for other ways of distinction.[250] Cultural expressions could also be used as tools of silent resistance against political and social change: after the settlement of the Sullan colony in Pompeii, the First Style of wall painting was preserved as a reminder of a past in which

245 Lomas 2003, 41. See Roth 2007a, 36–8 on the performance of social power.

246 Lomas 2003.

247 Lomas 1998, 76.

248 See Jouffroy 1986, 62–108.

249 Fracchia & Gualtieri 1998–9, 335; Nava & Poccetti 2001; Andrisani 2009, 122.

250 Wallace-Hadrill 1997, 323–8.

some Pompeians had enjoyed greater glory. It remained in use especially among the original Pompeian families, while the Sullan colonists preferred the Second Style.[251]

The main effects of the cultural integration taking place in Italy were not visible until the Augustan period. Indeed, it has been argued that 'the Augustan age represents the culmination of a long process of the gradual incorporation of the communities of Italy into the central systems of Roman power, which moves with different rhythms in different areas depending on the local pattern of historical contact with Rome'.[252] It was not until this period that we see a great unification in the material culture of Italy. This was expressed, for example, in public building, much of it in the standard Vitruvian style, which was of course itself a mix of many elements of Greek and Roman culture. An example is Etruscan burial rituals: the neighbouring towns of Pisae, Luna, and Volaterrae each had very different burial rituals until the first century, but by the Augustan period these had become uniform. The changes occurred at different paces; for example, at Volaterrae local ash urns were used for longer than in other nearby towns.[253]

Augustus emphasized the importance of *tota Italia*: all Italic peoples had contributed to Roman history, of which the Augustan age was the culmination. The uniformity of Italian culture that emerged in this period was to a certain extent the result of 'self-Romanization' and an internalization of Roman culture in Italy.[254] But this was acceptable for most Italians, because their contribution to the creation of *tota Italia* was recognized. This has often led to the belief that the separate identities of the Italians had disappeared by the first century AD: 'Certainly all Italic identity was submerged within Roman identity by the end of the Julio-Claudian era—especially as few Italians were identifying themselves by their old, particular Italic labels.'[255] However, some awareness of different cultural traditions was still present. In Neapolis, inscriptions of the first century AD record *agoranomoi* and archonts as local magistrates.[256] In Paestum, in the Augustan period, a conscious effort took place to preserve the memory of the past, by restoring Greek temples and using Greek titles. This was possibly done in order to link in with the Greek origins that Augustus' family claimed, in order to voice a similar claim for the local elites.[257]

The Italian languages finally disappeared as spoken languages in the Augustan period. Nevertheless, although Latin was now universally spoken in Italy, names still betrayed the different linguistic and ethnic backgrounds of the Italic peoples. In Capua, many names attested in the early Empire were the same Oscan names

[251] Zevi 1996; see Johannowsky 1976, 283.

[252] Wallace-Hadrill 1999, 292. See Lomas 1998, 68: More uniformity in public buildings, according to Vitruvian plans, reflects a 'new vision of both Roman identity and urbanism. Regional differences are not eradicated, but the idiom in which they are expressed is increasingly that of Roman urban culture'.

[253] Terrenato 2001b.

[254] Zanker 1990, 328–38.

[255] Farney 2007, 30.

[256] Sartori 1953, 48–52.

[257] Torelli 1996, 164–74.

that had been used here for centuries.[258] A remarkable degree of onomastic continuity thus existed between the Republican and Imperial periods.

Commemoration of local culture and identity continued even into the Imperial period, although it focused on different aspects of life than in earlier periods. Many towns celebrated their foundation long into the Imperial period. A relief from Aquileia, dating to the first century AD, for example, celebrates the foundation of the town in 181 by depicting the *sulcus primigenius*, the ceremonial first ploughing of a colony (see Fig 5.2).[259]

There was great respect for local history, as shown by continual reconstructions of old buildings. Even old inscriptions with no apparent current relevance were copied; in Pompeii an Oscan inscription referring to the erection of a building in the second century BC was copied and displayed after the earthquake of AD 62.[260] It is unlikely that many people still spoke Oscan at the time, but the desire to honour the memory of former donors to the community remained strong.[261]

Fig. 5.2. Relief from Aquileia, dating to the first century AD, celebrating the foundation of the town in 181 BC.

[258] Frederiksen 1959, 116. [259] Stek 2013a, 348–50.

[260] *Imagines* Pompei 24=Rix Po 3. See Adams 2003, 147. McDonald 2012 argues that the surviving inscription is the original, not a copy. In any case, it was deemed important enough to display it even after 150–200 years.

[261] *Dig.* 50.10.2–3 even forbids erasing the donor's name from a building.

Towns were strongly aware of their local history. Patavium in the Po Valley had two different origin myths, a Celtic and a Roman. It also used its own method of reckoning time, starting with the first treaty with Rome in 173.[262] An inscription from Interamna Nahars from AD 32 is dated to '704 years after the foundation of the town'.[263] Thus, Italian towns could realign themselves to Rome, but at the same time maintained a local identity.

Augustus thus allowed space for local traditions and variations, rather than imposing cultural homogeneity.[264] Still, the creativity of local expressions diminished in this period, so that local traditions became harmless folklore, rather than potential mechanisms for serious discontent. This occurred because 'monarchy viewed this continued pretense of independence within the Roman state as inimical to its control, and while... poets glorified the past of the Italian *populi*, their public aspects were surreptitiously degraded'.[265] An example of this is the fact that specific locations became known for certain characteristics, which were continuously repeated in literary works. Tibur becomes, in the works of Augustan writers, and Horace in particular, frozen as a *locus amoenus*, a place that exists mainly in and for philosophical and poetical inspiration. Its identity no longer is under the control of its inhabitants, but becomes fixed around a small number of *topoi*.[266]

'Italy' had now become an ethnic tag with which people could identify. It had become part of the homeland of the Romans, rather than a foreign land whose people should be held under tight control. Cicero describes both Rome and Italy as his patria: 'And as for my country, o immortal gods, it is scarcely possible to express how dear, how delightful it is to me. How great is the beauty of Italy!'[267] Horace, whose poetry embodies the ideals of Augustan Rome and Italy, could pride himself on his Italian heritage, as he was born in Venusia in Apulia: 'I'll be famous, I, born of humble origin, from where wild Aufidus roars, and where Daunus once, lacking in streams, ruled over a rural people, as the first to re-create Aeolian song in Italian verse.'[268] 'Italian' here seems to be a synonym for 'Latin'—that is, the language of the Roman state. Velleius Paterculus does the same: he emphasizes his origins from Campania and the fact that the Campanian cities, especially Cumae and Neapolis, had been loyal to Rome throughout their history. This matched Velleius' family's loyalty to Rome's cause.[269] The Roman Empire, and with it Italy, was given a sacred, civilizing mission:

[262] Strab. 5.1.4; CIL 5.2864, 2885. See Harris 1977; Laurence 1999, 172.

[263] CIL 11.4170. See Bradley 2000, 13–14.

[264] Bispham 2007, 443–4.

[265] Bispham 2007, 446.

[266] Buchet 2015.

[267] Cic. *Red. Quir.* 4: *ipsa autem patria, di immortales! dici vix potest quid caritatis, quid voluptatis habeat; quae species Italiae...*

[268] Hor. *Od.* 3.30.10–15. He also refers to himself as a *Lucanus an Apulus anceps* ('both Lucanian and Apulian') (Sat. 2.1.34), indicating that these two ethnic denominators still had a separate meaning at the time.

[269] Vell. 1.4.2. See Bispham 2011, 27–8.

> Italy is chosen to be at once the daughter and parent of all lands. This land is chosen by the gods to make even the sky clearer, to gather the scattered powers and pacify the customs and bring together the discordant and wild customs of so many peoples by the shared use of a language for communication, and to give civilization to mankind, and, in short, bring about a single nation from all the peoples of the whole world.[270]

For 'Italy', one might read 'the Roman Empire', but there was now little difference between the two: all Italy had become Roman.

This civilized, Roman-Italian culture was then propagated throughout the provinces of the Empire: 'The Hellenised culture of Italy and Rome was pumped out over the provinces,... thus aligning Romanization and Hellenization. This is what constitutes Wallace-Hadrill's cultural revolution: the transformation, through several inter-related stages, of a *koine* into a unified, dynamic cultural system.'[271] The Hellenistic cultural *koine* that had been shared by many Italians since the fourth century was appropriated by Rome—even though, as we have seen, the Romans were not the first people in Italy to engage with this culture—and was then infused with new messages of Roman-Italian unity in the Augustan period. This culture, with its new civilizing message, was spread through Italy and the provinces, using the military and administrative mechanisms created by Rome. It was only in the provinces that this culture was experienced as 'Roman'; the peoples of Italy were aware of their own contributions to it and the multiple meanings that it contained. It was in the Augustan period that art 'lost its direct relationship with the core culture of the society expressing it, and became instead a statement directed to a restricted audience with its own distinctive and autonomous discourse'.[272] Thus Hellenistic art was no longer seen as specifically connected to Greece, but was given new meanings relevant to the history and identity of Rome. Since Hellenistic art had been known among the Italians for a long time, they were familiar with its connotations. Thus both Romans and Italians could use it to express their own 'discourse', to advertise their belonging to a new, empire-wide elite, consisting of both Romans and Italians.

By the Augustan period, Italians and Romans were united in their control of the Roman state; the Italians now joined the Romans in governing the new Empire and exploiting its provinces. Although many Italians had suffered horrible atrocities at the hands of the Romans, they did not hesitate to inflict the same suffering on the peoples of the provinces, as long as it brought them material advantage. This behaviour was partially made acceptable by presenting the provincials as barbarians, much as the Italians themselves had been described earlier. Just like

[270] Plin. *NH* 3.39.

[271] Roth 2010, 225; see Wallace-Hadrill 2008, 18–27. See on the Augustan cultural revolution also Torelli 1999, 165–83. See Dench 2005, 173–217 on Italy's importance in the Augustan period.

[272] Terrenato 2001b, 59–60.

Cicero, cited above, Augustus too found it undesirable to admit people from outside Italy to Roman citizenship:

> Considering it also of great importance to keep the people pure and unsullied by any taint of foreign or servile blood, he was most reluctant in conferring Roman citizenship and set a limit to manumission. When Tiberius requested citizenship for a Greek dependent of his, Augustus wrote in reply that he would not grant it unless the man appeared in person and convinced him that he had reasonable grounds for the request; and when Livia asked it for a Gaul from a tributary province, he refused, offering instead freedom from tribute, and declaring that he would more willingly suffer a loss to his privy purse than the prostitution of the honour of Roman citizenship.[273]

There was, in Augustus' mind, a clear distinction between what was Greek and what was Roman, even if Roman culture was strongly influenced by the Greek world. In the visual arts, Augustus managed to create a coherent system of expression that clearly represented Roman values as separate from Greek, despite the Greek influence on Roman art.[274] Therefore, 'Roman' was certainly not only a legal or civic category, even though Roman culture was still influenced by Greek.[275]

Thus, in the first century AD Italians still enjoyed precedence over people from the provinces. When the emperor Claudius proposed to appoint senators from Gaul, this was cause for serious debate: people opposed that 'a mob of foreigners, a troop of captives, so to say, is now forced upon us'. As the Roman citizens had done before the Social War, the Italian citizens feared that their old privileges would be destroyed by newcomers:

> What distinctions will be left for the remnants of our noble houses, or for any impoverished senators from Latium? Every place will be crowded with these millionaires, whose ancestors of the second and third generations at the head of hostile tribes destroyed our armies with fire and sword, and actually besieged the divine Julius at Alesia . . . Let them enjoy indeed the title of citizens, but let them not vulgarize the distinctions of the Senate and the honours of office.[276]

Italy now shared the privileged position that Rome had enjoyed before the Social War. Italy had become a part of the Roman state, but the provinces could not yet be seen in the same way.

[273] Suet. *Aug.* 40.3–5.

[274] This huge topic cannot be addressed here; see Zanker 1990; Galinsky 1996; Wallace-Hadrill 2008.

[275] Osborne & Vout 2010, 237.

[276] Tac. *Ann.* 11.23–5; *cf.* the Lyons Tablet (CIL 13.1668), which purports to be an official record of Claudius' speech.

5.9. Conclusion

We have seen how the Italians, within a few decades, were transformed from a disadvantaged group within the Roman state to full participants in Rome's Mediterranean empire. In the late second century, the position of the Italians was unsatisfactory: their wealth and international status were not matched by their treatment within Italy. Apart from the insults to their dignity that came with Roman abuse, they also suffered economic disadvantages. Although most regions of Italy saw quick economic development in the second century, as we saw in chapter 4, the lack of Roman citizenship had significant negative effects on the economic activities of the Italians. The Roman state acknowledged these problems and created new methods of solving them, including new ways to gain citizenship, but this was not sufficient. Eventually the Italians realized that their problems could be solved only by gaining Roman citizenship; only in this way could they participate fully in all the material benefits that the Roman state created, as well as gain the status that they felt they deserved.

The Italians throughout this process were not helpless victims of Rome's policies: they manipulated Roman politicians into acting in their interest and assisted those who could help them gain their rights, if necessary with armed force. This was especially important in the 80s, when the Roman state made a last effort to stop the Italians from gaining influence in Roman politics. However, their power and influence could not be ignored, and they quickly gained the same civic rights as the old citizens. Many Italians quickly took advantage of the economic and political opportunities offered by their accession to the citizenship. Throughout the first century, people from Italy—some regions more quickly than others—entered Roman politics, often with the assistance of Roman leaders, but also on their own merits. Positive character traits were ascribed to people from Italian *municipia*; in the chaotic first century, where corruption and violence were rife, any claim to a good character was welcome.

However, this does not mean that the Italians wanted to become Roman: local politics remained important, even for those who were also active in Rome, such as Cicero. Pride in local history and achievements was advertised on coinage and in the public buildings that decorated the Italian landscape. The culture and language of Italy did indeed become more uniform, but this was a development especially of the Augustan period, not of the earlier first century. By the Augustan era, most Italians had been fully accepted into the Roman state and, as equals of the old Roman citizens, continued the exploitation of the provinces for their own gains.

6
General Conclusions

Although many issues discussed in this book have been the subject of earlier study, the importance of economic activities for the integration of Italy has never been studied in detail. Here I hope to have shown that economic affairs played a central role in the political, social, and cultural developments of Italy in the last three centuries BC. In chapter 2, we have seen that there were many opportunities for interaction between Romans and Italians. Many of these were economic in nature, such as seasonal migration for wage labour, transhumant pasturing, and attending markets and fairs. Even in the case of migration with a less explicitly economic aim, such as the settlement of colonies, there were many opportunities for interaction between Romans and locals. Many of these settlements attracted Italian immigrants, as attested by the growth of many colonies into important trading centres, such as Brundisium, Minturnae, Puteoli, and Aquileia. This created additional possibilities for interaction between Romans and Italians and between Italians from different parts of the peninsula.

Although this book has not attempted to give a general overview of economic developments in Italy in the Republican period, it is nevertheless clear that great economic changes occurred in Italy in the period between the fourth and first centuries (chapter 3). However, these varied widely from place to place, even over short distances; communities with the same administrative status often experienced very different economic and cultural developments. Latin colonies, for example, did not all develop in the same way: some became important international trade centres, such as Brundisium, others became production and/or trade centres for the region, such as Fregellae and Venusia, whereas others focused on agriculture on a smaller scale, such as Luceria. Some, like Paestum, even suffered economic decline. The same goes for colonies with Roman citizen rights: some fulfilled an important economic role, such as Minturnae and Puteoli, others became important production centres, such as Sinuessa, and yet others mainly played a role in the regional economy, such as Buxentum. In this respect, there was little difference between Latin and Roman colonies: when the circumstances were right, both types of settlement could grow into prosperous cities—as could allied communities. Thus, a colony's connections with Rome did not in all cases lead to prosperity. The presence of a colony could have a large impact on the surrounding territory's economy: many of the economic changes in central Apulia in the third and second centuries seem to have been caused by the settlement of

Italy's Economic Revolution. Saskia T. Roselaar, Oxford University Press (2019). © Saskia T. Roselaar.
DOI: 10.1093/oso/9780198829447.001.0001

Brundisium. Even small colonies could have an effect on the local settlement pattern, as in the case of Buxentum. On the other hand, some colonies hardly left their mark on the surrounding territory, such as the Latin colony Interamna Lirenas.

Developments in allied territory varied just as much as in colonies. In the case of *ager publicus*, non-intervention by the Romans seems to have been very common, so that in many such areas nothing changed after the confiscation of the land. In fact, developments on *ager publicus* differed little from areas that remained allied; settlement patterns developed in similar ways. In fact, some general trends can be discerned which occurred in most of Italy. The third century usually saw an increase in the number of sites, including towns, sanctuaries, and larger commercial farms. This was followed in the late third and early second centuries by a contraction in the size of villages and the abandonment of many sanctuaries and farms. Finally, in the later second and early first centuries, more farms for commercial production appeared in most areas. The disappearance of sanctuaries and farms, however, cannot be seen as a symptom of depopulation or a decline in the economic circumstances of small farmers, since small farms remained in use throughout Italy. Rather, this should be seen as a sign of expansion of the economic network and economic integration. Italy now became part of a larger network, which connected many parts of the Mediterranean. Thus, local and regional economies were more closely connected to other parts of the peninsula. This new economic framework was in part created by the Roman state: on the one hand, the conquest of large areas of the Mediterranean opened up new markets for products from all parts of Italy, not just central Italy, but also the Adriatic coast, Apulia, Lucania, and Bruttium. On the other hand, the creation of a system for the settlement of disputes meant that trade between peoples became easier. This allowed for the integration of the economy of the Italian peninsula, in the sense that the various regions of Italy became more connected to each other.

This enabled regional specialization for cash crops, a phenomenon that became especially visible in the second century. Some areas specialized in animal products, such as Apulia, while the coastal areas of southern Etruria and Campania, and to a lesser degree the coasts of Lucania, specialized in wine and olive oil. Harbours, such as Brundisium and Minturnae, facilitated the transport of products from their hinterlands, as well as the transport of Roman soldiers overseas. Each town and region gained its own niche in the economic system; the decline in the size of towns or the number of small farms in some areas could be seen as a sign of their changed role in the economic system of Italy. However, such decline on a local scale does not point to a general decline in economic well-being or in population numbers throughout Italy, as used to be assumed in older literature. Some fundamental changes took place in the economic system, and only those sites that could become part of the new economic network remained. The second century was clearly a turning point in the economic history of Italy, in which its economy became integrated more than ever before. This had an impact on all regions of Italy, and thus on all inhabitants of the peninsula, from the elites to the small farmers, although the exact effects varied greatly between the different regions and towns of Italy.

These general developments in the Italian and Mediterranean economy were an indirect result of Roman rule. We might therefore speak of 'economic Romanization': Rome created a new system of hegemony and influenced the economy of the peoples it controlled. However, economic developments in Italy did not depend on Rome's actions: it was the Italians themselves who took the initiative to profit from these opportunities. Local Italian elites interacted with Romans and people from other parts of Italy and the Mediterranean, leading to changes in the way they saw themselves and their position vis-à-vis the Roman state. However, this did not mean that they necessarily felt more 'Roman'; they had little reason to identify with Rome, since their lives remained focused on local economic and cultural activities. Therefore, even if economic 'Romanization' occurred, this does not mean that we can speak of cultural Romanization as well. Rome and its culture were not *a priori* more attractive than the culture of the Italians themselves; only elements of life that were of immediate (economic) use, such as coinage and laws, were adopted by Italians.

As discussed in chapter 4, the growth of economic interaction between Romans and Italians was accompanied by a need for more uniformity in commercial and institutional infrastructure, such as coinage and laws. Throughout the Republican period, Roman and Italian practice converged: Roman law created possibilities for business between Romans and Italians, Roman coinage came to dominate Italy, Roman weights and measures spread through Italy, and Latin administrative and business language influenced Italian practice. However, the speed with which these instruments of economic interaction spread through Italy was varied. Roman coinage only became dominant in the second century, while weights and measures remained variable until the late first. On the other hand, Italian laws and administration adapted to Roman practice slightly faster in the third and second centuries; in some areas of Italy, the Latin language was already in common use in the late third and early second centuries, although often local languages also remained in use.

There was no coordinated attempt by the Roman state to unify Italian administrative systems before the Augustan period, but many Italians realized the advantages that came with participating the laws and monetary systems of the Romans. The administrative and institutional sphere is thus another aspect of Italian life in which some degree of 'Romanization' can be discerned. For the Italians to profit from the new economic opportunities created by Rome's expanding power, it was necessary to adopt some of the innovations available, such as a unified coinage and inclusive legal system. On the other hand, Italians did not need to change fundamental elements of their culture, such as private language and material culture. Nevertheless, there was a limit to the degree of free agency that Italians held with regard to sharing the economic infrastructure of Rome. Even though many Italians until the late second century were not interested in Rome or becoming Roman, they had to adapt to Rome's institutions if they wanted to profit fully from the new economic advantages offered by Rome's expansion. Therefore, by adapting voluntarily to Roman practice, Italians acknowledged the changing power relations in the peninsula. Eventually, therefore, institutional changes in Italy, although they may seem superficial, could become a cause of resentment among the Italian elites.

It is clear that the economic, political, and institutional integration of Italy did not lead to feelings of similarity and identification between Romans and Italians. Italians did not see themselves as Romans; they considered themselves the social equals of the Roman elites, but they did not identify with Rome. There was no reason to, since many towns in Italy were wealthy and important in the economy and politics of their regions. A town like Praeneste had nothing to be ashamed of and its inhabitants could gain little by becoming Roman citizens. Many areas in Italy experienced cultural change during the Republic, but this cannot be attributed simply to 'Romanization': many of the cultural developments taking place in Italy were inspired by Greek models (see chapter 4). Italians encountered Hellenistic culture while travelling abroad, and this inspired many public and private cultural expressions, from public buildings to funerary art. Thus, cultural change in Italy was not stimulated by Rome; in many cases, new cultural developments appeared earlier in Italy than in the city of Rome itself. The Italian elites had plenty of reason to feel that they were up to date with the latest fashions; moreover, many of them were wealthy and respected individuals in their communities. They were in no way inferior to Romans—except for the fact that they were not recognized as such by Rome. Furthermore, Italians abroad often acted in a united group, putting up inscriptions in the name all *Italici*. This contributed to a new-found feeling of connection between the peoples of Italy, who had for most of the Republican period identified only with their own home towns and regions. This new Italian identity was one of the factors allowing the Italians to act in concert in the late second and early first centuries, especially during the Social War.

The Roman state was usually content to leave the Italians to pursue their activities. Rome recognized the importance of maintaining the economic well-being of its Italian allies, since this was essential to maintain Rome's military power. Therefore, the Romans protected Italians trading overseas and negotiated trade benefits for them, gave them a share in the spoils of successful wars, and maintained peace in the Mediterranean, which was then exploited by the Italians. The benefits of being loyal to the Roman state were sufficient, for a long time, to keep the Italians satisfied, even though they did not enjoy Roman citizenship. Its lack was not a major disadvantage, since they could easily continue their economic activities without it, as they had done for centuries.

However, in the late second century, the Italians started to feel dissatisfied with their position (chapter 5). Their most important grievance was that the economic benefits of being loyal to the Roman state had diminished, since the wars the Italians fought together with Rome at this time were not very profitable, and in fact had led to the death of many Italians. As non-citizens, the Italians had no say in Roman military and economic policy, despite the fact that this policy could have serious consequences for them. Other disadvantages added to their grievances: the most important of these were random abuse by Roman magistrates, and the fact that Italians could not directly participate in the exploitation of the provinces by becoming *publicani*. In the Gracchan period, moreover, they were threatened with the loss of private land by erroneous confiscations. The Roman state recognized that the Italians were unhappy with these developments and tried to satisfy them, for example, by issuing the *lex Acilia repentundarum* in 123 in order to stop abuse by magistrates, and by creating new methods for gaining Roman citizenship, such as the right to gain citizenship through holding a local magistracy. However, these measures were not very effective and were only available to a small number of Italians. But in any case, the Italians did not really want to become Roman citizens: what they wanted were equal opportunities in economic activities and the guarantee that their landholdings were safe.

By the first decade of the first century, the Italians realized that their problems could only be solved by gaining Roman citizenship, as they had come to realize that other solutions attempted by Rome had not been successful. Only by gaining citizenship could the Italians participate fully in all the material benefits that the Roman state created, and be protected against abuse. When the final attempt of Livius Drusus in 91 to give the Italians citizenship failed, the Italians had had enough of being manipulated by Roman politicians, while their grievances were ignored. They saw no other choice but to rise against Rome in revolt. The Social War most likely was not an attempt by the Italians to gain independence from Rome: they wanted a solution to their problems, and realized that without receiving full rights of citizenship, they would not reach the solution they wanted. By starting the war, they hoped to force Rome to accept them as fellow citizens. They did not desire citizenship in itself, but the reluctance of the Roman state to implement other solutions to their problems left the Italians no choice. When the Romans relented and eventually offered citizenship, this was an alternative that most Italians could accept, since it solved the problems that had caused their discontent in the first place.

When, after the Social War, the Romans continued to limit the Italians' influence, the latter again showed that they were not helpless victims of Rome's policies. They assisted Roman politicians who acted in their interests during the civil wars of the 80s. By the census of 70 at the latest, they had gained the same rights as the old citizens. Many Italians quickly took the opportunities offered by the citizenship by continuing their economic activities and exploiting new ones, such as becoming Roman *publicani*. Others entered Roman politics; many positive character traits were ascribed to people from Italian *municipia*, so that an Italian background could be used as propaganda to advertise someone's good character. This does not mean that all Italians wanted to become Roman, which had never been the main motivation in the Social War anyway: local politics remained important, even for those who were also active in Rome, such as Cicero. Participation in Roman society in itself was not always a cause for distinction on the local level. Local status was rather determined by economic factors such as landed property and conspicuous consumption, e.g. through funerary display and euergetism. Pride in local history and achievements was still advertised on coinage and in public buildings that decorated the Italian landscape. The culture and language of Italy did become more uniform, but this was a development especially of the Augustan period. By the Augustan era, most Italians had been fully accepted into the Roman state and, together with the old Roman citizens, continued the exploitation of the provinces as equals.

We may conclude that the impact of the Roman conquest on Italy was indeed large, since it changed the direction of economic development in all of Italy. New locations for contact between Romans and Italians and between Italians of different regions became possible, which led to more migration and interaction between different ethnic groups. The first changes adopted by the Italic peoples were practical: laws and coinage, as well as the emergence of Latin as a *lingua franca*. Furthermore, it cannot be denied that Rome exerted much influence on the politics of Italy, forcing all Italians to fight on its behalf. We can speak of military, institutional, administrative, and economic 'Romanization' to describe these processes. However, by no means did the Roman conquest of Italy lead to a loss of local identity; on the contrary, Italians exploited the economic opportunities created by Rome and the cultural possibilities of Hellenistic culture to express their identity and pride in their own communities and did so for their own purposes. The idea that 'Romanization' was a consequence of military, economic, and social 'weakness'[1] among the Italian elites could not be further from the truth.

In the Imperial period, the Romans continued their policy of exploitation of the resources of the provinces on the one hand, and the sharing of spoils with the inhabitants of the Empire on the other. Again, the Romans never intended to create one universal culture for the whole Empire. Its strength lay in the fact that it managed to unite particular local assets into a larger structure, which enabled the efficient exploitation of these assets: 'The Roman Empire becomes a highly variable series of local groups, roughly held together by directional forces of integration that formed an organized whole and lasted for several centuries. Heterogeneity becomes a binding force of imperial stability—a tool for the

[1] Torelli 1995, 89.

creation of perpetual imperial order.'[2] In the Imperial period, Roman citizenship remained, as in the Republic, an asset and privilege available to only a small elite. Yet, just like in the Republic, the Roman state eventually granted its precious citizenship to all inhabitants of the Empire—an acknowledgement of its continued importance.[3]

[2] Hingley 2010, 61.

[3] See, for a new re-evaluation of citizenship in the Imperial period, Lavan 2018.

Bibliography

Accardo, S., 2000. Villae romanae *nell'*ager Bruttius. *Il paesaggio rurale calabrese durante il dominio romano* (Rome).

Adams, J.N., 2003. *Bilingualism and the Latin language* (Cambridge).

Adams, J.N., 2007. *The regional diversification of Latin, 200 BC–AD 600* (Cambridge).

Albert, S., 1989. *Bellum iustum. Die Theorie des 'gerechten Krieges' und ihre praktische Bedeutung für die Auswärtigen Auseinandersetzungen Roms in republikanischer Zeit* (Kallmünz).

Ando, C., 2015. 'Fact, fiction, and social reality in Roman law', in: M. Del Mar & W. Twining (eds.), *Legal fictions in theory and practice* (New York) 295–323.

Andreau, J., 1985. 'Les financiers romains entre la ville et la campagne', in: Ph. Leveau (ed.), *L'origine des richesses dépensées dans la ville antique* (Aix-en-Provence) 177–201.

Andreau, J., 1987. *La vie financière dans le monde romaine: les metiers de manieurs d'argent (IVe siècle av. J.-C.—IIIe siècle ap. J.-C.)* (Rome).

Andreau, J., 1999. *Banking and business in the Roman world* (Cambridge).

Andreau, J., 2000. 'Les commerçants, l'élite et la politique romaine à la fin de le République', in: C. Zaccagnini (ed.), *Mercanti e politica nel mondo antico* (Rome) 217–43.

Andreau, J., 2002. 'Markets, fairs and monetary loans: cultural history and economic history in Roman Italy and Hellenistic Greece', in: P. Cartledge, E.E. Cohen, & L. Foxhall (eds.), *Money, labour, land. Approaches to the economies of ancient Greece* (London and New York) 113–29.

Andreussi, 1981. 'Stanziamenti agricoli e ville residenziali in alcune zone campione del Lazio', in: A. Giardina & A. Schiavone (eds.), *Società romana e produzione schiavistica I. L'Italia: insediamenti e forme economiche* (Rome) 349–70.

Andrisani, A., 2009. *Il santuario della Dea Mefitis a Rossano di Vaglio. Una rilettura degli aspetti archeologici e culturali* (Matera).

Antonacci Sanpaolo, E., 2001. 'Landscape changes: romanization and new settlement patterns at Tiati', in: S. Keay & N. Terrenato (eds.), *Italy and the West: comparative issues in romanization* (Oxford) 27–38.

Aprosio, M., 2008. *Archeologia dei paesaggi a Brindisi dalla romanizzazione al Medioevo* (Bari).

Arena, V., 2012. *Libertas and the practice of politics in the late Roman Republic* (Cambridge).

Arthur, P., 1991. *Romans in Northern Campania: settlement and land-use around the Massico and the Garigliano basin* (London).

Attema, P.A.J. & T. de Haas, 2005. 'Villas and farmsteads in the Pontine region between 300 BC and 300 AD', in: B. Santillo Frizell & A. Klynne (eds.), *Roman villas around the urbs. Interaction with landscape and environment* (Rome) 1–16.

Attema, P.A.J. & G.-J.L.M. Burgers, 2012. 'A comparative view of the Hellenistic and Roman landscape in three Italian regions', in: P.A.J. Attema & G. Schörner (eds.), *Comparative issues in the archaeology of the Roman rural landscape* (Portsmouth, RI) 107–16.

Attema, P.A.J., G.-J.L.M. Burgers, & P.M. van Leusen, 2010. *Regional pathways to complexity. Settlement and land-use dynamics in early Italy from the Bronze Age to the Republican period* (Amsterdam).

Badian, E., 1952. 'Notes on Roman policy in Illyria (230–201 B.C.)', *PBSR* 20, 72–93.
Badian, E., 1958. *Foreign clientelae (264–70 B.C.)* (Oxford).
Badian, E., 1970–1. 'Roman politics and the Italians', *Dialoghi di archeologia* 4–5, 373–409.
Badian, E., 1972. *Publicans and sinners. Private enterprise in the service of the Roman Republic* (Oxford).
Bakkum, G.C.L.M., 2009. *The Latin dialect of the ager Faliscus: 150 years of scholarship* (Amsterdam).
Bancalari Molina, A., 1987. 'Gli interventi degli Italici nella politica romana durante il tribunato di Livio Druso (91 a. C.)', *SCO* 37, 407–37.
Bandelli, G., 1983. 'Per una storia della classe dirigente di Aquileia repubblicana', in: M. Cébeillac-Gervasoni (ed.), *Les <<bourgeoisies>> municipales italiennes aux IIe et Ier siècle av. J.-C.* (Naples) 175–203.
Bang, P.F., 1997. *Antiquity between 'primitivism' and 'modernism'.* Århus.
Bang, P.F., 2009. 'The ancient economy and New Institutional Economics', *JRS* 99, 194–206.
Barker, G., J.A. Lloyd, & D. Webley, 1978. 'A classical landscape in Molise', *PBSR* 46, 35–51.
Baronowski, D.W., 1984. 'The *formula togatorum*', *Historia* 33, 248–52.
Basile, M., 1979. '*Mercatores, negotiatores, aratores, pecuarii* nella Sicilia di età repubblicana', *Archivio Storico Siciliano* 5, 5–15.
Baslez, M.F., 1996. 'La première présence romaine à Délos (vers 250-vers 140)', in: A.D. Rizakis (ed.), *Roman onomastics in the Greek East. Social and political aspects* (Athens) 215–24.
Battiloro, I., 2010. *Lucanian sanctuaries. History and evolution from the fourth century B.C. to the Augustan age* (University of Alberta PhD thesis).
Battiloro, I. & M. Osanna, 2015. 'Continuity and change in Lucanian cult places between the third and first centuries BC', in: T. Stek &. G.-J. Burgers (eds.), *The impact of Rome on cult places and religious practices in ancient Italy* (London) 169–97.
Bellini, G.R., A. Launaro, & M. Millett, 2014. 'Roman colonial landscapes: Interamna Lirenas and its territory through antiquity', in: T.D Stek &J. Pelgrom (eds.), *Roman Republican colonisation: new perspectives from archaeology and ancient history* (Portsmouth, RI) 255–75.
Benelli, E., 1994. *Le iscrizioni bilingui etrusco-latine* (Florence).
Benelli, E., 2001. 'The Romanization of Italy through the epigraphic record', in: S. Keay & N. Terrenato (eds.), *Italy and the West. Comparative issues in romanization* (Oxford) 7–16.
Bernardi, A., 1973. *Nomen Latinum* (Pavia).
Berry, D.H., 2003. '*Equester ordo tuus est*: did Cicero win his cases because of his support for the *equites*?' *CQ* 53, 222–34.
Bispham, E., 2006. '*Coloniam deducere*: how Roman was Roman colonization during the Middle Republic?', in: J.-P. Wilson & G. Bradley (eds.), *Greek and Roman colonization: origins, ideologies and interactions* (Swansea) 73–160.
Bispham, E., 2007. *From Asculum to Actium. The municipalization of Italy from the Social War to Augustus* (Oxford).
Bispham, E., 2011. 'Time for Italy in Velleius Paterculus', in: E. Cowan (ed.), *Velleius Paterculus.* Making history (Swansea) 17–57.
Bleicken, J., 1990. 'Tiberius Gracchus und die italischen Bundesgenossen', in: W. Ax (ed.), *Memoria rerum veterum. Neue Beiträge zur antiken Historiographie und alten Geschichte. Festschrift für Carl Joachim Classen zum 60. Geburtstag* (Stuttgart) 101–31.
Bodei Giglioni, G., 1977. '*Pecunia fanatica.* L'incidenza economica dei templi laziali', *RSI* 89, 33–76.

Boersma, J. & D. Yntema, 1987. *Valesio.* History of an Apulian settlement from the Iron Age to the late-Roman period (no place).

Boren, H.C., 1958. 'The urban side of the Gracchan economic crisis', *AHR* 63, 890–902.

Bouma, J.W. et al., 1995. 'The economy of an early Latin settlement, Borgo le Ferriere – Satricum', in: N. Christie (ed.), *Settlement and economy in Italy 1500 BC—1500 AD* (Oxford) 183–95.

Bourdin, S., 2012. *Les peuples de l'Italie préromaine: identités, territoires et relations inter-ethniques en Italie centrale et septentrionale (VIIIe-Ier s. av. J.-C.)* (Rome).

Bowman, A. & A. Wilson, 2009. 'Introduction. Quantifying the Roman economy: integration, growth, decline?' in: A. Bowman & A. Wilson (eds.), *Quantifying the Roman economy. Methods and problems* (Oxford) 3–84.

Bradeen, D.W., 1959. 'Roman citizenship *per magistratum*', *CJ* 54, 221–8.

Bradley, G.J., 1997. 'Archaic sanctuaries in Umbria', *CCG* 8, 111–29.

Bradley, G.J., 2000. *Ancient Umbria. State, culture, and identity in central Italy from the Iron Age to the Augustan Era* (Oxford).

Bradley, G.J., 2005. 'The Iuvanum survey project: an ancient community in Samnium', in: P. Attema, A. Nijboer, & A. Zifferero (eds.), *Papers in Italian archaeology IV: communinities and settlements from the Neolithic to the Early Medieval period* (Oxford) 1024–29.

Bradley, G.J., D. Fossataro, & O. Menozzi, 2008. 'The Iuvanum Survey Project, Chieti, Abruzzo, Italy', in: A. Faustoferri & G. Lock (eds.), *Archaeology and landscape in Central Italy: Papers in memory of John A. Lloyd* (Oxford) 137–49.

Brecciaroli Taborelli, L., 2000. 'La ceramica a vernice nera padana (IV-I secolo a.C.): aggiornamenti, osservazioni, spunti', in: G.P. Brogiolo & G. Olcese (eds.), *Produzione ceramica in area padana tra il II secolo a.C. e il VII sec. d.C.: nuovi dati e prospettive di ricerca* (Mantova) 11–30.

Breglia Pulci Doria, L., 1985. 'Per la storia di Atene alla fine del II sec. a. C. Il decreto sui pesi e misure: *IG* II^2 1013', *MEFRA* 97:1, 411–30.

Brennan, T.C., 2000. *The praetorship in the Roman Republic* (Oxford).

Briscoe, J., 1973. *A commentary on Livy, vol. I* (Oxford).

Broadhead, W., 2002. *Internal migration and the transformation of Republican Italy* (University College London PhD thesis).

Broekaert, W., 2013. 'Financial experts in a spider web. A social network analysis of the archives of Caecilius Iucundus and the Sulpicii', *Klio* 95, 471–510.

Bromberg, B., 1940. 'Temple banking in Rome', *Economic History Review* 10, 128–31.

Brown, F.E., 1980. *Cosa. The making of a Roman town* (Ann Arbor).

Brun, J.-P., 2000. 'The production of perfumes in antiquity: the cases of Delos and Paestum', *AJA* 104, 277–308.

Brunt, P.A., 1965. 'Italian aims at the time of the Social War', *JRS* 55, 90–109.

Brunt, P.A., 1982. '*Nobilitas* and *novitas*', *JRS* 72, 1–17.

Brunt, P.A., 1987^2. *Italian manpower 225 B.C. – A.D. 14* (Oxford).

Brunt, P.A., 1988. *The fall of the Roman Republic* (Oxford).

Bucher, G.S., 2000. 'The origins, program, and composition of Appian's *Roman History*', *TAPhA* 130, 411–58.

Buchet, E., 2015. 'Literary topoi and the integration of central Italy', in: S.T. Roselaar (ed.), *Processes of cultural change and integration in the Roman world* (Leiden) 278–87.

Burgers, G.-J.L.M., 1998. *Constructing Messapian landscapes. Settlement dynamics, social organization and culture contact in the margins of Graeco-Roman Italy* (Amsterdam).

Burnett, A., 1978. 'The first Roman silver coins', *Numismatica e antichità classiche* 7, 121–42.

Burnett, A., 1982. 'The currency of Italy from the Hannibalic War to the reign of Augustus', *AIIN* 29, 125–37.

Burnett, A., 1989. 'The beginnings of Roman coinage', *AIIN* 36, 33–64.

Burnett, A., 1991. 'La monetazione di Venosa e il suo rapporto con quella delle coeve colonie latine dell'area adriatica', in: M. Salvatore (ed.), *Il museo archeologico nazionale di Venosa* (Matera) 29–35 + plates.

Burnett, A., 1995. 'The unification of the monetary system of the Roman West: accident or design?' in: J. Swaddling, S. Walker, & P. Roberts (eds.), *Italy in Europe: economic relations 700 BC—AD 50* (London) 313–20.

Burnett, A., 1998. 'The coinage of the Social War', in: A. Burnett, U. Wartenberg, & R. Witschonke (eds.), *Coins of Macedonia and Rome: essays in honour of Charles Hersh* (London) 165–72.

Burnett, A., 2006. 'Reflections on the San Martino in Pensilis hoard', *RN* 162, 37–50.

Burnett, A., 2012. 'Early Roman coinage and its Italian context', in: W.E. Metcalf (ed.), *The Oxford handbook of Greek and Roman coinage* (Oxford) 297–314.

Cambi, F., 2002. 'La casa del colono e il paesaggio (III-II secolo a. C.)', in: A. Carandini & F. Cambi (eds.), *Paesaggi d'Etruria* (Firenze) 137–45.

Cambi, F., 2004. 'Le campagne di Falerii e di Capena dopo la romanizzazione', in: H. Patterson (ed.), *Bridging the Tiber. Approaches to regional archaeology in the Middle Tiber Valley* (Rome and London) 75–101.

Cambridge Dictionary, 2018. 'Integration.' Available online at: https://dictionary.cambridge.org/dictionary/english/integration.

Camodeca, G., 1999. Tabulae pompeianae Sulpiciorum *(TPSulp.): edizione critica dell'archivio puteolano dei Sulpicii* (Rome).

Campanelli, A., 1985. 'Il santuario italico-romano di Lecce nei Marsi', in: *Il Fucino e le aree limitrofe nell'antichità* (Avezzano) 325–30.

Campanile, E. & C. Letta, 1979. *Studi sulle magistrature indigene e municipali in area italica* (Pisa).

Cantilena, R., 1991. 'Le emissioni monetali di Larino e dei Frentani', in: S. Capini & A. Di Niro (eds.), *Samnium: archeologia del Molise* (Rome) 141–8.

Cantilena, R., 1996. 'I Sarrasti e le monete di Nuceria Alfaterna', in: L. Breglia Pulci Doria (ed.), *L'incidenza dell'antico. Studi in memoria di Ettore Lepore* (Naples) 319–24.

Capini, S., 2003. 'Il santuario di Ercole a Campochiaro', in: G. Cera, L. Petacco, & S. Quilici Gigli (eds.), *Santuari e luoghi di culto nell'Italia antica* (Rome) 233–50.

Capini, S. & A. Di Niro (eds.), 1991. *Samnium: archeologia del Molise* (Rome).

Carandini, A. (ed.), 1985. *Settefinestre: una villa schiavistica nell' Etruria romana* (Modena).

Carandini, A., 1988. *Schiavi in Italia. Gli instrumenti pensanti dei Romani fra tarda Repubblica e medio Impero* (Rome).

Carlsen, J., 1994. '*CIL* X 8217 and the question of temple land in Roman Italy', in: J. Carlsen, P. Ørsted & J.E. Skydsgaard (eds.), *Landuse in the Roman Empire* (Rome) 9–16.

Carre, M.B. & S. Pesavento Mattioli, 2003. 'Anfore e commerci nell'Adriatico', in: F. Lenzi (ed.), *L'archeologia dell'Adriatico dalla Preistoria al Medioevo* (Ravenna) 268–85.

Carter, J.C., 2005. *Discovering the Greek countryside at Metaponto* (Ann Arbor).

Càssola, F., 1962. *I gruppi politici romani nel III secolo a. C.* (Trieste).

Càssola, F., 1970–1. 'Romani e Italici in Oriente', *DdA* 4–5, 305–29.

Castrizio, D., 1995. *Reggio ellenistica* (Rome).

Catalli, F., 1995. *Monete dell'Italia antica* (Rome).

Cavalieri, M., 2012. *Nullus locus sine genio. Il ruolo aggregativo e religioso dei santuari extraurbani della Cisalpina tra protostoria, romanizzazione e piena romanità* (Brussels).

Cébeillac-Gervasoni, M., 1978. 'Problématique de la promotion politique pour les notables des cités du Latium à la fin de la République', *Ktèma* 3, 227–42.

Cébeillac-Gervasoni, M., 1991. 'Les travaux publics à la fin de la république, dans le Latium et la Campanie du Nord: la place de la classe dirigente et des familles de notables', *CCG* 2, 189–208.

Cébeillac-Gervasoni, M., 1998. *Les magistrats des cités italiennes de la seconde guerre punique à Auguste: le Latium et la Campanie* (Rome).

Celuzza, M., 2002. 'La romanizzazione: Etruschi e Romani fra 311 e 123 a. C.', in: A. Carandini & F. Cambi (eds.), *Paesaggi d'Etruria* (Firenze) 103–13.

Chiusi, T.J., 2011. 'Lo straniero come comparticipe dell'esperienza giuridica', in: A. Maffi & L. Gagliardi (eds.), *I diritti degli altri in Grecia e a Roma* (Sankt Augustin) 30–44.

Cipriano, M.T., 1994. 'La raccolta dei bolli sulle anfore italiche trovate in Italia', in: C. Nicolet (ed.), *Epigrafia della produzione e della distribuzione* (Rome) 205–18.

Cipriano, M.T. & M.B. Carre, 1989. 'Production et typologie des amphores sur la côte adriatique de l'Italie', in: *Amphores romaines et histoire économique. Dix ans de recherche* (Rome) 67–104.

Clackson, J. & G. Horrocks, 2007. *The Blackwell history of the Latin language* (Malden, MA and Oxford).

Coarelli, F., 1977. 'Public building in Rome between the Second Punic War and Sulla', *PBSR* 45, 1–23.

Coarelli, F., 1981. 'Il Vallo di Diano in età romana. I dati dell'archeologia', in: B. D'Agostini (ed.), *Storia del Vallo di Diano* I (Salerno) 217–49.

Coarelli, F., 1983. *Il foro romano* (Rome).

Coarelli, F., 1987. *I santuari del Lazio in età repubblicana* (Rome).

Coarelli, F., 1991. 'I Sanniti a Fregellae', in: G. D'Henry (ed.), *La Romanisation du Samnium aux IIe et Ier siècles av. J.-C.* (Naples) 177–85.

Coarelli, F., 1992. 'Praeneste in età repubblicana. Società e politica', in: *La necropoli di Praeneste. Periodi orientalizzante e mediorepubblicana* (Palestrina) 253–67.

Coarelli, F., 1996. Revixit ars. *Arte e ideologia a Roma. Dai modelli ellenistici alla tradizione repubblicana* (Rome).

Coarelli, F., 1998. 'La storia e lo scavo', in: F. Coarelli & P.G. Monti (eds.), *Fregellae I: Le fonti, la storia, il territorio* (Rome) 29–70.

Coccia, S. & D.J. Mattingly, 1992. 'Settlement history, environment and human exploitation of an intermontane basin in the central Apennines: the Rieti survey 1988–1991, part I', *PBSR* 60, 213–90.

Colavitti, A.M., 1999. *La presenza dei* negotiatores italici *nelle Sardegna di età romana* (Oristano).

Colivicchi, F., 2011. 'The long good-bye: the local élites of Daunia between continuity and change', in: F. Colivicchi (ed.), *Local cultures of south Italy and Sicily in the late Republican period: between Hellenism and Rome* (Portsmouth, RI) 112–37.

Colonna, G., 1984. 'Un 'trofeo' di Novio Fannio, comandante sannita', in: *Studi di antichità in onore di Guglielmo Maetzke* II (Rome) 229–41.

Compatangelo, R., 1989. *Un cadastre de pierre.* Le Salento romain. Paysage et structures agraires (Paris) 5.51.

Compatangelo-Soussignan, R., 1999. *Sur les routes d'Hannibal. Paysages de Campanie et d'Apulie* (Paris).

Cooley, A.E., 2002. 'The survival of Oscan in Roman Pompeii', in: A.E. Cooley (ed.), *Becoming Roman, writing Latin? Literacy and epigraphy in the Roman West* (Portsmouth, RI) 77–86.

Cornell, T.J., 1995. *The beginnings of Rome: Italy and Rome from the Bronze Age to the Punic Wars (C. 1000–264 BC)* (London and New York).

Cornell, T.J., 2004. 'Deconstructing the Samnite Wars: an essay in historiography', in: H. Jones (ed.), *Samnium: settlement and cultural change: proceedings of the third E. Togo Salmon conference on Roman studies* (Oxford) 115–31.

Cornell, T.J. (ed.), 2013. *The fragments of the Roman historians* (Oxford).

Coşkun, A., 2004. 'Zu den Rechtsgrundlagen der römischen Bürgerrechtsvergabe infolge des Bundesgenossenkrieges', *RIDA* 51, 101–32.

Coşkun, A., 2009a. *Bürgerrechtsentzug oder Fremdenausweisung? Studien zu den Rechten von Latinern und weiteren Fremden sowie zum Bürgerrechtswechsel in der Römischen Republik (5. bis frühes 1. Jh. v. Chr.)* (Stuttgart).

Coşkun, A., 2009b. *Großzügige Praxis der Bürgerrechtsvergabe in Rom? Zwischen Mythos und Wirklichkeit* (Stuttgart).

Coşkun, A., forthcoming. 'The Social War as a test case for the principles of Roman Republican citizenship policy', in: L. Cappelletti & S. Pyttia (eds.), *L'Italie entre déchirements et reconciliations. Revisiter la guerre sociale et ses lendemains* (Paris).

Cottier, M. et al. (eds.), 2008. *The Customs Law of Asia* (Oxford).

Crawford, M.H., 1969. *Roman Republican coin hoards* (London).

Crawford, M.H., 1974. *Roman Republican coinage* (Cambridge).

Crawford, M.H., 1981. 'Italy and Rome', *JRS* 71, 153–60 (Review of Galsterer 1976 and Humbert 1978).

Crawford, M.H., 1985. *Coinage and money under the Roman Republic. Italy and the Mediterranean economy* (London).

Crawford, M.H., 1991. 'Army and coinage in the late Republic', in: G. D'Henry (ed.), *La Romanisation du Samnium aux IIe et Ier siècles av. J.-C.* (Naples) 135–7.

Crawford, M.H., 1996. 'Lex agraria', in: M.H. Crawford (ed.), *Roman statutes* I (London) 113–80.

Crawford, M.H., 2006. 'From Poseidonia to Paestum via the Lucanians', in: J.-P. Wilson & G. Bradley (eds.), *Greek and Roman colonization: origins, ideologies and interactions* (Swansea) 59–72.

Crawford, M.H. (ed.), 2011. Imagines italicae. *A corpus of Italic inscriptions* (London).

Crawford, M.H. & R. Coleman, 1996. 'Lex Osca Tabulae Bantinae', in: M.H. Crawford (ed.), *Roman statutes* 1 (London) 271–92.

Crawford, M.H., et al., 1996. 'Lex de provinciis praetoriis', in: M.H. Crawford (ed.), *Roman statutes* 1 (London) 231–70.

Crimaco, L., 2002. 'Il territorio di Sinuessa tra storia ed archeologia', *Bollettino sezione Campania ANISN* 23, 83–122.

Curti, E., E. Dench, & J.R. Patterson, 1996. 'The archaeology of central and southern Italy: recent trends and approaches', *JRS* 86, 170–89.

Dall'Aglio, P.L., S. De Maria, & M. Podini, 2007. 'Territory, city and private life at Suasa', *JRA* 20, 177–201.

D'Andria, F., 1979. 'La Puglia romana', in: D. Adamesteanu (ed.), *La Puglia dal Paleolitico al Tardoromano* (Milan) 273–360.

Dart, C.J., 2014. *The Social War, 91 to 88 BCE. A history of the Italian insurgency against the Roman Republic* (Farnham).

Daube, D., 1951. 'The peregrine praetor', *JRS* 41, 66–70.

David, J.-M., 2006. 'La prise en compte des intérêts des Italiens par le gouvernement de Rome', in: M. Jehne & R. Pfeilschifter (eds.), *Herrschaft ohne Integration?* Rom und Italien in republikanischer Zeit (Frankfurt) 95–110.

De Benedittis, G., 1990. 'Monte Vairano: tratturi economia e viabilità', in: *Giornate internazionali di studio sulla transumanza. Atti del convegno 4–7 Nov. 1984* (Padova) 107–28.

De Cazanove, O., 2000. 'I destinatari dell'iscrizione di Tiriolo e la questione del campo d'applicazione del senatoconsulto *de Bacchanalibus*', *Athenaeum* 88, 59–69.

De Cazanove, O., 2004. 'Le aree interne dal III al I sec. Il quadro archeologico', in: *Tramonto della Magna Grecia. Atti del 44 convegno di studi sulla Magna Grecia* (Taranto) 763–99.

Decorte, R., 2015. 'Sine dolo malo: the influence and impact of Latin legalese on the Oscan law of the Tabula Bantina', *Mnemosyne* 69, 1–16.

De Gennaro, R. & A. Santoriello, 2003. *Dinamiche insediative nel territorio di Volcei* (Paestum).

De Lachenal, L., 1993. *Da Leukania a Lucania. La Lucania centro-orientale fra Pirro e i Giulio-Claudii* (Venosa).

De Laet, S.J., 1949. *Portorium.* Étude sur l'organisation dounanière chez les Romains surtout à l'époque du Haut-Empire (Bruges).

Dell 'Aglio, A. & E. Lippolis, 1989. 'Il commercio del vino rodio a Taranto', in: *Amphores romaines et histoire économique. Dix ans de recherche* (Rome) 544–7.

de Ligt, L., 1993. *Fairs and markets in the Roman Empire. Economic and social aspects of periodic trade in a pre-industrial society* (Amsterdam).

de Ligt, L., 2004. 'Poverty and demography: the case of the Gracchan land reforms', *Mnemosyne* 57, 725–57.

de Ligt, L., 2012. *Peasants, citizens and soldiers. Studies in the demographic history of Roman Italy 225 BC–AD 100* (Cambridge).

Dench, E., 1995. *From barbarians to new men. Greek, Roman and modern perceptions of peoples of the Central Apennines* (Oxford).

Dench, E., 1997. 'Sacred springs to the Social War; myths of origins and questions of identity in the Central Appennines', in: T. Cornell & K. Lomas (eds.), *Gender and ethnicity in ancient Italy* (London) 43–51.

Dench, E., 2005. *Romulus' asylum. Roman identities from the age of Alexander to the age of Hadrian* (Oxford).

D 'Ercole, M.C., 1990. *La stipe votive del Belvedere a Lucera* (Rome).

Derow, P.S., 2003. 'The arrival of Rome; from the Illyrian Wars to the fall of Macedon', in: A. Erskine (ed.), *A companion to the Hellenistic world* (Malden MA) 51–70.

De Simone, C. & S. Marchesini, 2002. *Monumenta Linguae Messapicae* (Wiesbaden).

De Souza, P., 1999. *Piracy in the Graeco-Roman world* (Cambridge).

Desy, P., 1993. *Recherches sur l'économie apulienne au IIe et au Ier siècle avant notre ère* (Brussels).

Desy, P. & P. De Paepe, 1990. 'Torre di San Giovanni (Ugento): les amphores commerciales hellénistiques et républicaines', *Stud. Ant. Lecce* 6, 187–234.

Di Fazio, M., 2006. *Fondi e il suo territorio in età romana. Profilo di storia e economia e sociale* (Oxford).

Di Giuseppe, H., 2012. *Black-gloss ware in Italy. Production management and local histories* (Oxford).

Dondin, M., 1979. 'Les Atilii Glabriones de Pérouse: ascension sociale et relations sénatoriales de magistrats municipaux', *MEFRA* 91:2, 651–70.

Dyson, S.L., 1992. *Community and society in Roman Italy* (Baltimore & London).

Eberle, L.P. & E. Le Quéré, 2017. 'Landed traders, trading agriculturalists? Land in the economy of the Italian diaspora in the Greek East', *JRS* 107, 27–59.

Eckstein, A.M., 2008. *Rome enters the Greek East. From anarchy to hierarchy in the Hellenistic Mediterranean, 230–170 BC* (Malden, MA).

Edlund, I.E.M., 1984. 'Sacred and secular: evidence of rural shrines and industry among Greeks and Etruscans', in: T. Hackens, N.D. Holloway, & R.R. Holloway (eds.), *Crossroads of the Mediterranean* (Providence RI and Leuven) 277–90.

Edlund, I.E.M., 1987. *The gods and the place. Location and function of sanctuaries in the countryside of Etruria and Magna Graecia (700–400 B.C.)* (Stockholm).

Eilers, C., 1991. 'Cn. Domitius and Samos: a new extortion trial (IGR 4, 968)', *ZPE* 89, 167–78.

Ellis, S., 2011. 'The rise and re-organization of the Pompeian salted fish industry', in: S. Ellis (ed.), *The making of Pompeii: studies in the history and urban development of an ancient town* (Portsmouth, RI) 59–88.

Empereur, J.-Y. & A. Hesnard, 1987. 'Les amphores hellénistiques du monde grec', in: P. Lévêque & J.-P. Morel (eds.), *Céramiques hellénistiques et romaines* II (Paris) 10–71.

Ercolani Cocchi, E., 2000. 'Romanizzazione e moneta', in: M. Marini Calvani (ed.), *Aemilia. La cultura romana in Emilia Romagna dal III secolo a. C. all'età costantiniana* (Bologna) 37–47.

Erdkamp, P., 1998. *Hunger and the sword. Warfare and food supply in Roman Republican wars (264–30 BC)* (Amsterdam).

Erdkamp, P., 2007. 'Polybius and Livy on the allies in the Roman army', in: L. de Blois, E. Lo Cascio, & O. Hekster (eds.), *The impact of the Roman army (200 BC–AD 476): economic, social, political, religious and cultural aspects* (Leiden) 47–74.

Erdkamp, P., 2008. 'Mobility and migration in Italy in the second century BC', in: L. de Ligt & S. Northwood (eds.), *People, land, and politics. Demographic developments and the transformation of Italy 300 BC–AD 14* (Leiden and Boston) 417–49.

Erdkamp, P., 2011. 'Soldiers, Roman citizens, and Latin colonists in mid-Republican Italy', *AncSoc* 41, 108–46.

Errington, R.M., 1988. 'Aspects of Roman acculturation in the east under the Republic', in: P. Kneissl & V. Losemann (eds.), *Alte Geschichte und Wissenschaftsgeschichte.* Festschrift für K. Christ zum 65. Geburtstag (Darmstadt) 140–57.

Estienne, S. & O. De Cazanove, 2009. 'Offrandres et amendes dans les sanctuaires du monde romain à l'époque républicaine', *ARG* 11, 5–35.

Facella, A., 2001. 'Note sul territorio kauloniate in età ellenistica romana', in: M.C. Parra (ed.), *Kaulonía, Caulonia, Stilida (e oltre). Contributi storici, archeologici e topografici I* (Pisa) 59–101.

Farney, G.D., 2007. *Ethnic identity and aristocratic competition in the Roman Republic* (Cambridge).

Fearon, J.D., 1999. 'What is identity (as we now use the word)?' Stanford working paper. Available online.

Fentress, E., 2000. 'Introduction: Cosa and the idea of the city', in: E. Fentress (ed.), *Romanization and the city. Creation, transformations and failures* (Portsmouth RI) 9–24.

Finley, M.I., 1999^2. *The ancient economy* (Cambridge) 1st ed. 1973.

Flambard, J.-M., 1983. 'Les collèges et les élites locales à l'époque républicaine d'après l'exemple de Capoue', in: M. Cébeillac-Gervasoni (ed.), *Les «bourgeoisies» municipales italiennes aux IIe et Ier siècle av. J.-C.* (Naples) 75–89.

Flohr, M., 2013. *The world of the fullo. Work, economy, and society in Roman Italy* (Oxford).

Flohr, M., 2017. 'Quantifying Pompeii: population, inequality, and the urban economy', in: M. Flohr & A. Wilson (eds.), *The economy of Pompeii* (Oxford) 53–84.

Flohr, M. & A. Wilson, 2017. 'Introduction: investigating an urban economy', in: M. Flohr & A. Wilson (eds.), *The economy of Pompeii* (Oxford) 1–19.

Fracchia, H., 2013. 'Survey, settlement and land use in Republican Italy', in: J. DeRose Evans (ed.), *A companion to the archaeology of the Roman Republic* (Malden, MA) 181–97.

Fracchia, H. & M. Gualtieri, 1998–9. 'Roman Lucania and the upper Bradano Valley', *MAAR* 43–4, 295–343.

Fracchia, H. & M. Gualtieri, 2011. 'The countryside of Regio II and Regio III (c. 300 B.C.–A.D. 14)', in: F. Colivicchi (ed.), *Local cultures of south Italy and Sicily in the late Republican period: between Hellenism and Rome* (Portsmouth, RI) 11–29.

Franchi De Bellis, A., 1990. 'Il cippo abellano: il santuario di Ercole', in: M. Tagliente (ed.), *Italici in Magna Grecia: lingua, insediamenti e strutture* (Venosa) 111–15.

Fraschetti, A., 1981. 'Le vicende storiche', in: B. D'Agostini (ed.), *Storia del Vallo di Diano* I (Salerno) 201–15.

Frayn, J.M., 1993. *Markets and fairs in Roman Italy: their social and economic importance from the second century BC to the third century* AD (Oxford).

Frederiksen, M.W., 1959. 'Republican Capua: a social and economic study', *PBSR* 37, 80–125.

Frederiksen, M.W., 1981. 'I cambiamenti delle strutture agrarie nella tarda Repubblica: la Campania', in: A. Giardina & A. Schiavone (eds.), *Società romana e produzione schiavistica I. L'Italia: insediamenti e forme economiche* (Rome) 265–87.

Fronda, M.P., 2010. *Between Rome and Carthage: Southern Italy during the Second Punic War* (Cambridge).

Fronda, M.P., 2011. 'Privata hospicia, beneficia publica? Consul(ar)s, local elite and Roman rule in Italy', in: H. Beck et al. (eds.), *Consuls and res publica. Holding high office in the Roman Republic* (Cambridge) 232–55.

Gabba, E., 1954. 'Le origini della guerra sociale e la vita politica romana dopo l'89 a. C.', *Athenaeum* 32, 41–114.

Gabba, E., 1956. *Appiano e la storia delle guerre civile* (Firenze).

Gabba, E., 1976. *Republican Rome, the army and the allies*, trans. P.J. Cuff (Berkeley).

Gabba, E., 1977. 'Considerazioni sulla decadenza della piccola proprietà contadina nell'Italia centro-meridionale del II sec. a. C.', *Ktèma* 2, 269–84.

Gabba, E., 1987. 'La città italica', in: P. Rossi (ed.), *Modelli di città* (Turin) 109–26.

Gabba, E., 1989. 'Rome and Italy in the second century BC', in: A.E. Astin, F.W. Walbank, M.W. Frederiksen, & R.M. Ogilvie (eds.), *Cambridge Ancient History* VIII (Cambridge) 197–243.

Gabba, E., 1994. 'Rome and Italy: the Social War', in: J. Crook, A. Lintott, & E. Rawson (eds.), *Cambridge Ancient History* IX (Cambridge) 104–28.

Gagliardi, L., 2006. *Mobilità e integrazione delle persone nei centri cittadini romani. Aspetti giuridichi I: la classificazione degli* incolae (Milan).

Galinsky, K., 1996. *Augustan culture: an interpretive introduction* (Princeton).

Gallone, A., 2007. 'Agricultural landscapes in Hellenistic Messapia: socio-economic structures and cultural implications', in: P. van Dommelen & N. Terrenato (eds.), *Articulating local cultures: power and identity under the expanding Roman republic* (Portsmouth, RI) 23–32.

Galsterer, H., 1976. *Herrschaft und Verwaltung im republikanischen Italien. Die Beziehungen Roms zu den italischen Gemeinden vom Latinerfreuden 338 v. Chr. bis zum Bundesgenossenkrieg 91 v. Chr.* (Munich).

Garnsey, P., 1980. 'Non-slave labour in the Roman world', in: P. Garnsey (ed.), *Non-slave labour in the Graeco-Roman world* (Cambridge) 34–47.

Gasparri, D., 1994. 'Nuove acquisizioni sulla divisione agraria di Paestum', in: *La ravitaillement en blé de Rome et des centres urbains des débuts de la République jusqu'au haut Empire* (Naples and Rome) 149–58.

Gatti, S. & M.T. Onorati, 1992. 'Praeneste medio-repubblicana: gentes e attività produttive', in: *La necropoli di Praeneste. Periodi orientalizzante e mediorepubblicana* (Palestrina).

Gauthier, F., forthcoming. 'Plunder, common soldiers, and military service in the middle and late Republic', in: S.T. Roselaar & M. Helm (eds.), *Spoils in the Roman Republic—a re-evaluation* (Stuttgart).

Gianfrotta, P.A., 1981. 'Commerci e pirateria: prime testimonianze archeologiche sottomarine', *MEFRA* 93:1, 227–42.

Giannotta, M.T., 1980. *Metaponto ellenistico-romana: problemi topografici* (Galatina).

Giardina, A., 1981. 'Allevamento ed economia della selva in Italia meridionale: trasformazioni e continuità', in: A. Giardina & A. Schiavone (eds.), *Società romana e produzione schiavistica I. L'Italia: insediamenti e forme economiche* (Rome) 87–113.

Giardina, A. & A. Schiavone (eds.), 1981. Società romana e produzione schiavistica I. L'Italia: insediamenti e forme economiche (Rome).

Gleba, M., 2009. 'Textile tools in ancient Italian votive contexts: evidence of dedication or production?' in: M. Gleba & H. Becker (eds.), *Votives, places and rituals in Etruscan religion. Studies in honor of Jean MacIntosh Turfa* (Leiden) 69–84.

Glinister, F., 1997. 'What is a sanctuary?' *CCG* 8, 61–80.

Glinister, F., 2003. 'Gifts of the gods. Sanctuary and society in archaic Tyrrhenian Italy', in: J.B. Wilkins & E. Herring (eds.), *Inhabiting symbols: symbol and image in the ancient Mediterranean* (London) 137–47.

Goffredo, R., 2008. 'Persistenze e innovazioni nelle modalità insediative della valle dell'Ofanto tra fine IV e I sec. A.C.', in: G. Volpe, M.J. Strazulla, & D. Leone (eds.), *Storia e archeologia della Daunia in ricordo di Marina Mazzei* (Bari) 287–301.

Goffredo, R., 2010. 'Persistence and change in settlement patterns in the Ofanto valley near Canusium and Cannae (Apulia) (late 4th c. B.C. - 1st c. B.C.)', *JRA* 23, 7–33.

Göhler, J., 1939. *Römische Politik im bundesgenössischen Italien. Von der Gründung des Italischen Bundes bis zur Gracchenzeit* (Würzburg).

Granino Cerere, M.G., 2009. 'Pecunia sacra e proprietà fondiaria nei santuari dell'Italia centrale. Il contributo dell'epigrafia', *ARG* 11, 37–62.

Greco, E., 1988. 'Archeologia della colonia latina di Paestum', *DdA* 6.3, 79–86.

Greco, G., 2004. 'Paestum ed Elea tra Magna Grecia e Roma', in: *Tramonto della Magna Grecia. Atti del 44 convegno di studi sulla Magna Grecia* (Taranto) 577–641.

Green, J.R., 1976. *Gnathia pottery in the Akademisches Kunstmuseum Bonn* (Bonn).

Grelle, F., 1981. 'Canosa. Le instituzioni, la società', in: A. Giardina & A. Schiavone (eds.), *Società romana e produzione schiavistica I. L'Italia: insediamenti e forme economiche* (Rome) 181–225.

Grelle, F., 2008. 'Le colonie latine e la romanizzazione della Puglia', in: G. Volpe, M. J. Strazzulla, & D. Leone (eds.), *Storia e archeologia della Daunia* (Bari) 365–87.

Grelle, F. & A. Giardina, 1993. *Canosa romana* (Rome).

Gros, P., 1978. *Architecture et société à Rome et en Italie centro-méridionale aux deux derniers siècles de la République* (Brussels).

Gruen, E.S., 1974. *The last generation of the Roman Republic* (Berkeley).

Gruen, E.S., 1984. *The Hellenistic world and the coming of Rome* (Berkeley).

Gruen, E.S., 1990. *Studies in Greek culture and Roman policy* (Leiden).

Gualtieri, M., 2003. *La Lucania romana. Cultura e società nella documentazione archeologica* (Naples).

Gualtieri, M., 2008. 'Contesti della ceramica tardo-apula: il 'caso Arpi' e la Lucania', in: G. Volpe, M.J. Strazzulla, & D. Leone (eds.), *Storia e archeologia della Daunia* (Bari) 221–31.

Gualtieri, M. & H. Fracchia, 2001. *Roccagloriosa II. L'oppidum lucano e il territorio* (Naples).

Guerrini, C. & L. Mancini, 2007. 'La ceramica di età romana', in: *Introduzione allo studio della ceramica in archeologia* (Siena) 197–234.

Guidobaldi, M.P., 2005. 'La diffusione del modello romano e l'unificazione amministrativa', in: F. Pesando (ed.), *L'Italia antica. Culture e forme del popolamento nel I millennio a. C.* (Rome) 267–73.

Guidobaldi, M.P. & F. Pesando, 1989. 'La *colonia civium Romanorum*', in: F. Coarelli (ed.), *Minturnae* (Rome) 35–66.

Guzzo, P.G., 1984. 'Lucanians, Brettians and Italiote Greeks in the fourth and third centuries B.C.', in: T. Hackens, N.D. Holloway, & R.R. Holloway (eds.), *Crossroads of the Mediterranean* (Providence, RI and Leuven) 191–246.

Guzzo, P.G., 1991. 'Documentazioni ed ipotesi archeologiche per la più antica romanizzazione di Bari, Brindisi, Taranto', in: J. Mertens & R. Lambrechts (eds.), *Comunità indigene e problemi della romanizzazione nell'Italia centro-meridionale (IVo- IIIo sec. av. C.)* (Brussels and Rome) 77–88.

Guzzo, P.G., 2000. 'Alla ricerca della Pompei sannitica', in: R. Cappelli (ed.), *Studi sull'Italia dei Sanniti* (Rome) 107–17.

Hall, J.M., 2002. *Hellenicity between ethnicity and culture* (Chicago and London).

Hantos, T., 1983. *Das römische Bundesgenossensystem in Italien* (Munich).

Harris, W.V., 1971. *Rome in Etruria and Umbria* (Oxford).

Harris, W.V., 1977. 'The era of Patavium', *ZPE* 27, 283–93.

Harris, W.V., 1984. 'The Italians and the Empire', in: W.V. Harris (ed.), *The imperialism of mid-republican Rome* (Rome) 89–109.

Harris, W.V., 1991^2. *War and imperialism in Republican Rome 327–70 B.C.* (Oxford).

Harris, W.V., 1993. 'Between archaic and modern: some current problems in the history of the Roman economy', in: W.V. Harris (ed.), *The inscribed economy: production and distribution in the Roman Empire in the light of instrumentum domesticum* (Ann Arbor) 11–29.

Harris, W.V., 2000. 'Roman governments and commerce, 300 B.C. – A.D. 300', in: C. Zaccagnini (ed.), *Mercanti e politica nel mondo antico* (Rome) 275–305.

Harris, W.V., 2006. 'A revisionist view of Roman money', *JRS* 96, 1–24.

Harris, W.V., 2007. 'Quando e come l'Italia divenne per la prima volta Italia? Un saggio sulla politica dell'identità', *Studi Storici* 48:2, 301–22.

Harriss, J., J. Hunter, & C.M. Lewis, 1995. 'Introduction: development and significance of NIE', in: J. Harriss, J. Hunter, & C.M. Lewis (eds.), *The new institutional economics and third world development* (London and New York) 1–13.

Hasenohr, C., 2007. 'Italiens et Phéniciens à Délos: organisation et relations de deux groupes d'étrangers résidents (IIe-Ier siècles av. J.-C.)', in: R. Compatangelo-Soussignan & C.-G. Schwentzel, *Étrangers dans la cité romaine* (Rennes) 77–90.

Hatzfeld, J., 1912. 'Les Italiens résidant à Délos mentionnés dans les inscriptions de l'île', *BCH* 36:1, 5–218.

Hatzfeld, J., 1919. *Les trafiquants Italiens dans l'Orient Hellenique* (Paris).

Haverfield, F., 1908. *The Romanization of Britain* (Oxford).

Heady, P., 2005. 'Barter', in: J.G. Carrier (ed.), *A handbook of economic anthropology* (Cheltenham and Northampton, MA) 262–74.

Helly, B., 1983. 'Les Italiens en Thessalie au IIe et au Ier s. av. J.-C.', in: M. Cébeillac-Gervasoni (ed.), *Les «bourgeoisies» municipales italiennes aux IIe et Ier siècle av. J.-C.* (Naples) 355–80.

Herring, E., 2007. 'Identity crises in SE Italy in the 4th c. B.C.: Greek and native perceptions of the threat to their cultural identities', in: R. Roth & J. Keller (eds.), *Roman by integration: dimensions of group identity in material culture and text* (Portsmouth RI) 11–25.

Hesnard, A. et al., 1989. 'Aires de production des Gréco-italiques et des Dr 1', in: *Amphores romaines et histoire économique: dix ans de recherche* (Rome) 21–65.

Heurgon, J., 1952. 'Les Lassii pompéiens et l'importation des vins italiens en Gaule', *PdP* 23, 113–18.

Heurgon, J., 1969. 'Inscriptions étrusques de Tunisie', *CRAI* 113–14, 526–51.

Hin, S.C., 2013. *The demography of Roman Italy. Population dynamics in an ancient conquest society (201 BCE—CE 14)* (Cambridge).

Hingley, R., 2005. *Globalizing Roman culture. Unity, diversity and Empire* (London and New York).

Hingley, R., 2010. 'Cultural diversity and unity: empire and Rome', in: S. Hales & T. Hodos (eds.), *Material culture and social identities in the ancient world* (Cambridge) 54–75.

Hodos, T., 2010. 'Local and global perspectives in the study of social and cultural identities', in: S. Hales & T. Hodos (eds.), *Material culture and social identities in the ancient world* (Cambridge) 3–21.

Holleran, C., 2012. Shopping in ancient Rome: the retail trade in the late Republic and the Principate (Oxford).

Hopkins, K., 1978. *Conquerors and slaves* (Cambridge).

Hoyos, B.D., 1998. *Unplanned wars. The origins of the first and second Punic wars* (Berlin).

Humbert, M., 1978. Municipium *et* civitas sine suffragio. *L'organisation de la conquête jusqu'à la guerre sociale* (Rome).

Huskinson, J., 2000. 'Looking for culture, identity and power', in: J. Huskinson (ed.), *Experiencing Rome. Culture, identity and power in the Roman Empire* (London and New York) 3–27.

Ilari, V., 1974. Gli italici nelle strutture militari romane (Milan).

Isaac, B., 2004. The invention of racism in classical antiquity (Princeton and Oxford).

Isayev, E., 2007. *Inside ancient Lucania: dialogues in history and archaeology* (London).

Isayev, E., 2010. 'Unintentionally being Lucanian. Dynamics beyond hybridity', in: S. Hales & T. Hodos (eds.), *Material culture and social identities in the ancient world* (Cambridge) 201–26.

Isayev, E., 2017. *Migration, mobility and place in ancient Italy* (Cambridge).

Jaeger, M., 2006. 'Livy, Hannibal's monument, and the Temple of Juno at Croton', *TAPA* 136, 389–414.

Jefferson, E., 2012. 'Problems and audience in Cato's Origines', in: S.T. Roselaar (ed.), Processes of integration and identity formation in the Roman Republic (Leiden and Boston) 311–26.

Jehne, M., 2006. 'Römer, Latiner und Bundesgenossen im Krieg. Zu Formen und Ausmass der Integration in der republikanischen Armee', in: M. Jehne & R. Pfeilschifter (eds.), Herrschaft ohne Integration? Rom und Italien in republikanischer Zeit (Frankfurt am Main) 243–67.

Jehne, M. & R. Pfeilschifter (eds.), 2006. *Herrschaft ohne Integration? Rom und Italien in republikanischer Zeit* (Frankfurt am Main).

Jiménez, A., 2010. 'Reproducing difference. Mimesis and colonialism in Roman Hispania', in: P. van Dommelen & A.B. Knapp (eds.), *Material connections in the ancient Mediterranean. Mobility, materiality and identity* (London and New York) 38–63.

Johannowsky, W., 1976. 'La situazione in Campania', in: P. Zanker (ed.), *Hellenismus in Mittelitalien* (Göttingen) 267–99.

Jongman, W., 1988. *The economy and society of Pompeii* (Amsterdam).

Jongman, W., 2003. 'Slavery and the growth of Rome. The transformation of Italy in the second and first centuries BCE', in: C. Edwards & G. Woolf (eds.), *Rome the cosmopolis* (Cambridge) 100–22.

Jongman, W., 2017. 'The benefits of market integration', in: G. Tol & T. de Haas (eds.), *The economic integration of Roman Italy. Rural communities in a globalizing world* (Leiden) 15–27.

Jordan, B., forthcoming. 'The revenues of Asia and the evolution of the res publica', in: S.T. Roselaar & M. Helm (eds.), *Spoils in the Roman Republic—a re-evaluation* (Stuttgart).

Jouffroy, H., 1986. *La construction publique en Italie et dans l'Afrique romaine* (Strasbourg).

Kaimio, J., 1975. 'The ousting of Etruscan by Latin in Etruria', in: *Studies in the Romanization of Etruria* (Rome) 85–245.

Kaser, M., 1953. 'Vom Begriff des commercium', in *Studi in onore di V. Arangio-Ruiz nel XLV anno del suo insegnamento* II (Naples) 131–67.

Kaser, M., 1960. *Das römische Privatrecht I: das altrömische, das vorklassische und klassische Recht* (Munich).

Kaser, M. (ed. R. Hackl), 1996. *Das römische Zivilprozessrecht* (Munich).

Kay, P., 2014. *Rome's economic revolution* (Oxford).

Keaveney, A., 1987. *Rome and the unification of Italy* (London and Sydney).

Keay, S. & N. Terrenato (eds.), 2001. *Italy and the West: comparative issues in Romanization* (Oxford & Oakville, CT).

Keller, J., 2007. 'Rome and her Italian allies: conflicting interests and disintegration', in: R. Roth & J. Keller (eds.), *Roman by integration: dimensions of group identity in material culture and text* (Portsmouth, RI) 43–58.

Kendall, S., 2013. *The struggle for Roman citizenship. Romans, allies, and the wars of 91–77 BCE* (Piscataway, NJ).

Kirbihler, F., 2007. 'Die Italiker in Kleinasien, mit besonderer Berücksichtigung von Ephesos (133 v. Chr. – 1. Jh. n. Chr.)', in: M. Meyer (ed.), *Neue Zeiten—neue Zitten. Zu Rezeption und Integration römischen und italischen Kulturguts in Kleinasien* (Vienna) 19–35.

Kremer, D., 2006. *Ius latinum:* le concept de droit latin sous la République et l'empire (Paris).

Kremer, D., 2014. 'À propos d'une tentative recente de deconstruction des privileges latins et en particulier du *ius migrandi*', *Athenaeum* 102, 226–37.

Laffi, U., 1995. 'Sull'esegesi di alcuni passi di Livio relativi ai rapporti tra Roma e gli alleati Latini e Italici nel primo quarto del II sec. a. C.', in: A. Calbi & G. Susini (eds.), *Pro poplo arimenese* (Faenza) 43–77.

La Greca, F., 2006. 'I beneficiari della legge agraria di Tiberio Gracco e le assegnazioni in Lucania', *RSS* 23, 11–42.

Lamboglia, N., 1952. 'Per una classificazione preliminare della ceramica campana', in: *Atti del I congresso internazionale degli studi liguri* (Bordighera) 139–206.

Lamboley, J.-L., 1996. *Recherches sur les Messapiens IVe-IIe siècle avant J.-C.* (Rome).

Lampela, A., 1998. *Rome and the Ptolemies of Egypt. The development of their political relations, 273–80 B.C.* (Helsinki).

Langslow, D., 2012. 'Integration, identity, and language shift: strengths and weaknesses of the 'linguistic' evidence', in: S.T. Roselaar (ed.), *Processes of integration and identity formation in the Roman Republic* (Leiden and Boston) 289–309.

La Regina, A., 1976. 'Il Sannio', in: P. Zanker (ed.), *Hellenismus in Mittelitalien* (Göttingen) 219–54.

La Regina, A., 2000. 'Il trattato tra Abella e Nola per l'uso comune del santuario di Ercole e di un fondo adiacente', in: R. Cappelli (ed.), *Studi sull'Italia dei Sanniti* (Rome) 214–22.

La Torre, G.F., 1997. 'La romanizzazione del Bruzio: gli aspetti urbanistici', in: L. Quilici & S. Quilici Gigli (eds.), *Architettura e pianificazione urbana nell'Italia antica* (Rome) 25–34.

Launaro, A., 2011. *Peasants and slaves. The rural population of Roman Italy (200 BC to AD 100)* (Cambridge).

Laurence, R., 1999. *The roads of Roman Italy: mobility and cultural change* (London).

Lauter, H., 1976. 'Die hellenistischen Theater der Samniten und Latiner in ihrer Beziehung zur Theaterarchitektur der Griechen', in: P. Zanker (ed.), *Hellenismus in Mittelitalien* (Göttingen) 413–30.

Lavan, M., 2018. 'The foundation of empire? The spread of Roman citizenship from the fourth century BCE to the third century CE', in: K. Berthelot & J. Price (eds.), *Citizenship and political-religious self-definitions in the Roman empire* (Leuven) 21–54.

Leigh, M., 2004. *Comedy and the rise of Rome* (Oxford).

Lejeune, M., 1976. *L'anthroponymie osque* (Paris).

Lejeune, M., 1978. *Ateste à l'heure de la romanisation* (étude anthroponymique) (Florence).

Lepore, E., 1981. 'Geografia del modo di produzione schiavistico e modi residui in Italia meridionale', in: A. Giardina & A. Schiavone (eds.), *Società romana e produzione schiavistica I. L'Italia: insediamenti e forme economiche* (Rome) 79–85.

Le Roux, P., 2004. 'La romanisation en question', *Annales HSS* 59, 287–311.

Lesk, A., 1999. *The anatomical votive terracotta phenomenon: healing sanctuaries in the Etrusco-Latial-Campanian region during the fourth through first centuries B.C.* (University of Cincinnati MA thesis).

Letta, C. & S. D'Amato,1975. *Epigrafia della regione dei Marsi* (Milan).

Levi, M.A., 1997. 'L'agricoltura italiana, G. Lelio e i Gracchi', *Rendiconti dell'accademia nazionale dei Lincei.* Classe di scienze morali, storiche e filologiche ser. 9, vol. 8, 467–72.

Lewis, R.G., 1968. 'Appian B.C. 1, 49, 214 *dekateuontes*: Rome's new tribes 90–87 B.C.', *Athenaeum* 46, 273–91.

Lintott, A.W., 1999. *The constitution of the Roman Republic* (Oxford).

Lippolis, E., 1997. *Fra Taranto e Roma. Società e cultura urbana in Puglia tra Annibale e l'età imperiale* (Taranto).

Livi, V., 2006. 'Religious locales in the territory of Minturnae: aspects of Romanization', in: C.E. Schultz & P.B. Harvey (eds.), *Religion in republican Italy* (Cambridge) 90–116.

Lloyd, J. & G. Barker, 1981. 'Rural settlement in Roman Molise: problems of archaeological survey', in: G. Barker & R. Hodges (eds.), *Archaeology and Italian society* (Oxford) 289–314.

Lloyd, J.A., G. Lock, & N. Christie, 1997. 'From the mountain to the plain: landscape evolution in the Abruzzo. An interim report on the Sangro Valley Project (1994–95)', *PBSR* 65, 1–57.

Lo Cascio, E., 1978. 'Moneta e politica monetaria nel principato', *AIIN* 25, 241–52.

Lo Cascio, E., 2006. 'The role of the state in the Roman economy: making use of New Institutional Economics', in: P. Bang, M. Ikeguchi, & H.G. Ziche (eds.), *Ancient economies, modern methodologies: archaeology, comparative history, models and institutions* (Bari) 215–36.

Lomas, K., 1993. *Rome and the western Greeks 350 BC—AD 200. Conquest and acculturation in southern Italy* (London and New York).

Lomas, K., 1998. 'Roman imperialism and the city in Italy', in: R. Laurence & J. Berry (eds.), *Cultural identity in the Roman Empire* (London and New York) 64–78.

Lomas, K., 2003. 'Public building, urban renewal and euergetism in early imperial Italy', in: K. Lomas & T. Cornell (eds.), *'Bread and circuses'. Euergetism and municipal patronage in Roman Italy* (London) 27–45.

Lomas, K., 2012. 'The weakest link: elite social networks in Republican Italy', in: S.T. Roselaar (ed.), *Processes of integration and identity formation in the Roman Republic* (Leiden and Boston) 197–213.

Loomis, W.T., 1994. 'Entella Tablets VI (254-241 B.C.) and VII (20th century A.D.?)', *Harvard Studies in Classical Philology* 96, 127–60.

Loughton, M.E., 2000. *Republican amphorae in the Auvergne central France: an archaeological and petrological study* (University of Bournemouth PhD thesis).

Mac Sweeney, N., 2011. *Community identity and archaeology: dynamic communities at Aphrodisias and Beycesultan* (Ann Arbor).

Malkin, I., 2002. 'A colonial Middle ground: Greek, Etruscan, and local identities in the Bay of Naples', in: C.L. Lyons & J.K. Papadopoulos (eds.), *The archaeology of colonialism* (Los Angeles) 151–81.

Malrieu, A., 2005. 'Le rôle économique des sanctuaires romains: thésaurisation et investissement des fonds sacrés', *Topoi* 12–13, 95–116.

Manacorda, D., 1981. 'Produzione e proprietari nell'ager Cosanus', in: A. Schiavone & A. Giardina (eds.), *Società romana e produzione schiavistica II: merci, mercato e scambi nel Mediterraneo* (Rome) 3–54.

Manacorda, D., 1988. 'Per uno studio dei centri produttori delle anfore brindisine', in: C. Marangio (ed.), *La Puglia in età romana* (Mesagne) 91–108.

Manacorda, D., 2003. 'Schiavi e padroni nell'antica Puglia roman: produzione e commerci', in: F. Lenzi (ed.), *L'archeologia dell'Adriatico dalla Preistoria al Medioevo* (Ravenna) 297–316.

Manacorda, D. & C. Panella, 1993. 'Anfore', in: W.V. Harris (ed.), *The inscribed ecnomy. Production and distribution in the Roman empire in the light of the instrumentum domesticum* (Ann Arbor) 55–64.

Marasco, G., 1986. 'Interessi commerciali e fattori politici nella condotta romana in Illiria (230–219 a. C.)', *SCO* 36, 35–112.

Marchetti, P., 1993. 'Numismatique romaine et histoire', *CCG* 4, 25–65.

Marchi, M.L., 2010. *Ager Venusinus II (Forma Italiae)* (Florence).

Marchi, M.L. & G. Sabbatini, 1996. *Venusia (Forma Italiae 37)* (Rome).

Marengo, S.M. & G. Paci, 2008. 'Per la circolazione delle anfore rodie e tardo-repubblicane in area adriatica', in: *Est enim ille flos Italiae... Vita economica e sociale nella Cisalpina romana. Atti delle giornate di studi in onore di Ezio Buchi* (Verona) 313–29.

Marichal, R., 1988. *Les graffites de la Graufesenque* (Paris).

Marshall, A.J., 1976. 'Livius Drusus and the Italian question', *Historical Papers* 11, 93–103.

Marzano, A., 2013. *Harvesting the sea: the exploitation of marine resources in the Roman Mediterranean* (Oxford).

Masseria, C. & M.C. D'Anisi,2001. 'Santuari e culti dei Lucani', in: M.L. Nava & M. Osanna (eds.), *Rituali per una dea. Il santuario di Torre di Satriano* (Potenza) 123–34.

Mattingly, D.J., 1997. 'Introduction: dialogues of power and experience in the Roman Empire', in: D.J. Mattingly (ed.), *Dialogues in Roman imperialism. Power, discourse, and discrepant experience in the Roman Empire* (Portsmouth, RI) 7–24.

Mattingly, D.J., 2002. 'Vulgar and weak 'Romanization', or time for a paradigm shift?', *JRA* 15, 536–40.

Mattingly, D.J., 2011. *Imperialism, power, and identity: experiencing the Roman Empire* (Princeton).

Mayer-Maly, T., 2003. 'Commercium', *Tijdschrift voor Rechtsgeschiedenis* 71:1, 1–6.

Mazzei, M., 1991. 'Indigeni e Romani nella Daunia settentrionale', in: J. Mertens & R. Lambrechts (ed.), *Comunità indigene e problemi della romanizzazione nell'Italia centro-meridionale (IVo- IIIo sec. av. C.)* (Brussels and Rome) 109–24.

Mazzei, M., 2002. 'La collina del Serpente. Dalle prime scoperte al Parco di Dauni', in: M. Fabbri & M. Osanna (eds.), *Ausculum I: L'abitato daunio sulla collina del Serpente di Ascoli Satriano* (Foggia) 15–18.

Mazzei, M., J. Mertens, & G. Volpe, 1990. 'Aspetti della romanizzazione della Daunia', in: M. Salvatore (ed.), *Basilicata. L'espansionismo romano nel sud-est d'Italia. Il quadro archeologico* (Venosa) 177–225.

McDonald, K., 2012. 'The testament of Vibius Adiranus', *JRS* 102, 40–55.

Meijer, F., 2011. *Lessen uit Rome. Vreemdelingen in het Romeinse Rijk en in de Europese Unie* (Amsterdam).

Mele, A., 1993. 'Crotone greca negli ultimi due secoli della sua storia', in: *Crotone e la sua storia tra IV e III secolo a. C.* (Naples) 235–91.

Metzger, E., 2013. 'An outline of Roman civil procedure', *Roman Legal Tradition* 9, 1–30.

Michetti, L.M., 2007. 'Scambi e interferenze culturali tra ambiente etrusco-italico e mondo punico: alcuni esempi nell'artigianato artistico di età recente (IV–III sec. a. C.)', in: G. M. Della Fina (ed.), *Etruschi, Greci, Fenici e Cartaginesi nel Mediterraneo centrale* (Orvieto) 325–63.

Millett, M., 1990. *The Romanization of Britain: an essay in archaeological interpretation* (Cambridge).

Mitchell, S., 1999. 'The administration of Roman Asia from 133 BC to AD 250', in: W. Eck (ed.), *Lokale Autonomie und römische Ordnungsmacht in den kaiserzeitlichen Provinzen vom 1. bis 3. Jahrhundert* (Munich) 17–46.

Mogetta, M., 2015. 'A new date for concrete in Rome', *JRS* 105, 1–40.

Momigliano, A., 1975. *Alien wisdom: the limits of Hellenization* (Cambridge).

Morel, J.-P., 1969. 'Etudes de céramique campanienne I: l'atelier des petits estampilles', *MEFRA* 81, 59–117.

Morel, J.-P., 1976. 'Le sanctuaire de Vastogirardi (Molise) et les influences hellénistiques en Italie centrale', in: P. Zanker (ed.), *Hellenismus in Mittelitalien* (Göttingen) 255–66.

Morel, J.-P., 1980. 'La céramique campanienne: acquis et problèmes', in: *Céramiques hellénistiques et romaines* I (Paris) 85–115.

Morel, J.-P., 1981. 'La produzione della ceramica campana: aspetti economici e sociali', in: A. Giardina & A. Schiavone (eds.), Società romana e produzione schiavistica II. Merci, mercati e scambi nel Mediterraneo (Rome) 81–97.

Morel, J.-P., 1983a. 'Les producteurs de biens artisanaux en Italie à la fin de la République', in: M. Cébeillac-Gervasoni (ed.), *Les «bourgeoisies» municipales italiennes aux IIe et Ier siècle av. J.-C.* (Naples) 21–39.

Morel, J.-P., 1983b. 'Les relations économiques dans l'Occident grec', in: G. Nenci (ed.), *Modes de contacts et processus de transformation dans les sociétés anciennes* (Pisa and Rome) 549–80.

Morel, J.-P., 1988. 'Artisanat et colonisation dans l'Italie romaine aux IVe et IIIe siècles av. J.-C.', *DdA* 6.3, 49–63.

Morel, J.-P., 1991a. 'Artisanat, importations et Romanisation dans le Samnium aux IIe et Ier siècles av. J.-C.', in: G. D'Henry (ed.), *La Romanisation du Samnium aux IIe et Ier siècles av. J.-C.* (Naples) 187–203.

Morel, J.-P., 1991b. 'La romanisation du Samnium et de la Lucanie aux IVe et IIIe siècles av. J.-C. d'après l'artisanat et le commerce', in: J. Mertens & R. Lambrechts (eds.), *Comunità indigene e problemi della romanizzazione nell'Italia centro-meridionale (IVo- IIIo sec. av. C.)* (Brussels and Rome) 125–44.

Morel, J.-P., 1998. 'Le commerce à l'époque hellénistique et romaine et les enseignements des épaves', in: G. Volpe (ed.), *Archeologia subacquea, Come opera l'archeologo sott'acqua, Storie delle acque VIII*[e] *ciclo di lezioni sulla ricerca applicata in Archeologia* (Florence) 485–529.

Morel, J.-P., 2007. 'Early Rome and Italy', in: W. Scheidel, I. Morris, & R. Saller (eds.), *The Cambridge economic history of the Greco-Roman world* (Cambridge) 487–510.

Morel, J.-P., 2009. 'Céramiques à vernis noir et histoire' (review of Roth 2007a), *JRA* 22, 477–88.

Morley, N.D.G., 1996. *Metropolis and hinterland. The city of Rome and the Italian economy 200 B.C.—A.D. 200* (Cambridge).

Morris, I., R.P. Saller, & W. Scheidel, 2007. 'Introduction', in: W. Scheidel, I. Morris, & R. P. Saller (eds.), *The Cambridge economic history of the Greco-Roman world* (Cambridge) 1–12.

Morstein Kallet-Marx, R., 1995. *Hegemony to empire: the development of the Roman Imperium in the east from 148 to 62 B.C.* (Berkeley).

Mouritsen, H., 1998. *Italian unification. A study in ancient and modern historiography* (London).

Mouritsen, H., 2006. 'Caius Gracchus and the *cives sine suffragio*', *Historia* 55, 418–25.

Müller, C., 2002. 'Les Italiens en Béotie du IIe siècle av. J.-C. au Ier siècle ap. J.-C.', in: C. Müller & C. Hasenohr (eds.), *Les Italiens dans le monde grec, IIe siècle av. J.-C.—Ier siècle ap. J.-C.* (Athens) 89–100.

Müller, C. & C. Hasenohr, 2002. 'Gentilices et circulation des Italiens: quelques réflexions méthodologiques', in: C. Müller & C. Hasenohr (eds.), *Les Italiens dans le monde grec, IIe siècle av. J.-C.—Ier siècle ap. J.-C.* (Athens) 11–20.

Musco, S. & P. Zaccagni, 1985. 'Caratteri e forme di insediamenti rustici e residenziali nel suburbio orientale tra il IV ed il I secolo a. C.', in: R. Bussi & V. Vandelli (eds.), *Misurare la terra: centuriazione e coloni nel mondo romano. Città, agricoltura, commercio: materiali da Roma e dal suburbio* (Modena) 90–106.

Musti, D., 1980. 'Il commercio degli schiavi e del grano: il caso di Puteoli', in: *The seaborne commerce of ancient Rome* (Rome) 197–215.

Naerebout, F.G., 2014. 'Convergence and divergence: one Empire, many cultures', in: G. de Kleijn & S. Benoist (eds.), *Integration in Rome and in the Roman World* (Leiden and Boston) 263–81.

Nagle, D.B., 1973. 'An allied view of the Social War', *AJAH* 77, 367–78.

Nava, M.L. & P. Poccetti, 2001. 'Il santuario lucano di Rossano di Vaglio. Una nuova dedica osca ad Ercole', *MEFRA* 113:1, 95–122.

Nicolet, C., 1966. *L'ordre équestre à l'époque républicaine (312–43 av. J.-C.)* (Paris).

Nicolet, C., 1967. 'Arpinum, Aemilius Scaurus et les Tullii Cicerones', *REL* 45, 276–304.

Nicolet, C., 1978. 'Le stipendium des alliés italiens avant la Guerre Sociale', *PBSR* 33, 1–11.

Nicolet, C., 1989. *Rome et la conquête du monde méditerranéen* (Paris).

Nocita, M., 2012. *Italiotai e Italikoi. Testimonianze greche nel Mediterraneo orientale* (Rome).

Nolla, J.M. & F.J. Nieto, 1989. 'La importación de ánforas romanas en Cataluña', in: *Amphores romaines et histoire économique*. Dix ans de recherche (Rome) 367–91.

Nonnis, D. & S. Sisani, 2012. 'Manufatti iscritti e vita dei santuari: l'Italia centrale tra media e tarda repubblica', in: G. Baratta & S.M. Marengo (eds.), *Instrumenta inscripta III. Manufatti iscritti e vita dei santuari in età romana* (Macerata) 41–91.

North, D.C., 1990. *Institutions, institutional change and economic performance* (Cambridge).

North, J.A., 1992. 'Deconstructing stone theatres', in: *Apodosis: studies presented to Dr W. W. Cruickshank to mark his eightieth birthday* (London) 75–83.

Northwood, S., 2008. 'Census and tributum', in: L. de Ligt & S. Northwood (eds.), *People, land, and politics. Demographic developments and the transformation of Italy 300 BC—AD 14* (Leiden and Boston) 257–70.

Nucera, E., 2008. *Locri in età romana. La civitas romana nel cuore dello polis magnagreca* (Reggio Calabria).

Oakley, S.P., 1995. *The hill-forts of the Samnites* (London).

Olcese, G., 2004. 'Anfore greco-italiche antiche: alcune osservazioni sull'origine e sulla circolazione alla luce di recenti ricerche archaeologiche ed archaeometriche', in: E.C. De Sena & H. Dessales (eds.), *Metodi e approci archeologici: l'industria e il commercio nell'Italia antica* (London) 173–91.

Olcese, G., 2005–6. 'The production and circulation of Greco-Italic amphorae of Campania (Ischia/Bay of Naples)', *Skyllis* 7, 60–75.

Osanna, M. & M.M. Sica (eds.), 2005. *Torre di Satriano I: il santuario lucano* (Venosa).

Osborne, R. & C. Vout, 2010. 'A revolution in Roman history?' *JRS* 100, 233–45.

Paci, G., 2008. *Ricerche di storia e di epigrafia romana delle Marche* (Rome).

Pailler, J.-M., 1988. *Bacchanalia. La répression de 186 av. J.-C. à Rome et en Italie: vestiges, images, tradition* (Rome).

Palazzo, P., 1994. 'Insediamenti artigianali e produzione agricola', in: C. Marangio & A. Nitti (eds.), *Scritti di antichità in memoria di Benita Sciarra Bardaro* (Fasano) 53–60.

Pandolfini Angeletti, M. & A. Maggiani (eds.), 2002. *La tabula Cortonensis e il suo contesto storico-archeologico: atti dell'incontro di studio, 22 giugno 2001* (Rome).

Pareti, L. (ed. A. Russi), 1997. *Storia della regione Lucano-Bruzzia nell'antichità* (Rome).

Parker, A.J., 1992. *Ancient shipwrecks of the Mediterranean and the Roman provinces* (Oxford).

Patterson, J.R., 2006a. 'The relationship of the Italian ruling classes with Rome: friendship, family relations and their consequences', in: M. Jehne & R. Pfeilschrifter (eds.), *Herrschaft ohne Integration. Rom und Italien in Republikanischer Zeit* (Frankfurt am Main) 139–53.

Patterson, J.R., 2006b. 'Rome and Italy', in: N. Rosenstein & R. Morstein-Marx (eds.), *A companion to the Roman Republic* (Malden, MA) 606–24.

Pausch, D., 2011. *Livius und der Leser: narrative Strukturen in Ab Urbe Condita* (Munich).

Peacock, D.S. & D.F. Williams, 1986. *Amphorae and the Roman economy* (London and New York).

Pedley, J.G., 1990. *Paestum. Greeks and Romans in southern Italy* (London).

Pedroni, L., 2001. *Ceramica calena a vernice nera: produzione e diffusione* (Naples).

Pelgrom, J., 2008. 'Settlement organization amd land distribution in Latin colonies before the Second Punic War', in: L. de Ligt & S. Northwood (eds.), *People, land, and politics. Demographic developments and the transformation of Italy 300 BC—AD 14* (Leiden and Boston) 333–72.

Pelgrom, J., 2014. 'Roman colonization and the city-state model', in: Stek, T.D. & J. Pelgrom (eds.), *Roman Republican colonization: new perspectives from archaeology and ancient history* (Rome) 73–85.

Perkins, P. & L. Nevett, 2000. 'Urbanism and urbanization in the Roman world', in: J. Huskinson (ed.), *Experiencing Rome. Culture, identity and power in the Roman Empire* (London and New York) 213–44.

Pesando, F., 1997. *Domus. Edilizia privata e società pompeiana fra III e I secolo a. C.* (Rome).

Pfeilschifter, R., 2007. 'The allies in the republican army and the Romanization of Italy', in: R. Roth & J. Keller (eds.), *Roman by integration: dimensions of group identity in material culture and text* (Portsmouth RI) 27–42.

Pietra, G., 2010. 'I Romani a Olbia: dalla conquista della città punica all'arrivo dei Vandali', *Bollettino di archeologia on line* 47–62.

Pina Polo, F., 2006. 'Deportation, Kolonisation, Migration. Bevölkerungsverschiebungen im republikanischen Italien und Formen der Identitätsbildung', in: M. Jehne & R. Pfeilschrifter (eds.), *Herrschaft ohne Integration. Rom und Italien in Republikanischer Zeit* (Frankfurt am Main) 171–206.

Pinzone, A., 1999. 'L'immigrazione e i suoi riflessi nella storia economica e sociale della Sicilia del II sec. a. C.', in: M. Barra Bagnasco, E. De Miro, & A. Pinzone (eds.), *Magna Grecia e Sicilia. Stato degli studi e prospettive di ricerca* (Messina) 381–402.

Pitts, M. & M.J. Versluys (eds.), 2014. *Globalisation and the Roman World. World history, connectivity and material culture* (Cambridge).

Pobjoy, 1997. 'A new reading of the mosaic inscription in the temple of Diana Tifatina', 65, 59–88.

Poccetti, P., 1984. 'Romani e Italici a Delo. Spunti linguistici da una pubblicazione recente', *Athenaeum* 62, 646–56.

Porzio Gernia, M.T., 1970. 'Aspetti dell'influsso latino sul lessico e sulla sintassi osca', *Archivio glottologico italiano* 55, 94–144.

Principal, J., 1998. 'Tarraco, las cerámicas del Grupo Hercúleo y el comercio romano-itálico anterior a la Segunda Guerra Punica', *JRA* 11, 233–44.

Purcell, N., 1994. 'South Italy in the fourth century B.C.', in: D.M. Lewis, J. Boardman, S. Hornblower, & M. Ostwald (eds.), *Cambridge Ancient History VI: the fourth century B. C.* (Cambridge) 381–403.

Quilici, L. & S. Quilici Gigli, 2006. 'Ricerche nella valle del Sinni', in: *Problemi della chora coloniale dall'Occidente al Mar Nero* (Taranto) 793–806.

Raggi, A., 2010. 'Praetor qui inter peregrinos et cives ius dicit nel trattato tra Roma e i Lici (46 a.C.)', in: D. Mantovani & L. Pellecchi (eds.), *Eparcheia, autonomia e civitas Romana. Studi sulla giurisdizione criminale dei governatori di provincia (II sec. a.C.—II d.C)* (Pavia) 45–67.

Rathbone, D., 1983. 'The slave mode of production in Italy', *JRS* 73, 160–8.

Rathbone, D., 1993. 'The census qualifications of the *assidui* and the *prima classis*', in: H. Sancisi-Weerdenburg et al. (eds.), *De agricultura: in memoriam Pieter Willem De Neeve (1945–1990)* (Amsterdam) 121–52.

Rathbone, D., 2008. 'Poor peasants and silent sherds', in: L. de Ligt & S. Northwood (eds.), *People, land, and politics. Demographic developments and the transformation of Italy 300 BC—AD 14* (Leiden and Boston) 305–32.

Rauh, N.K., 1986a. 'Cicero's business friendships: economics and politics in the late Roman Republic', *Aevum* 60, 3–30.

Rauh, N.K., 1986b. *Senators and business in the Roman Republic: 264–44 B.C.* (University of North Carolina PhD thesis).

Rauh, N.K., 1993. *The sacred bonds of commerce. Religion, economy, and trade society at Hellenistic Roman Delos* (Amsterdam).

Rawson, E., 1975. 'Architecture and sculpture: the activities of the Cossutii', *PBSR* 43, 36–47.

Regoli, E., 2002. 'Il paesaggio delle ville (II secolo a. C. – metà I a. C.)', in: A. Carandini & F. Cambi (eds.), *Paesaggi d'Etruria* (Firenze) 145–54.

Renda, G., 2004. 'Il territorio di Caiatia', in: G. Cera, S. Quilici Gigli, & G. Renda (eds.), *Carta archeologica e ricerche in Campania* I (Rome) 237–423.

Rich, J., 2008. 'Treaties, allies and the Roman conquest of Italy', in: P. De Souza & J. France (eds.), *War and peace in ancient and medieval history* (Cambridge) 51–75.

Rich, J., 2011. 'Velleius' history: genre and purpose', in: E. Cowan (ed.), *Velleius Paterculus. Making history* (Swansea) 73–92.

Richardson, J.S., 1976. 'The Spanish mines and the development of provincial taxation in the second century B.C.', *JRS* 66, 139–52.

Richardson, J.S., 1987. 'The purpose of the lex Calpurnia de repetundis', *JRS* 77, 1–12.

Richardson, J.S., 2008. *The language of empire: Rome and the idea of empire from the third century BC to the second century AD* (Cambridge).

Riggs, C., 2005. *The beautiful burial in Roman Egypt* (Oxford).

Rix, H., 1991. *Etruskische Texte* (Tübingen).

Rix, H., 2000. 'Tribù', 'stato', 'città' e 'insediamento' nelle lingue italiche', *Archivio glottologico italiano* 85, 196–231.

Rix, H., 2002. *Sabellische Texte* (Heidelberg).

Robinson, E.S.G., 1964. 'Carthaginian and other south Italian coinages of the Second Punic War', *NC* 4, 37–64.

Roselaar, S.T., 2008. 'Regional variations in the use of *ager publicus*', in: L. de Ligt & S. Northwood (eds.), *People, land and politics. Demographic developments and the transformation of Roman Italy, 300 BC—AD 14* (Leiden and Boston) 557–86.

Roselaar, S.T., 2009. '*Assidui* or *proletarii*? Property in Roman citizen colonies and the *vacatio militiae*', in *Mnemosyne* 62, 609–23.

Roselaar, S.T., 2010. *Public land in the Roman Republic: a social and economic history of ager publicus in Italy, 396–89 BC* (Oxford).

Roselaar S.T., 2011. 'Colonies and processes of integration in the Roman Republic', *MEFRA* 123, 527–55.

Roselaar, S.T., 2012. 'Mediterranean trade as a mechanism of integration between Romans and Italians', in Roselaar, S.T. (ed.), *Processes of integration and identity formation in the Roman Republic* (Leiden and Boston) 141–58.

Roselaar, S.T., 2013a. 'The concept of *commercium* in the Roman Republic', *Phoenix* 66, 381–413.

Roselaar, S.T., 2013b. 'The concept of *conubium* in the Roman Republic', in: P. Du Plessis (ed.), *New frontiers: law and society in the Roman World* (Edinburgh) 102–22.

Roselaar, S.T., 2017. 'Lex Valeria de provocatione', in: *Oxford Classical Dictionary* (Oxford and New York) Available online at: http://classics.oxfordre.com/view/10.1093/acrefore/9780199381135.001.0001/acrefore-9780199381135-e-8191.

Roselaar, S.T., 2017. 'Pride and prejudice in Cicero's speeches', in: A. Gavrielatos (ed.), *Self-presentation and identity in the Roman world* (Newcastle upon Tyne).

Rosenstein, N., 2004. *Rome at war. Farms, families, and death in the Middle Republic* (Chapel Hill & London).

Rosenstein, N., 2008. 'Aristocrats and agriculture in the Middle and Late Republic', *JRS* 98, 1–26.

Rosenstein, N., 2012. 'Integration and armies in the middle Republic', in: S.T. Roselaar (ed.), *Processes of integration and identity formation in the Roman Republic* (Leiden and Boston) 85–103.

Rossiter, J.J., 1981. 'Wine and oil processing at Roman farms in Italy', *Phoenix* 35, 345–61.

Roth, R.E., 2007a. *Styling Romanisation. Pottery and society in central Italy* (Cambridge).

Roth, R.E., 2007b. 'Varro's *picta Italia* (*RR* I.ii.1) and the odology of Roman Italy', *Hermes* 135, 286–300.

Roth, R.E., 2010. 'Review of A. Wallace-Hadrill, *Rome's Cultural Revolution*', *Classical Review* 60, 224–27.

Roth, R.E., 2012. 'Regionalism: towards a new perspective of cultural change in central Italy, c. 350–100 BC', in: S.T. Roselaar (ed.), *Processes of integration and identity formation in the Roman Republic* (Leiden and Boston) 17–34.

Russo, F., 2012. 'The beginning of the First Punic War and the concept of *Italia*', in: S.T. Roselaar (ed.), *Processes of integration and identity formation in the Roman Republic* (Leiden and Boston) 35–50.

Russo Tagliente, A., 1995. *Armento. Archeologia di un centro indigeno* (Bollettino di Archeologia 35–6).

Rutter, N.K., 2001. *Historia numorum. Italy* (London).

Sabbatini, G., 2001. *Ager Venusinus I: Mezzana del Cantore (Forma Italiae)* (Firenze).

Salmon, E.T., 1958. 'Notes on the Social War', *TAPhA* 89, 159–84.

Salmon, E.T., 1962. 'The cause of the Social War', *Phoenix* 16, 107–19.

Salmon, E.T., 1967. *Samnium and the Samnites* (Cambridge).

Salmon, E.T., 1969. *Roman colonization under the Republic* (London).

Salmon, E.T., 1982. *The making of Roman Italy* (London).

Sangineto, A.B., 1994, 'Per la ricostruzione del paesaggio agrario delle Calabrie romane', in: S. Settis (ed.), *Storia della Calabria antica età italica e romana* (Rome) 557–93.

Santangelo, F., 2006. 'Sulla and the Senate: a reconsideration', *CCG* 17, 7–22.

Santangelo, F., 2009. *Sulla, the elites and the Empire. A study of Roman politics in Italy and the Greek East* (Leiden).

Sartori, F., 1953. *Problemi di storia costituzionale italiota* (Rome).

Sartori, F., 1975. 'Le città italiote dopo la conquista romana', in: *La Magna Grecia nell'età romana* (Naples) 83–136.

Scheers, S., 1995. 'La circolazione monetaria', in: J. Mertens (ed.), *Herdonia. Scoperta di una città* (Bari) 327–31.

Scheidel, W., 2005. 'Human mobility in Roman Italy II: The slave population', *JRS* 95, 64–79.

Scheu, F., 1964. 'The coinage of the Lucanians', *NC* 4, 65–73.

Scopacasa, R., 2014. *Ancient Samnium: settlement, culture, and identity between history and archaeology* (Oxford).

Scopacasa, R., 2015. 'An allied view of integration: Italian elites and consumption in the second century BC', in: S.T. Roselaar (ed.), *Processes of cultural change and integration in the Roman world* (Leiden and Boston) 39–57.

Scopacasa, R., 2016. 'Falling behind: access to formal burial and falteringelites in Samnium', in: E. Perego & R. Scopacasa (eds.), *Burial and social change in first-millennium BC Italy: approaching social agents* (Oxford).

Senatore, F., 2004. 'Note sulle origini di Potentia: le premesse indigenee l'istituzione del municipium', *SCO* 50, 303–19.

Settis, S. (ed.), 1984. *Misurare la terra: centuriazione e coloni nel mondo romano* (Modena).

Sewell, J., 2014. 'Gellius, Philip II and a proposed end to the 'model-replica' debate', in: T.D. Stek & J. Pelgrom (eds.), *Roman Republican colonization. New perspectives from archaeology and ancient history* (Rome) 125–39.

Sherk, R.K., 1969. *Roman documents from the Greek East:* senatus consulta *and* epistulae *to the age of Augustus* (Baltimore).

Sherwin-White, A.N., 1972. 'The date of the Lex Repetundarum and its consequences', *JRS* 62, 83–99.

Sherwin-White, A.N., 1973². *The Roman citizenship* (Oxford) 1st ed. 1939.

Silvestrini, M., 1990. '*Gentes*', in: M. Chelotti, V. Morizio, & M. Silvestrini, *Le epigrafi romane di Canosa* II (Bari) 257–65.

Simelon, P., 1993. *La propriété en Lucanie depuis les Gracques jusqu'à l'avènement des Sévères* (Brussels).

Sirks, A.J.B., 2014. 'Review of P. Du Plessis (ed.), *New frontiers: law and society in the Roman World*', *Tijdschrift voor Rechtsgeschiedenis* 82, 171–7.

Sisani, S., 2007. *Fenomenologia della conquista. La romanizzazione dell'Umbria tra il IVsec. a.C. e la guerra sociale* (Rome).

Sisani, S., 2008. 'Romanizzazione e latinizzazione: linee dei fenomeni di acculturazione linguistica in area etrusco-italica', in: J. Uroz, J.M. Noguera, & F. Coarelli (eds.), *Iberia e Italia. Modelos romanos de integración territorial* (Murcia) 101–26.

Sisani, S., 2009. Umbrorum gens antiquissima Italiae. *Studi sulla società e le istituzioni* (Perugia).

Small, A.M., 1992. 'Botromagno: an introduction', in: A.M. Small (ed.), *Gravina.* An Iron Age and Roman Republican settlement in Apulia I: the site (London) 3–18.

Small, A.M., 1994. 'Villa building in Roman Lucania', in: A.M. Small & R.J. Buck (eds.), *The excavations of San Giovanni di Ruoti I: The villas and their environment* (Toronto) 37–42.

Small, A.M., 2014. 'From Silvium to Vagnari: sheep, wool and weaving on the saltus', in: A.M. Small (ed.), *Beyond Vagnari. New themes in the study of Roman South Italy* (Bari) 99–110.

Small, A.M. & R.J. Buck (eds.), 1994. *RicThe excavations of San Giovanni di Ruoti I: the villas and their environment* (Toronto).

Small, A. & C. Small, 2002. 'The Basentello Valley survey (Apulia, Basilicata)', in: P. Attema et al. (eds.), *New developments in Italian landscape archaeology* (Oxford) 83–6.

Smith, A.D., 1986. *The ethnic origins of nations* (Oxford).

Smolicz, J., 1981. 'Core values and cultural identity', *Ethnic and Racial Studies* 4:1, 75–90.

Smurra, R., 1989. 'Contributo per una carta delle "ville" romane nella provincia di Calabria', *Studi e materiali di geografia storica della Calabria* I (Cosenza) 115–84.

Solin, H., 1982. 'Appunti sull'onomastica romana a Delo', in: F. Coarelli, D. Musti, & H. Solin (eds.), *Delo e l'Italia* (Rome) 101–17.

Soricelli, G., 2007. 'Comunità orientale a Puteoli', in: R. Compatangelo-Soussignan & C.G. Schwentzel (eds.), *Étrangers dans la cité romaine* (Rennes) 129–44.

Sotty, R., 1977. *Ricerche sur les utiles actiones. La notion de l'action utile en droit romain classique* (Grenoble).

Stannard, C., 2013. 'Are Ebusan and pseudo-Ebusan coin at Pompeii a sign of intensive contacts with the Island of Ebusus?' in: A. Arévalo González, D. Bernal Casasola, & D. Cottica (eds.), *Ebusus y Pompeya, ciudades marítimas.Testimonios monetales de una relación* (Cádiz) 125–55.

Stazio, A., 1955. 'Rapporti fra Pompei ed Ebusus nelle Baleari alla luce dei rinvenimenti monetali', *AIIN* 2, 33–57.

Stazio, A., 1970. 'Monetazione e circolazione monetale dell'antico Salento', in: *Atti del II convegno dei comuni Messapici, Peuceti e Dauni* (Bari) 61–89.

Steiger, O., 2006. 'Property economics versus New Institutional Economics: alternative foundations of how to trigger economic development', *Journal of Economic Issues* 40:1, 183–208.

Steingräber, S.,2000. *Arpi-Apulien-Makedonien. Studien zum unteritalischen Grabwesen in hellenistischer Zeit* (Mainz).

Stek, T.D., 2009. *Cult places and cultural change in Republican Italy. A contextual approach to religious aspects of rural society after the Roman conquest* (Amsterdam).

Stek, T.D., 2013a, 'Material culture, Italic identities and the Romanization of Italy', in: J. DeRose Evans (ed.), *A companion to the archaeology of the Roman Republic* (Malden, MA) 337–53.

Stek, T.D., 2013b. 'Monumental architecture of non-urban cult places in Roman Italy', in: R.B. Ulrich & C.K. Quenemoen (eds.), *A companion to Roman architecture* (Malden, MA) 228–47.

Stek, T.D., 2014. 'Roman imperialism, globalization and Romanization in early Roman Italy. Research questions in archaeology and ancient history', *Archaeological Dialogues* 21, 30–40.

Stek, T.D., 2015. 'The importance of rural sanctuaries in structuring non-urban society in ancient Samnium: approaches from architecture and landscape', *Oxford Journal of Archaeology*, 34, 397–406.

Stek, T.D. & J. Pelgrom (eds.), 2014. *Roman Republican colonization: new perspectives from archaeology and ancient history* (Rome)

Strazzulla, M.J., 1981. 'Le produzioni dal IV al I a.C.', in: A. Schiavone & A. Giardina (eds.), *Società romana e produzione schiavistica II: merci, mercato e scambi nel Mediterraneo* (Rome) 187–94.

Strazzulla Rusconi, M.J., 1982. 'Onocles Dindi Tiberi servus. Note su alcune presenze prenestine ad Aquileia in età repubblicana', *ArchClass* 34, 98–138.

Suolahti, J., 1956. *The junior officers of the Roman army in the Republican period* (Helsinki).

Swain, S., 1989. 'Plutarch: chance, providence, and history', *AJPh* 110, 272–302.

Sweetman, R.J., 2011. '100 years of solitude: Roman colonies in the first century of their foundation', in: R.J. Sweetman (ed.), *Roman colonies in the first century of their foundation* (Oxford) 1–6.

Swidzinski, A., 2007. 'Italian aims in the First Civil War 87–82 BC', *Hirundo* 5, 118–46.

Tagliamonte, G., 1989–90. 'Iscrizioni votive italiche su armi', in: G. Bartoloni & G. Colonna (eds.), *Atti del convegno internazional anathema: regime delle offerte e vita dei santuari nel Mediterraneo antico (Scienze dell'Antichità* 3–4 (Rome) 519–34.

Tagliamonte, G., 1994. *I figli di Marte. Mobilità, mercenari e mercenariato italici in Magna Grecia e Sicilia* (Rome).

Taliercio Mensitieri, M., 1998. 'Le emissioni romano-campane di bronzo', in: *La monetazione romano-campana. Atti del convegno del centro internazionale di studi numismatici—Napoli 18–19 giugno 1993* (Rome 1998) 49–139.

Tan, J., forthcoming. 'The *dilectus-tributum* system and the settlement of fourth-century Italy', in: J. Armstrong & M. Fronda (eds.), *Romans at war: soldiers, citizens, and society in the Roman Republic* (Abingdon).

Tarpin, M., 2014. 'Strangers in paradise. Latins (and some other non-Romans) in colonial context: a short story of territorial complexity', in: T.D. Stek & J. Pelgrom (eds.), *Roman*

Republican colonization: new perspectives from archaeology and ancient history (Portsmouth, RI) 160–91.

Tchernia, A., 1983. 'Italian wine in Gaul at the end of the Republic', in: P. Garnsey, K. Hopkins, & C.R. Whittaker (eds.), *Trade in the ancient economy* (London) 87–104.

Tchernia, A., 1986. *Le vin de l'Italie romaine* (Rome).

Tellegen-Couperus, O.E., 2002. *A short history of Roman law* (London).

Termeer, M.K., 2015. *Latin colonization in Italy before the end of the Second Punic War: colonial communities and cultural change* (University of Groningen PhD thesis).

Termeer, M.K., forthcoming. 'Roman warfare and coinage production in Italy', in: S.T. Roselaar & M. Helm (eds.), *Spoils in the Roman Republic—a re-evaluation* (Stuttgart).

Terpstra, T., 2013. *Trading communities in the Roman world: a micro-economic and institutional perspective* (Leiden).

Terrenato, N., 1998. 'The Romanization of Italy: global acculturation or cultural *bricolage*?', in: C. Forcey, J. Hawthorne, & R. Witcher (eds.), *TRAC* 7, 20–7.

Terrenato, N., 2001a. 'The Auditorium site in Rome and the origins of the villa', *JRA* 14, 5–32.

Terrenato, N., 2001b. 'A tale of three cities: the romanization of northern coastal Etruria', in: S. Keay & N. Terrenato (eds.), *Italy and the West: comparative issues in romanization* (Oxford) 54–67.

Terrenato, N., 2007. 'The clans and the peasants: reflections on social structure and change in Hellenistic central Italy', in: P. van Dommelen & N. Terrenato (eds.), *Articulating local cultures: power and identity under the expanding Roman Republic* (Portsmouth RI) 13–22.

Terrenato, N., 2012. 'The enigma of 'Catonian' villas: the De agri cultura in the context of second-century BC Italian architecture', in: J.A. Becker & N. Terrenato (eds.), *Roman Republican villas. Architecture, context, and ideology* (Ann Arbor) 69–93.

Terzani, C., 1991. 'La colonia Latina di Aesernia', in: S. Capini & A. Di Niro (eds.), *Samnium: archeologia del Molise* (Rome) 111–12.

Thiel, J.H., 1954. *A history of Roman sea-power before the Second Punic War* (Amsterdam).

Thomas, Y., 1996. *'Origine' et 'commune patrie'. Étude de droit public romain (89 av. J.-C.—212 ap. J.-C.)* (Rome).

Thomsen, R., 1957–61. *Early Roman coinage: a study of the chronology* (Copenhagen).

Tocco, G., 1990. 'La villa di Moltone (Tolve)', in: M. Salvatore (ed.), *Basilicata. L'espansionismo romano nel sud-est d'Italia. Il quadro archeologico* (Venosa) 95–100.

Tol, G. & T. de Haas, 2017. 'Introduction', in: G. Tol & T. de Haas (eds.), *The economic integration of Roman Italy. Rural communities in a globalizing world* (Leiden) 1–12.

Torelli, M., 1977. 'Greci e indigeni in Magna Graecia: ideologia religiosa e rapporti di classe', *Studi storici* 18, 45–61.

Torelli, M., 1982. 'Regio IV (Samnium)', in: *Epigrafia e ordine senatorio* II (Rome) 165–99.

Torelli, M., 1983. 'Edilizia pubblica in Italia centrale tra guerra sociale ed età augusta. Ideologia e classi sociali', in: M. Cébeillac-Gervasoni (ed.), *Les «bourgeoisies» municipales italiennes aux IIe et Ier siècle av. J.-C.* (Naples) 241–50.

Torelli, M., 1990. 'La formazione della villa', in: A. Momigliano & A. Schiavone (eds.), *Storia di Roma 2: L'impero mediterraneo 1: La repubblica imperiale* (Turin) 123–32.

Torelli, M., 1995. *Studies in the Romanization of Italy* (Edmonton).

Torelli, M., 1996. 'Donne, domi nobiles ed evergeti a Paestum tra la fine della Repubblica e l'inizio dell'Impero', in: M. Cébeillac-Gervasoni (ed.), *Les élites municipales de l'Italie péninsulaire des Gracques à Néron: actes de la table ronde de Clermont-Ferrand (28–30 novembre 1991)* (Rome) 153–78.

Torelli, M., 1999. *Tota Italia: Essays in the cultural formation of Roman Italy* (Oxford).
Torelli, M., 2006. 'Topography and archaeology of Rome', in: N. Rosenstein & R. Morstein-Marx (eds.), *A companion to the Roman Republic* (Malden, MA) 81–101.
Toynbee, A.J., 1965. *Hannibal's legacy. The Hannibalic War's effects on Roman life* (London) 2 vols.
Travaglini, A., 1982. *Inventario dei rinvenimenti monetali del Salento. Problemi di circolazione* (Rome).
Travaglini, A., 1990. 'La monetazione di ORRA', *Studi antichità Università di Lecce* 6, 235–55.
Tweedie, F., 2012. 'The *Lex Licinia Mucia* and the *Bellum Italicum*', in: S.T. Roselaar (ed.), *Processes of integration and identity formation in the Roman Republic* (Leiden and Boston) 123–39.
Uguzzini, A. & F. Ghinatti, 1968. *Le tavole greche di Eraclea* (Rome).
Valenti, M., 2003. *Ager Tusculanus (Forma Italiae)* (Rome).
Vandermersch, C., 1994. *Vins et amphores de Grande Grèce et de Sicile, IVe-IIIe s. avant J.-C.* (Naples).
Van Kerckhove, J., 2004. 'The development of 'vernice nera'-pottery in the Marches', *BaBesch* 79, 59–73.
Van Wonterghem, F., 1992. 'Il culto di Ercole fra i popoli osco-sabellici', in: C. Bonnet & C. Jourdain-Annequin (eds.), *Héraclès. D'une rive à l'autre de la Méditerranée* (Brussels and Rome) 319–51.
Verboven, K., 2002. *The economy of friends. Economic aspects of amicitia and patronage in the late Republic* (Brussels).
Verbrugghe, G.P., 1973. 'The *elogium* from Polla and the first slave war', *CPh* 68, 25–35.
Versluys, M.J., 2013. 'Material culture and identity in the late Roman Republic (c. 200–c. 20)', in: J. DeRose Evans (ed.), *A companion to the archaeology of the Roman Republic* (Malden, MA) 429–39.
Vicari, F., 2001. *Produzione e commercio dei tessuti nell'Occidente romano* (Oxford).
Vicente Jordá, T., 1999. *Ius commercii* (PhD thesis, University of València).
Vollmer, D., 1990. *Symploke. Das Übergreifen der römischen Expansion auf den griechischen Osten* (Stuttgart).
Volpe, G., 1990. *La Daunia nell'età della romanizzazione. Paesaggio agrario, produzione, scambi* (Bari).
Volpe, G., 2001. 'Linee di storia del paesaggio dell'Apulia romana: San Giusto e la Valle del Celone', in: E. Lo Cascio & A. Storchi Marino (eds.), *Modalità insediative e strutture agrarie nell'Italia meridionale in età romana* (Bari) 315–61.
Volpe, G. & J. Mertens, 1995. 'Il territorio, la viabilità, la produzione agraria', *Herdonia. Scoperta di una città* (Bari) 291–320.
Walbank, F.W., 1957. *A historical commentary on Polybius* I (Oxford).
Wallace-Hadrill, A., 1997. 'Rethinking the Roman atrium house', in: R. Laurence & A. Wallace-Hadrill (eds.), *Domestic space in the Roman world. Pompeii and beyond* (Portsmouth, RI) 219–40.
Wallace-Hadrill, A., 1999. 'The Roman revolution and material culture', in: F. Millar (ed.), *La révolution romaine après Ronald Syme* (Vandoeuvres-Geneva) 283–313.
Wallace-Hadrill, A., 2008. *Rome's cultural revolution* (Cambridge and New York).
Watson, A., 1961. *Contract of mandate in Roman law* (Oxford).
Webster, J., 2001. 'Creolizing the Roman provinces', *AJA* 105, 209–25.
Wegner, M., 1969. *Untersuchungen zu den lateinischen Begriffen socius und societas* (Göttingen).

Whitehouse, R.D., J.B. Wilkins, & E. Herring (eds.), 2000. *Botromagno. Excavation and survey at Gravina in Puglia 1979–1985* (London).

Wiedemann, T., 2003. 'The patron as banker', in: K. Lomas & T. Cornell (eds.), *'Bread and circuses'. Euergetism and municipal patronage in Roman Italy* (London) 12–27.

Wightman, E.M. & J.W. Hayes, 1995. 'Settlement patterns and society', in: J.W. Hayes & I.P. Martini (eds.), *Archaeological survey in the Lower Liri Valley, central Italy* (Oxford) 34–40.

Wikander, Ö., 1989. 'Senators and equites III: the case of the Saufeii', *Opuscula Romana* 17, 205–12.

Will, E.L., 1982. 'Greco-Italic amphoras', *Hesperia* 52, 338–56 + plate.

Will, E.L., 1987. 'The Roman amphoras', in: A.M. McCann et al. (eds.), *The Roman port and fishery of Cosa: a center of ancient trade* (Princeton) 171–219.

Williams, J.H.C., 2001. *Beyond the Rubicon. Romans and Gauls in Republican Italy* (Oxford).

Wilson, A.J.N., 1966. *Emigration from Italy in the Republican age of Rome* (Manchester).

Winkel, L., 2013. 'Some thoughts on the *formulae ficticiae* of citizenship in Gaius 4.37: a form of reception?' in: A. Burrows, D. Johnston, & R. Zimmermann (eds.), *Judge and jurist. Essays in memory of Lord Rodger of Earlsferry* (Oxford) 299–308.

Wiseman, T.P., 1969. 'The census in the first century B.C.', *JRS* 59, 59–75.

Wiseman, T.P., 1971. *New men in the Roman senate, 139 B.C. – A.D. 14* (Oxford).

Wiseman, T.P., 1983. '*Domi nobiles* and the Roman cultural elite', in: M. Cébeillac-Gervasoni (ed.), *Les «bourgeoisies» municipales italiennes aux IIe et Ier siècle av. J.-C.* (Naples) 299–307.

Witcher, R.E., 2000. 'Globalisation and Roman imperialism. Perspectives on identities in Roman Italy', in: E. Herring & K. Lomas (eds.), *The emergence of state identities in Italy in the first millennium BC* (London) 213–25.

Witcher, R.E., 2006. 'Broken pots and meaningless dots? Surveying the rural landscapes of Roman Italy', *PBSR* 74, 39–72.

Witcher, R., 2017. 'The global Roman countryside: connectivity and community', in: G. Tol & T. de Haas (eds.), *The economic integration of Roman Italy. Rural communities in a globalizing world* (Leiden) 28–50.

Woods, M., 2007. 'Engaging the global countryside: globalization, hybridity and the reconstitution of rural place', *Progress in Human Geography* 31:4, 485–507.

Woolf, G., 1995. 'The formation of Roman provincial cultures', in: M. Millett et al. (eds.), *Integration in the early Roman west. The role of culture and ideology* (Luxembourg) 9–18.

Woolf, G., 1997. 'Beyond Romans and natives', *World Archaeology* 28:3, 339–50.

Woolf, G., 1998. *Becoming Roman. The origins of provincial civilization in Gaul* (Oxford).

Woytek, B.E., 2012. 'The denarius coinage of the Roman Republic', in: W.E. Metcalf (ed.), *The Oxford handbook of Greek and Roman coinage* (Oxford) 315–34.

Yntema, D., 1993. *In search of an ancient countryside* (Amsterdam).

Yntema, D., 1995. 'Salento and the Eastern Mediterranean in the middle and late Hellenistic period: some 'Eastern' ceramic evidence (fine wares) from Valesio, province of Brindisi', *Studi di Antichità, Università di Lecce* 8:2, 387–404.

Yntema, D., 2006. 'The birth of a Roman southern Italy: a case study. Ancient written sources and archaeological evidence on the early Roman phase in the Salento district, southern Italy (3rd – 1st century BC)', *BABesch* 81, 91–133.

Yntema, D., 2009. 'Material culture and plural identity in early Roman southern Italy', in: T. Derks & N. Roymans (eds.), *Ethnic constructs in antiquity. The role of power and tradition* (Amsterdam) 144–66.

Zanker, P. (ed.), 1976. *Hellenismus in Mittelitalien* (Göttingen).

Zanker, P., 1990. *The power of images in the age of Augustus* (Ann Arbor).

Zevi, F., 1973. 'P. Lucilio Gamala seniore e i 'quattro tempietti' di Ostia', *MEFRA* 85:2, 555–81.

Zevi, F., 1996. 'Pompei dalla città sannitica alla colonia sillana: per un'interpretazione dei dati archeologici', in: M. Cébeillac-Gervasoni (ed.), *Les élites municipales de l'Italie péninsulaire des Gracques à Néron: actes de la table ronde de Clermont-Ferrand (28–30 novembre 1991)* (Rome) 125–38.

Zevi, F., 2000. 'Pompei: Casa del Fauno', in: R. Cappelli (ed.), *Studi sull'Italia dei Sanniti* (Rome) 118–38.

Zoumbaki, S., 1998. 'Die Niederlassung römischer Geschäftsleute in der Peloponnes', *Tekmeria* 4, 112–73.

Index

The manufacturer's authorised representative in the EU for product safety is Oxford University Press España S.A. of el Parque Empresarial San Fernando de Henares, Avenida de Castilla, 2 – 28830 Madrid (www.oup.es/en or product.safety@oup.com). OUP España S.A. also acts as importer into Spain of products made by the manufacturer.

www.ingramcontent.com/pod-product-compliance
Lightning Source LLC
LaVergne TN
LVHW011915200926
848484LV00002B/629

* 9 7 8 0 1 9 8 8 2 9 4 4 7 *